PACIFIC BRIDGES

The New Immigration from Asia and the Pacific Islands

The Center for Migration Studies is an educational, non-profit institute founded in New York in 1964 to encourage and facilitate the study of sociological, demographic, economic, historical, legislative and pastoral aspects of human migration, refugee movements, and ethnic group relations everywhere.

The East-West Center is a public, nonprofit educational institution established by the U.S. Congress in 1960 to promote cultural and technical interchange between the United States and the nations of Asia and the Pacific through cooperative study, training, and research. The Population Institute, a unit of the East-West Center, conducts multidisciplinary research and training in the field of population, placing emphasis on economic, social, psychological, and environmental aspects of population in the Asian and Pacific region.

The opinions expressed in this text are those of the authors.

Pacific Bridges:
The New Immigration
from Asia and the Pacific Islands

First Edition

Copyright © 1987, reprint 1990 by
The Center for Migration Studies
of New York, Inc.

Center for Migration Studies
209 Flagg Place, Staten Island, N.Y. 10304

Library of Congress Cataloging-in-Publication Data

Pacific bridges.
    Includes bibliographies and index.
    1. Asia—Emigration and immigration.   2. Islands of
the Pacific—Emigration and immigration.   I. Fawcett,
James T., 1935–   .   II. Cariño, Benjamin V.,
1942–   .   III. Center for Migration Studies (U.S.)
JV8490.P33   1986   325′.25   86–26402
ISBN 0-934733-10-4
ISBN 0-934733-09-0 (pbk.)

Printed in the United States of America

Contents

List of Figures

List of Tables

PREFACE

The topic of international migration has drawn increasing attention in recent years, partly because of rapid growth in the number of people crossing national boundaries. Interest has been stimulated too by a recognition of the diversity among international migrants: immigrants, refugees, temporary workers, tourists, executives of multinational corporations, students, and so on. Each type is important for different reasons and each demands separate consideration with respect to policies of sending and receiving countries. In some countries, public controversy has arisen because of illegal immigration or purposeful overstaying of visitors with tourist visas or temporary work permits, calling further attention to international migration. The drama of the "boat people" fleeing Vietnam and their subsequent resettlement has also been a major media story over the past decade.

International migrants from Asia have been in the spotlight recently. On the one hand, Asians have been singled out as the most "successful" group among contemporary immigrants to the United States and some other countries. On the other, Asian refugees from Afghanistan, Laos, Kampuchea, and (to a lesser extent) Vietnam have been identified as groups having severe adaptation problems in countries of first asylum or countries of eventual resettlement. In another sphere, Asians have received plaudits for their exceptional performance as temporary workers in the oil-exporting countries of the Middle East. These contrasting pictures reflect the real diversity among Asian international migrants.

International migrants from the Pacific Islands are less well known, except perhaps in New Zealand. Their numbers are not large in absolute terms but are substantial relative to the populations of their island homes. Thus the impact of out-migration is very noticeable in the Pacific. And, in areas of destination, Pacific Islanders often form an underclass, owing to their poor preparation for the job markets outside their home countries.

Public and scholarly interest in international migration has been accompanied by the appearance of numerous publications, both popular and scientific, over the past ten years. Surprisingly, though, no publication is available that assesses comprehensively contemporary immigration flows in the Asian and Pacific region. This book is designed to fill that gap. In Chapter 1, we discuss Asian and Pacific immigration in the context of social and economic development in the region and in relation to other forms of population movement. We also provide an overview of the book by summarizing the contents of each chapter.

The preparation of this book was carried out as part of a larger program in international migration at the East–West Population Institute. That program has as its goals the development of a comprehensive data base, the conduct of a wide variety of original research studies, and the dissemination of relevant findings to interested scholars and policymakers. As part of the institute's program, an international Conference on Asia–Pacific Immigration to the United States was convened in September 1984. This book draws on papers from that conference for about half the chapters, with the remaining chapters being either entirely new contributions or substantial modifications of conference presentations.

We are grateful to many people for their efforts in the preparation and production of this book. The authors have responded in good grace to our requests for revision and, in many cases, shortening of chapters. Both style and substance of the book have been greatly enhanced by the meticulous and intelligent editing done by Don Yoder and Sandra Ward. The dedicated secretarial staff of the East–West Population Institute—particularly Kathy Martinez, who assumed special responsibility—have cheerfully and competently reworked the manuscripts again and again, as we went through various stages of editing and revision. Russell Fujita designed the book, and Lois Bender carefully prepared the camera copy.

Among our professional colleagues, we owe particular thanks to Fred Arnold and Robert Gardner. Dr. Arnold was a co-coordinator of the conference from which the book is derived and would have been a co-editor if he had not been too busy editing another book on Asian labor migration. Dr. Gardner contributed a great deal to the planning for the conference; we have also benefited from his research on Asian Americans.

Dr. Lee-Jay Cho, director of the East–West Population Institute, has given unfailing encouragement to our efforts and has made possible institutional support for this project. The School of Urban and Regional Planning, University of the Philippines, facilitated Dr. Cariño's work on the book by awarding him a sabbatical leave at the East–West Population Institute. Dr. Mary Kritz has been a wise advisor during the course of our work and helped arrange Rockefeller Foundation support for this project (Grant RF 83043 Allocation 23). To these colleagues and others too numerous to name, we wish to express our deep thanks.

Honolulu and Manila
August 1986

James T. Fawcett
Benjamin V. Cariño

INTRODUCTION

1

International Migration and Pacific Basin Development

James T. Fawcett
and Benjamin V. Cariño

Asia is home to more than half of the world's people; it is also the world's main source region for international migrants—those leaving home in search of a better life through temporary employment or permanent residence in another country. Immigration—a relatively permanent type of international migration—is the focus of this book, with special reference to immigration flows to and from countries in the Pacific Basin.

In the last century and the early part of this century, immigration was a more prominent feature of global affairs than it is today. As colonial empires have shrunk and wilderness frontiers have disappeared, nations have instituted stronger and more effective controls over immigration. Even for the adventurous in spirit, there are today relatively few options for permanent resettlement, with the prospect of eventually attaining the rights of citizenship in a new country. The opportunities that do exist, moreover, are nearly all found in four Pacific Basin nations: Australia, New Zealand, Canada, and the United States. Among these, the United States admits most of the world's immigrants.

Asia is now the primary source region for immigration to the United States, contributing close to half of all legal immigrants. This predominance of Asians is the outcome of a dramatic realignment of U.S. immigration patterns that has taken place in just the past twenty-five years. In 1960 Europe was still the main source of immigrants to America, as it had been throughout U.S. history. In that year, European nations constituted seven out of the top ten source countries for U.S. immigration. By 1985, six of the ten major source countries were Asian and none was European.

These numerical shifts in immigration to the United States are closely paralleled by recent changes in immigration to Canada and Australia. The growth of Asian immigration to all three countries was made possible by similar policy changes, which eliminated earlier discriminatory provisions. The new policies provide, in effect, equal opportunities for admission regardless of the immigrant's nationality or ethnicity. It is no surprise that these policy reforms produced significant shifts in immigration patterns, but the predominance of Asians was not really anticipated, at least in the United States. Even today, more than twenty years after the U.S. immigration reform of 1965, we know little about why Asian immigration grew faster than immigration from other regions or why, for example, immigration from South Korea grew by 200 percent in the 1970s while Japanese immigration barely grew at all.

Most Asian immigrants to the United States come from just five countries. The major source countries in 1984, in rank order, were the Philippines, Vietnam, China, South Korea, and India. These five countries (with Taiwan included as part of China) accounted in 1984 for 73 percent of Asian admissions and 32 percent of admissions from all countries. Filipinos are currently the second-largest group among all legal immigrants to the United States, after Mexicans.

The pattern is different for Canada, Australia, and New Zealand—all members of the British Commonwealth. Canada's top-ranked Asian admissions in 1984 were from Vietnam, Hong Kong, and India. The recent picture from Australia puts India and Vietnam at the top, followed by Malaysia. In New Zealand, the number of Pacific Islanders greatly exceeds the number of Asians, with Samoa, the Cook Islands, and Fiji being the major sources. Indians, the largest Asian group, rank just below Fijians among the foreign-born in New Zealand.

Although Asians are the dominant group in permanent immigration streams in the Pacific Basin, the actual numbers involved are not large relative to the size of the populations of Asian sending countries. The proportion of international migrants *is* large in the Pacific Islands, however, where perhaps 10 percent of the total ethnic population has moved away. In the Pacific, most of the movers are not immigrants in the legal sense, owing to political arrangements providing free movement between the home islands and specified destinations, notably New Zealand and the United States. They are immigrants in another sense, however, since the trend among Pacific Islanders who have left seems to be toward permanent resettlement in the destination country.

The changes that are taking place in the Pacific Basin reflect to some degree a worldwide increase in international population movements, involving not only immigrants and refugees but also contract workers, business people, students, tourists, and illegal or undocumented migrants. The volume of such movements is sufficient to have impacts on the demographic structure of small countries, to affect population growth rates in larger industrialized countries where birth rates are low, and to have a noticeable influence on various other aspects of sending and receiving societies.

This book aims to bring together in one place a body of knowledge that will advance our understanding of Asian and Pacific immigration and related forms of population movement. In pursuit of that aim, we give prominence to analysis of the basic demographic facts—the size of international migration flows and counterflows, the characteristics of the people who make up the flows, and the changes over time in both size and composition of the flows. We also examine the historical, political, economic, and social conditions that are associated with major immigration flows, drawing upon theoretical conceptualizations and comparative empirical analyses. Further, we emphasize distinctively in this book the perspective of immigrant sending countries, with respect both to the impetus for emigration and the consequences for the society of an outflow of people.

Before presenting a chapter-by-chapter preview of the book, we sketch in the following section the broader context within which Pacific Basin immigration flows are taking place. Topics discussed include political and economic linkages between countries and trends in transpacific population movements. Our aims here are to provide an appreciation of the macrostructural influences on immigration and to highlight the connections between immigration and other forms of population movement in the region. Issues raised in a general way in this introductory chapter are examined more systematically in the book's concluding chapter.

THE CONTEXT OF ASIAN AND PACIFIC IMMIGRATION

Policies on Population Movement

In 1875, the first effective U.S. immigration law was enacted. Only seven years later the first racial basis for excluding immigrants was added, aimed at barring Chinese laborers. Asian immigration has thus demonstrably been a policy issue in the United States since the earliest days of immigration policy formulation. Similar observations can be made about the other major immigrant-receiving countries: Canada, Australia, and New Zealand. Yet, immigration policy is only one aspect of the legal, economic, political, and cultural context that influences international migration.

Policies on *emigration* from Asian and Pacific countries have not been systematically studied, although a compilation of formal and informal policies derived from the U.S. State Department's *Human Rights Report* was recently made available (Fawcett et al., 1985). In general, the trend is toward greater freedom of movement. Some Asian countries previously had highly restrictive policies on issuance of passports and exit permits, because of brain drain concerns or domestic political considerations. Today, however, such places as South Korea and India have loosened their constraints and instituted essentially laissez-faire emigration policies. Some evidence even exists of coordination of emigration and immigration policies in the region, as in the case of a Korean policy change to accommodate emigration of investors to Canada. There are some exceptions to the generalization about loosening of emigration controls, mainly in socialist or communist countries such as Burma and Vietnam. The policies in China have been relaxed recently, however, to allow a fairly free outflow of those who have permission to immigrate to another country.

In general, emigration and immigration policies are decided by individual countries, based on perceptions of their own national interest. While this undoubtedly will continue to be the dominant pattern, some shifts in emphasis are indicated, as noted by Papademetriou (1984:421):

What is needed . . . is a better understanding of the place of each country in an increasingly interdependent world and the responsibilities that migration imposes on actors at both ends of the flow. In view of this mutuality of responsibilities, migration becomes a matter virtually impervious to satisfactory solution by unilateral action.

Policies on refugees have been a dominant regional concern since 1975, when U.S. forces withdrew from Saigon. In that case, policy coordination was required not between sending and receiving countries, but between countries of first asylum and receiving countries. More recently, however, attention has been directed to enlarging the legal channel for emigration from Vietnam (the Orderly Departure Program) as a means of reducing the number of "boat people" and other clandestine departures. Even so, political conflicts continue to provoke significant refugee flows from Kampuchea, Laos, and Afghanistan.

It is worth noting in this context that the major refugee flows in Asia since World War II have been between Asian countries—notably the mass population movements between India and Pakistan. Other significant flows include those between North and South Korea, between Tibet and India, between Indonesia and China, between China and

Hong Kong, between India and Sri Lanka, and between Bangladesh and India. Thus, the recent prominence of refugee policy issues is unusual only because it involves massive resettlement in third countries—a fact that is often cited as actually enhancing refugee flows from Indochina.

Legal constraints on emigration and immigration are undoubtedly a major factor in regulating the size and composition of many international population flows. It does not follow, however, that the element of border control makes international migration uniquely policy-directed. In some instances, movements within a country's borders, through such means as residence permits and government-directed employment controls, are almost as tightly controlled as movements across the border. In other instances, long-distance international moves are not subject to immigration controls, as in migration from certain Pacific Islands to countries with which they have special political connections. And, of course, some land borders are so permeable that immigration controls have little practical effect.

Immigration policies are often discussed in the context of labor market forces, but they reflect cultural and social forces as well. As Weiner (1985b:449) remarks, "Indeed, governments often choose entry and exit rules that economists would regard as inefficient, because the government seeks to maximize values other than economic efficiency." Immigration policies are in fact one of the main mechanisms for maintaining the social, cultural, and political integrity of sovereign states. At the same time, however, changing immigration policies are both a cause and a reflection of differing national perspectives on ethnicity and assimilation. Richmond (1984:519–520) notes that:

Today more than ever it is important to recognize the polyethnic and culturally diversified character of both sending and receiving countries. There is no single "American way of life" into which immigrants arriving in the United States must eventually be assimilated. The United States is ethnically stratified, culturally pluralistic and exhibits a diversity of life-styles. The same applies to other countries such as Australia, Canada, France, the United Kingdom, and many others who have experienced large-scale immigration in the last three decades.

Recently the constraining powers of emigration and immigration policies seem to have weakened owing to the fluidity and ease of other kinds of cross-border movements, such as tourism, business travel, and contract labor migration—all of which act as facilitators of long-term settlement, whether legal or illegal. With these trends in mind, and with the "foreignness" of distant places diminishing because of the influence of modern communication technology (such as satellite-transmitted television), there is a strong case for looking at international migration in a broad conceptual or theoretical context that is applicable to other forms of population movement as well.

International Linkages

Immigration in the modern world is one dimension of myriad international connections that exist in many forms and at many levels. A significant body of contemporary scholarship looks at these connections in a "world systems" framework that highlights economic and political subordination of some nations to others (Cheng and Bonacich, 1984; Petras, 1981). From this perspective, international migration is seen largely as a labor flow that is accounted for by the workings of the international capitalist system, which seeks to minimize the costs of labor in its drive to maximize profits. One need not fully agree with this perspective to recognize that it has had the important consequence of directing our attention to the migration impacts of economic connections that transcend national boundaries. As noted by Kritz (1985:5):

Growing interdependence among countries contributes to increased international population mobility. Increased international flows of capital, technology, goods, services, and resources have been accompanied by increased flows of people, in order to manage these other transfers, to provide labor, and to take advantage of differentials in opportunities. . . .

The immigration flows that are the focus of this book take place within the Pacific Basin, the most dynamic region of the contemporary world from the standpoint of economic growth (East-West Center, 1986). Indeed, it is common for pundits to speak of the late twentieth century as the "Age of the Pacific." The high level of economic growth in the Pacific Basin has occurred during a period of greatly increased economic interdependency among nations, which itself is a function of technological advances that have made possible the easy international movement of information, capital, commodities, and people. The emergence of transnational corporations that readily transfer personnel and goods across national boundaries is testimony to the connection between a global economic system and the growth of international population movements.

The "economic miracle" in Asia has radically transformed patterns of world trade. As recently as 1970, the volume of transatlantic trade (exports and imports between countries of North America and countries of Europe, the Middle East, and Africa) was nearly double the volume of transpacific trade. By 1984 the Pacific Basin had essentially caught up, with transpacific trade being about equal to transatlantic trade. This shift reflects not only the rapid economic growth in Asian countries, but also the extent to which that growth has been export-oriented and therefore closely linked to the world economic system. Japan continues to dominate transpacific trade, but recent figures show that other Asian countries now account for nearly half of the total.

The connections between immigration or resettlement and various temporary international movements of people in the Pacific Basin is an important topic. Tourism, business travel, and short-term residence for study or work are all on the increase. Economic growth in Asian countries has produced a burgeoning middle class whose members are sufficiently affluent to afford international travel for pleasure. At the same time, the expansion of multinational corporations and companies devoted to the export and import of goods has fostered an increase in international business travel. It is not possible to distinguish accurately these two types of travel, because many business trips are taken on tourist visas, many tourist visas are issued to family members going along on a business trip, and often travel is for both business and pleasure. Nonetheless, the overall trends for temporary visitors, as described in U.S. immigration statistics, provide a useful picture of economically significant circular migration. For simplicity, the United States is used consistently as an example in the paragraphs that follow; many of the same trends could be documented for Canada, Australia, and New Zealand.

The number of Asians admitted to the United States as temporary visitors increased almost threefold between 1973 and 1983, when the total reached 2.2 million. The largest categories among 1983 visitors from Asia were tourists (1.6 million), business people (318,000), and students (118,000). Japan was the primary source of Asian visitors to the United States in all three categories, with China in second place across the board. India ranked third in tourists, South Korea ranked third in business visitors, and Malaysia ranked third in student admissions in 1983.

Students are an especially important type of temporary visitor. They stay much longer than tourists or business visitors, they represent a highly selected, elite segment of their home country's population, they come to the host country at an impressionable age, and they participate in one of the host society's major socializing institutions—the educational system.

Asian students have outnumbered other foreign students in the United States for the past thirty years. Although only 10,000 Asians were studying in the United States in 1955, they comprised 30 percent of all foreign students at that time. Current figures put the number of Asian students at 132,000, about 39 percent of the total number of foreign students in American schools. In the academic year 1981–1982, Iran was the top source country. Among East and South Asian countries, Taiwan was first (20,500), followed by Japan (14,000), India (11,300),

Malaysia (9,400), Hong Kong (9,000), South Korea (8,100), and Thailand (6,700). These figures should be viewed not only as an indicator of important international linkages, but also in light of a recent estimate that one out of every three Asian students in the United States will eventually become an immigrant.

Immigration is a cause as well as a consequence of student admissions, since the population of previous immigrants who are residents of the United States—Asian Americans—can provide information, financial sponsorship, and hospitality to potential students from the home country. Recent estimates put the number of Asian Americans at just over five million (Gardner et al., 1985). Other causes of the popularity of the United States among Asians seeking higher education have been identified by Cummings and So (1985) as: (1) political affinity between many Asian countries and the United States, an aspect of which has been government-sponsored scholarships for Asians to study in the United States; (2) economic ties, particularly the scale of Asian exports to the United States; (3) similarities between Asian and U.S. educational systems, in combination with the popularization of English as an international language; (4) the size and absorptive capacity of the American educational system; and (5) the perceived quality and diversity of programs in U.S. universities. With such factors as these at work, and with the school-age population in Asia continuing to expand, Asians studying in the United States will continue to be an important feature of international connections in the Pacific Basin.

Our focus in this discussion is on movements of people to the United States, but we should not forget that much transpacific travel originates in the United States. Included in this out-migration are previous Asian immigrants who are returning home. Warren and Kraly (1985) estimate that 239,000 persons who were not U.S. citizens emigrated from the United States to Asia during the period 1970–1980, most of whom would be return migrants. Additional outbound travelers would include Asian-born U.S. citizens returning home, native-born Americans emigrating to countries in the Asian–Pacific region, and those leaving for shorter periods, such as business people and tourists. The volume of such travel is difficult to estimate because the United States does not maintain exit statistics and data on the Asian side are not always available or comparable.

One indication of the scale and impact of U.S. visitors in Asia can be gained by taking an Asian receiving country as an example. South Korea, where data are reliable, showed a tripling of the number of Americans entering the country as tourists over a recent ten-year period. About 190,000 Americans entered South Korea on tourist visas in 1982. Korean data on the growth in international communications are also worth noting, since they are a reflection of either the presence of foreigners in the country or direct contacts between Koreans and persons overseas. During the 1972–1982 decade, the number of international telephone calls received in South Korea increased tenfold, as did the number of telex messages received.

South Korea also provides an important example of the impact of U.S. military alliances, an international connection that is not often emphasized in immigration studies. About 40,000 U.S. troops are stationed in South Korea at present, accounting for one-third of the total American military personnel in Asia. (Japan and the Philippines are the other major countries of concentration.) The "stock" of U.S. military personnel is a conservative indicator of impact, because many military men and women are accompanied by dependents, military personnel are supported by a substantial overseas staff of American civilians, and troops are rotated on a regular basis.

One of the military's impacts is discernible in South Korean government emigration statistics, which show 85,000 Korean women emigrating to the United States during 1962–1983 under the category of "international marriage," most of them brides of G.I.'s. Also monitored are departures of children for adoption by Americans—50,000 from 1962 to 1983—many of whom are Amerasian children.

Another potentially significant U.S. military influence in the Pacific Basin is the Pentagon's International Military Education and Training Program (IMET), under which foreign military personnel receive U.S.-oriented training and indoctrination. The Department of Defense's 1984 congressional presentation on this program describes it as a "valuable channel of communication and influence with a significant elite, especially in the Third World," and notes that ". . . the English language training which is essential to much of the training [provides] a common language for increased knowledge of the American people, and, in the long run, a greater understanding of the United States." Over 300,000 Asian military personnel have participated in IMET programs since 1950, composing over half of the program's worldwide total. The countries of Indochina have supplied more than half of the Asian trainees, followed by South Korea (35,500), Taiwan (25,600), Thailand (19,000), the Philippines (17,600), and Japan (19,700).

The examples given above indicate that international migration and permanent immigration in the Asian–Pacific region are related in complex ways to other kinds of country-to-country connections, not all of which fit comfortably into existing theoretical frameworks for migration. This lack of fit may be attributed to the fact that not all immigration is labor migration. Further, international migration is regulated by public policies that may have purposes, such as cultural protection, that are unrelated to economic forces. The scale and diversity of international population movements have increased so rapidly that models based on earlier experience seem inadequate to explain contemporary trends. Along these lines, Kritz (1985:22–23) has noted that, "The growing numbers of persons of all nationalities partaking in international travel for work, study, or touristic purposes results in a new form of movement unique to the modern era. How international mobility and circulation interact with international migration requires further consideration and measurement."

Sending Country Issues

The perspective of immigrant-sending countries is of course quite different from the perspective of receiving countries, although both are concerned with the general issues of transfer of human resources and intercountry linkages. While the brain drain continues to be a matter of concern in some sending countries, it does not seem to be the major issue it was a few years ago. There is a growing recognition that many emigrants are people whose skills are surplus in the home country, that emigration to some extent acts as a safety valve to relieve pressures of unemployment or political dissatisfaction, and that remittances from emigrants (or temporary workers) can have a positive economic impact at home. These facts carry substantial weight among national policymakers, even though the problems alleviated by out-migration may be a consequence of the country's dependent status vis-à-vis the receiving country in the world economic structure.

A recent comprehensive study of the overseas Indian community—estimated to number more than 13 million—concluded that, "although emigration on the whole seems to have been beneficial to India, particularly in relieving the pressure of unemployment and in enabling the country to enjoy an improved foreign exchange reserve position, one cannot be conclusive about its long-term effects" (Madhavan, 1985:474–475).

An overseas population can sometimes serve as an effective political lobby in the host country for issues important to the home country. Some of these issues involve trade and tariff measures and may affect immigration directly. The Taiwanese lobby in Washington, for example, played a role in gaining U.S. Congressional approval for an immigration quota for Taiwan that is separate from the quota for mainland China.

There are also potential benefits to a country's international trade relationships in having a cadre of business people resident in overseas locations. Weiner (1985b:452) notes that, "Third World countries initially concerned primarily with the flow of remittances have become increasingly interested in the role that migrant businessmen and professionals can play in investment and in the transfer of technology. The governments of China and India, for example, now actively work with their overseas communities to promote investment and technology transfers." Evidence of this connection was recently noted (Kotkin, 1986:25) in a U.S. business magazine: "With their cultural, linguistic, and family ties to China, Chinese-American entrepreneurs are proving to be America's secret weapon in recapturing a predominant economic role in the world's most populous nation."

On the negative side, some sending countries are concerned about undesirable cultural influences transmitted home by emigrants or students and workers abroad. Western values are not universally admired in Asian and Pacific countries, especially as they impinge on family relationships and religious or cultural beliefs. Cultural domination by the West is a real worry, and it reinforces fears of economic and political domination. The tenets of dependency theory, which put Third World development at the mercy of marketplace decisions made in the "core" industrialized nations, have been readily accepted by many Asian and Pacific scholars because of the obvious economic interdependence of countries in the region. Increasingly, then, international migration is evaluated by sending countries from a much broader perspective than transfer of human resources, taking into account also the complex international linkages of which migration is but a small part. Weiner (1985a:194–199) summarizes the contemporary assessment of immigration as follows:

. . . the gains are short-term, while the costs come later; . . . the gains are mainly economic, while the costs are both political and social; . . . employers and migrants are the primary gainers, while the costs are borne by others; and . . . the receiving countries are greater beneficiaries than the sending countries, who bear a disproportionate share of the costs.

Although emigration flows have long been recognized as a public policy concern in Asian countries, the more recent temporary labor flows have generated a much higher level of official government involvement (Arnold and Shah, 1986). This involvement seems to stem from two considerations: The sending government can continue to exercise some control over temporary contract workers, in view of their expected return home; and this control can include requirements for repatriation of overseas earnings. Remittances have grown tremendously in some countries in recent years. For example, remittances in Pakistan in 1981 reached a level equivalent to 70 percent of merchandise exports. In Bangladesh in 1985, remittances were second only to jute exports as an earner of foreign exchange (Appleyard, 1986). Worldwide, Tabbarah (1984:437) has concluded that, ". . . remittances constitute a major transfer of funds from more developed to less developed countries, which has recently been exceeding the total value of development assistance." The scale of remittances has drawn the attention of Asian policymakers to issues connected with international migration, including issues that involve both temporary migration and emigration.

Most of the topics just discussed are dealt with more fully in various chapters of this book, which addresses a wide range of theoretical, empirical, and policy concerns. We summarize each chapter in the paragraphs that follow, so that the reader may see where each part fits within the whole.

PREVIEW OF THE BOOK

The four chapters composing Part I, Factors Influencing International Migration Flows, provide a general framework within which subsequent chapters can be better understood. Although much of the material in this section emphasizes Asia, the perspective is global and comparative.

Chapter 2 by Kritz provides a quantitative framework, looking at international migration flows since 1960 and recent data on the foreign-born component of national populations. Kritz's worldwide analysis shows important shifts in permanent immigration, with recent trends favoring Third World immigrants, especially those from Asia. Only a few countries admit significant numbers of permanent immigrants, among which the United States is the unquestioned leader. However, many more countries admit "temporary" workers, a phenomenon that has led to an unexpected surge in international movements of people. The growing significance of temporary migration is one of three factors Kritz identifies as shaping contemporary international migration. The others are interdependence among nations and social networks linking sending and receiving areas. Kritz rejects the view that economic inequalities between places adequately explain migration flows, and she identifies some of the key components of a new immigration paradigm.

This theme is carried forward in Chapter 3 by Portes, who attempts to distill from the literature on international migration some common themes and contrasting elements. In this insightful essay, Portes looks at explanations for migration under four rubrics: the origins of flows, the causes of their stability, the uses of immigrant labor, and adaptation of immigrants to the host society. Like Kritz, he finds the classical economic explanations inadequate, but sees more promise in theories that look to the linkages and dependencies that may be found through analysis of the global economic system. To an understanding of the stable or temporary nature of migration, however, social networks are the key. Social networks also facilitate access to the opportunities provided through the economic system, as well as create new opportunities that can support a migration flow running counter to economic trends.

The uses of labor migration are a topic that has dominated the theoretical literature on migration in recent years, introducing such concepts as the split labor market and the dual economy. Although economic at bottom, these writings introduce elements of ideology and commitment into the immigration literature. As portrayed by Portes, they are unduly narrow, not allowing for different "modes of incorporation" that parallel the diversity of migrants and types of international migration. A similar ferment is apparent in the area of immigrant adaptation, where value judgments about the desirability of assimilation into the host culture have been replaced by a recognition that individuals and groups can be incorporated in a new society in diverse ways, some of which are rooted in ethnic solidarity and imply continuation of "old culture" norms.

Although a wide net is cast by Portes, his chapter still does not address the perspective taken in Chapter 4 by Teitelbaum, whose topic is international relations. Teitelbaum identifies three themes: the effect of foreign policy on migration, the effect of migration on foreign policy, and migration as an instrument of foreign policy. Telling examples of each are given from recent Asian history, e.g., the refugee exodus prompted by U.S. policy in Indochina, the impact of the "Taiwanese lobby" on U.S. foreign policy, and the planned settlement of Vietnamese in Kampuchea to assure political domination.

The significance of the relationship between international migration and international relations is highlighted by examining recent and potential crises: the Korean War, the Soviet invasion of Afghanistan, the decline of the U.S.-supported regime in the Philippines, the drama of the boat people, and the possible exodus related to China's political absorption of Hong Kong. From Teitelbaum's analysis, it appears that national purposes related to foreign policy "explain" a substantial part of Asian immigration to the United States, as well as some other international migrations. Yet, this perspective has somehow eluded both theoretical modelers and empirical analysts.

A partial exception is the work on refugees, which so potently involves international relations that this dimension has almost been taken for granted. Chapter 5 by Suhrke and Klink reminds us, however, that understanding refugee flows is not a simple task. In an enlightening comparison of the Vietnamese and Afghan cases, Suhrke and Klink show how the direction and size of refugee flows are influenced by policies in the receiving countries. These policies on refugee admissions are shaped by foreign policy considerations based on the nature of the conflict and the posture of other countries. Tracing such considerations, Suhrke and Klink arrive at important conclusions about why Indochinese have been rapidly and massively absorbed in third-country resettlement schemes, while Afghanistan's refugees mostly remain in their countries of first asylum, Pakistan and Iran.

Part II, Immigration Trends and Policies, looks at immigrant and refugee flows from the perspective of the four major receiving countries: the United States, Australia, New Zealand, and Canada. Together, these countries account for the vast majority of the total intake of legal immigrants in recent years. They have in common many factors related to Asian immigration that become apparent through an examination of the historical development of their current immigration policies.

Chapter 6 by Arnold, Minocha, and Fawcett shows the clear relationship between immigration policies in the United States and the number of immigrants admitted from specific countries. A drop in admission of Chinese after passage of the Chinese Exclusion Act in 1882 is hardly surprising, but the impact of eliminating preferences by national origin in 1965 was harder to foresee. In the event, Asians have been the main beneficiaries of the latter change, with their numbers jumping from only 17,000 in 1965 to about a quarter of a million annually in recent years. Arnold et al. document the change from predominantly European to predominantly Asian immigration to the United States. This dramatic shift has come about mainly through the use by Asian Americans of the family reunification provisions of U.S. immigration law, which give priority to close relatives of persons already resident in the United States. Filipino Americans and Chinese Americans have made especially good use of these provisions, taking advantage of their historical ties. The equally well-established Japanese Americans have not made much use of family reunification provisions, however, whereas the more recently arrived Koreans are using the family provisions to achieve a very rapid rate of growth. After carefully reviewing such trends, Arnold and his colleagues discuss the multiple factors that appear to be responsible for the dramatic increase in Asian immigration, concluding that these mutually reinforcing influences should produce a continuing strong inflow for the foreseeable future.

Refugees from Indochina have been a significant component of Asian immigration to the United States since 1975, when U.S. troops withdrew from Saigon and Vietnam was unified under a regime dominated by northerners. Gordon's Chapter 7 provides a careful analysis of this important and dramatic chapter in U.S. immigration history. In only ten years, more than 700,000 Asians—mainly Vietnamese—were admitted in refugee status, profoundly changing the Asian American profile. Whereas many of the Vietnamese refugees were ethnic Chinese with high levels of education and skills, others were not so well equipped for life in the United States and were in need of assistance. The proportion of Laotians (many of them Hmong) and Kampucheans has also grown in recent years, and an estimated quarter-million have now been admitted. Massive programs have been mounted to facilitate the adaptation of Indochinese refugees and to foster their acceptance in the communities where they settle. Gordon draws upon a body of solid research to show that although refugees start off very low on the socioeconomic ladder, most of them move toward comparability with the native population fairly quickly—in part because more persons in the household become income earners. Overall, refugees are still disadvantaged in U.S. society. Nonetheless, they continue to seek entry to the United States, causing a substantial annual flow and a large backlog in the camps in countries of first asylum and in the "pending" files of the Orderly Departure Program.

Refugees from Indochina have also had a substantial impact in Australia, which has admitted more refugees per capita than any other country. It is not only refugees, however, who have stirred up public debate over Asian immigration. As Price points out in Chapter 8, Australia's introduction of nondiscriminatory immigration policies in 1973 has resulted in a big jump in Asian admissions through family reunification provisions, much like the increase in the United States. In a recent year, fully one-third of the new settlers arriving in Australia came from Asian and Pacific countries—an enormous change for a country known for its earlier White Australia policy. One interesting facet is the high proportion of females among Filipino and Thai immigrants, which is related to an overall pattern among Asian immigrant women of marrying outside their own groups. From this and other evidence, Price presents a portrait of a society evolving toward multiculturalism.

Such evolution does not seem to be occurring in New Zealand, or at least is taking place more slowly there. One evidence for this is a low rate of out-marriage among ethnic groups. And, as Trlin points out in Chapter 9, New Zealand's immigration policies continue to preclude large-scale Asian immigration. Nevertheless, New Zealand does give priority to the admission of some Pacific Islanders and has taken an active role in training students from some Asian countries. The complexities of New Zealand's immigration policies are traced by Trlin, who examines recent census data to provide evidence that the barriers erected through formal and informal immigration policies have proven to be quite effective. Trlin believes that New Zealand will continue to give special consideration to Pacific Island nations but that substantial Asian immigration is unlikely except for particular situations, such as the resettlement of refugees.

Asian immigration to Canada has followed a course similar to that in the United States, owing partly to parallel conditions. In Chapter 10, Kubat traces the early history of a Chinese Exclusion Act and a Gentlemen's Agreement with Japan, very much like those in the United States and stimulated by similar West Coast racial prejudices and economic fears. Distinctively evident in the Canadian case was the development of a more urban industrial economy and a consequent adjustment of immigration provisions to foster the importation of appropriate skills. The current policies are ethnically nondiscriminatory and have facilitated a surge in Asian immigration under family reunification provisions. Kubat shows that over 40 percent of Canada's recent immigrants are from Asian and Pacific countries, up from about 20 percent a decade ago. He also presents data on the geographic concentration of Asian groups, a factor that is an important issue with respect to adaptation patterns because of related effects such as ethnic solidarity and visibility in the host community.

The next part of the book provides a detailed empirical look at Asian immigrant adaptation, focusing on Asians in the United States. In the two chapters that constitute this section, recent U.S. census data and other statistical sources are analyzed to provide an Asian American socioeconomic profile and to project the future growth of the Asian American population.

Chapter 11 by Xenos and his colleagues is based mainly on the 1980 census but includes comparisons with previous census analyses. The chapter compares Asian Americans with other major immigrant groups—blacks, Hispanics, and non-Hispanic whites—and includes comparisons among the six largest Asian American groups. The analyses make important distinctions between immigrant and nonimmigrant Asians and between recent immigrants and those who arrived earlier. The chapter confirms what is by now widely known—that most Asian American families are doing well economically—but also shows important differences among groups, notably the relatively low status of Vietnamese refugees, particularly in the years immediately following arrival. Among Asian immigrants in general, the participation of women in the labor force is perhaps the most important aspect of the immigrant family's successful economic adjustment. Moreover, immigrants tend to have larger households and to obtain income from members who are not of the immediate family. A somewhat surprising finding is the evidence of a shift in residential preference toward the southern United States, although California continues to be the major Asian American destination.

This picture of the current status of Asian Americans is extended into the future in Chapter 12 by Bouvier and Agresta, who base their analysis on statistical projections. Using assumptions that seem reasonable, they project growth of the Asian American population from 3.5 million in 1980 to about 10 million in the year 2000 and to perhaps 20 million by the year 2030. This sixfold increase in fifty years would contribute to a proportional increase, with Asian Americans growing from 1.6 percent to 6 percent of the U.S. population. On the basis of recent information about the demographic patterns for particular ethnic groups, Bouvier and Agresta project Filipinos to become the largest Asian American group by the late 1980s. By the year 2000 Vietnamese may be the second largest, followed by Koreans. If the three Indochinese groups (Vietnamese, Laotian, Kampuchean) are combined, then the Indochinese would be the largest Asian American contingent in 2030, accounting for fully one-third of the total Asian American population. The cultural implications of these projections are discussed by Bouvier and Agresta, who point out that the proportions of blacks, Hispanics, and Asian Americans will increase significantly by the middle of the next century, while the proportion of non-Hispanic whites decreases. The options for different forms of a multicultural society in the United States require careful examination.

The next part of the book, Sending Country Perspectives, is designed to add a supply-side view to explanations for the trends and projections in Asian immigration as well as to look at the impacts of emigration on the home countries. The Asian situation is covered in three chapters. The first focuses on the Philippines, with some attention to other countries in Southeast Asia; the second focuses on South Korea, with some attention to Japan, China, Hong Kong, and Taiwan; and the third focuses on India, with some attention to other countries in South Asia. Finally, the situation in the Pacific Islands is reviewed in a chapter that gives particular attention to Polynesia while looking also at Micronesia and Melanesia.

The Philippines is a special case among Asian sending countries, owing to its previous colonial relationship with the United States. As Cariño points out in Chapter 13, this long historical connection has produced, among other factors, a pervasive Americanization of Philippine culture. In addition, the early roots of the immigration stream—Filipino plantation workers imported to Hawaii and California—provided a strong U.S. network that was able to take quick advantage of the 1965 changes in U.S. immigration law. The colonial heritage has also meant close business ties between the United States and the Philippines, as well as prominent military and political connections. The overall picture of the effects of emigration on the Philippines is not very clear, but remittances seem to be important and there is evidence of substantial return migration and repatriation of earnings. These personal and institutional networks help explain why the Philippines is the largest current source of Asian immigrants to the United States. Cariño's chapter also discusses what little is known about immigration from other Southeast Asian countries (excluding Indochina). The next largest stream is from Thailand, but that is only one-tenth the size of the Philippine stream and much more recent, probably arising mainly as a by-product of the war in Vietnam. Both the Philippines and Thailand send more females than males to the United States, many of them through marriage connections.

In Chapter 14 on South Korea and East Asia, Kim prefers a multifactor approach to the causes of international migration. Rejecting conventional theories as too simplistic, he builds a convincing case for the complex, mutually reinforcing factors that have caused South Korea to become a major source of immigrants to the United States. Kim describes a variety of premigration factors—kinship, mass culture, economic development, political conditions, military alliances—and discusses their relevance to "emigration connections." Ties to the United States through military and political alliances and trade have been important in all East Asian countries. A singular connection has been the large numbers of marriages of Korean and Japanese women to U.S. military personnel. The U.S. military has also been partly responsible for the spread of American mass culture in South Korea and Japan that fosters emigration by reinforcing such "push" factors as population density and political instability. With these multiple factors at work and a labor supply that fitted with U.S. labor force requirements, the seeds were sown for a Korean emigration stream that has grown faster than any other except that of refugees.

India dominates the South Asian picture, over 80 percent of U.S. immigrants from that region being Indian. Differences in the history of immigration may account for the substantial difference in size of immigration streams between India and the next largest South Asian sending country, Pakistan. Chapter 15 by Minocha pulls together the scanty information that is available about immigration from the region, focusing on India.

The important and striking descriptive difference between South Asian and other Asian streams is the high proportion of professional and technical workers among South Asian immigrants—generally two-thirds or more, many of whom are physicians, engineers, and scientists. The political connections with the United States are not so strong in India as they are in South Korea and the Philippines, but the United States has had a longstanding interest in providing economic and technical support to India, a very populous and poor country with a democratic political system. Along with economic aid has come a variety of American connections, notably scholarships and training programs for Indians to study in the United States, which have undoubtedly helped to start immigration networks. The push factors have also been substantial, not only because of poverty, but also because of an oversupply of professionals. Concern about the brain drain seems to have subsided in India, partly because of a recognition that there are benefits in emigration of people whose skills cannot be absorbed at home. Indians are perhaps the least known among major Asian immigrant groups in the United States, owing to their employment in the primary sector and their residential scatter (as opposed to settlement in ethnic enclaves). As Minocha points out, however, the influence of Indian immigrants on the United States could be substantial as a result of their high-status positions.

The situation of the Pacific Island nations is unusual, owing to their physical isolation, their imbalanced and fragile economies, their close political and economic links to "metropolitan" countries (especially the United States and New Zealand), and their very high proportions of emigrants. These factors come to the fore in a comprehensive survey by Connell, who in Chapter 16 discerns a new structure of international dependence that has emerged in the Pacific over the past twenty years or so. Migration is an important—indeed essential—aspect of this structure, since it has allowed for relief of population pressures and has provided a major source of outside income through remittances. About 10 percent of Pacific Islanders now live outside their home countries, and currently the United States is the main destination. (A brief profile of Pacific Islanders in the U.S. is included in Chapter 11 by Xenos et al.) Despite the great diversity among Pacific Island countries, Connell finds many similarities in their situations with respect to migration, especially in the negative economic and social consequences. These consequences are easier to see in the Pacific, where rates of outmigration are high and whole societies can be more easily studied. Outmigration appears to be a rational household strategy, however, and Connell believes it will continue at high levels.

In the last part of the book, Research Issues, the first chapter focuses on the perspective of sending countries and the second on the United States as a receiving country, with each chapter deriving conclusions about gaps in knowledge and priorities for future research. The third chapter in this section pulls together a variety of research issues and discusses them in the context of a migration systems approach.

Cariño's Chapter 17 provides a useful framework for organizing knowledge about impacts of emigration on the sending society. Four areas are identified for review: migrant selectivity, repatriated earnings, skills and ideas brought back, and activities of emigrants abroad.

Migrant selectivity usually entails movement of the younger and better-educated segment of the population and sometimes involves unequal proportions of males and females. This aspect has received substantial attention, especially the out-migration of skilled workers known as the brain drain, but still it is difficult to draw general conclusions about costs and benefits because much depends on the economic conditions in the area of origin.

The significance of repatriated earnings has become a prominent issue in Asia in recent years, mainly because of the rapid growth of labor migration to the Middle East. Remittances have been shown to be of meaningful magnitude, but it is not at all clear that they have important long-term positive economic effects (as opposed to short-term effects on consumption and household welfare). Cariño points out, though, that use of remittances for education may be a highly productive long-term investment in human capital. As for skills and ideas brought back by returning migrants, the skimpy evidence available does not indicate a significant positive effect. Even less is known about the business and trade connections established by immigrants, but anecdotal evidence on this topic and on immigrants' political lobbying activities indicates that they could be important to the sending country. Cariño's chapter discusses some of the research designs that are needed to produce gains in knowledge for each impact of emigration on the sending countries.

Chapter 18 by Sullivan takes as its theme a comparison of research on Asians and Hispanics in the United States, while also addressing the overarching issue of research problems in the field of U.S. immigration studies. A fundamental structural problem is the separation of data producers from data analysts, compounded by inadequate communications between the groups. To put it simply, the best immigration data are produced by U.S. government agencies, but those agencies do little useful analysis; the best analyses are done in the academic community, but academic researchers do not have access to much data and have had little effect in suggesting improvements in data production. This problem has recently been recognized in a report of the National Research Council, which also contains recommendations (summarized by Sullivan) that would, if adopted, go a long way toward improving knowledge about immigrants.

The greater research attention given to Hispanics, in comparison with Asians, is attributed by Sullivan to both perceived and actual differences between the two groups. The prevailing stereotype of Asian Americans pictures them as the "golden minority": hardworking, family oriented, intelligent, and successful. Hispanics tend to be seen as a disadvantaged minority (similar to blacks), who have low education and high fertility, and are likely to be on the welfare rolls. These public perceptions may be related to the difference between "easy" border crossings and long-distance transoceanic travel to enter the United States, with the latter suggesting greater motivation and commitment by Asians and an intention to remain in the United States. Sullivan also points out that Hispanics are seen as a culturally more homogeneous group, owing to their common language and religion, and are therefore more subject to the fears and prejudices connected with the image of "growing hordes" of immigrants. In more practical research terms, we actually know much less about Asians than we do about Hispanics. This ignorance about Asian immigrants stems partly from methodological problems, such as how ethnic groups are coded in existing data sources, but also from the lower level of domestic policy interest in Asians and a related shortage of research funding. Sullivan's chapter says why this situation must change and provides guidelines for learning more about the impact of Asian immigration to the United States.

In the final chapter, Fawcett and Arnold point out that, while theoretical work on international migration has shown significant advances in recent years, many discontinuities remain between the sweeping generalizations of current theories and the empirical diversities apparent in the flows and counterflows of people in the Asian–Pacific region. Immigration theorists need to give greater attention to the noneconomic conditions in sending countries, for example, and especially to take account of kinship networks functioning not only as a passive linkage but also as a pro-active shaper of migration flows. Fawcett and Arnold argue for a migration systems paradigm that incorporates such considerations, and they review the macrolevel and microlevel factors that should be assessed in an examination of the sending and receiving societies and the linkages between them.

REFERENCES

Appleyard, R. T.

  1986   "The Impact of International Migration on Developing countries." Paper prepared for a meeting of the Organization for Economic Cooperation and Development, Paris, May.

Arnold, F., and N. M. Shah

  1986   *Asian Labor Migration: Pipeline to the Middle East.* Boulder: Westview Press.

Cheng, L., and E. Bonacich

  1984   *Labor Immigration Under Capitalism: Asian Workers in the United States Before World War II.* Berkeley: University of California Press.

Cummings, W., and W. C. So

1985   "The Preference of Asian Overseas Students for the United States: An Examination of the Context." *Higher Education*, 14 (August): 403–423.

East–West Center

1986   *Asia–Pacific Report: Trends, Issues, Challenges.* Honolulu.

Fawcett, J. T., B. V. Cariño, and F. Arnold

1985   *Asia–Pacific Immigration to the United States: A Conference Report.* Honolulu: East–West Population Institute, East–West Center.

Gardner, R. W., B. Robey, and P. C. Smith

1985   "Asian Americans: Growth, Change, and Diversity." *Population Bulletin*, 40(4), October.

Kotkin, M.

1986   "The New Yankee Traders." *Inc.*, March: 25–28.

Kritz, M. M.

1985   "International Migration Theories: Conceptual and Definitional Issues." Paper presented at the IUSSP Seminar on Emerging Issues in International Migration, Bellagio, Italy, April 22–26.

Madhavan, M. C.

1985   "Indian Emigrants: Numbers, Characteristics, and Economic Impact." *Population and Development Review*, 11(3):457–481.

Papademetriou, D. G.

1984   "International Migration in a Changing World." *International Social Science Journal*, 36(3):409–423.

Petras, E. M.

1981   "The Global Labor Market in the Modern World-Economy." In M. M. Kritz et al. (eds.), *Global Trends in Migration: Theory and Research on International Population Movements.* New York: Center for Migration Studies.

Richmond, A. H.

1984   "Socio-cultural Adaptation and Conflict in Immigrant-Receiving Countries." *International Social Science Journal*, 36(3):519–536.

Tabbarah, R.

1984   "Prospects of International Migration." *International Social Science Journal*, 36(3):425–440.

Warren, R., and E. P. Kraly

1985   *The Elusive Exodus: Emigration from the United States.* Population Trends and Public Policy, No. 8. Washington: Population Reference Bureau.

Weiner, M.

1985a "Exit—The Gains and Losses of International Migration." In E. Cohen et al. (eds.), *Comparative Social Dynamics.* Boulder: Westview Press.

1985b "On International Migration and International Relations." *Population and Development Review,* 11(3):441–455.

PART I. FACTORS INFLUENCING INTERNATIONAL MIGRATION FLOWS

2

The Global Picture of Contemporary Immigration Patterns

Mary M. Kritz

Thirty years ago, social scientists considered the era of international migration to have ended. Given the context at that time, this undoubtedly was a reasonable assumption. During the great global depression of the 1930s and World War II, U.S. immigration had fallen to its lowest level since the 1820s. Intercontinental movements to other permanent immigration countries also had declined. Argentina, Chile, Brazil, and Uruguay had shifted away from their pro-immigration stance of the late 1800s and closed their doors to European immigration. Although Australia and New Zealand, underpopulated states in the South Pacific, continued to allow immigration from England and from other European countries considered to have culturally compatible peoples, only small numbers migrated in spite of travel and relocation assistance offered by the host countries.

Viewed with hindsight in the 1980s, it is clear that international migration has not only not ended, it has surged to historically high levels and taken on new patterns that social scientists and policymakers are

Several people assisted with the preparation of this chapter. The professional staff of the United Nations Statistical Office, particularly William Seltzer, Alice Clague, and K. S. Gnanasekaran, facilitated access to data from the 1980 round of censuses. Valuable comments were provided by James Fawcett, Benjamin Cariño, Douglas T. Gurak, and participants in the Conference on Asia–Pacific Immigration to the United States.

just beginning to understand. Today there are very few countries that neither send nor receive international migrants. The numbers may be small relative to global population and the migrants may not settle permanently, but the evidence shows increasing international migration in most countries. At the same time, the policy trend has been toward increasing restrictions on permanent entry. How can this apparent anomaly be understood? What are the patterns and characteristics of contemporary international migrations? Are there continuities between current global population flows and those of earlier epochs?

Drawing on a comparative perspective, this chapter provides an overview of contemporary international migration patterns. First, data are reviewed on recent immigration trends and patterns: transit statistics on flows to permanent migration countries from 1950 to 1980 and census data on the foreign-born composition of selected countries in 1970 and 1980. Of particular interest here are the new types of migration flows—contract labor, illegal, intraregional, and refugee—which tend to be shorter in duration than international migration flows in the past. Some of the political, economic, and policy issues underlying contemporary immigration patterns are discussed. It will be argued that international migration should be seen as one of many exchanges taking place among nation-states and is related to growing global interdependence. The emphasis here is on global patterns, since other chapters will provide detailed analyses of Asian flows.

OVERVIEW OF INTERNATIONAL MIGRATION

Trends in Permanent Immigration Countries

Permanent immigration refers to the movement of persons to another country for long-term settlement. But the concept has a broader policy connotation in that it usually refers to immigration to countries that grant immigrants upon entry most of the legal rights of citizens, including the right to work, reside, and participate in community affairs. Only the right to vote is generally withheld until the immigrant becomes a naturalized citizen.[1] By this definition of permanent migration, only four countries—Australia, Canada, New Zealand, and the United States—would qualify. Israel could also be considered a permanent immigration country, but immigration is limited largely to persons of Jewish background. Although significant numbers of immigrants may be

---

1. Most countries do not have comparable definitions of immigrants, nor do they define juridically how foreigners can become citizens. The problems confronted in Western European countries with assimilation of second-generation foreigners result, in part, from the treatment of the children of immigrants as foreigners, even if they have been born and raised and have lived all of their lives in the host country.

entering, residing, and even remaining permanently in many other countries, they do so under regulatory provisions that differ from those of the four permanent immigration countries, which grant the right of long-term settlement upon approval for entry.

Total immigrant admissions to the four permanent immigration countries have increased since 1956, but the patterns by country diverge sharply (Table 2.1). While permanent admissions to the United States increased by 42 percent from 1956 to 1980, those to Canada, Australia, and New Zealand decreased by 24 percent. Consequently, by 1980 two out of every three permanent immigrants were being admitted to the United States compared with one out of two in 1956–1960. In all four countries, however, demand for permanent residency visas is high, waiting lists are long, and only a small number of interested migrants receive admission annually.

The origins of permanent immigrants have also shifted since the mid-1950s, when the vast majority came from developed countries. All four countries have experienced increasing immigration from developing countries, but their rates differ (Table 2.1). In the 1976–1980 period, the United States was the most likely to receive its immigrants from developing countries—80.1 percent compared with only 26.5 percent in New Zealand and 56.5 and 41.7 percent, respectively, in Canada and Australia. This trend toward increased numbers of immigrants from developing countries was already under way in the United States in the early 1960s even though the national-origin quota system remained in effect until 1968. In the other countries, however, ethnic liberalization of immigration policies occurred later and it is only in the past decade that increased immigration from developing regions can be noted.

Regarding the geographic region of origin, the Americas have been the primary source of immigrants to the United States since 1960, but Asia was almost as likely to be the origin region in 1980 (Table 2.1). The classification of Asian countries adopted in Table 2.1 draws on that of the United Nations and includes countries in Southwest Asia—a scheme that differs from that recommended in Chapter 6. Shifts occurred in the geographic origins of immigrants to the other permanent immigration countries as well. Although Europe continued to be the major source of immigrants to Australia and New Zealand in the 1976–1980 period, the proportions have steadily decreased since the 1950s. The Asian region showed the largest gain in emigration to all four countries, accounting for one-third or more of all immigrants to the United States, Canada, and Australia by 1980. Of interest in the Australian and New Zealand flows is the movement between these two countries, as well as immigration from their island neighbors in the South Pacific.

Table 2.1 Admissions of Permanent Immigrants, by Development Level and Geographic Region of Origin, to Australia, Canada, New Zealand, and the United States: 1956–1980

Region of Origin	Receiving Country	1956–1960	1961–1965	1966–1970	1971–1975	1976–1980[a]
		(Number in thousands)				
All countries	Total	2,826.6	2,713.6	3,748.3	3,404.7	3,095.8
	U.S.	1,427.8	1,450.3	1,871.4	1,936.3	2,026.4
	Canada	782.9	498.8	910.8	834.5	605.9
	Australia	500.0[b]	594.2	807.0	494.7	402.7
	New Zealand	115.9	170.3	159.1	139.2	60.8

Development Region of Origin

(Number in thousands)

Region of Origin	Receiving Country	1956–1960	1961–1965	1966–1970	1971–1975	1976–1980[a]
More-developed countries	Total	2,292.9	1,951.9	2,340.7	1,495.0	945.2
	U.S.	979.6	809.6	776.3	532.0	402.5
	Canada	738.1	437.8	722.7	470.4	263.4
	Australia	470.0[b]	550.6	697.2	368.4	234.6
	New Zealand	105.2	153.9	144.5	124.2	44.7
Less-developed countries	Total	533.8	761.8	1,407.6	1,909.6	2,150.6
	U.S.	448.3	640.7	1,095.1	1,404.2	1,623.9
	Canada	44.8	61.0	188.1	364.0	342.5
	Australia	30.0[b]	43.6	109.8	126.4	168.1
	New Zealand	10.7	16.5	14.6	15.0	16.1

(Percentages)

Region of Origin	Receiving Country	1956–1960	1961–1965	1966–1970	1971–1975	1976–1980[a]
More-developed countries	Total	81.1	71.9	62.4	43.9	30.5
	U.S.	68.6	55.8	41.5	27.5	19.9
	Canada	94.3	87.8	79.3	56.4	43.5
	Australia	94.0[b]	92.7	86.4	74.5	58.3
	New Zealand	90.8	90.3	90.8	89.2	73.5
Less-developed countries	Total	18.9	28.1	37.6	56.1	69.5
	U.S.	31.4	44.2	58.5	72.5	80.1
	Canada	5.7	12.2	20.7	43.6	56.5
	Australia	6.0[b]	7.3	13.6	25.5	41.7
	New Zealand	9.2	9.7	9.2	10.8	26.5

TABLE 2.1 (*continued*)

Region of Origin	Receiving Country	1956– 1960	1961– 1965	1966– 1970	1971– 1975	1976– 1980[a]
		Geographic Region of Origin[c]				
		(Percentages)				
Europe	U.S.	55.6	41.8	33.8	22.4	14.5
	Canada	85.8	73.1	64.9	40.1	31.9
	Australia	NA	88.7	80.0	65.1	41.3
	New Zealand	61.8	53.9	45.7	68.9	45.0
Oceania	U.S.	0.4	0.5	0.7	0.8	0.9
	Canada	1.4	1.9	2.6	2.1	1.8
	Australia	NA	2.3	3.8	5.4	14.9
	New Zealand	30.1	36.4	45.0	20.0	35.1
Africa	U.S.	0.7	0.9	1.4	1.7	2.2
	Canada	0.9	2.6	2.2	4.8	4.6
	Australia	NA	2.6	3.0	3.6	4.9
	New Zealand	1.1	1.3	0.6	1.8	3.0
Americas	U.S.	35.5	49.1	46.3	43.4	43.6
	Canada	9.1	16.2	18.8	30.1	24.8
	Australia	NA	2.1	4.1	9.9	5.6
	New Zealand	3.1	4.1	4.4	5.7	5.8
Asia	U.S.	7.8	7.8	17.8	31.6	38.8
	Canada	2.7	5.5	11.3	22.6	36.9
	Australia	NA	4.0	8.3	15.6	32.2
	New Zealand	3.1	2.8	3.3	3.1	10.9

Source: United Nations (1983:tables V.2 and V.3).

Note: More-developed countries include Australia, Canada, Japan, New Zealand, the USSR, the United States, and all of Europe. Less-developed countries include all other countries.

[a]For the United States the data refer to 1976–1979.

[b]The 1956–1960 figure for Australia is an estimated total.

[c]The receiving country percentages sum to 100 by period and by region of origin.

In summary, then, permanent immigration is high in these four countries and growing in the United States. Immigrants are increasingly coming from developing regions, particularly the Americas and Asia, although only a small number originates in Africa. Of special interest is the growing importance of Asian emigration. In the 1976–1980 period, Asian countries provided about 1.1 million immigrants to the four permanent immigration countries, the largest number from any region. Given the volume of Asian contract-labor migrations to the Middle East (Arnold and Shah, 1984), Asia is the major source of today's intercontinental migrants. Viewed from a demographic perspective, the potential for further Asian emigration is very high, considering that Asia has 60 percent of the world's population and is growing at the rate of 1.8 percent annually.

These differentials in volume, trends, and composition among the four permanent immigration countries illustrate the importance of the policy context. Regardless of the economic or social forces that may propel or attract immigrants, ultimately the numbers and characteristics of immigrants are shaped by the immigration policy of the receiving country. The specific policy contexts of these receiving countries will be examined in detail in the chapters by Kubat (Canada), Price (Australia), and Trlin (New Zealand). Some of their major features are examined here.

Many similarities can be noted in the immigration policies of the four permanent immigration countries. In recent years, all four countries have had lengthy internal debates over their immigration policies, and all except the United States have revised their policies several times. These internal debates have been dominated by three concerns: Is there a continuing need for immigration and, if so, what number should be admitted? Do immigrants hurt the economy, particularly in periods of rising domestic unemployment? And what are the long-term implications of increasing ethnic diversity for the social and political fabric? Each of the countries has shown a continued willingness to maintain some immigration, although the justification is increasingly formulated in terms of humanitarian interests. The symbolic importance of immigration cannot be discounted given its historic role in populating these countries.

Essentially there are three criteria for admitting immigrants in these countries: family reunification, skill and occupation, and refugee status. The relative importance of these three factors, however, differs in each country. The United States favors family reunification criteria; indeed, 86 percent of all U.S. immigrants qualified under such provisions in 1980. All four countries gave priority to refugee admissions during the 1970s and early 1980s, but these admissions have declined subsequently. Canada, Australia, and New Zealand gave priority to the occupational and skill criterion during the 1970s, but this factor has played less of a role since the economic crisis beginning in the late 1970s. In fact, there has been a convergence in all four countries toward immigration for family reunification purposes. At least half of Canada's immigrants are admitted for family reunification (Chapter 10), and New Zealand and Australia are admitting increasing numbers of family members of Indochinese refugees (Chapters 8 and 9).

A further policy similarity is the increasing tendency to ignore origin in selection. The United States became the leader in developing policies that are blind to ethnicity and race with the passage of the Immigration Act of 1965, which abolished the national-origin quota system. Canada followed with a nondiscriminatory bill in 1967, shifting its emphasis to migrant human capital—education, skill, investment—and historical and familial ties. Although Australia and New Zealand favored British immigration during most of their history, by the mid-1970s Australia had dismantled its white ethnic-restrictive policies and opened admissions to migrants from other countries, basing selection on skill characteristics and assimilation potential. Subsequent shifts expanded opportunities for family reunificiation, which contributed to increased Asian immigration (Chapter 8 in this volume; Birrell, 1984). These policy shifts reflected, in part, Australia's changing geopolitical role in the Pacific Basin, particulariy its interest in expanding trade and other ties with Asian countries.

New Zealand's immigration policies have also been revised several times in recent decades, shifting away from its pro-British immigration bias toward the selection of immigrants with skills required for economic growth and with cultural characteristics considered compatible with those of earlier immigrant groups (Farmer, 1984). In practice, New Zealand continues to favor immigrants from Europe and from the South Pacific islands with which it has close historic ties.

Foreign-Born Composition of Selected-Immigration Countries

Many other countries have become receivers of international migrants in recent years. These countries generally do not grant permanent residency to immigrants nor do many of their immigrants intend to stay permanently. Some countries, such as those of Western Europe and the Middle East, have developed contract-labor programs because of real labor shortages; others, such as Malaysia, Nigeria, and Venezuela, have become recipients of large numbers of illegal migrants from neighboring countries because of their relatively strong labor markets; and many others, particularly less-developed countries in sub-Saharan Africa, Central America, and Asia, have received large numbers of political refugees. These flows are poorly documented, but they are generally believed to be large and increasing. To assess levels and trends of international migration in a broad range of countries, data are examined on the foreign-born composition of selected countries—those for which

data could be obtained—for two recent census periods (see Table 2.2).
Census data on the foreign-born composition of the population give
some indication of the magnitude of these flows. Although census data
cannot capture the dynamics of immigration flows, they do provide
valuable information on cross-sectional patterns and on immigrant
trends and characteristics if comparisons are made across more than
one census period.[2]

Of the thirty-one countries for which data are presented in Table 2.2,
almost two-thirds experienced absolute increases in foreign-born population between their two most recent censuses. Many of the countries
with declines in foreign-born population—Argentina, Panama, and
Uruguay—experienced considerable immigration earlier in this century.
Thus their decreases reflect the mortality patterns among aging cohorts
of earlier immigrants rather than low rates of recent immigration. In
fact, during the 1970s Argentina was a major recipient of migrants from
neighboring countries. In Switzerland, however, the declining foreign-
born composition reflects policy shifts adopted in the 1970s to encourage
the return home of guest workers and to reduce the number of new
entrants.

A considerable range exists in the foreign-born composition of countries. The highest proportions are found in five Middle Eastern countries: United Arab Emirates (72 percent), Qatar (70 percent), Kuwait (53
percent), Saudi Arabia (36 percent), and Bahrain (32 percent). Hong
Kong and Israel are the only other countries included in Table 2.2 with
populations that are over one-third foreign-born. The Western European countries that received guest workers in the 1960s and 1970s have
foreign-born populations ranging from a high of 15 percent in Switzerland to a low of 3.8 percent in the Netherlands, but most are between
5 and 8 percent foreign-born. European countries generally have discouraged admissions of new guest workers since 1973 but have continued to experience increases in foreign stock because of immigration
of family members of permanent-contract holders (Tapinos, 1983).

The experience of the Western European countries suggests that some
permanent and long-term settlement develops from contract-labor programs. In the case of the Middle Eastern labor importers, however, it
remains unclear how much long-term settlement will result from their

---

2. Data on foreign-born composition can be misleading if examined out of context. Several
   factors confound the interpretation of such data and make comparisons across countries difficult. The definition of foreign-born employed in censuses may vary; classification of children born to nationals residing abroad may inflate the foreign-born share;
   and seasonal migrants may be residing in their home country at the time of the census. Despite these limitations and although such data are likely to be underestimates,
   no better data are available.

sizable foreign-born populations. The policy intent in the Middle East is to avoid permanent settlement, and foreign-labor strategies have been devised that facilitate return migration. These measures include the shift in recruitment from Middle Eastern countries to Asia and sub-Saharan Africa and the growth of turnkey programs that grant foreign contractors full responsibility for development of projects, including the temporary importation of workers and managers, with the condition that these foreign workers return home when the projects are completed.

Intraregional migrations of labor migrants and refugees, largely taking place between contiguous or geographically proximate countries, have also increased significantly since the 1950s. Indeed, a growing number of countries are experiencing such flows in every region. These flows appear similar to internal migration inasmuch as they respond largely to market forces, are initiated by the migrants rather than the government, and operate outside the official immigration policy. In ad-

Table 2.2 Foreign-Born Composition of Population for Selected Immigration Countries in Two Recent Censuses

Region and Country	Latest Census		Earlier Census		% Change in Foreign-Born[a]
	Year	Foreign-Born (%)	Year	Foreign-Born (%)	
Americas					
Argentina	1980	6.8	1970	9.5	–12.3
Bahamas	1970	18.4	1963	12.1	97.1
Bermuda	1980	26.2	1970	27.7	–2.2
Canada	1981	16.1	1971	15.3	17.3
Panama	1980	2.7	1970	3.4	–5.5
United States	1980	6.2	1970	4.7	46.4
Uruguay	1975	5.0	1963	8.0	–36.8
Venezuela	1981	7.2	1971	5.6	74.2
Europe					
France	1982	8.2[b]	1974	7.7[b]	10.0
Germany (Fed. Rep.)	1982	7.6[b]	1974	6.7[b]	13.1
Netherlands	1982	3.8[b]	1974	2.6[b]	57.3
Sweden	1982	4.9[b]	1974	4.9[b]	1.1
Switzerland	1982	14.7[b]	1974	16.5[b]	–13.1
United Kingdom	1981	6.6	1971	5.5	9.0
Asia					
Hong Kong	1981	42.8	1971	43.6	24.2
Israel	1982	42.0[c]	1970	52.8	22.7
Malaysia	1980	5.2	1970	7.4	–11.9
Singapore	1980	21.8	1970	25.5	–0.2

Table 2.2   (*continued*)

Region and Country	Latest Census		Earlier Census		% Change in Foreign-Born[a]
	Year	Foreign-Born (%)	Year	Foreign-Born (%)	
Middle East					
Bahrain	1981	32.0	1971	17.5	196.5
Kuwait	1980	53.0	1970	42.4	10.1
Libya	1980	20.0[d]	1964	2.4	NA
Qatar	1984	70.0[d]	1975	57.0	NA
Saudi Arabia	1983	36.0[d]	1963	7.0	NA
United Arab Emirates	1980	72.0[d]	1975	64.0	NA
Oceania					
Australia	1981	20.9	1971	20.2	5.4
New Zealand	1981	14.9	1971	14.6	12.3
Africa					
Gambia	1973	10.2[e]	1963	11.3	48.9
Ghana	1975	5.7[e]	1970	4.1	67.8
Malawi	1977	4.1	1966	7.3	−22.3
Swaziland	1976	5.3	1966	10.6	−33.9
Togo	1975	7.7[e]	1970	7.4	20.9

Sources: Data for the 1980 round of censuses are from United Nations Statistical Office, *Demographic Yearbook,* migration questionnaires; data for 1970 and 1960 census rounds of Americas countries were obtained from published country census reports or 1977 *Demographic Yearbook;* data for some 1970 and 1960 census rounds were obtained from *Trends and Characteristics of International Migration Since 1950,* table 6.

[a]This column presents the percentage change in the absolute size of the foreign-born population between the two censuses.

[b]Estimates on stocks of foreign population are from OECD (1983:table A.6).

[c]Data from Friedlander and Goldscheider (1984). Estimate refers to Jewish population only.

[d]Estimate provided in Galaleldin (1984).

[e]The 1975 data for Gambia, Ghana, and Togo are from *United Nations* (1983:table V.19). That report indicates that data are from censuses around 1975.

dition to being circumscribed territorial flows, these movements generally take place between social units that share some sociocultural characteristics, although they are likely to differ in levels of economic development (stimulating illegal labor migrants) or political stability (creating refugee flows).

Such flows have always occurred. During the early stages of nation-state development, border flows of agricultural workers or nomads took place with scant attention from government authorities. What have changed in recent years—and, consequently, received increasing governmental attention—are the volume, destination, and permanency of intraregional flows. Numerous examples can be cited of the conversion of former border flows to rural areas into long-distance moves to larger metropolitan areas, of immigrants' shift from seasonal work in agriculture to year-round work in services and construction, and of the increasing number of years that such migrants, largely undocumented, remain in receiving countries. In Latin America, this pattern has occurred in the case of Colombian flows to Venezuela (Kritz, 1975), Paraguayan and Bolivian flows to Argentina (Marshall, 1981), and Mexican migration to the United States.

The magnitude of intraregional migration flows in developing countries is captured to some extent by the foreign-born data in Table 2.2. Venezuela and Argentina are the largest receivers of intraregional migrants in Latin America, as is reflected in the size of their foreign-born populations, 7.2 and 6.8 percent, respectively, in 1980. In both countries, the growth of foreign-born populations has been facilitated by government amnesty programs for illegal migrants. Argentina is one of the few recipients of intraregional migrants that have maintained a relatively favorable stance toward unsolicited immigration. From a desire to increase its population, Argentina has been receptive to immigrants from neighboring countries. Even during periods of economic recession, Argentina has not closed its door on immigrants, although economic conditions have slowed the volume. Venezuela, in contrast, has had an ambivalent attitude toward immigration. It encouraged immigration in the 1950s and early 1970s, but discouraged it in the 1960s and after the mid-1970s. Despite an ability to provide jobs and absorb immigrants, a xenophobia exists in Venezuela regarding long-term consequences of immigration for national identity.

Elsewhere in the Americas, some of the larger foreign-born compositions are found on the English and French-speaking islands of the Caribbean, most of which are also major sources of emigrants in the region. These Caribbean islands receive labor migrants from neighboring islands and U.S. nationals retiring to the islands, as well as return immigration of children born abroad to emigrants who have subsequently returned (Kritz, 1981).

Several Asian countries, too, have relatively large foreign-born populations. In their latest censuses, Singapore and Hong Kong had foreign-born populations of 21.8 and 42.8 percent, respectively. Historically, intraregional migrations have played an important role in Asian societies, as can be witnessed in the multiethnic composition that characterizes most of them. Currently Afghan refugee flows to Pakistan and Indochinese refugee migrations are of particular prominence in Asia, but labor migrations between neighboring Asian countries are growing. Malaysia is the major recipient of labor migrants, particularly from the Philippines and Indonesia (Lim, 1984). Japan stands out as a special case because it alone among the industrialized countries gives priority to maintenance of its homogeneous population and relies on alternatives to migrant labor: high rates of labor force participation, robotics, and export of capital.[3]

Since the population size of sending and receiving countries and that of immigrant groups differs considerably, comparisons of the proportion foreign-born say little regarding the role of these countries in the global immigration system. The populations examined in Table 2.2, for example, range from a high of 226 million in the United States to a low of 54,000 in Bermuda. While Bermuda has a foreign-born composition of 26 percent, this figure represents only 14,170 foreigners, an insignificant share of the world's total immigrants. In contrast, the 14.1 million foreigners in the United States in 1980, while constituting only 6.2 percent of the total U.S. population, is the largest immigration group in the world—one that is four times larger than the foreign-born population of Saudi Arabia (3.5 million), the country with the next largest total. Moreover, the long-range implications of U.S. immigration differ from those of countries experiencing temporary migration with high return rates. It could also be argued that the absolute size of immigrant communities may be of greater importance than their relative share of the total population when social and economic consequences are considered. Since large immigrant groups have the potential for developing enclave communities, consideration has to be given to the effects of such settlements on long-term social and economic integration.

Not only does the United States have the largest number of immigrants in the world; several U.S. foreign-born groups are now larger in size than the total immigrant populations of most receiving countries and even of the total population of several sending countries (Table 2.3). For example, the 2.2 million foreign-born Mexicans in the United States are a larger immigrant group than the foreign-born populations of all but five countries (Australia, Saudi Arabia, France, Federal Republic of Germany, and Canada). Considering that the Mexican-heritage population comprised 8.7 million in 1980, it is clear that continued immigration from a specific country can contribute significant

---

3. Compared with other industrial countries, Japan has high rates of participation, particularly among older workers. In 1980, some 40.8 percent of Japanese males 65 years old and over were in the labor force compared with only 7.5 percent in West Germany, 9 percent in Great Britain, 11 percent in Australia, and 19 percent in the United States. Moreover, 14.9 percent of Japanese women age 65 and over were in the labor force compared with 2 to 4 percent in most other industrialized countries (Sorrentino, 1983).

Table 2.3 Native and Foreign-Born Composition of U.S. Population, Absolute and Relative Change, and Legal Immigration: 1970–1980 (in Thousands)

Origin	U.S. Population		Absolute Change, 1980–1970	% Change, 1980–1970	Legal Immigration 1970–1980
	1980	1970			
Native-Born	212,465.9	193,616.0	18,849.9	9.7	NA
Foreign-Born	14,079.9	9,619.3	4,460.6	46.4	4,493.3
Europe	4,743.6	5,248.6	-505.0	-9.6	800.4
Germany	849.4 (2)	833.0 (2)	16.4	2.0	74.4
Greece	211.0	177.3	33.7	19.0	92.4
Hungary	144.4	183.2	-38.9	-21.2	11.6
Ireland	197.8	251.4 (9)	-53.6	-21.3	11.5
Italy	831.9 (4)	1,008.5 (1)	-176.6	-17.5	129.4
Poland	418.1 (8)	548.1 (6)	-130.0	-23.7	37.2
Portugal	177.4	91.0	86.4	94.9 (7)	101.7
Sweden	77.2	127.1	-49.9	-39.3	6.5
United Kingdom	669.0 (5)	686.1 (5)	-17.1	-2.5	137.4
USSR	406.0 (9)	463.5 (7)	-57.4	-12.4	39.0
Yugoslavia	153.0	153.7	-0.8	-0.5	30.5
Asia	2,539.8	824.9	1,714.9	207.9	1,588.2
China	286.1	172.1	114.0 (7)	66.2	124.3
India	206.1	51.0	155.1 (5)	304.1 (2)	164.1 (7)
Japan	221.8	120.2	101.6 (9)	84.5 (8)	49.8
Korea	289.9	38.7	251.2 (3)	648.8 (1)	272.0 (4)
Philippines	501.4 (7)	184.8	316.6 (2)	171.3 (6)	360.2 (2)
Vietnam	231.1	NA	NA	NA	179.7 (5)

Table 2.3 (continued)

Origin	U.S. Population		Absolute Change, 1980–1970	% Change, 1980–1970	Legal Immigration 1970–1980
	1980	1970			
West Indies	1,258.4	675.1	583.3	86.4	741.1
Cuba	607.8 (6)	439.0 (8)	168.8 (4)	38.4	276.8 (3)
Dominican Republic	169.1	61.2	107.9 (8)	176.3 (5)	148.0 (8)
Jamaica	196.8	68.6	128.2 (6)	187.0 (4)	142.0 (9)
South America	561.0	255.2	305.8	119.8	345.5
North and Central America	4,664.9	2,361.2	2,303.8	97.6	944.9
Canada	842.9 (3)	812.4 (3)	30.4	3.7	169.9 (6)
Mexico	2,199.2 (1)	759.7 (4)	1,439.5 (1)	189.0 (3)	640.3 (1)

Sources: U.S. Census of Population, 1980. *U.S. Summary: General Social and Economic Characteristics*, table 79; and *1980 Statistical Yearbook of the Immigration and Naturalization Service*, table 2.

Note: Numbers in parentheses represent rank order. Regional totals do not sum because not all regions are included.

numbers in the course of time. Moreover, the relative growth of native and foreign-born populations differs considerably in the United States—increasing by 10 and 46 percent, respectively, from 1970 to 1980 (Chapter 12 in this volume). Sharp differentials, however, characterize growth patterns of specific immigrant groups. The most rapidly growing U.S. immigrant communities come from Asia, followed by those from Latin America and the West Indies. Many of the European immigrant groups continue to be among the larger ones, representing the legacy of earlier U.S. immigration waves, although few of them experienced an increase in size from 1970 to 1980.

SHIFTS IN THE DETERMINANTS OF MIGRATION

The foregoing overview suggests that current forms and patterns of international migration differ from those of the intercontinental migration era, which was characterized by permanent migration to newly emergent countries needing settlers and workers. Labor recruitment in the sending countries and open immigration policies in the receiving countries encouraged migrants to leave European countries that were more developed than the frontier lands awaiting them in the Americas or the South Pacific. Travel to these new lands was slow and arduous, and diseases struck down many before arrival. Few came just to visit or look around; the intent of the receiving countries and the immigrants was to make permanent homes in these new lands.

The context in which international migration now takes place differs considerably from that of the eighteenth and nineteenth centuries. While only four countries continue to receive permanent immigrants in the mode of the intercontinental period, more countries are senders or receivers of international migration than at any point in the past. The dominant flow today is from less developed to more developed countries, but increasingly flows are taking place among developing countries and movements from developed to developing countries are also present. Jet age travel allows persons from the most remote regions of the world to reach New York, Sydney, Düsseldorf, London, Buenos Aires, or Riyadh within a few hours. In the past, most international movement consisted of permanent migrants journeying to a new land; today most international movement consists of little more than vacation travel for a couple of weeks or a summer, business travel to check on company operations in other countries, and professional travel to international conferences and meetings. Even commuting to work from a residence in a neighboring country has become a common pattern, as can be seen along the Mexican–United States and other borders.

It could be argued that immigration specialists have been so preoccupied with a particular type of migration—permanent settlement—

that we failed to see the full range of population movements taking place among countries today and to consider the implications of these different flows. International migration tends to be compared with European intercontinental migrations of the nineteenth century. Viewed over a longer sweep of history, however, it could be argued that intercontinental migration was an anomaly rather than the dominant historical pattern. In fact, as McNeill (1984) notes, migrations have always characterized the globe's populations, but most of these movements had a different character prior to the development of the nation-state system. Moreover, intercontinental migration was closely associated with the efforts of European countries to extend their economic and political hegemony over distant territories by settling their own nationals in these sparsely populated territories. Thus sending and receiving countries had political and demographic objectives in addition to economic aims.

Although numerous economic, political, and social forces shape contemporary international migration, this study highlights the importance and implications of three factors: interdependence among nation-states and its relationship to international population movement; the salience of social networks linking sending and receiving communities; and the growing significance of temporary migrations and the regulatory mechanism facilitating them.

Global Interdependence

The period since the 1950s can be considered a watershed in international migration inasmuch as it marks the point when economic and political transformations in the nation-state system began gathering momentum, which resulted in expanding interdependence among states. If data were available on nation-state exchanges of capital, goods, technology, services, and resources over the past thirty or forty years, they would likely show a geometric increase in these exchanges. Whether this increase stems from the penetration of capital into peripheral regions, as Portes discusses in Chapter 3, or from the changing mode of technology and complex organizations that has evolved is open to debate. The point to be made here is that this growing interdependence among nation-states is intertwined with contemporary international population movements.

While the global system continues to be composed of separate nation-states, the organized linkages and exchanges among states have increased dramatically and contribute to increased integration and diminishing social distance among states. Improvements in transportation are but one reflection of the improved linkages among nation-states. Development in Third World countries has not significantly improved the lot of most of the world's peoples, but it has brought them the technology and information that facilitate both internal and international migration. Most developing countries have experienced substantial expansions in their road and public transport systems over the past twenty or thirty years. These roads, intended to expand market access and public services, also allow people to move toward urban and international centers believed to hold greater opportunity.

While growing interdependence among nation-states is generally recognized in policy and academic circles, it tends to be seen in terms of the economic and political linkages and dependencies among states. Less understood, however, is the role played by increasing global circulation of people to manage these other exchanges, to provide labor, or to take advantage of differentials in opportunities that present themselves in other countries. A wide array of international population movement, most of which would be classified as short-term moves and not migration, is taking place in the world today. How these differing forms of international movement relate to other exchanges among states or to each other has really not been addressed.

The study of international migration would be advanced by directing greater attention to international population movement. International migration is in fact a component of international population movement, the basic distinction between them being their duration. Tourism and business travel constitute the two most prevalent forms of short-term movement. Yet there are many other moves that would be considered long enough to be classified as international migration, using the United Nations' recommended standard of one year—including those by contract workers, foreign students, diplomats, entertainers, artists, and professionals and managers transferred by their employers to another country. Yet these moves are usually not considered by the receiving country or the migrants as international migration. If scholars begin to shift their attention toward the full range of international population movement, we may begin to understand the processes that lead to shifts from short-term to long-term movement and to the two-way flows between developed and developing and sending and receiving countries.

Structural Differentials and Social Processes

Given the growing importance of south-to-north flows of migrants, there has been a tendency to associate these flows with other north–south differentials. Arguments have been developed, for example, that emphasize the importance for migration of differentials in levels of economic development (Hofstetter, 1984), technology (Travis, 1984), and population growth rates (Demeny, 1983). Generally there is agreement that the number of potential emigrants in developing countries is growing and that economic and demographic disparities between north–south countries are not being reduced. There is disagreement, however, on the extent to which these differentials cause emigration or whether emigration is induced by the labor needs of receiving countries.

Inequalities—economic, social, political—between and within nation-states may shape international migration, but they do not explain why some countries rather than others become prominent within certain flows. Rather than focusing on structural differentials between nation-states, it may be more fruitful to consider the macro and microprocesses linking them. In the previous section the growing interdependence among nation-states at the macrolevel was discussed. At the microlevel, the operation of cross-national social networks linking individuals and households is the process of particular importance to international migration.

The household is a key social group that intervenes between the macroeconomic forces that set the stage for migration and the individuals who ultimately move (Wood, 1982; Tienda, 1983). Not only can the family or household unit influence whether one of its members moves, it can also serve as a link to society at large and furnish information about opportunities in other areas. Moreover, numerous migration studies have noted the importance of chain migration between migration nodes in sending and receiving countries (MacDonald and Mac-Donald, 1964). Chain migration refers to movements organized primarily by the migrants themselves and is believed to account for differential selectivity of migrants across and within communities in sending countries. Links between kin and social groups in the sending and receiving communities serve, on the one hand, as channels for communicating information about opportunities and, on the other, as the means for facilitating the transfer and settlement of migrants. To the extent that family networks are critical in shaping migration processes, established migration flows could be expected to continue for some time even if there is a change in the macroeconomic and institutional forces that stimulated migration in the first place.

Temporary Migration: The Evolving Norm?

Generally those who argue that opportunities for international migration are declining in the modern era base their rationale on the increasing restrictions placed on immigration by nation-states. The data presented earlier, however, support a different argument—that population movement is generally increasing in the world, although legally it has a temporary character. Growing interdependence among nation-states creates a need for increased international population movement, and governments have generally responded to this need by developing elaborate regulatory systems. Although considerable research supports the argument that migrants have long seen their movements to other lands as temporary and that significant numbers of earlier permanent migrants returned home, the current temporary pattern results, in large part, from government policy. Immigrants are now admitted to most countries with work permits or visas that grant them temporary residency rights and specify the terms for work, study, family reunification, and length of residence. The formal expectation on the part of the receiving governments and most of the immigrants is that they will return to their home country upon completion of the specified period. Most indeed probably do return home, but many other temporary migrants find ways of staying on, legally or illegally, and thereby become de facto permanent migrants.

Over the past three decades, nation-states have devised elaborate regulatory systems to facilitate population inflows considered desirable and to restrict or prohibit those that are not (Bohning, 1983).[4] The dilemma confronted by governments is how to control entry, and numerous policy strategies have been devised. Since many flows are perceived to be in the national interest, governments want to maintain relatively open borders and easy access in order to facilitate these entries—business, investment, tourism, study, technical assistance, and cultural exchange—and their regulatory systems readily accommodate them. It is with regard to long-term work and permanent settlement, however, that governments are reluctant to extend unlimited entry privileges to foreigners.

Given this context of increasing population movement among countries for short periods and regulatory systems that place compliance largely in the hands of the traveler, it is hardly surprising to see growing numbers of visitors who stay on after their visas have expired and become undocumented migrants. Others, largely the poor who are unable to obtain proper travel documents, enter by land and add to undocumented populations. Essentially most persons who wish to enter another country, for whatever purpose, do so on temporary entry visas that specify the activity in which they can engage and the period of time they can stay. In lieu of obtaining official authorization to enter, foreigners may ignore a country's entry regulations and enter surreptitiously for work or other purposes.

International migrants employ a wide range of strategies to gain entry into the more developed countries, where restrictions on entry tend

---

4. I am referring here to all visa and entry controls employed by nation-states to restrict or control entries. These include proof of financial solvency, waiting periods, affidavits, limited entry periods, and the like.

to be greatest. Entering as a tourist and remaining as an illegal migrant is only one of many strategies. Even higher education becomes a means for some to gain access to another country. The number of foreign students in the United States and other developed countries, for example, has expanded considerably in recent decades. In the case of the United States, not only do foreign students remain for years to complete their studies, but also many have permanent residence as their objective from the very beginning and others get interested in long-term settlement after their arrival. Many factors encourage students to stay: They may be attracted by the quality of life and job opportunities in the United States; their U.S. training may be more appropriate for the American job market than for their home country; they may fall in love and marry an American; or they may fear political and economic uncertainties in their home countries. Many of these factors represent nothing other than more attractive alternatives for foreigners once they enter the international system. While ulterior motives may be involved in some cases, a more likely explanation for most students is shifting interests and priorities once they become exposed to a different sociocultural system. Falling in love and marrying a U.S. national, for example, is unlikely to be a planned event. The data on intermarriage among persons of different nationalities suggest that rates are increasing and can be expected to rise in the future (Gurak and Fitzpatrick, 1982). Cross-national intermarriage necessarily leads to an international move on the part of at least one partner or, at least, solidifies the permanence of a move that has already occurred.

CONCLUDING COMMENTS

International migrations are undergoing change. While permanent immigrants continue to be received by Australia, Canada, New Zealand, and the United States, only the last country has accepted growing numbers. Most international migrants in the world today are not moving as permanent migrants but rather as temporary migrants with work permits or visas that grant them temporary residency rights to carry out their business, study, work, or other objectives. Others, particularly undocumented migrants, may not have formal state approval to enter and work; but, as their growing numbers in every region substantiates, this does not deter them from migrating. The growing interdependency among nation-states both sets the stage for people exchanges, facilitating the information and means that enable them to move, and generates the need for international migration in order to manage other exchanges, provide technical and social assistance, and benefit from opportunities that present themselves in other countries. Whereas macrolinkages and exchanges among nation-states set the context for international migration, it is the social networks among families and communities, stretching across national boundaries, that largely determine who actually moves and where.

What will immigration patterns be like in fifty years? Given the growing number of immigration countries that have emerged over the past twenty or thirty years, it is easy to imagine a scenario that extends these patterns to an even larger number of countries and migrants. Restricting such flows is difficult and, at best, seems to slow the volume rather than stop the flows, particularly temporary migrations. If sharp economic disparities between northern and southern countries continue, it is unlikely that immigration policies will be able to reduce immigration. In any case, as I have argued here, nation-states need and *want* to receive international migrants for entrepreneurial, managerial, professional, and many other activities. Thus states will likely continue to accept such migrants in the future.

A more distant scenario—one that assumes significant economic development and declines in population growth—could lead to increased competition for workers comparable to the pre-nineteenth-century mode when countries competed with one another for population and labor, frequently resorting to military means to obtain additional people. In such a context, more countries may place restrictions on exits. Even in this era, one sees limitations on the right to exit in Eastern European countries and growing doubts in industrialized democracies whether immigration is an appropriate means of obtaining workers when there is little or no natural increase of their native-born populations.

REFERENCES

Arnold, F., and N. M. Shah

    1984   "Asian Labor Migration to the Middle East." *International Migration Review,* 18(2):294–318.

Birrell, R.

    1984   "A New Era in Australian Migration Policy." *International Migration Review,* 18(1):65–84.

Bohning, W. R.

    1983   "International Migration: A Suggested Typology." *International Labour Review,* 122(5):641–650.

Demeny, P.

    1983   "International Development and Population Policy." Paper presented at the Harvard–Draeger Conference on Population Interactions Between Poor and Rich Countries, Cambridge, Massachusetts. New York: Population Council. Mimeographed.

Farmer, R. S. J.

1984   "Social Consequences of Alternative Types of Immigration for In-
        tegration and Acculturation: The New Zealand Experience." Paper
        presented at the IUSSP Workshop on the Consequences of Interna-
        tional Migration, Canberra, Australia. Hamilton, N.Z.: University
        of Waikato. Mimeographed.

Friedlander, D., and C. Goldscheider

1984   "Israel's Population." *Population Bulletin,* 39(2):1–39.

Galaleldin, M.

1984   "Demographic Consequences of Alternative Types of International
        Migration in the Middle East." Paper presented at the IUSSP Work-
        shop on the Consequences of International Migration, Canberra, Aus-
        tralia. Safat, Kuwait: Arab Planning Institute. Mimeographed.

Gurak, D. T., and J. P. Fitzpatrick

1982   "Intermarriage Among Hispanic Ethnic Groups in New York City."
        American Journal of Sociology, 87(4):921–934.

Hofstetter, R. R.

1984   "Economic Underdevelopment and the Population Explosion: Im-
        plications for U.S. Immigration Policy." In R. R. Hofstetter (ed.), *U.S.
        Immigration Policy.* Durham, N.C.: Duke University Press.

Kritz, M. M.

1975   "The Impact of International Migration on Venezuelan Demographic
        and Social Structure." *International Migration Review,* 9(4):513–543.

1981   "International Migration Patterns in the Caribbean Basin: An Over-
        view." In M. M. Kritz et al. (eds.), *Global Trends in Migration: Theory
        and Research on International Population Movements.* New York: Center
        for Migration Studies.

Lim, L. L.

1984   "The Consequences of International Migration for Social Change:
        The Case of Malaysia." Paper presented at the IUSSP Workshop on
        the Consequences of International Migration, Canberra, Australia.
        Kuala Lumpur: University of Malaya. Mimeographed.

MacDonald, J. S., and L. D. MacDonald

1964   "Chain Migration, Ethnic Neighborhood Formation, and Social Net-
        works." *Milbank Memorial Fund Quarterly,* 42(1):82–97.

Marshall, A.

    1981   "Structural Trends in International Labor Migration: The Southern Cone of Latin America." In M. M. Kritz et al. (eds.), *Global Trends in Migration: Theory and Research on International Population Movements.* New York: Center for Migration Studies.

McNeill, W. H.

    1984   "Human Migration in Historical Perspective." *Population and Development Review,* 10(1):1–18.

Organisation for Economic Co-operation and Development (OECD)

    1983   *Continuous Reporting System on Migration (SOPEMI).* Paris.

Sorrentino, C.

    1983   "International Comparisons of Labor Force Participation, 1960–1981." *Monthly Labor Review,* 106(2):23–36.

Tapinos, G. P.

    1983   "European Migration Patterns: Economic Linkages and Policy Experiences." In M. M. Kritz (ed.), *U.S. Immigration and Refugee Policy: Global and Domestic Issues,* Lexington, Mass.: Lexington Books.

Tienda, M.

    1983   "Socioeconomic and Labor Force Characteristics of U.S. Immigrants: Issues and Approaches." In M. M. Kritz (ed.), *U.S. Immigration and Refugee Policy: Global and Domestic Issues.* Lexington, Mass.: Lexington Books.

Travis, W. P.

    1984   "Migration, Income Distribution, and Welfare Under Alternative International Economic Policies." In R. R. Hofstetter (ed.), *U.S. Immigration Policy.* Durham, N.C.: Duke University Press.

United Nations (UN)

    1983   *World Population Trends and Policies: 1983 Monitoring Report.* IESA/P/WP.82. New York: United Nations.

Wood, C. H.

    1982   "Equilibrium and Historical-Structural Perspectives on Migration." In A. Portes and C. Hirschman (eds.), *Theory and Methods in Migration and Ethnic Research.* Special issue of *International Migration Review,* 16(2):298–319.

Zolberg, A.

    1981   "International Migrations in Political Perspective." In M. M. Kritz et al. (eds.), *Global Trends in Migration: Theory and Research on International Population Movements.* New York: Center for Migration Studies.

3

One Field, Many Views: Competing Theories of International Migration

Alejandro Portes

International migration is not a homogeneous process. It includes refugee movements forced by political repression and by dire economic conditions. It also includes colonizing movements bent on occupying territory in less-advanced countries and profiting from their land and labor. It comprises as well flows of skilled technicians and professionals moving in search of opportunities denied to them in their home countries. It includes, finally, massive displacements of manual labor moving, permanently or temporarily, to meet labor needs in the receiving economy. Many a contemporary treatise on international migration has focused exclusively on one or another of these flows without explicitly recognizing its distinct character and its differences from other movements.

It is not surprising that the bulk of theorizing about international migration has focused on the origins, uses, and effects of labor flows. Refugee movements, professional emigration, and the few remaining colonizing migrations tend to be conceptualized at present as variants of the models applied to labor migration. Current theories generally

An earlier version of this chapter was published in A. Portes and R. L. Bach, *Latin Journey: Cuban and Mexican Immigrants in the United States* (Berkeley: University of California Press, 1985).

do not attempt to encompass the process in its totality but concentrate instead on one of its specific aspects.

At present four major issues are of theoretical interest: the origins of migrant flows, the determinants of their stability, the uses of immigrant labor, and the adaptation of immigrants to the host society. While these topics may overlap at times, each serves as a primary focus of attention for different theoretical perspectives. The diversity of social and national origins of Asian migrants to the United States and of their reception at different times offers fertile ground for the empirical application and testing of these perspectives.

ORIGINS OF LABOR MIGRATION

The most widely held approach to the causes of migration is that of push–pull theories. Generally they consist of a compilation of economic, social, and political factors believed to force individuals to leave their native region or country and a similar list impelling them toward another.

Orthodox economic theories of migration also emphasize the gap in wage incentives between sending and receiving regions. The notion of unlimited supplies of labor, common in analysis of both internal and international migrations, is based on the existence of a permanent large differential in favor of receiving countries. The existence of unlimited labor supplies implies that the initiation of migrant flows will depend, almost exclusively, on labor demand in receiving areas. When such demand exists, migration will take place. Thus these economic theories downplay the push factors and concentrate instead on the pull exercised by receiving economies.

These theories on the causes of migration present several problems, however. Lists of push and pull factors are drawn almost invariably after the fact to explain existing flows. Seldom are they used to predict the beginnings of such movements. The limitations of these theories boil down, ultimately, to their inability to explain why certain countries and regions experience sizable migrations while others in similar or even worse conditions fail to produce them.

Modern history is replete with instances in which the pull of higher wages has failed to attract migration from less-developed regions. When labor has been needed, it has had to be coerced out of them. The forced employment of native peoples from Africa and the Americas in mines and plantations offers multiple examples. This failure of push–pull theories to provide adequate explanations has led others to propose an alternative interpretation based on deliberate labor recruitment. According to this theory, differentials of advantage between sending and receiving regions determine only the *potential* for migration. Actual flows begin with planned recruitment by the labor-scarce (and generally more ad-vanced) country. Recruiters inform prospective migrants of the oppor-tunities and advantages to be gained by the movement and facilitate it by providing free transportation and other inducements.

While more persuasive than push–pull theories, this explanation of the origins of migration also runs into problems. First, not all early migrant flows were based on recruitment through economic incen-tives—some required outright coercion. Second, recent labor migrations from several countries, especially those involving undocumented work-ers, have been initiated without any apparent recruitment effort.

Migrant recruitment on the basis of economic inducement can be seen as the midpoint of a process that has ranged from forced labor extraction to the spontaneous initiation of a flow on the basis of labor demand in the receiving country. The central difficulty with push–pull and labor recruitment theories is not that they fail to identify impor-tant forces but that they do not consider the changing historical con-texts of migration.

For each of these theories, migration occurs between two distinct so-cial units: that which supplies labor and that which receives it. The possibility that such flows may actually be part of a broader system to which both units belong is not usually contemplated. An alternative conceptualization of the origins of migration requires a grasp of the character of this changing global system and an understanding of how different areas fit into it.

The gradual articulation of an international economic system has resulted in changing forces underlying labor migrations. The effects of this articulation have not been limited to the diffusion of new standards and expectations. Indeed, the penetration of outlying regions by capital-ism has produced imbalances in their internal social and economic struc-tures. Though first induced from the outside, these imbalances become internal to the incorporated societies and lead in time to migratory pres-sures. Hence the pull from advanced economies is not based primar-ily on invidious comparisons of advantage with the outside world but on the solution that migration represents to otherwise insoluble problems *inside* the sending countries.

The changing character of push and pull, the obsolescence of labor recruitment, and the "spontaneous" origins of recent migrant flows are all consequences of the development of an international economy and the shifting modes of incorporation of countries into it. It is this rela-tional dynamics within a global order that appears to offer the most satisfactory explanation of the origins of international migrations.

STABILITY OF MIGRATION

A second aspect discussed by current theories of migration concerns the direction of these flows and their stability. Orthodox analysts tend to view migration in fairly simple terms: People leave their home country to escape economic or political conditions, move to another with the hope of a better life, and struggle for years or generations to attain equality within the new society. Once initiated, the movement can be expected to continue as long as push and pull factors remain and as long as the receiving nation permits it. Massive returns of immigrants to their home country occur only under conditions of deliberate repatriation or severe economic depression.

The massive immigrations from peripheral to advanced countries since World War II have given rise to a different theoretical emphasis. Most of the labor migrations in this period have taken place under guest-worker arrangements or as a surreptitious flow. These immigrants are labeled *target-earners* because they are assumed to be motivated by the accumulation of money with which to fulfill goals in the home country. Certainly a high proportion of their earnings are sent home as remittances, either to subsidize consumption needs or for investment. This characterization of the immigrant as Economic Man is accompanied by an emphasis on the immigrant's failure to integrate and general indifference to the institutions of the host society.

This new theory has accorded central importance to return migration. Unlike earlier analyses, it views return to the home country as part of the normal sequence of labor displacements. This ebb-and-flow characterization of immigration advances our understanding in comparison with earlier descriptions of a simple unidirectional movement.

Still, this alternative theory too runs into difficulties. First, there is evidence that many immigrants do stay in the host country precisely because they have been economically successful. Second, the movement in many cases involves not a single coming-and-going but a series of displacements, frequently in a seasonal pattern. (See Dinerman, 1978; Cornelius, 1981; Bustamante, 1976.)

This new theory, like earlier ones, is based on the perspective of the receiving country and hence fails to capture the process in its totality. It does not take into account, for instance, the true nature of return migration, which may be to the actual place of origin or to another destination. Similarly, it does not consider common patterns in which individuals alternate internal with international migration or in which households select some members to travel abroad and some to journey to cities within the country (Rhoades, 1978; Dinerman, 1978; Sassen-Koob, 1978). These omissions stem from the fact that this theory conceives of international migration as a process occurring between two separate national units.

The progressive articulation of a global economic order allows individuals and families in remote areas to gain access to a much broader range of economic opportunities and to deliberately plan their use. Today villages in the interior of Mexico maintain regular contact with ethnic communities in Chicago. Remote towns in the mountains of the Dominican Republic are well informed about labor market conditions in Queens and the Bronx (Rhoades, 1978; Roberts, 1976; Cornelius, 1976).

A full understanding of how these ties are established and how multiple displacements take place requires, in addition, the concept of social networks. Networks link populations distributed widely across the system. It is through networks that the economic opportunities of migration are often actualized.

Labor migration can thus be conceptualized as a process of network building that depends on and, in turn, reinforces social relationships across space. The microstructures thus created not only permit the survival of migrants but also constitute a significant undercurrent often running counter to dominant economic trends.

This alternative perspective helps explain a phenomenon that escapes earlier theories: the resilience of migrant flows after original push and pull forces have disappeared or after original opportunities for target earning have been removed. The fact that migrant flows do not respond automatically to such changes is related to their organization through social networks. Once in place, these structures stabilize such movements by adapting to shifting economic conditions and by generating new opportunities apart from the original incentives. Although they are not indifferent to the broader context, the network structures of migration have frequently led to outcomes quite different from those anticipated by conventional economic hypotheses.

USES OF LABOR MIGRATION

Most contemporary theorizing on international migration has focused neither on its origins nor on its directionality and stability. Instead it has dealt with the two remaining aspects—uses of migration for the receiving economy and the adaptation of new immigrants. The different theoretical positions on these issues are both more complex and more controversial since each lays claim to a supporting body of evidence.

The orthodox economic perspective regards immigrant labor as a supplement to an insufficient domestic labor force. Immigrants are recruited to fill jobs in an expanding economy that has run out of hands in its own population. This situation has been assumed since the time of classic political economy. John Stuart Mill, for example, defended labor emigration in these terms.

Orthodox economic theory explains the gravitation of immigrants toward the worst jobs as a natural consequence of an expanding economy. In this situation, native workers move upward toward better-paid, more prestigious, or more autonomous positions. In the United States, the existence of a frontier played a central role in maintaining an open economic structure and abundant opportunities for advancement. Even in the absence of cheap land this situation can occur, at least in theory, through the expansion of an industrial economy.

Because labor scarcity occurs at the bottom, wages for unskilled and semiskilled workers tend to rise as a result of competition between employers. This process has the dual consequences of attracting prospective immigrants while compelling employers to seek new sources of labor as means of controlling wages. Both trends encourage further immigration. (See Lebergott, 1964; Chiswick, 1980.) From this perspective, immigrant workers are not qualitatively different from native laborers except that they are newer entrants in the labor force and have less experience and perhaps less education. With time, immigrants can acquire the experience and qualifications to move upward as well, leaving the bottom of the occupational structure to new labor flows.

A second perspective has focused on the experience of immigrant groups who have not come of their own free will or have been made to work under conditions of slavery, servitude, or peonage. These "colonized minorities" also meet a labor demand, but one that is qualitatively distinct from that described by orthodox theory. They occupy positions at the bottom of the occupational structure. These are not, however, positions vacated by domestic workers but require a specific class of worker since no free domestic labor can be found to occupy them.

The incorporation of a colonized minority into the receiving economy has been marked in general by two central features: First, it is employed in nonurban extractive tasks, primarily mining and agriculture. Second, production is organized along precapitalist lines where labor is subject, under various legal arrangements, to the will of employers. The existence of this kind of labor gives rise, in turn, to ideologists who justify the situation on the grounds of racial or cultural differences and the need to educate and control the inferior group.

The central feature of the colonial perspective on immigration is that it regards the use of this labor as valuable for the dominant racial or cultural group *as a whole.* Its different classes benefit from the colonial situation in different ways. Employers gain because they have at their disposal a cheap and exploitable source of labor to which they can dictate their own terms. Workers belonging to the dominant group also benefit in various ways. First, they gain symbolically by the existence of an inferior group with whom they can compare their own lot. Hence they can entertain feelings of superiority and enjoy a vicarious identification with the dominant classes. Second, they stand to gain materially through three mechanisms: the exclusion of the colonized from competition for the better-paid menial and supervisory jobs; the lower cost of goods and services produced with colonized labor; and the redistribution of part of the surplus extracted from that labor by the employer class in the form of higher wages and other benefits for workers belonging to the dominant group.

A third perspective on the uses of migrant labor stresses the significance of racial or cultural differences and a racist ideology as well, but it interprets their effects differently. Employment of migrants from culturally and racially distinct origins is defined here as a common strategy by the employer class *against* the organizations of domestic workers. Hence the benefits brought about by a subordinate minority in the labor market do not accrue to all members of the dominant group but are accorded only to the employer class. These benefits are extracted precisely against the interests of the domestic proletariat that is pitted against the new sources of labor.

Immigrant workers, whether free or coerced, are generally in a weaker position than domestic ones to resist employers' dictates. First, immigrants lack familiarity with their new economic and social conditions and do not have the means to resist exploitation. Second, they are separated from the domestic working class by linguistic and cultural barriers and by the all too common prejudices among the latter. Third, conditions in their places of origin are frequently so desperate that immigrants willingly accept whatever occupation is given them. Fourth, an immigrant labor force is usually brought under legal constraints that place it from the start in a vulnerable position.

This perspective on labor immigration does not necessarily contradict the colonialist view, since each applies to a different historical period. This last perspective does, however, call attention to an important outcome neglected by most analysts of colonialism: a "cultural division of labor" that works to the direct advantage of certain classes within the racially dominant group and to the direct disadvantage of others. In this version of things, ideology is used less to legitimize the privileges of one race or cultural group over another than to sustain the separation between two segments of the working class and to fragment organizations based on class solidarity. The widespread existence of racism among domestic workers is thus, ultimately, an ideology directed against themselves. The most systematic version of this perspective has been

presented by Edna Bonacich in her analysis of Southern black migration in cities in the American North. Bonacich labels her thesis a *split
labor market* interpretation.

The fourth and last perspective on immigrant labor combines elements of the preceding two, though it focuses primarily on contemporary situations. There are different versions of this perspective, but
the most coherent one is based on an analysis of the increasing segmentation of social relationships of production under advanced capitalism. The core of this *dual economy* thesis is the observation that advanced
economies have created an oligopolistic segment where control of the
different aspects of production and commercialization is far more extensive than among typical capitalist firms of earlier times (O'Connor,
1973; Edwards, 1979; Stone, 1975).

The emergence of oligopolies in different segments of the economy
is a process common to all the industrialized capitalist countries. These
firms control a significant portion of their respective markets, rely on
capital-intensive technology to enhance productivity, and are able to
pass on increases in the wage bill to consumers through their control
of markets. Oligopolistic corporations are able to create internal markets because of their size and because increases in labor costs are compensated by increases in productivity, by higher prices for the final
product, or both. Wages in this sector of the economy are thus higher
and fringe benefits and work conditions more desirable (O'Connor,
1973; Gordon, 1972).

A second segment of the economy is formed by smaller competitive
enterprises that more faithfully reflect the structural conditions under
early industrial capitalism. They operate in an environment of considerable economic uncertainty. Their markets are usually local or regional,
they do not generate their own technology, and they often rely on labor-
intensive processes of production. Firms in this sector do not have internal markets. Because they also lack a monopoly position, they face
greater difficulties in passing on increases in their wage bill. Not only
are wages lower than in the oligopolistic sector, but also they do not
increase with time. For workers in the secondary sector, seniority is
not a guarantee of higher income or job security. High labor turnover
in these firms is a joint consequence of employers' dismissals and workers' dissatisfaction (Sassen-Koob, 1980; Portes and Bach, 1980).

Entrance into the oligopolistic labor market is primarily a function
of the requirements of firms and not the qualifications of workers. As
part of its control over the work process, management has systematically opted for capital-intensive technology that reduces labor demand.
As many analysts have noted, the adoption of technological innovations is determined not by their availability but by the fact that they

represent a rational strategy for capital when confronted with an organized labor force. The supply of qualified workers for available positions in the oligopolistic sector consistently exceeds demand. Hence it is perfectly possible that individuals with equal qualifications are rewarded unequally depending on the segment of the economy in which they are located (Sassen-Koob, 1980; Bach, 1978).

Students of immigration in the United States have noted the increasing reliance of competitive firms on immigrants, primarily illegal ones, as a source of labor. This process accelerated in the mid-1960s and reached both numerical importance and notoriety during the 1970s. It coincided with the exhaustion of certain labor sources—teenagers and rural migrants—and the increasing resistance of others to accept conditions of employment in these firms. Women and blacks, previously available as pliant sources of labor, have increasingly refused to accept these jobs at those wages. The availability of protective social legislation ("welfare") and other devices have enabled them to withhold their labor from what they perceive as harsh and unfair working conditions (Badillo-Veiga et al., 1979; Bonacich, 1976).

More recent structural theories have accepted the basic division posited by proponents of the dual economy perspective as well as their assertion that immigrants have become increasingly the mainstay of the secondary labor market. Structural theorists have noted, however, other distinct modes of incorporating immigrants into the receiving economy not emphasized by either orthodox or neo-Marxist views.

First, thousands of professionals, technicians, and artisans migrate abroad every year. This flow, known as brain drain in countries of origin, possesses several distinct characteristics. In the United States, in particular, immigrant professionals and technicians do not tend to form concentrated ethnic communities but are usually dispersed throughout cities and regions and follow diverse career paths. More important, they generally enter the primary labor market, where they help to alleviate shortages in specific occupations. Although immigrants usually start at the bottom, they have access in time to the same professional mobility ladders available to domestic workers (Stevens et al., 1978; Portes, 1976).

Second, certain small groups of immigrants insert themselves as commercial intermediaries in particular countries or regions. These "middleman minorities" are distinct in nationality, culture, and sometimes race from both the superordinate and subordinate groups to which they relate (Light, 1972; Bonacich and Modell, 1980). They can be used by elites as a buffer to deflect mass frustration and also as an instrument to conduct commercial activities in impoverished areas. Middlemen accept these risks in exchange for the opportunity to share in the commercial and financial benefits gained through such instruments as taxation, higher retail prices, and usury. Contemporary examples include Indian merchants in East Africa and Chinese entrepreneurs in Southeast Asia and throughout the Pacific Basin. In the United States, they comprise Jewish, Korean, and other Oriental merchants in inner-city ghetto areas and Cubans in Puerto Rico (Light, 1979; Bonacich and Modell, 1980; Kim, 1981; Cobas, 1985).

Third, sizable entrepreneurial immigrant groups tend to form ethnic enclaves characterized by an extensive division of labor and the production of goods and services for both the ethnic and outside markets. Enclaves typically develop through a successful transplantation of an entrepreneurial class from origin to destination during the first waves of migration. Unlike middleman minorities, enclaves tend to be physically concentrated, to encompass manufacturing and agriculture as well as commerce and finance, and to compete with rather than complement domestic firms. (See Portes, 1981; Wilson and Portes, 1980.)

As exemplified by turn-of-the-century histories of Jews in New York and Japanese in California, and contemporary experiences of Koreans in Los Angeles and Cubans in Miami, the formation of enclaves is based on the principle of ethnic solidarity. Immigrant entrepreneurs employ this principle to inhibit unionization and fight opposition among their workers. Ethnic solidarity also provides the basis for effective forms of capital accumulation through pooled savings and rotating credit systems (Light, 1972; Petersen, 1971; Rischin, 1962; Bonacich, 1978). The same principle also prescribes, however, the promotion by successful entrepreneurs of members of the same minority and the support of their economic activities. Skills and contacts acquired in ethnic firms furnish the basis for frequent moves into self-employment. In this way, a class of low-wage earners in an ethnic enclave may move up, in a matter of years, to managerial jobs or into petty enterprise.

The experience of professional immigrants, middleman minorities, and ethnic enclaves reveals possibilities not contemplated by either orthodox, colonialist, or segmented labor market theories about the uses of immigrant labor. These experiences illustrate the possibility of occupational and economic mobility *in the first generation* through use of the immigrants' individual skills and collective resources. The instances of entrepreneurial minorities, in particular, show how immigrants may respond to the threat of exploitation in the open capitalist market with a capitalism of their own that offers possibilities for economic survival and advancement. In general, the theory of alternative modes of structural incorporation captures the growing diversity of situations experienced by recent immigrant groups and identifies explanations for these different outcomes (Wilson and Martin, 1982; Light, 1984).

IMMIGRANT ADAPTATION

The last set of theories deals with the social relationships between immigrants and members of the native majority and their cultural interactions. Different perspectives on immigrant adaptation correspond to different theories on the uses of immigrant labor. Thus the theory that views immigrants essentially as a supplement to the domestic labor force is complemented by a perspective on adaptation that emphasizes social and cultural assimilation. This *assimilationist school* comprises most of the classic studies of immigrants in the United States.

The assimilationist perspective defines the situation of immigrants as a clash between conflicting cultural values and norms. The native majority represents the core; immigrants are the periphery. By osmosis, as it were, the new cultural forms are gradually absorbed by immigrants, bringing them closer to the majority. The process, sometimes called acculturation, is generally seen as irreversible though it may take different lengths of time for different groups. (See Hechter, 1977: chap. 2; Geschwender, 1978.)

In the most extensive treatise on assimilation, Milton Gordon (1964) defines *acculturation* as a precondition for other forms of assimilation. Next in line comes *structural assimilation,* or extensive participation of immigrants in primary groups of the core society. This stage is followed, in a loose sequence, by *amalgamation,* or intermarriage between immigrants and natives, and by *identificational assimilation,* the development of a common national identity based on the symbols of the core group. *Attitudinal assimilation* reflects the absence of prejudice toward immigrants while *behavioral assimilation* represents the absence of discrimination against them.

Gordon examines three alternative outcomes of the assimilation process labeled, respectively, *Anglo conformity,* the *melting pot,* and *cultural pluralism.* As the label indicates, Anglo conformity refers to the complete surrender of immigrants' symbols and values and their absorption of the core culture. The process culminates in identificational assimilation, though it may not lead to structural assimilation or the total elimination of discrimination and prejudice.

The melting pot thesis holds that assimilation results in a blend of the values, norms, life-styles, and institutions of the different groups, both core and peripheral. This integration is manifested, for example, in "American" food, in the incorporation into the language of foreign expressions, and in the adoption of symbols and festivities brought by different immigrant groups.

Cultural pluralism refers to a situation in which immigrants are able to retain their own culture, modified by contact with the core but still preserving its distinct character. Under pluralism, these differences do

not result in prejudice or discrimination; each group is allowed to function in a plane of equality with limited structural assimilation and amalgamation among them. While cultural pluralism is the option favored
by most immigrants, Gordon argues that it has never really existed in
the United States. In his view, the acculturation process has led to outcomes best reflected in the Anglo conformity thesis: The basic values,
norms, and symbols taught to immigrants and fully absorbed by their
children correspond to those of the dominant culture.

Despite the many qualifications and typologies that pervade this literature, its basic insight is that contact between a new foreign minority
and an established majority will lead, through a series of stages, to an
eventual merging of values, symbols, and identities. This integration
into a single society and culture or perhaps into several major segments
is held to be a good thing. For the majority, it represents a guarantee
of social stability and the enrichment provided by elements of new cultures. For the minority, it offers the possibility of access to positions
of higher prestige and power and the promise of a better future for their
children. The assimilationist perspective reflects a view of society as
a consensual structure. Social change consists of attempts to restore
equilibrium disrupted by external forces. The massive arrival of people with a foreign culture represents such a disruption. Assimilation
is the process by which equilibrium is restored.

The colonialist, split labor market, and dual economy perspectives
on immigrant labor correspond to a very different analysis of immigrant
adaptation. From this alternative viewpoint, greater knowledge of the
core language and culture by new immigrants and greater familiarity
with members of the dominant group do not necessarily lead to more
positive attitudes and more rapid assimilation. Indeed, they can lead
to precisely the opposite as immigrants learn their true economic position and are exposed to racist ideologies directed against them as instruments of domination. This perspective on immigrant adaptation
emphasizes ethnic consciousness and the resilience of ethnic culture
as instruments of political resistance by exploited minorities.

At this point, the ethnicity literature splits into two currents. One
notes the functional advantages of ethnicity—ranging from the moral
and material support provided by ethnic networks to political gains
made through ethnic bloc voting. It *pays* to preserve ethnic solidarity,
for this is often the only advantage that immigrants and their descendants have for advancement in society at large. (See Greeley, 1971;
Glazer and Moynihan, 1970; Suttles, 1968.)

A second current generally agrees with these statements but focuses
on the origins of ethnic solidarity. It emphasizes the experience of immigrant groups, which, though acculturated to dominant values and

norms, have been rebuffed in their attempts to enter the core society. In the present version of things, this rejection is an inevitable consequence of the subordinate position of immigrant minorities in the labor market and of the ideologies employed to legitimize it.

The rejection experienced by immigrants and their descendants in their attempts to become fully assimilated constitutes a central element in the reaffirmation of ethnic culture. As several scholars have noted, this culture is not a mere continuation of that originally brought by immigrants but represents a distinct emergent product. It is forged in the interaction of the immigrant group with the dominant majority and incorporates certain aspects of the core culture while retaining those from the past that appear most suited in the struggle for self-worth and mobility. "Nationalities" thus emerge among immigrants who shared only the most tenuous link in the old country. They are brought together by the imputation of a common ethnicity by the core society and its use to justify their exploitation (Hechter, 1977:chaps. 2,10,11; Barrera, 1980; Blauner, 1972).

The central insight of this perspective is that the same ideology employed to justify the condition of colonized and other immigrant groups is eventually turned around as an instrument of solidarity and struggle. As immigrant minorities discover assimilation to be a deceptive path, they come to rely on in-group cohesiveness and cultural reassertion as the only effective means to break out of their situation.

Finally, the theory of alternative modes of structural incorporation is associated with possibilities not contemplated by either the assimilationist or ethnic resilience perspectives. Both perspectives tend to predict greater probability of discontent and mobilization on an ethnic basis when immigrant groups remain isolated from the social mainstream. Depending on the theory, this situation would represent a failure of the assimilation process to materialize or the continuing subordination and exploitation of the minorities. On the other hand, the modes of incorporation represented by middleman groups and, in particular, ethnic enclaves indicate that a measure of isolation need not work to the disadvantage of immigrant communities and hence need not form the basis for political mobilization. On the contrary, it is when immigrants or their descendants begin to leave the relative protection of their enclosures to enter the economic and social mainstream that chances for conflict and mobilization are greatest. This is so because in the process of competition with the domestic majority for positions of relative advantage, discrimination and mobility barriers become more evident. This view, labeled the *ethnic competition* hypothesis, has received consistent support in the recent research literature (Despres, 1975:209–212; Hannan, 1979:253–275; Nielsen, 1980; Olzak, 1983; Portes, 1984).

Although segmented at present, the trend exemplified by the theory of alternative modes of incorporation points toward increasing integration between conflicting perspectives on the uses of immigrant labor and on the process of immigrant adaptation. This trend is the result of the accumulation of empirical knowledge, which has selectively supported different predictions in different times and social contexts. What the sum total of research findings indicates is, above all, the wide diversity of immigration histories and experiences, a fact that precludes blanket generalizations and compels us to draw on different theoretical traditions for their understanding.

REFERENCES

Bach, R. L.

1978   "Mexican Immigration and the American State." *International Migration Review,* 12:536–558. Winter.

Badillo-Veiga, A., J. DeWind, and J. Preston

1979   "Undocumented Immigrant Workers in New York City." *NACLA Report on the Americas,* 13:2–46. November–December.

Barrera, M.

1980   *Race and Class in the Southwest: A Theory of Racial Inequality.* Notre Dame: Notre Dame University Press.

Blauner, R.

1972   *Racial Oppression in America.* New York: Harper & Row.

Bonacich, E.

1976   "Advanced Capitalism and Black/White Relations: A Split Labor Market Interpretation." *American Sociological Review,* 41:34–51. February.

————————— .

1978   "U.S. Capitalism and Korean Immigrant Small Business." Riverside: Department of Sociology, University of California. Mimeographed.

Bonacich, E., and J. Modell

1980   *The Economic Basis of Ethnic Solidarity: Small Business in the Japanese-American Community.* Berkeley: University of California Press.

Bustamante, J. A.

1976   "Espaldas Majadas: Materia Prima para la Expansion del Capital Norteamericano." *Cuadernos del CES,* 9:3–6.

Chiswick, B. R.

1980   *An Analysis of the Economic Progress and Impact of Immigrants.* Final report to the U.S. Department of Labor, Employment and Training Administration. Chicago Circle: Department of Economics, University of Illinois. Mimeographed.

Cobas, J. A.

1985   "A New Test and Extension of Propositions from the Bonacich Synthesis." *Social Forces*, 64(2):432–441.

Cornelius, W. A.

1976   "Mexican Migration to the United States: The View from Rural Sending Communities." Working paper. Cambridge, Mass.: Center for International Studies, M.I.T.

1981   "Immigration, Mexican Development Policy, and the Future of U.S.–Mexican Relations." In R. H. McBride (ed.), *American Assembly of Mexico and the United States*. Englewood Cliffs, N.J.: Prentice-Hall.

Despres, L.

1975   "Toward a Theory of Ethnic Phenomena." In L. Despres (ed.), *Ethnicity and Resource Competition*. The Hague: Mouton.

Dinerman, I. R.

1978   "Patterns of Adaptation Among Households of U.S.-Bound Migrants from Michoacan, Mexico." *International Migration Review*, 12:485–501. Winter.

Edwards, R. C.

1979   *Contested Terrain: The Transformation of the Workplace in the Twentieth Century.* New York: Harper & Row.

Geschwender, J. A.

1978   *Racial Stratification in America.* Dubuque, Iowa: William C. Brown.

Glazer, N., and D. P. Moynihan

1970   *Beyond the Melting Pot: The Negroes, Puerto Ricans, Jews, Italians, and Irish of New York City.* Cambridge, Mass.: M.I.T. Press.

Gordon, D. M.

1972   *Theories of Poverty and Underemployment: Orthodox, Radical and Dual Labor Market Perspectives.* Lexington, Mass.: D. C. Heath.

Gordon, M. M.

1964   *Assimilation in American Life: The Role of Race, Religion, and National Origins.* New York: Oxford University Press.

Greeley, A.

1971   *Why Can't They Be Like Us? America's White Ethnic Groups.* New York: E. P. Dutton.

Hannan, M. T.

1979   "The Dynamics of Ethnic Boundaries in Modern States." In J. W. Mayer and M. T. Hannan (eds.), *National Development and World System*. Chicago: University of Chicago Press.

Hechter, M.

1977   *International Colonialism: The Celtic Fringe in British National Development: 1536–1966.* Berkeley: University of California Press.

Kim, I.

1981   *New Urban Immigrants: The Korean Community in New York.* Princeton, N.J.: Princeton University Press.

Lebergott, S.

1964   *Manpower in Economic Growth: The American Record Since 1800.* New York: McGraw-Hill.

Light, I. H.

1972   *Ethnic Enterprise in America: Business and Welfare Among Chinese, Japanese, and Blacks.* Berkeley: University of California Press.

———.

1979   "Disadvantaged Minorities in Self-Employment." *International Journal of Comparative Sociology,* 20:31–45.

———.

1984   "Immigrant and Ethnic Enterprise in North America." *Ethnic and Racial Studies,* 7:195–216. April.

Nielsen, F.

1980   "The Flemish Movement in Belgium After World War II: A Dynamic Analysis." *American Sociological Review,* 45:76–94.

O'Connor, J.

1973   *The Fiscal Crisis of the State.* New York: St. Martin's Press.

Olzak, S.

1983   "Contemporary Ethnic Mobilization." *Annual Review of Sociology,* 9:355–374.

Petersen, W.

1971   *Japanese Americans: Oppression and Success.* New York: Random House.

Portes, A.

1976   "Determinants of the Brain Drain." *International Migration Review,* 10:489–508. Winter.

———.

1981   "Modes of Structural Incorporation and Present Theories of Labor Immigration." In M. M. Kritz et al. (eds.), *Global Trends in Migration: Theory and Research on International Population Movements.* New York: Center for Migration Studies.

————— .

1984 "The Rise of Ethnicity: Determinants of Ethnic Perceptions Among Cuban Exiles in Miami." *American Sociological Review,* 49:383–397. June.

Portes, A., and R. L. Bach

1980 "Immigrant Earnings: Cuban and Mexican Immigrants in the United States." *International Migration Review,* 14:315–341. Fall.

————— .

1985 *Latin Journey: Cuban and Mexican Immigrants in the United States.* Berkeley: University of California Press.

Rhoades, R. E.

1978 "Intra-European Return Migration and Rural Development: Lessons from the Spanish Case." *Human Organization,* 37:136–147. Summer.

Rischin, M.

1962 *The Promised City: New York Jews, 1870–1914.* Cambridge, Mass.: Harvard University Press.

Roberts, B. R.

1976 "The Provincial Urban System and the Process of Dependency." In A. Portes and H. H. Browning (eds.), *Current Perspectives in Latin American Urban Research.* Austin: Institute of Latin American Studies of the University of Texas.

Sassen-Koob, S.

1978 "The International Circulation of Resources and Development: The Case of Migrant Labor." *Development and Change,* 9(4):509–545. October.

————— .

1980 "Immigrant and Minority Workers in the Organization of the Labor Process." *Journal of Ethnic Studies,* 1:1–34. Spring.

Stevens, R., L. W. Goodman, and S. S. Smith

1978 *The Alien Doctors: Foreign Medical Graduates in American Hospitals.* New York: Wiley.

Stone, K.

1975 "The Origins of Job Structure in the Steel Industry." In R. C. Edwards et al. (eds.), *Labor Market Segmentation.* Lexington, Mass.: D. C. Heath.

Suttles, G. D.

1968 *The Social Order of the Slum: Ethnicity and Territory in the Inner City.* Chicago: University of Chicago Press.

Wilson, K. L., and W. A. Martin

1982   "Ethnic Enclaves: A Comparison of the Cuban and Black Economies in Miami." *American Journal of Sociology,* 88:135–160. July.

Wilson, K. L., and A. Portes

1980   "Immigrant Enclaves: An Analysis of the Labor Market Experiences of Cubans in Miami." *American Journal of Sociology,* 86:259–319. September.

4

International Relations and Asian Migrations

Michael S. Teitelbaum

From time to time, new issues arise in international relations among nation-states. In the 1970s, international issues of economics, energy, and terrorism took pride of place. In the 1980s, international migration appears to be joining them—especially in the case of the United States—and recent events on the Asian continent have had much to do with this trend.

In one sense international migration is a creature of the nation-state system that appeared in Europe several centuries ago and spread to the rest of the world in this century. A migration from Europe to South Asia or from East Bengal to West Bengal is now an international movement between sovereign states, with implications that did not attach to earlier human movements across the same territory. Over the last few decades, however, there has been a rapid increase in the numbers of potential international migrants—a function of the rapid population growth that has more than doubled the population of the developing world since World War II (and especially since the large surviving birth cohorts of the 1950s and 1960s have reached labor force age). Also responsible for this increase in migration are improvements in international transportation that have transformed international migrations from long, dangerous, and expensive sea journeys to quick, safe, and convenient jet flights. Moreover, improved communication and eco nomic growth have made such travel, previously restricted to a few, available to large proportions of the population.

Over the same few decades, rapid economic advance in Western countries coupled with development problems elsewhere has led to large and frequently increasing disparities in living standards, thereby providing economic incentives for international migration from the Third World to the West. Meanwhile, most of the traditional Western countries of immigration—sparsely populated and resource-rich countries such as nineteenth-century America, Australia, and Canada—have indicated their desire for sharp curtailment of further immigration, especially since the global recession of the 1970s and early 1980s.

These changes have been brought home to policymakers by a series of recent migration "crises," many of them in Asia. For example:

- The mass migration of the Indochinese "boat people." More than one million persons are known to have fled Vietnam, with the possibility that additional thousands died in the attempt. International concern was accentuated in 1978–1979 when officials from certain Southeast Asian countries ordered that boats full of Vietnamese be pushed back out into the sea.

- The flight of 20 percent of the population of Afghanistan to Pakistan and Iran after the 1980 Soviet intervention—perhaps 3.5 million persons in all.

- The long-standing pattern of illegal migration from Bangladesh into the Indian state of Assam, leading in 1983 to serious civil strife, suspension of the constitution and voting rights, and horrific reports of communal riot and massacre.

Migration crises also occurred in other regions: the 1983 expulsion by Nigeria of between 1 and 1.5 million foreign nationals from Ghana, Chad, Niger, and other countries; the second such expulsion in 1985, this time affecting an estimated 700,000 people; the seemingly perennial fate of a similar number of Ethiopian refugees seeking to survive in refugee camps in Somalia and the Sudan; the out-migration of several hundred thousand Salvadorans and Guatemalans escaping from political and economic problems in those countries; the saga of thousands of Haitians landing on Florida beaches in small boats, some of them drowning in tragic mass accidents; and the infamous pushout and mass exodus of more than 125,000 Cubans to the United States in 1980.

All these experiences have had important political repercussions in the states involved and have also affected the tenor and content of their relations with other states. These reverberations highlight the sometimes intimate connections between foreign policies and international migrations. The effects flow in both directions: Foreign policies have both stimulated and restrained international migrations, and migrations in turn have had important impacts upon foreign policies. In the recent past, such effects have been far more important than generally perceived, and they show every sign of being on the increase.

Lest the mistaken impression be conveyed of a world of footloose masses roaming uncontrollably across borders, it is worth stating that most people in the world do not migrate across international borders. Only a small minority of the world's 4.9 billion souls have done so, and perhaps 100 million now live outside their homelands. Few countries have "exported" more than 10 or 15 percent of their people. But even a small fraction of the great populations of Asia imply huge numbers in absolute terms. Five percent of India's population would number more than 38 million people—a small minority of Indians, but an enormous number of migrants. Similarly, even a relatively small number of in-migrants can constitute a large percentage of population in a small country. Only 360,000 migrants, many of them from Asia, constituted nearly 80 percent of Abu Dhabi's 1980 population (Emirate of Abu Dhabi, 1981).

Immigrants in the traditional sense (that is, permanent settlers with legal rights of residence) may no longer be the largest component of international migration. Over the past decade, perhaps 10 million persons have fallen into this category—about a half of this total to a single country, the United States. Those forced to leave their homelands for reasons of persecution, and hence designated as refugees, may be at least as numerous. The world's refugee population in need of assistance was estimated conservatively to be about 10.1 million persons in 1985 (U.S. Committee for Refugees, 1985). Many of them originated in Asia, especially the estimated 3.5 million refugees from Afghanistan and the hundreds of thousands from Kampuchea and Laos. Moreover, more than 1.3 million have left the Socialist Republic of Vietnam since 1975 and 1 million have now resettled permanently outside Southeast Asia— about 50 percent in the United States, 25 percent in China, and the rest mainly in Western Europe.

The largest category of international migrants is probably represented by "temporary workers" and by illegal, undocumented, or "irregular" (to use the United Nations' term) migrants. Some 20 to 30 million persons now live and usually work outside their homelands on such temporary (and sometimes unlawful) bases. Perhaps 10 to 15 million have been lawfully admitted as temporary workers, mostly in Western Europe and the Persian Gulf. Increasingly these workers are coming from Asian countries as diverse as India, Pakistan, Bangladesh, the Philippines, and South Korea. Another 10 to 15 million or so (the numbers here are very uncertain) are in an illegal, undocumented, or "irregular" status, concentrated heavily in the United States, Venezuela, India, France, and a few other countries (Martin and Houstoun, 1982; United Nations, 1983:para. 40).

As for the future prospects for Asian migration, it is worth considering two sets of demographic projections—for the economically active and the urban populations—both of which are highly relevant to assessing future pressures for international migration. Projections for the economically active population of Asia prepared by the International Labour Office (ILO) show an increase of some 599 million between 1985 and 2010—from 1,299 million to 1,898 million. This represents a 46 percent increase over the twenty-five-year projection period. If China and Japan are excluded, the comparable projected increase is from 621 million in 1985 to 1,026 million in 2010—a twenty-five-year increase of 405 million, or 65 percent (ILO, 1986). The most recent UN projections for Asian cities show a Calcutta of 16.6 million by 2000, up 75 percent from 9.5 million in 1980; a Bombay of 16.0 million, up 88 percent from 8.5 million in 1980; and a Shanghai and Seoul of 13.5 million each, up 14 and 59 percent from 11.8 and 8.5 million respectively (United Nations, 1984:table 26). These are projections, however, not predictions. The UN projections of urban growth, though statistically conservative, may well prove to be unreliable as predictions, since numerous economic, political, and other developments that cannot be anticipated may have major impacts on urbanization trends. The ILO projections of the economically active population are more robust because they involve forward projection of populations already born.

MIGRATION AND FOREIGN RELATIONS AFFECTING ASIA

The links of foreign policies to immigration and refugee policies may be visualized in three components (Teitelbaum, 1984): foreign policy as it affects international migration; international migrations as they affect foreign policies; and international migrations as instruments of foreign policy.

Foreign Policy As It Affects Migration

Military or political intervention can generate large outflows of refugees or economic migrants. There are also cases of the converse—when interventions restrain existing or potential outflows or, put in another way, cases in which the *absence* of intervention can generate outmigrations as effectively as intervention itself.

Asia provides good examples of both types. The most obvious case of the first is Vietnam, where the departure of some 1.3 million persons was stimulated by foreign intervention—depending upon the perspective of the observer, either by U.S. intervention in a Vietnamese civil war or by North Vietnamese intervention in the affairs of South Vietnam. This mass migration from Vietnam was then affected by further foreign policy interventions of various types. Western nations urged countries in the Association of Southeast Asian Nations (ASEAN) to allow the entry of desperate Vietnamese boat people. ASEAN countries in turn informed Western countries that the boat people's entry would be allowed only if the West undertook to provide third-country resettlement of such migrants. Finally, a large number of countries sought to deter the Socialist Republic of Vietnam from coercing additional thousands of Vietnamese to depart. The most effective actions took place at the 1979 Geneva Conference on Indochinese Refugees.

The 1980 intervention by the Soviet Union in Afghanistan led both to the breakdown of U.S.–USSR detente and also to the departure of 3.5 million Afghans. In contrast, the failure of other nations to intervene in the Pakistani Civil War of 1971 may be said to have contributed to the flight of up to 10 million Pakistanis to India, which led eventually to direct and decisive military intervention by Indian military forces. The absence of foreign intervention in response to interventions by the Soviet Union and Vietnam may also be said to have contributed to mass refugee movements out of Afghanistan and Kampuchea.

Foreign policy initiatives also have stimulated nonrefugee migrations, often unintentionally.

First, there are cases in which close political, military, or economic ties have facilitated immigration. The long-standing and increasingly unlawful immigration to the United States from one of its few former colonies, the Philippines, provides an obvious example of such effects, and proposed U.S. measures to restrain this migration have reportedly been opposed by the Philippine government. (See Chapter 13 in this volume.) A second example is the dramatic growth of Korean migration to the United States accompanying the close political and economic ties that have developed between the two countries since the Korean War. A third example of such effects could arise in the future as an unintended consequence of the proposed Compact of Free Association between the United States and the Pacific Trust Territories of the Marshall Islands and the Federated States of Micronesia. This agreement, under negotiation for some fifteen years now, includes a provision allowing unlimited migration to the United States (Compact of Free Association, sec. 141). This provision has the support of the governments of the Trust Territories, but it has provoked opposition in the United States and may fail to obtain congressional approval.

A second case of foreign policy stimulating migration is provided by bilateral treaties and less formal arrangements that have been negotiated among various countries desiring temporary workers and a number of Asian sending countries. Recent reports suggest that such an arrangement may be facilitating migration from Indonesia to Malaysia (*Economist*, 1984). There are large flows of temporary workers to the oil-rich states of the Persian Gulf from India, Pakistan, Bangladesh, the Philippines, and South Korea, all involving the tacit or explicit agreement of the governments involved. Numerous experiences with such migrations have existed in the past, including the *Gastarbeiter* policy of the Federal Republic of Germany and the *bracero* program between Mexico and the United States. It is now generally agreed that these "temporary worker" policies turned into unintentional incentives of permanent immigration—on the part of both temporary workers who acquire permanent legal status and those who choose to migrate illegally along migration pathways and networks established by legal temporary workers.

Countries from which illegal migrants originate have also sought to employ foreign policy instruments to facilitate or legitimize such flows. The most recent example involves India and Bangladesh. The government of India has sought to calm anti-immigrant agitation in Assam by promising to build a 2,000-mile border fence to restrain illegal immigration by Bangladeshis. This proposal has brought strong criticism from officials of Bangladesh, who maintain that there is little or no migration of this type and that the building of such a border fence is an unfriendly act. Similar criticism has been expressed by the Mexican government about proposals to replace decrepit border fences on the U.S.–Mexican border.

Finally, it has frequently been argued that one of the most effective uses of foreign policy to curb pressures for international migration lies in the realm of foreign assistance, trade, and direct investment. The goal of such proposals is to accelerate the development of countries experiencing heavy out-migration pressures by more rapid job creation and hence domestic opportunities for those who might otherwise seek them abroad.

Such proposals are afflicted by substantial uncertainties regarding the size, speed, and even the direction of their effects. There is, first, doubt as to the development impact of much foreign assistance and direct investment. But there are even more profound questions regarding the effect on migration if such development does occur. While the evidence is hardly definitive, it appears that the impact of such development over two to three decades is the opposite of that intended; the effect is to *accelerate* out-migration (Morrison, 1982; Weintraub, 1983).

Indeed, many countries with the most rapid pace of out-migration, South Korea for example, have been distinct success stories of economic development. The large migrations to the United States from such places as the Philippines, South Korea, Hong Kong, and Taiwan do appear to have been stimulated in part by substantial American investment, trade, and foreign assistance or by close political and military ties. Effects such as these should not be surprising to those who appreciate the importance of social networks in migration decision making. The migration-restraining effects of foreign assistance, trade, and investment policies, if they do occur, could be expected only in the much longer term.

Migration As It Affects Foreign Policy

The presence in a country of large numbers of nationals of another country inevitably affects relations between the two. The migrants' presence may improve relations and understanding between the countries involved, but it also may stimulate bilateral tensions because of perceived mistreatment of the migrants.

There may also be broad foreign policy effects, in which the attention of the receiving country is focused toward the sending region by the presence of large numbers of immigrants. An American senator widely respected for his knowledge of foreign relations recently described as "plausible" the argument that immigration is the single most important determinant of U.S. foreign policy (Mathias, 1981:979). Such views converge with expectations that the predominance of Latin Americans and Asians among immigrants in the United States may redirect American foreign policy away from its traditional European focus and toward Latin America and Asia.

Other, less obvious, effects have also become apparent.

First, sending countries often seek to mobilize their expatriate populations in political relations with the host country. Such efforts usually take the form of subtle or not so subtle support of ethnic-group advocacy involving issues of concern to the sending country. It has been alleged, for example, that in the 1960s the People's Republic of China engaged in such activities among the Chinese expatriate population resident in Indonesia and elsewhere in Southeast Asia, and the government of Vietnam made similar allegations during the 1970s in justification of its treatment of Vietnamese nationals of Chinese origin (Teitelbaum, 1985).

Second, the presence in the United States of several hundred thousand Taiwanese immigrants, a highly educated and influential group, has allegedly contributed to the formulation of U.S. foreign policy toward Taiwan and the People's Republic of China over the past three decades. Until the 1970s, Taiwanese American efforts were directed toward defending Taiwan in its ideological and occasionally military contests with the People's Republic. Over the past decade, opposition has arisen among Taiwanese Americans to the continued state-under-siege political structure maintained by the Kuomintang leadership on Taiwan, which continues to aspire to the dream of someday recapturing the mainland. Some critics now reject the position (held in common, ironically enough, by the governments of both the People's Republic and Taiwan) that Taiwan is an integral part of China. Taiwanese American opposition to the current government of Taiwan has found resonance among influential members of the U.S. Congress and in the State Department, from which concerns have repeatedly been expressed about political repression of Taiwanese dissidents. Such pressures reportedly have already had some impact in moderating the policies of the Taiwan government (*Asian Wall Street Journal*, 22 August 1983, p. 10).

Similar political activities favoring reform in the homeland have energized the large population of Filipino immigrants in the United States. These efforts have achieved greater press attention in the United States than those of Taiwanese Americans—in part because of the larger numbers of Filipino immigrants and in part owing to the highly publicized assassination of Senator Benigno Aquino, a prominent anti-Marcos politician, as he returned to the Philippines after years of exile in the United States. The subsequent events, in which Marcos himself was sent into controversial exile in Hawaii after being overthrown by Corazón Aquino, called further attention to the role of Filipino Americans in home-country politics.

Third, many of the countries with large immigrant or refugee populations lack traditions of political stability—the small oil-producing states on the Persian Gulf are a good example—and in such settings expatriate populations can be employed as instruments to destabilize or pressure the host governments. Efforts to this end include conventional political mobilization of the migrant populations and also the use of unconventional methods such as terrorism or sabotage.

Migration As an Instrument of Foreign Policy

Migrations become instruments of foreign policy when they are seen as serving primarily foreign policy goals. Such uses of migrations have been made by both sending and receiving countries.

First, there is the explicit encouragement of out-migration to another country for the purpose of exercising greater political influence there. Such actions reflect a recognition that the presence of large numbers of immigrants in a receiving country often directs its attention toward the sending country in a way that might otherwise not occur. Ideally, closer political and economic ties can be forged on the basis of such population movements. Such an approach is particularly attractive to a country that finds itself dependent upon the goodwill of another country owing to the latter's superior economic or political power. It has been suggested, for example, that the governments of India, Pakistan, and Bangladesh have encouraged worker migration to the oil-producing states of the Persian Gulf in order to strengthen political ties with countries holding enormous wealth and influence over essential energy supplies (Weiner, 1982).

Second, there is the use of civilian migration and settlement for purposes of asserting either formal sovereignty or de facto control over a geographical area. In Asia, the reported migration of Vietnamese civilians into Kampuchea may be of this type, though it has not been explicitly acknowledged as such. Such migrations make unlikely the withdrawal of the Vietnamese from Kampuchea, and that unlikelihood in turn has stalled negotiations over the international standing of the Kampuchean government and prevented relations between the United States and Vietnam from improving. In some respects, this apparent policy of Vietnamese civilian settlement in Kampuchea is similar to the more open policy of civilian settlement on the West Bank of the Jordon River pursued by successive governments of Israel since the 1967 Middle East War, although security reasons are far more compelling in the West Bank case than in Kampuchea.[1]

Third, there is the use of mass expulsion of nationals into neighboring countries in order to destabilize or embarrass adversaries. A related approach is the deliberate facilitation of illegal migration into a neighboring hostile nation by nationals of a third country. It has been alleged, for example, that the massive outflows of Vietnamese nationals in the past several years were intended in part to destabilize adversaries, and concerns about such effects upon Thailand may have been a factor in determining the willingness of the U.S. government to guarantee permanent resettlement for such migrants. Moreover, some high ASEAN officials and the *People's Daily* of Beijing have reported evidence that the Vietnamese boat people were used as covers to insert communist political and espionage agents into ASEAN nations (*Far East Economic Review*, 15 June 1979, pp. 21–27). Similar allegations have been made about the 1980 Cuban migration to the United States (Fauriol, 1983). Whatever may have been the true motivations in these specific cases (and we shall probably never know for sure), it is clear that mass migra-

---

1. An explicit case is provided in Africa by the 1975 "peaceful march of conquest" of 350,000 unarmed Moroccan civilians into the disputed territory of the former Spanish Sahara.

tions uncontrolled by the receiving country provide attractive opportunities for international destabilization and subversion.

Countries admitting refugees have also viewed them as instruments of foreign policy. Sometimes the refugees serve to discredit the regime of the country from which they have departed. On other occasions, refugees from hostile neighbors have been welcomed to maintain indigenous opposition to that country's government or in support of long-standing border disputes. Sometimes support is also provided for guerrilla operations across international borders, or a blind eye is turned to such activities. Alternatively, migrant groups may be seen as human buffers against hostile military incursions. In most of these cases, it is difficult to distinguish between measures adopted for foreign policy reasons and those adopted out of simple humanitarian concern; usually the receiving country claims that the latter sentiments motivate its policy.

LOOKING TO THE FUTURE

Several issues related to Asian migration deserve concerted attention, as they involve important elements of U.S.–Asian relations. Certainly the continued out-migration of Indochinese poses significant problems for ASEAN nations, for the United States, and for U.S.–ASEAN relations. A recent report prepared by the staff of Senator Edward Kennedy embraces what many ASEAN leaders have been saying for years—that Vietnamese out-migration has been transformed from the flight or coerced departure of refugees into a continuing stream of migrants moving for more traditional reasons of economic attraction or family reunification (U.S. Senate, 1984). The report concludes that there remain genuine political refugees needing assistance, but these people are now forced to compete for resettlement with nonrefugee immigrants. For this reason, the report urges measures to limit nonrefugee migrant flows while facilitating the orderly departure and resettlement of bona fide refugees. Such goals should prove challenging to policymakers in Southeast Asia and Washington.

The civil war and Soviet intervention in Afghanistan appear to have reached a bloody stalemate, leaving in limbo the 3.5 million Afghani refugees in Pakistan and Iran. The foreign policy issues involved are both global and regional in scope; at stake are the future relations between the superpowers, between the USSR and China, and between India and Pakistan, as well as the views of the West and the Muslim world of the Soviet Union's intentions.

Migration by South Asian (and also East Asian) temporary workers to the Persian Gulf has become significant and now contributes a substantial proportion of the foreign currency earnings of such countries as India and Pakistan. Persian Gulf labor importers have made clear their intention to keep such migrations temporary, but the experience of previous importers of "temporary" labor suggests that this intention may prove difficult to implement. Should labor-importing countries conclude that imported labor is no longer needed, serious tensions may arise between them and labor exporters seeking to protect their for-eign currency earnings and limit the destabilizing impacts of mass return migration into their already underemployed labor forces. Given the political and economic sensitivity of the Persian Gulf, such tensions are likely to involve the United States and other Western countries.

The political future of Hong Kong, which has been the subject of active negotiations between the People's Republic of China and the British government, is already raising the prospect of substantial out-migration. Largely because of the uncertainties about the crown colony's future, the British government undertook a major reform of its antiquated nationality laws to make clear that possession of a British passport does not entitle its holder to residence in the United Kingdom. Recent press reports indicate that those in Hong Kong with financial means are already taking precautions to assure the option of international migration to countries such as the United States, Canada, Australia, and Singapore.

Delicate issues affecting U.S. relations with the People's Republic of China and with Taiwan could increasingly be affected by political activities within the United States by Chinese immigrants. One issue of central importance is whether Taiwan will continue to be viewed by the United States, as well as by the governments of both the People's Republic and Taiwan, as an integral part of China, or instead as an independent nation-state as urged by many Taiwanese critics of the Taiwan government.

The immigration provisions of the proposed Compact of Free Association between the United States and the Pacific Trust Territories may well generate opposition in the U.S. Congress, especially given past experience with unlimited migration from American Samoa. This opposition in turn may cause diplomatic complications in the already convoluted negotiations over the future status of the Trust Territories.

Continuation of large-scale legal migrations from the Philippines and South Korea to the United States, described earlier, poses potential political problems for the countries involved. Already proposals have been put forth in the United States to curtail not only illegal immigration, but also the unlimited legal immigration of immediate family members that comprises a large proportion of East Asian migration streams. Such measures can be expected to be opposed by governments that regard this out-migration as a safety valve for political dissidents and underemployed citizens. Certain Asian countries (the Philippines, India, and

Sri Lanka stand out) appear, willy-nilly, to have become producers-for-export of skilled labor; their educational systems produce far too many graduates in certain professions to be absorbed locally, and they therefore depend upon the continuing out-migration of these graduates to limit middle-class dissatisfaction.

As can be seen from this brief discussion of urgent issues, many of the matters involved are at the very core of American relations with Asian countries. They concern some of the most delicate matters on the foreign policy agenda, such as those involving China, Taiwan, the Philippines, Vietnam, and Afghanistan. Although migration issues appear to be growing in importance, they do not fit well within the traditional structure of international affairs and generally are considered only as afterthoughts (if at all) by many foreign policy professionals. In the case of U.S.–Asian relations, such inattention can no longer be justified. Indeed, it poses substantial peril for the interests of the countries involved.

REFERENCES

Economist

1984 "Indonesia's Loss, Malaysia's Gain." 292(7353):62.

Emirate of Abu Dhabi

1981 *Statistical Yearbook.* Abu Dhabi: Department of Planning.

Fauriol, G.

1983 "U.S. Immigration Policy and the National Interest." Immigration Policy Paper No. 2. Washington, D.C.: Center for Strategic and International Studies.

International Labour Office (ILO)

1986 *Economically Active Population: Estimates 1950–1980, Projections 1985–2025.* Geneva: ILO.

Martin, P. L., and M. F. Houstoun

1982 "Law and Contemporary Problems." *European and American Immigration Policies,* 45(2):29.

Mathias, C., Jr.

1981 "Ethnic Groups and Foreign Policy." *Foreign Affairs,* 59(5):979.

Morrison, T. K.

1982 "The Relationship of U.S. Aid, Trade and Investment to Migration Pressures in Major Sending Countries." *International Migration Review,* 16(1):4–26.

Teitelbaum, M. S.

1984 "Immigration, Refugees and Foreign Policy." *International Organization*, 38(3):429–450.

1985 "Forced Migration: The Tragedy of Mass Expulsions." In N. Glazer (ed.), *Clamor at the Gates: The New American Immigration.* San Francisco: ICS Press.

United Nations (UN)

1983 "Recommendation of the Expert Group on Population Distribution, Migration and Development." E/CONF. 76/PC/7, 27 July. New York: Economic and Social Council.

1984 *The World Population Situation in 1983.* New York: United Nations.

U.S. Committee for Refugees

1985 *World Refugee Survey: 1985 in Review.* New York: U.S. Committee for Refugees.

U.S. Senate

1984 *Refugee and Migration Problems in Southeast Asia: 1984.* Committee Report. Committee on the Judiciary, Subcommittee on Immigration and Refugee Policy. Washington: D.C.: Government Printing Office.

Weiner, M.

1982 "Migration and Development in the Gulf." *Population and Development Review*, 8(1):1–36.

Weintraub, S.

1983 "U.S. Foreign Economic Policy and Illegal Migration." *Population Research and Policy Review*, 2:211–231.

5

Contrasting Patterns of Asian Refugee Movements: The Vietnamese and Afghan Syndromes

Astri Suhrke
and Frank Klink

This chapter examines the main international migrations of Vietnamese after 1975 and Afghans after 1978. The two population flows are similar in many respects. They resulted from the same type of social conflict, consisting of revolutionary struggle compounded by foreign intervention. Both conflicts, moreover, became closely tied to the globalized confrontation between the two superpowers, and the people leaving both Vietnam and Afghanistan have been widely recognized as refugees by intergovernmental and governmental agencies. A striking difference between the two movements, however, is that most of the Afghans outside their country have remained in Asia, whereas few of the Vietnamese have.

Apart from forming an interesting pair in and of themselves, the two cases are theoretically significant. They reveal crucial relationships between the causes and the directions of movement in certain types of migrations that are formally recognized as consisting of refugees. The Vietnamese represent the classic resettlement case involving a large-scale, organized movement of people from Asia to Western Europe and the United States. The Afghans provide the contrasting case. Millions are concentrated in refugee camps or have spontaneously settled in neighboring countries, while only a tiny proportion has been resettled elsewhere.

It may be objected that the contrast does not constitute an interesting theoretical formulation because one can easily explain why the Vietnamese were resettled whereas the Afghans languish in camps. The outflow from Afghanistan peaked a few years later than the Vietnamese (1982 as opposed to 1979). By that time the so-called compassion fatigue in the industrialized states made it politically impossible to mount another large-scale resettlement program. That answer is superficially correct, but it begs the obvious question of why, in that case, a different mix of Vietnamese and Afghans was not admitted under existing programs?

More fundamentally, the different directions of the two population movements can be better understood if regarded not as accidental—a quirk of historical timing—but as a logical element in the overall refugee situation. Each situation appears as an entity with several closely interrelated parts, a syndrome, in other words, which usually is identified precisely with reference to its outcome.

In seeking to explain the differences between the Vietnamese resettlement syndrome and the Afghan camp syndrome, one soon realizes that foreign policy considerations of outside, interested states played an important role. The fundamental reasons for this stem from definitional characteristics of "refugees" versus "migrants." It is therefore useful at this point to consider briefly the definitional problem, which a chapter on refugees in a book largely devoted to migrants scarcely can avoid. (For a fuller discussion see Zolberg and Suhrke, 1985.)

Both migrants and refugees can be defined legally or sociologically, for they have certain social properties independent of their legal status. For instance, a labor migrant is commonly defined sociologically as someone who moves primarily in order to sell his labor, and a refugee as someone who moves mainly to escape immediate, physical violence. These sociological definitions may not coincide with legal practice; hence customary language allows for the existence of legal as well as illegal migrants. Nobody, however, speaks of illegal refugees. At first glance this is puzzling. Quite obviously refugees as well as migrants can be illegal or undocumented, in the sense that they can meet a given sociological criterion but not be recognized as refugees in law.

Conventions of language express the confused state of the public and scholarly discourse about refugees. Sociological and legal definitions are melted into one, vague usage of the word. A recent publication of two serious scholars in the field of refugee studies is illustrative. Starting by proclaiming this a "century of refugees," it proceeds to describe "refugees" as follows: They are "among the world's most disadvantaged people," they "do not voluntarily leave their homes to seek economic opportunity in another country," and "they flee because of persecution or fear of it" (Loescher and Loescher, 1982:1). The description contains a contemporary Western legal code for refugees (fear of persecution), while the rest ("disadvantaged" and involuntary flight) are sociological criteria laid down by the observer. The indiscriminate merging of the two kinds of definitions gives the impression that there is only one kind of refugee: the legally recognized refugee who also needs aid (*qua* sociological refuge) and consequently is recognized and assisted for humanitarian reasons. He who does not meet this description is merely a migrant.

Such terminology serves to mystify the nature of refugee movements. The terms *legal* and *illegal* as applied to refugees are analytically more promising by calling attention to the reasons why sociological and legal definitions coincide or not. Some sociological refugees are legally recognized while others are not; and some who would not meet a sociological criterion of refugee nevertheless may be given legal status as such. The variations are not random. The legal codes in themselves are the product of historical experiences that have varied over time and place, as reflected in the different principles of contemporary legal codes as well as earlier ones (Goodwin-Gill, 1983). Whether or not an individual or group is recognized as having refugee status according to prevailing laws is a policy decision, a variable determined by the values, demands, and pressures in a given society, as well as an appreciation of the "objective" (sociological) condition of the claimant(s).

Since persons asking for asylum or refugee status originate from a conflict in a foreign country, considerations of foreign policy inevitably will influence the response by third countries. In some cases the foreign policy element may be marginally important alongside domestic policy pressures or humanitarian concern. The outflows from Vietnam and Afghanistan, however, acquired much international political significance because the conflicts in those countries were closely linked to the wider relationship between the United States and the USSR, as well as to regional politics in West Asia and Southeast Asia.

In the case studies that follow, the term *refugee* is used to identify the peoples of Afghanistan and Vietnam who are recognized by the UN agencies and supportive governments as such. Unlike the terms *legal refugees* and *illegal refugees*, the use of the unmodified term here does not imply a judgment that all or some of them are refugees in a legal or sociological sense. The purpose of the chapter is to explain policies of recognition and support, not to evaluate their merit.

THE VIETNAMESE SYNDROME

The Vietnamese flow, as noted, has become the classic resettlement case. Of the more than 1 million Vietnamese who have left Vietnam since 1975, about 700,000 have been resettled in Western countries—about 457,500 in the United States (as of FY 1984) and the remainder mainly in France, Canada, and Australia, with smaller numbers in other European countries. Moreover, approximately 250,000 have gone to China directly from Vietnam. As of early 1985, some 48,000 remained in first asylum areas, mainly in Southeast Asia, and in refugee processing centers in the region.[1] There have been no formal repatriations and no efforts to integrate them permanently in the areas of first asylum provided by neighboring countries. In recent years the outflow from Vietnam has stabilized at a fairly low level: Boat arrivals in Southeast Asia averaged 2,288 a month in FY 1984 and 2,920 in FY 1983, as against 60,000 for the month of June alone at the 1979 peak. The Orderly Departure Program (ODP), started in 1979, has grown to a monthly average outflow of 1,303 in FY 1983 and 2,262 in FY 1984. The policy of the United States toward admissions likewise seems to have stabilized at a lower level: 23,000 in FY 1983 and 24,900 in FY 1984 as compared with 95,200 in FY 1980 and 86,100 in FY 1981.

Classic cases often appear, on closer examination, to be singular cases. Such also is the history of the Vietnamese refugees. The point has been reiterated by the office of the UN High Commissioner for Refugees (UNHCR), which insists that massive resettlement of Third World refugees to the West must be an exceptional solution, not a standard remedy. To understand why this occurred in the Vietnamese case, it is necessary to recapitulate the sequence of the outflow. (The following sources were useful for the ensuing account: Hugo, 1983; Grant, 1981; Condominas and Potter, 1982; Commission on Human Rights, 1981; Suhrke, 1981.)

The first flow took the form of evacuation to the United States in 1975 of about 125,000 persons associated with the South Vietnamese government and its American supporters. It was followed by a much smaller outflow over the next couple of years (5,100 in 1976–1977) consisting of individuals likewise closely linked with the former regime as well as urban, middle-class professionals.

By mid-1978 it was apparent that other social groups in the South could not easily be integrated into the new order and a second outflow

---

1. Statistics are taken from the FY 1984 and FY 1985 reports of the Office of the U.S. Coordinator for Refugee Affairs, *Country Reports on the World Refugee Situation* (Washington, D.C.), from the monthly reports prepared by the Department of State (RP/TR), and from Chapter 7 in this volume.

developed. Between March 1978 and June 1979, about 163,000 people sought first asylum in Southeast Asia and Hong Kong; another 250,000 ended up in China. This was a mass exodus rather than a displaced elite belonging to the *ancien régime* as narrowly defined. Most came from a sociologically distinct segment of the population: the ethnic Chinese whose prominence in the private economic sector conflicted with the government's socialist economic policies and whose general position was further undercut by the evolving hostilities between Vietnam and China.

A third flow probably started at the same time but emerged more clearly after the July 1979 Geneva conference, at which Vietnam agreed to try to halt further outflows. As it became increasingly dangerous and difficult to leave Vietnam, and as the anti-Chinese measures developed into a more predictable policy that allowed for some accommodation, the remaining ethnic Chinese in South Vietnam (estimated to be about 1 million) generally chose to remain for the time being. A substantial outflow of ethnic Vietnamese materialized, however, drawn overwhelmingly from the middle and lower classes to include teachers, clerks, soldiers, peasants, and fishermen. Some lower level associates of the *ancien régime* who had been in labor camps continued to come out, but the outflow as a whole consisted of a much broader population segment.

The general conditions encouraging this third flow involve both so-called pull and push factors. There was much economic hardship in Vietnam associated with the enormous task of reconstruction and development in a war-devastated country. The problems were worsened by a series of natural disasters in 1977–1978, a virtual economic embargo by Western countries and major international lending institutions (the World Bank and the Asian Development Bank), ideological rigidities of socialist transformation at home (at least until the 1979 reforms), and continuous warfare in neighboring Kampuchea (after the December 1978 invasion). It still may seem surprising that a population that had endured more or less continuous, brutalizing warfare for the last thirty years would find it so difficult to accept the austerity of relative peace. The many years of warfare themselves provide part of the answer. Vietnamese society had been profoundly uprooted in a social, economic, and political as well as geographical sense. An estimated 10 million people had become internal refugees within South Vietnam in the 1960–1975 period owing to bombing, defoliation, and ground combat. Many of them had taken refuge in southern cities permeated by the American presence and its accompanying culture. When this population was confronted after the war with extreme economic austerity, political discipline, a return to the countryside, and possible conscription for a war in Kampuchea, many viewed the alternative of flight—frequently destined for California—as not merely as an attractive option but also as one that in some sense was a logical continuation of the previous *déraciné* condition.

The salient pull factor lies in the availability of a choice. Flight paths became established and well known. One crucial bit of widely shared information was that virtually all Vietnamese who succeeded in reaching a neighboring noncommunist country had a good chance of being resettled in the country of their choice. The U.S. processing system for admission of Vietnamese at first was based on a four-category priority system that included the residual category of "other." Admission thus was practically open-ended. (See U.S. Senate, Joint Economic Committee, 1980:2–4.) A predictable reaction in the United States of domestic political and bureaucratic forces led to the development of a more discriminating seven-category system in 1981, and a streamlined six-category system was established in 1982 for all refugee admissions. This system retained a residual category of people who could be admitted as refugees because their admission was "otherwise in the national interest," although this category was much less frequently used for the Vietnamese than before.[2]

For all practical purposes, however, resettlement in Western countries continued to be the solution for all Vietnamese who reached first asylum in neighboring states. The logic was simple and compelling. The governments of the first asylum countries—principally the ASEAN (Association of Southeast Asian Nations) states of Thailand, Malaysia, Singapore, Indonesia, and the Philippines—were unwilling to absorb the social, economic, and political costs of accepting the Vietnamese on a long-term basis (see Suhrke, 1983). Traditional rivalries and current problems made the Vietnamese unwelcome. Nor did the Vietnamese want to stay. And since there was neither a desire nor the means to return unwilling Vietnamese to their homeland, the only alternative was resettlement. The waiting time in camp had become longer, and an increasing number could circumvent the camps altogether by qualifying for the ODP, but resettlement remained the norm.

The Vietnamese flow sequence fits a pattern typical of social revolutionary conflicts, as has been analyzed more fully elsewhere (Zolberg et al., 1985). The first outflow of *ancien régime* supporters usually has

2. Persons who otherwise qualify as refugees may be admitted to the United States according to a system of priorities enumerated in the 1982 Worldwide Refugee Processing Priorities. The list starts with persons whose lives are in immediate danger for political reasons, proceeds to those with previous association with the United States, and then cites family reunification cases. The last priority is the residual category VI for persons whose admission is "otherwise in the national interest" (Office of the U.S. Coordinator for Refugee Affairs, 1982:29).

independent financial means. More important, they can draw on the sympathy of the foreign states that provided material and political assistance to the *ancien régime* when it was in power. The more established the international links, the more compelling the claims that even rank and file members of the old order can make on the foreign patrons. For this reason alone, it is perhaps not surprising that the United States after two decades of indirect or direct military involvement in Vietnam accepted both the first and the second flow of Vietnamese for resettlement. The Vietnamese experience here resembles that of previous émigré flows, which after the French and Russian revolutions were accepted in countries ruled by conservative or counterrevolutionary forces.

Nevertheless, an element of surprise lingers that calls for further explanation. The earlier émigrés had been European; that the Vietnamese were not was significant, particularly in the context of U.S. admissions, given the long history of exclusionary provisions for Asian immigrants. Moreover, whereas many Vietnamese in the first and second flow had various ties to the United States, the third flow consisted of persons with minimal Western acculturation, resembling ordinary Third World migrants rather than the typical émigré (see Tinker, 1985). Still, there was never really any question but that the Vietnamese would continue to be given priority for admission to the United States as refugees, even though the overall intake went down as domestic political pressure mounted.[3] Not only had Secretary of State George Shultz in September 1984 committed the United States to take 10,000 persons still in so-called reeducation camps in Vietnam, but also for the time being there was no solution except resettlement for those already in first asylum areas.

The explanation for this unusual aspect of the Vietnamese refugee flow is threefold.

First, in the generally intensified U.S.–Soviet confrontation after 1979–1980, it was good foreign policy to accept refugees from Vietnam. The refugee flow was cited as proof of the bankruptcy of Vietnamese socialism and its alliance with the Soviet Union. The point served retrospectively to vindicate American involvement in Vietnam as well as to emphasize the moral superiority of the United States over the Soviet Union. The lesson learned in Vietnam was employed in arguments supporting American policy closer to home. Unless the United

---

3. Thus for FY 1985 Congress authorized a total intake of 70,000 refugees, 50,000 of them Indochinese. The Vietnamese were expected to form a majority, with Khmer and Laotians arriving in smaller numbers. The authorized levels for FY 1984 were a total of 72,000 with 52,000 for the Indochinese; for FY 1983 a total of 90,000 was authorized with 64,000 for the Indochinese. The trend continued in 1985, when the administration proposed to admit only 40,000 Indochinese during FY 1986.

States intervened to prevent the establishment of communist regimes in Central America, officials of the Reagan administration repeatedly warned, the "feet people" would flood the United States as had the boat people from Vietnam.[4] Thus the Vietnamese refugee flow to the United States had some foreign policy utility.

Second, the intense and controversial nature of American involvement in Vietnam made it difficult for those taking either hawkish or dovish positions on that war to criticize a liberal U.S. intake of Vietnamese refugees.[5] For both it represented an obligation, though of two different kinds. Moreover, bureaucratic constituencies had developed in the course of that war that, almost imperceptibly, shifted to organize and defend the resettlement program for the Vietnamese (see U.S. Senate, Joint Economic Committee, 1980:4).

The third explanation for the high priority given to Vietnamese refugees in the United States relates to the conditions of first asylum. It is generally recognized that the unwillingness of the first asylum countries in Southeast Asia to accept the Vietnamese on a permanent basis made large-scale resettlement necessary. But we need to take the analysis beyond this stage to its proper starting point—namely, that the conflict in Vietnam was over and the outcome was irreversible. The outflow of refugees was equally permanent and irreversible; not even a political mythology promising a return to a "free Vietnam" survived after the 1975 communist victory. This was the context that shaped the policy alternatives for the first asylum countries.

In theory, the first asylum countries had several options. They could forcefully return the refugees to Vietnam; they could pass them on to the rich, powerful patron of the anti-communist struggle in Vietnam; or they could absorb the economic and social costs of permitting the Vietnamese to settle locally. The first was a dubious course of action from a legal and political perspective. Since the Vietnamese had been recognized as refugees by the United Nations and its major supporting governments, but not by the first asylum countries themselves, the international legal prohibition on involuntary repatriation of refugees

---

4. See, for example, the speech by Secretary George Shultz commemorating the fall of Saigon, "The Meaning of Vietnam," 25 April 1985 (Department of State, Bureau of Public Affairs, *Current Policy*, no. 694).

5. Two examples are illustrative. In an article in *Foreign Policy* (fall 1979), James R. Kurth wrote under the title "Refugees: America Must Do More" that a greater U.S. intake of Vietnamese would help to transcend an unhappy period in American and Vietnamese history, effectively atoning for the war. A contrary sentiment was stated bluntly by Senator S.I. Hayakawa on 24 October 1979: "By welcoming Indonchinese refugees to the United States we will once and for all show up the present government of Vietnam as the totalitarian, racist tyranny that it is. Morally, we shall have won the Vietnam war."

was not, strictly speaking, relevant. The political stigma associated with returning unwilling subjects to a communist country was, however, and the governments of all the ASEAN countries were firmly anti-communist. Nor did the Vietnamese government want to accept returning refugees unconditionally. Hanoi indicated it would discuss the matter only in the much broader context of a normalization of relations with the United States. That left the ASEAN countries with only the options of local integration or third country resettlement. The choice was demonstrated to the world with increasingly great resolve in 1979, when the authorities in some first asylum areas allowed refugee boats to be towed out to sea.

The United States responded to the ASEAN countries' firm refusal to accept the Vietnamese on a permanent basis by increasing its own intake enormously. In addition to compelling humanitarian reasons, there were weighty foreign policy considerations. The ASEAN countries were important to American economic and strategic interests in Asia because their governments were the only ones in Southeast Asia that remained friendly to the United States after the Vietnam War.

As we shift the analysis to the Afghan refugee flow, two factors seem especially significant in determining the quite different direction that this movement took: the nature of previous American involvement in the area, and the degree of finality associated with the outcome of the conflict.

THE AFGHAN SYNDROME

The most massive refugee outflows from the conflict in Afghanistan occurred after the Soviet intervention in December 1979. Moving primarily into Pakistan, the refugees were estimated to number 1.4 million at the end of 1980 and 2.7 million at the end of 1982. Anywhere from 0.5 to 1.5 million were said to be in Iran.[6] The outflow subsequently stabilized, and by early 1985 close observers concluded the exodus was "probably substantially over" (Coldren, 1985:170).

The antecedents of this flow must be noted. (For a lucid account that also comments on later refugee movements, see Ghani, 1984.) Two political events stand out. First a republican coup in 1973 ousted the monarchy, sending some of the aristocracy as well as old and new religious leaders into exile, mainly in Pakistan. Then, in 1978, Marxists seized power and instituted radical social change. In the process, the republican leaders were executed or went into exile, as did some of the remaining members of the elite from the monarchical period. Largely

6. These numbers are based on UNHCR estimates that are recognized to have a wide margin of error (see U.S. Committee for Refugees, 1982).

because of the feudal (or, more precisely, clan) structure of society, some exiled leaders could take with them client populations across the border to Pakistan. Along with the Islamic organizations, they shaped the popular resistance to the revolutionary regime. They were part of the general Afghan population in Pakistan that collectively came to be considered as "refugees" by the UNHCR and most of its contributing member governments, including the United States.

The subsequent Soviet intervention—which installed a rival Marxist faction and slowed down the tempo of the revolution—enabled the resistance to mobilize a much larger constituency around an emerging nationalism. In the ensuing intensified warfare, the Soviet Union applied high-technology weapons of indiscriminate firepower in areas where the guerrillas were active. The political and military developments caused huge outflows of the population, equivalent to the third stream noted in the Vietnam case. Members of the former elite, both urban based and drawn from local tribal families, continued to come out, but the overwhelming majority of the outflow since 1980 has consisted of entire social segments: Whole villages, with their secular and religious leadership structures intact, have relocated.

Political conflict, warfare, and concomitant economic and social dislocation formed powerful push factors. Although this situation persisted, and indeed worsened in early 1985 when the military campaign intensified, the flow of people across the border abated. People continued to move within the country, however, seeking the relative safety of some cities, notably Kabul, which had doubled in size to about 2 million (Coldren, 1985). As this indicates, the direction of refugee movements is determined not only by the elementary desire for physical safety. By going to Pakistan or Iran it was possible to organize a resistance in exile, and many of those opposed to either the first revolutionary regime or its Soviet-backed successor probably had left by 1985.[7] Ethnic affinities, economic ties, and readily available asylum also facilitated movement across the eastern and the western borders.

The routes to Pakistan and Iran traditionally have been heavily traveled by exiles, migrants, and traders. Similarities in language and culture encouraged a substantial labor migration from the western provinces of Afghanistan to Iran. The flow increased markedly during

7. Some of the reduced outflow could be illusory. Inflated figures for the camp population in Pakistan in previous years were adjusted downward in 1983, and Pakistani authorities refused to register new arrivals for a period in 1983–1984. As for 1985, increased fighting and bombing along the Pakistani border made crossing more hazardous. Little is revealed to Western observers about movements across the border with Iran. Most observers nevertheless accept a secular downward trend in arrival figures since 1982.

Iran's economic boom in the 1970s, and many people simply elected to stay after the 1978–1979 upheavals in Afghanistan. Revolutionary Iran generally has given asylum to these and subsequent groups; the rate of arrival has fluctuated with the ebb and flow of warfare in Afghanistan. Most of the cost of the relief program is absorbed by the Iranian government, which prefers an independent program to one relying on foreign finance and supervised by the UNHCR. Only in 1983 did the government ask for UNHCR assistance, and a modest international program was established.

On the Pakistani side, ethnic ties and traditional cross-border traffic are even more marked. The Durand line drawn by the British in 1893 separated the ethnically distinct Pathan population into two parts. They came to form the politically dominant majority of contemporary Afghanistan (about 8 million of the 18 million population). In Pakistan, the 8.5 million Pathans are concentrated in the Northwest Frontier Province (NWFP), and although they comprise only about 10 percent of the population they retain significant local power and some leverage on national politics. This constellation led to close social and economic interaction: Migrant labor moved from Afghanistan into Pakistan, Afghan nomads crossed in large numbers to bring sheep for winter pasture, and exiles from both sides found ready asylum. The contemporary trek from Afghanistan, which consists mainly of Pathans, followed and mingled with these flows to reach physical safety and material support on the Pakistani side. Since Pakistan in April 1979 asked for its assistance, the UNHCR has coordinated substantial international aid to the refugees.[8]

Although no precise figures are available, it is clear that a tiny proportion of those who have left Afghanistan since the late 1970s have settled in Western countries, and even fewer of these have formal refugee status. Both categories of settlers are drawn primarily from an urbanized elite with ties to the West.[9] As of January 1985, only 16,716 had been admitted as refugees to the United States. Admission ceilings for the last two years are representative of the very limited space reserved for Afghans in United States resettlement policy: For FY 1984 the proposed

8. The main governmental components came under the budget of the UNHCR and the World Food Programme (WFP). The UNHCR has averaged almost $75 million annually since 1981; the WFP budget is around $100 million annually (United Nations, General Assembly, Executive Committee of the High Commissioner's Program, *Report on UNHCR Assistance Activities and Proposed Voluntary Funds Programmes*, annually).

9. This population segment was in itself quite small. Louis Dupree (1973:5) estimated the old elite (urban and rural) to number only around 3,000 in the early 1970s and the entire middle class, broadly defined, to include perhaps 1 million persons. The total population was estimated to be 15 to 18 million, with an estimated 90 percent illiteracy rate.

ceiling for refugees from the Near East and South Asia (mainly Irani-
ans and Afghans) was 6,000 out of a total of 72,000; the corresponding
figures for FY 1985 were 5,000 out of 70,000 (Office of the U.S. Coordinator for Refugee Affairs, 1984). The admissions process likewise is more
restrictive for Afghans than for Vietnamese. Afghan refugees are
processed for resettlement on the basis of only the first four of the six
general priorities—that is, excluding a wider family reunification
category and the residual "national interest" category.

The main characteristic distinguishing the Afghan from the Vietnamese refugee syndrome lies in the differential opportunity for the
two populations to remain in first asylum areas. The governments of
Iran and Pakistan generally permit not only free movement of people
across their borders but also the channeling of material support to the
guerrillas who are using Iranian and Pakistani territory as sanctuary
for themselves and their dependents. In both cases, substantial de facto
local settlement of Afghans has taken place in addition to the establishment of camps. The costs incurred by the host countries are substantial, especially in the case of Pakistan (see Male, 1981). The Afghan
arrivals, mainly Pathans but also Baluchi, meant that the central government progressively lost control over independent-minded minorities
in the border region; economic pressures built up with the rapid inflow of more than 2 million persons; and relations with the Soviet Union
deteriorated sharply.

The reasons for nevertheless extending liberal first asylum were compelling. Traditional local ties, discussed above, supported such a policy, as did considerations of domestic political expediency and religious
legitimacy. Finally, and in sharp contrast to the situation in Vietnam,
the military conflict in Afghanistan has not ended. Although few observers anticipate a clear-cut victory for the resistance movements, the
guerrillas have powerful patrons that are not willing to concede political or military defeat. These patrons include the United States, China,
several Middle Eastern governments and nongovernmental groups
(notably the Muslim Brotherhood organizations), and various Western
European states.

As long as the conflict continues, there is a chance—however remote—that a settlement will enable the refugee population to return
home. A more salient consideration, however, is that without a sizable
refugee population concentrated near the border it would be difficult
to sustain a prolonged resistance. The refugee population represents
what elsewhere have been called "refugee-warrior" communities: whole
population segments that have relocated to a place from where they
can continue the struggle (Zolberg and Suhrke, 1984.) The United States
alone has channeled an estimated $100 million annually in covert funds

to the resistance since 1980; the Middle East is the other main source of weapons and funds (see *Washington Post*, 10 May 1985; *New York Times*, 4 May 1983). In a less instrumental and more symbolic sense, the refugees represent a rejection of the legitimacy of the Soviet-supported regime in Kabul as long as they are *not* formally resettled elsewhere or locally integrated. (For a recent example of this point see Bernstein, 1985). The same principle is evident in the case of the Palestinians.

In general, then, foreign policy considerations influence the refugee policy of outside states for a simple reason. Recognition and material support for the refugees—without which they scarcely could appear in the first place, and certainly not in very large numbers—become a means to condemn or oppose the political order in the country of origin. When the refugees emerge from a conflict that involves intense international rivalries, refugee policy can become a particularly salient instrument of foreign policy. It can be a symbolic testimony against the political order in the country of origin (as in the case of Vietnam)—a usage consonant with a policy of large-scale resettlement. On the other hand, if the opposition is to be both symbolic and instrumental (as in Afghanistan), large numbers of refugees must remain in the area to carry on the struggle.

For the United States, other considerations have reinforced this policy. The Afghan refugees started to accumulate in large numbers from 1980 onward, just after the United States had committed itself to a huge intake of Vietnamese and had become the first asylum country for thousands of Cubans and Haitians as well. An additional large-scale resettlement project was politically impossible. The Afghans would have to compete for space within a refugee program swollen to an authorized admissions level of 217,000 for FY 1981. That only 4,500 places were allotted for the entire Near East in that year reflects the underlying differences in the Vietnamese and Afghan situations. Moreover, the United States had evidenced little prior interest in Afghanistan; there was no sense of a sustained moral and political obligation created by previous involvement. Arrangements for prolonged first asylum in Pakistan could be worked out in return for military, economic, and diplomatic support to Islamabad.[10] The U.S. government also paid for approximately

---

10. The Pakistani government's international image, tarnished by the 1979 execution of former Prime Minister Bhutto and a poor human rights record, improved greatly as Pakistan emerged as the frontline state against Soviet expansionism and generous home for more than 2 million Afghan refugees. American aid, previously terminated on the grounds that Pakistan appeared to be developing nuclear weapons, was resumed in 1981 with the conclusion of a five-year agreement for $4.4 billion in military and economic assistance.

one-half of the annual World Food Programme's budget and about one-third of the UNHCR budget for Afghans in Pakistan.

Although little is known of the attitudes of the Afghans in Iran, among those in Pakistan there has not been a large-scale demand for resettlement to the United States. Many are comfortably settled in familiar environments either in camps or in towns. Afghan resistance leaders in Pakistan have explicitly opposed resettlement as a defeatist solution, expressing the foreign policy logic noted above. And although Afghan society has been uprooted by war and political conflict, it has not been systematically exposed to the pull of Western society through a pervasive and prolonged foreign presence in its country. Feudal or clan structures remained strong after 1978 partly because the revolution was of the putschist kind; traditional patron–client relationships frequently survived the refugee experience as entire villages moved together. In both respects, the South Vietnamese experience is strikingly different.

The UNHCR, moreover, has discouraged large-scale resettlement after the frustrations encountered with the Vietnamese experience. About 95 percent of the funds disposed by the UNHCR for refugees are earmarked by individual governments for particular flows.[11] Funds therefore cannot easily be shifted around (from the Vietnamese to the Afghan program, for example), and overall contributions for relief assistance and quota commitments for refugee resettlement are quite limited. The Vietnamese refugee program had absorbed large quantities of both and cut into potential resources for other programs. Moreover, the self-perpetuating pull elements in the Vietnamese program were creating concern in the UNHCR. There was a growing awareness that it resembled an assisted migration process which, for political and historical reasons, disproportionately favored a small group in the universe of needy. By the time the flow of Afghan refugees became massive, some of these reservations had come to be shared by U.S. officials.

CONCLUSIONS

The Afghans and the Vietnamese were recognized and assisted as refugees by a U.S.-led international coalition not merely because of their obvious need, but also because Western states generally opposed the revolutions that the Vietnamese and Afghans sought to escape or fight. These two factors—the nature of the social conflict and its link to the structure of international rivalries—provide the basic explanation for

11. In 1970, almost 30 percent of the total UNHCR expenditure was covered by the regular contribution from the UN budget, but by 1980 the figure had fallen to less than 5 percent (UN/GA A/AC.96/577 ADD.1).

why the millions of legal refugees appeared in the first place. They also suggest why the movements took such different directions. The conflict in Vietnam had definitely ended (whereas in Afghanistan the war continues), and the United Stated had been deeply involved in Vietnam (but not in Afghanistan). These combinations largely explain why the Vietnamese were resettled in large numbers, whereas the Afghans were not.

This analysis departs from much of the existing literature that emphasizes humanitarian concern and domestic political pressures to explain the admissions policy of third countries. (See, for example, N.F. Zucker, 1983; N.L. Zucker, 1983; Leibowitz, 1983; and Stein, 1983. The article by Scanlan and Loescher [1983] in the same source is a notable exception.) In the Afghan and Vietnamese cases, a detailed analysis of the "absorptive capacity" of third countries would not alter the general thrust of the argument. The analysis, moreover, could easily be extended to other cases. The Khmer situation, for instance, appears to lie somewhere between the Afghan and the Vietnamese syndromes. The conflict in Kampuchea continues, although at a lower level than in Afghanistan, and all the large powers are involved to a degree. The population movement reflects the indeterminate state of the Kampuchea question. Many Khmer have been resettled as refugees in Western countries, but a substantial refugee-warrior community remains in Thailand.

Nevertheless, foreign policy uses of refugee policy that involve large-scale admission of legal aliens will clash with some domestic interests. The mounting pressure within the United States against a large intake of Vietnamese is a case in point. Similar tension is evident in a first asylum country such as Pakistan. In neither case, however, can the tension be resolved readily except through foreign policy adjustments. In the Afghan case it would mean a settlement permitting a more or less voluntary return of the refugees. As for the Vietnamese, an expansion of the Orderly Departure Program or a repatriation agreement from first asylum areas that would lessen the pressure on the U.S. refugee program seems to require a modification of U.S.-Vietnamese relations more generally.

The theoretical implication for the study of legal and illegal refugee movements is clear. Analysis of such movements must recognize the external dimensions of the conflict that produced the flows in the first place and must systematically incorporate the foreign policy considerations of third countries that affect the eventual disposition of the refugees. An analogous international perspective is increasingly recognized in the field of migration studies—namely, the notion that pull–push factors as between sending and receiving countries operate only at certain levels of international integration (see Chapter 3 by Portes and Chapter 16 by Connell in this volume).

REFERENCES

Annals of the American Academy of Political and Social Science

    1983   *The Global Refugee Problem: U.S. and World Response,* special issue, May.

Bernstein, R.

    1985   "Remaking Afghanistan in the Soviet Image." *New York Times Magazine,* 24 March.

Coldren, L. O.

    1985   "Afghanistan in 1984," *Asian Survey,* 25:2. February.

Commission on Human Rights

    1981   *Study on Human Rights and Massive Exoduses.* (Aga Khan, Special Rapporteur.) E/CN.4/1503. Geneva: UN Economic and Social Council.

Condominas, G., and R. Potter

    1982   *Les réfugiés originaires de l'Asie du Sud-Est.* Paris: La Documentation française.

Dupree, L.

    1973   *The Emergence of Technocrats in Modern Afghanistan,* AUFS Reports, vol. 28, no. 5.

Ghani, A.

    1984   "The Afghan State, Islam, and Legitimacy." Paper presented to the Asia Society, Washington, D.C., March.

Goodwin-Gill, G. S.

    1983   *The Refugee in International Law.* Oxford: Clarendon Press.

Grant, B.

    1981   *The Boat People of the Indochina Refugees.* New York: Simon & Schuster.

Hugo, G.

    1983   "Postwar Refugee Migration in Southeast Asia: Patterns, Problems, and Policy Consequences." Paper prepared for the Population Commission of the International Geographical Union.

Leibowitz, H.

    1983   "The Refugee Act of 1980: Problems and Congressional Concerns." In *The Global Refugee Problem: U.S. and World Response.* Special issue of *Annals of the American Academy of Political and Social Science,* May.

Loescher, G., and A. D. Loescher

1982   *The World's Refugees: A Test of Humanity.* New York: Harcourt, Brace, Jovanovich.

Male, B.

1981   A Tiger by the Tail: Pakistan and the Afghan Refugees." In *Refugees: Four Political Case Studies.* Canberra: Australian National University, Department of International Relations.

Office of the U.S. Coordinator for Refugee Affairs

1982   *Proposed Refugee Admissions and Allocations for FY 1983.* Washington, D.C., August.

————.

1983   *Proposed Refugee Admissions and Allocations for FY 1984.* Washington, D.C., August.

————.

1984   *Proposed Refugee Admissions and Allocations for FY 1985.* Washington, D.C., August.

Scanlan, J., and G. Loescher

1983   "U.S. Foreign Policy, 1959–80: Impact on Refugee Flow from Cuba." In *The Global Refugee Problem: U.S. and World Response.* Special issue of *Annals of the American Academy of Political and Social Science,* May.

Stein, B. N.

1983   "The Commitment to Refugee Resettlement." In *The Global Refugee Problem: U.S. and World Response.* Special issue of *Annals of the American Academy of Political and Social Science,* May.

Suhrke, A.

1981   "Indochinese Refugees and American Policy." *World Today,* 37:2. February.

————.

1983   "Indochinese Refugees: The Law and Politics of First Asylum." *Annals of the American Academy of Political and Social Science,* 467. May.

Tinker, J.

1985   U.S. Refugee Policy: Coping with Migration." *Indochina Issues,* 55. March.

U.S. Committee for Refugees

1982   *Afghan Refugees in Pakistan: Will They Go Home Again?* New York: U.S. Committee for Refugees.

U.S. Senate, Joint Economic Committee

1980   *Indochinese Refugees: The Impact on First Asylum Countries and Implications for American Policy.* Washington, D.C.: Government Printing Office.

Zolberg, A., and A. Suhrke

1984   "Social Conflict and Refugees in the Third World: The Cases of Ethiopia and Afghanistan." Paper prepared for the Center for Migration and Population Studies, Harvard University, 22 March.

1986   "Genesis of Refugee Movements in the Third World: Implications for U.S. Policy." *Proceedings of the Eighth Annual National Legal Conference on Migration and Refugee Policy (1985).* New York: Center for Migration Studies.

Zolberg, A., A. Suhrke, and S. Aguayo

1985   "Roots of Refugee Movements: An International Perspective." Paper delivered at the International Political Science Association, Paris, 15–20 July 1985.

Zucker, N. F.

1983   "The Haitians Versus the United States: The Courts of Last Resort." In *The Global Refugee Problem: U.S. and World Response.* Special issue of *Annals of the American Academy of Political and Social Science,* May.

Zucker, N. L.

1983   "Refugee Resettlement in the United States: Policy and Problems." In *The Global Refugee Problem: U.S. and World Response.* Special issue of *Annals of the American Academy of Political and Social Science,* May.

PART II.   IMMIGRATION TRENDS AND POLICIES

6

The Changing Face of Asian Immigration to the United States

Fred Arnold,
Urmil Minocha,
and James T. Fawcett

More than 3 million Asians have immigrated to the United States since 1920.[1] This flow may seem insignificant compared with the nearly 50 million immigrants to the United States from other parts of the world during the same period. The proportion of Asians among all immigrants has changed dramatically, however, since the 1965 overhaul of U.S. immigration law. Asians now constitute the largest stream of immigrants to the United States, comprising nearly half of all annual admissions.

Perhaps because of the recency of large-scale immigration from Asia, most previous studies have focused on immigrants from Europe, Latin

The authors are thankful to Robert W. Gardner for his helpful comments and to Irma Peña and Shanta Danaraj for their assistance in the preparation of the tables.

1. For the purposes of this chapter, Asia includes all countries in East Asia, Southeast Asia, and Middle South Asia (including Iran as the westernmost country). This definition differs in many respects from the one used by the Immigration and Naturalization Service. The INS definition of Asia includes these countries plus all of Southwest Asia. From 1931 to 1963, the INS also included parts of the USSR in Asia. Wherever possible, we have adjusted the "all Asia" category to make it consistent with our definition. This could not always be done, however, because the "other Asia" INS category includes data from different regions and also includes a different set of countries in different years and in different tables. These problems may cause minor inconsistencies between tables in the "all Asia" and "other Asia" categories. The Pacific Islands, which the INS classifies as part of Oceania, are excluded in our definition of Asia as well. See Chapter 16 for a discussion of Pacific Islands migration.

America, and the Caribbean. This chapter reviews recent immigration trends from Asia in a comparative framework that includes immigration from all regions of the world. Because immigrant streams from various Asian countries differ substantially in their characteristics, we also compare trends among the major sending countries (Vietnam, the Philippines, China, Korea, and India). In this study we have organized the data in a new way to highlight the major shift in immigration trends since 1965.

We begin with an overview of the historical trends in Asian immigration to the United States and a survey of the racially restrictive legislation that has affected the trend at various times. We then examine the revolution in recent immigration trends and patterns. The chapter concludes with a discussion of the current debate about immigration policies and the implications for the future of Asian immigration to the United States.

HISTORICAL OVERVIEW

Prior to 1875, few statutory limitations on immigration existed and entry into the United States was virtually unrestricted (Cafferty et al., 1983; Select Committee on Population, 1978). Nevertheless, between 1820, when the United States began collecting immigration statistics, and 1853, fewer than 200 Asians were recorded as arriving in American ports (see Appendix Table 6.1). Until 1850, immigration statistics were based entirely on the arrival of ships at Atlantic and Gulf ports and did not include arrivals at Pacific ports. Although estimates of the total amount of Asian immigration during this period vary substantially, it was evidently not until 1849–1852 that large numbers of Asians began arriving on U.S. shores. These early flows originated in South China, and they were spurred on by economic depression, political unrest, famine, and flooding in that area, as well as by the lure of the gold rush in California.

The annual trend in total Asian immigration since 1854 is shown in Figure 6.1, along with historical landmarks in U.S. immigration legislation. Figure 6.2 shows annual totals separately for three countries with a long history of immigration to the United States—China, Japan, and India. Figure 6.3 shows annual totals for five major Asian source countries since 1960—the Philippines, China, Korea, India, and Japan. (Vietnam, another major source country in the recent period, is included in the overall total in Figure 6.1 but is not analyzed separately here. See Chapter 7 for a detailed study of refugee admissions.)

During the initial thirty years of significant Asian immigration (1854–1883), nearly 300,000 aliens from China entered the United States, but only a few thousand Asians from outside China made the journey across the Pacific (U.S. Bureau of the Census, 1975:108). The import

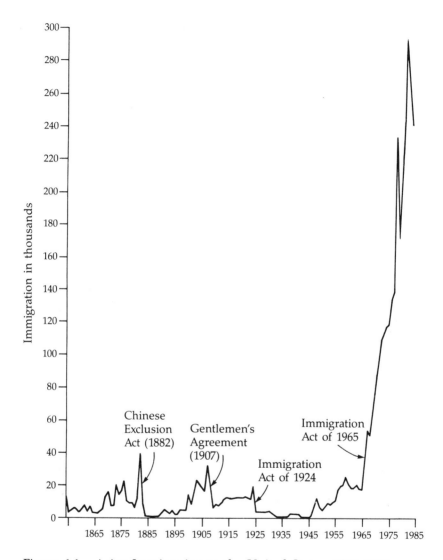

Figure 6.1. Asian Immigration to the United States: 1854–1984

Source: Appendix Table 6.1.

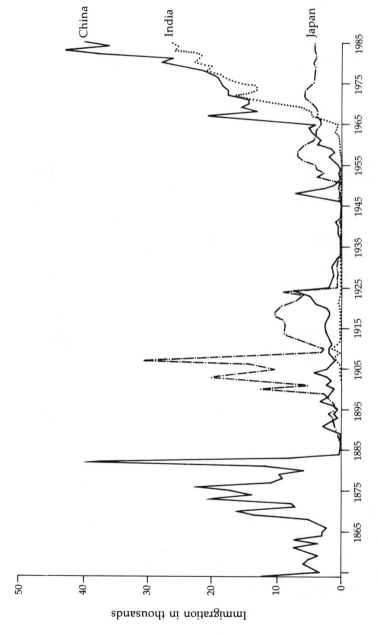

Figure 6.2. U.S. Immigration from China, Japan, and India: 1854–1985

Sources: Appendix Table 6.1; INS (1986:table 4).

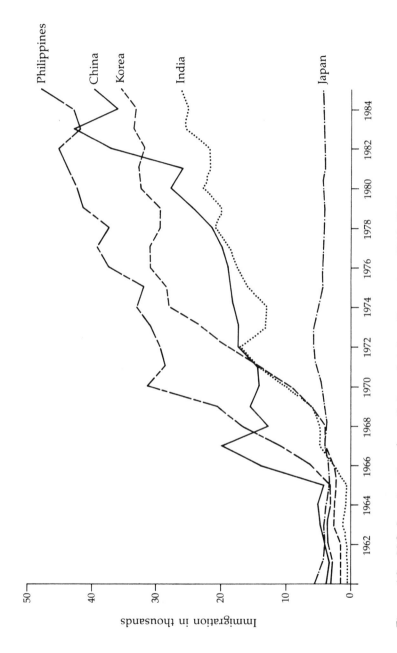

Figure 6.3. U.S. Immigration from Selected Asian Countries: 1960–1985

Sources: Appendix Table 6.1; INS (1986:table 4).

of Chinese workers was encouraged by a severe shortage of labor in the rapidly developing West. Chinese laborers were brought in to work on the railroads and mines, and in construction, manufacturing, and agriculture. These early Chinese immigrants also provided a variety of personal services as domestic servants and operators of restaurants and laundries. Perhaps because most Chinese considered themselves to be only temporary sojourners in the United States, they made little attempt to acculturate (Brown and Pannell, 1985). Chinese immigrants during this period were stereotyped as being clannish and alien. Their willingness to work for low wages brought them into conflict with organized labor, particularly in times of economic recession. These factors, together with the intense nationalism that characterized the period, created the conditions that led to the eventual passage of racially restrictive immigration legislation.

In 1882, Congress passed the Chinese Exclusion Act, which barred additional Chinese laborers from entering the United States and prevented Chinese aliens from obtaining American citizenship. This act remained in effect until 1943, two years after China became a wartime ally of the United States. The act almost entirely terminated immigration from China soon after its passage, and not until the late 1960s did Chinese immigration regain the levels it had reached before the Exclusion Act was implemented.

Much of the slack in Asian immigration after 1882 was picked up a few years later by the rapidly expanding immigration stream from Japan, which reached a height of 13,000 arrivals per year in the first decade of the twentieth century. A few immigrants from Japan were officially recorded as arriving in the United States beginning in 1861 (just eight years before Commodore Perry's historic visit to Japan), but the annual flow did not exceed one hundred immigrants until after 1885 when the Japanese government began officially to permit its subjects to leave Japan. Japanese workers were brought into the United States in lieu of Chinese laborers, who were no longer permitted to immigrate. They were also imported to work on the rapidly expanding sugarcane plantations in Hawaii and the fruit and vegetable farms in California (Nishi, 1985). Many of the sentiments behind legislation to restrict Chinese immigration, however, eventually led to similar demands to limit further immigration from Japan. The Gentlemen's Agreement with Japan in 1907 curtailed Japanese immigration temporarily, but the numbers began to increase again after 1910.

The National Origins Act of 1924 was targeted mainly against the new immigrants from Southern and Eastern Europe, but it also placed severe restrictions on Asian immigration, which dropped from a level of 19,245 in 1924 to only 3,527 the following year. Annual immigration from Asia did not substantially exceed this new level until after World War II. The McCarran–Walter Act of 1952 liberalized immigration regulations for Asians and set up quotas for the Asia–Pacific Triangle (Chandrasekhar, 1981). Within a few years after the passage of the McCarran–Walter Act, Asian immigration reached an annual level of about 20,000 admissions, finally regaining the heights it had reached in the first decade of the century. This increase, however, was only a minor harbinger of the radical changes on the horizon. The 1965 amendments to the 1952 act abolished the national-origins quota system and ended the strict numerical limits on immigrants from Asian countries. This legislation significantly changed the face of U.S. immigration.

RECENT ASIAN IMMIGRATION TO THE UNITED STATES

The contours of recent immigration from Asia have been shaped primarily by the 1965 changes in U.S. immigration law and the political changes that took place in Indochina in the 1970s.[2] Asian immigration has grown dramatically from just over 17,000 in 1965 to an average of more than a quarter of a million annually since 1981 (Appendix Table 6.2). No other region of the world has matched this rapid rise in immigration. In fact, during the same period immigration from Europe declined from 114,329 to less than 65,000. In 1978, Asia overtook North and Central America (including the Caribbean) as the largest source of U.S. immigrants, and it has maintained its predominance ever since. In 1984, more than 44 percent of all immigrants to the United States came from Asia, 31 percent from North and Central America, 12 percent from Europe, and 13 percent from other regions. The rapid rise in the importance of Asian immigration, the decline in the prominence of European immigration, and the slower decline in the proportion of immigrants from North and Central America are depicted graphically in Figure 6.4.

As for individual countries, the transformation has been no less dramatic. In 1960, none of the ten largest sending countries was in Asia (see Figure 6.5). By 1985, however, six of the ten largest streams of immigrants to the United States (and four of the five largest streams) had their origin in Asia. Mexico, with a total of 61,077 legal immigrants in 1985, was the only non-Asian country in the top five.

Recent trends in immigration from individual Asian countries are shown in Appendix Table 6.3. In 1984, some 239,722 Asians immigrated to the United States. The major sending countries in Asia were the

---

2. We deal here only with the incoming flows of Asian immigrants but exclude a detailed analysis of Indochinese refugees, whose annual flows are analyzed in Chapter 7. For a complementary perspective on the stock of U.S. residents of Asian ancestry, see Chapter 11.

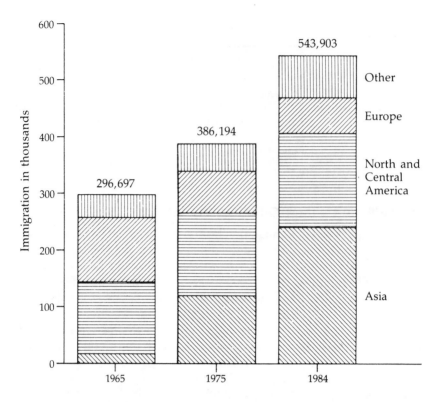

Figure 6.4.   Region of Origin of U.S. Immigrants: 1965–1984

Source: Appendix Table 6.2.

Philippines (42,768); Vietnam (37,236); China, including Taiwan (35,841); Korea (33,042); and India (24,964). The most rapid gains have been registered by Indochina: from fewer than 1,000 immigrants in 1960–1964 to more than 60,000 in 1984 alone. Most of these immigrants arrived from refugee camps in countries of first asylum, but increasing numbers are coming under the aegis of the Orderly Departure Program (see Chapter 7).

Aside from Vietnamese refugees, the largest recent flow of Asian immigrants is from the Philippines. Historically, Filipinos were brought into the United States in response to massive recruiting campaigns in the early 1900s by agricultural interests in Hawaii and California (particularly by the sugar industry). The status of the Philippines as a U.S. territory (the country was ceded to the United States by the Treaty of Paris at the end of the Spanish–American War in 1898) established the political, economic, and social linkages that also encouraged migration

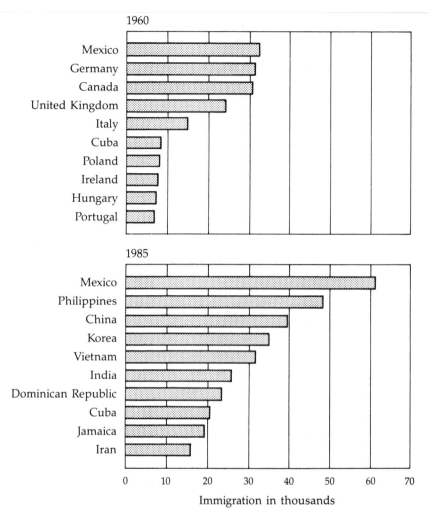

Figure 6.5.   Major Countries of Origin of U.S. Immigrants: 1960 and 1985

Sources: INS (1960:table 6; 1986:table 4).

of Filipino labor to the United States (Pido, 1985). Despite the restrictions placed on the immigration of workers from other parts of Asia, Filipinos were allowed to move to the United States freely as U.S. nationals until 1934.

Immigration from the Philippines dropped to a mere trickle from the years of the Great Depression through World War II. The immigration stream then began a steady rise to its current place of prominence. Since 1960, more immigrants have come to the United States from the Philippines than from any other country except Mexico. Moreover, the recent deterioration of the Philippine economy and continuing political uncertainties are likely to keep the demand for emigration strong in the coming years.

Japan is the only Asian country that has not shown a substantial increase in the number of immigrants to the United States since the passage of the 1965 amendments to the Immigration and Nationality Act. Japan was the largest Asian sending country in 1960–1964, but by 1984 eleven other Asian countries were sending more immigrants to the United States.

EMIGRATION AND ILLEGAL IMMIGRATION

The flow of officially recorded Asian immigrants, as discussed above, tells only part of the story about the volume and impact of international migration. Two additional components of mobility—emigration and illegal immigration—are of numerical importance, although relatively little is known about either of them. Another important component—temporary visits by nonimmigrants—is discussed in a later section.

Only indirect methods can be used to estimate the extent of recent emigration among Asians in the United States. The U.S. government has not collected any emigration statistics since 1958, and the alien address registration program, which might have been used to estimate one component of emigration, was never very complete and in any case was discontinued in 1981. There is no doubt, however, that the emigration of both American citizens and permanent resident aliens is substantial. Warren and Kraly (1985) estimate that since 1900 the ratio of U.S. immigration to emigration for all countries was about 3 to 1. In other words, while 30 million persons immigrated to the United States between 1900 and 1980, about 10 million persons left the United States to live in other countries. Between 1965 and 1979, Warren and Kraly estimate, 1,686,000 residents who were not American citizens emigrated from the United States.

Emigration of permanent resident aliens to Asia is less prominent than is emigration to other regions of the world. According to Warren and Kraly, from 1970 to 1980, 34 percent of legal immigrants were from Asia but only 20 percent of non-U.S. citizen emigrants were Asian. Nevertheless, emigration of Asian non-U.S. citizens was 17.9 percent as high as the flow of legal immigrants from Asia during that same period. Alternative estimates by Jasso and Rosenzweig (1982) confirm the importance of emigration from the United States. They used indirect methods to estimate the range of plausible cumulative net emigration rates of the FY 1971 cohort of legal immigrants to the United States as of January 1979. Emigration rates for Asians were estimated to be lowest for Chinese (7 to 12 percent) and Koreans (8 to 22 percent), considerably higher for Filipinos (20 to 39 percent) and Indians (21 to 40 percent), and higher still for Asians from other countries (41 to 53 percent).

Thus emigration clearly acts to reduce the size of the Asian population in the United States. Moreover, there are thought to be a large number of Asians—particularly residents of Taiwan and Hong Kong—who have obtained immigrant visas to the United States but have never moved to this country. These people continue to live and work in their countries of origin and travel to the United States only often enough to avoid losing their green cards (i.e., their permanent resident status). If the economic or political situation in their home country should deteriorate, or if kinship ties so dictate, they maintain the option of moving to the United States at a moment's notice. They cannot, however, be considered U.S. residents in any real sense.

On the other hand, the size of the Asian community in the United States is bolstered by a large number of Asians who are in the country without proper documents. Illegal immigration from Asia is somewhat restricted by geographical factors—the distance and cost of travel and the difficulty of entering the United States surreptitiously without inspection by immigration officials. Nevertheless, a substantial number of Asians enter the United States with fraudulent documents, slip across the land borders from Canada or Mexico, or overstay their nonimmigrant visas.

The extent of illegal immigration from Asia and other areas of origin is a matter of continuing conjecture. A myriad of estimates have been published, but all of them are based on questionable assumptions. A recent report by the National Academy of Sciences (NAS) indicates that the extent of illegal immigration may have been overestimated. The NAS report concludes that a population of 1.5 to 3.5 million undocumented residents in the United States in 1980 is reasonably consistent with most reliable studies (Hill, 1985). Moreover, there is no empirical evidence to support the contention that illegal immigration has increased sharply in the late 1970s and early 1980s.

The extent of illegal immigration from Asia is even less certain than the amount of illegal immigration overall. Undocumented immigration from Mexico, undoubtedly the source of the largest number of illegal immigrants, has received much more attention than the Asian situation. Relatively few undocumented immigrants who are apprehended by the Immigration and Naturalization Service (INS) come from Asia. Of the 1.25 million deportable aliens located by the INS in FY 1984, for example, fewer than 1 percent were Asians (INS, 1984). This statistic may be misleading, however, since it reflects the enforcement priorities of the INS more than the actual distribution of illegal immigrants in the United States. Estimates of the stock of illegal immigrants from Asia provide a fairer assessment of the situation. Slater (1985) reports that only about 10 percent of illegal immigrants who were counted in the 1980 census came from Asia. Other conjectural estimates are of the same order of magnitude, but none of them can claim a high degree of accuracy. It is evident, however, that illegal immigration from Asia is less important numerically and politically than, for example, illegal immigration from Mexico.

PREFERENCE CATEGORIES FOR LEGAL IMMIGRANTS

The Immigration and Naturalization Service data recognize two types of immigrants to the United States—those subject to a numerical limitation of 20,000 persons per year from any one country, and those who are not subject to numerical limitation. The latter category of immigrants consists primarily of parents, spouses, and unmarried minor children of U.S. citizens and specially admitted refugees.

Immigrants who are subject to numerical limitation are admitted according to a preference system that was established when the national-origins quota system was abolished in 1965. This system was set up to facilitate family reunification, to admit workers with skills needed in the United States, and to make provision for the admission of refugees. Four of the preference categories (first, second, fourth, and fifth) are for relatives of U.S. citizens and permanent resident aliens, and two of the preferences (third and sixth) are for persons in specified occupations and their dependents.[3] If the quota of immigrants is not filled by persons in the preference categories, space may be available for the admission of immigrants who do not meet the qualifications required by any of the preference categories. The nonpreference quota, however, has totally dried up in recent years.

In 1984, substantially more Asian immigrants were being admitted to the United States outside the numerical limitation than within the limitation (see Appendix Table 6.4). The percentage of Asians immigrating outside the numerical limitation has increased rapidly since the mid-1970s as the number of refugee admissions has soared. Not counting admissions from Indochina, 59 percent of all immigrants from Asia were admitted subject to the numerical limitation in 1984.

---

3. The seventh preference, which was reserved for refugees, was abolished by the Refugee Act of 1980. At that time, a separate category for refugees was established with a ceiling that is set each year by the president after consultation with Congress.

These overall percentages mask substantial differences in the method of admission among countries. Among the major sending countries, the South Asian countries and China generally had the lowest percentages of admissions outside the numerical limitation in 1984 (25.9 percent for India, 34.8 percent for Pakistan, and 23.3 percent for China). At the other end of the spectrum, 93.6 percent of all Indochinese immigrants were exempt from the numerical limitation.

Among immigrants subject to the numerical limitation, the majority of Asians who immigrated between 1970 and 1974 came under the occupational preferences and the nonpreference category (Appendix Table 6.5). That situation has changed rapidly, to the point where the vast majority of Asian preference immigrants now enter under the family (or relative) preferences. Immigrants from Europe, Africa, and Oceania are much more likely than Asians to enter under the occupational preference categories, but those who come from North and South America make even less use of occupational preferences.

With regard to the family preferences, almost 90 percent of Asians in this category are either second-preference immigrants (spouses and unmarried sons and daughters of permanent resident aliens and their children) or fifth-preference immigrants (brothers and sisters of U.S. citizens and their spouses and children). The fifth preference and the second preference have registered more rapid increases in the absolute number of immigrant admissions than any other preference categories. There have also been significant gains in the immigration of sons and daughters of U.S. citizens (first and fourth preferences), but the absolute number of immigrants in these categories is relatively small. Among Asians entering under the occupational preferences, third-preference immigrants, including professionals and highly skilled workers (and their dependents or beneficiaries—that is, their spouses and children) have declined steadily since 1970. The number of sixth-preference immigrants (workers in short supply and their dependents) has continued to increase, however.

Individual Asian countries exhibit distinct patterns of immigration under the preference system despite the fact that in each of the major sending countries more than 80 percent of preference immigrants fell within the family preferences in 1984. The proportion entering under the occupational preferences varies from 2.3 percent for Vietnamese to 19.7 percent for Filipinos. The Philippines provides a particularly vivid example of the transformation that has taken place in recent years. From 1970 to 1974, more than half of all preference immigrants from the Philippines were admitted under the occupational preferences and virtually all of these were in the professional and highly skilled worker category. By 1980, the proportion had dropped to a mere 1.6 percent before rebounding to nearly 20 percent since that time. Moreover, within the occupational categories the relative emphasis has shifted away from professionals and toward workers in short supply. There has also been a trend, both in the Philippines and in Asia as a whole, for occupational preference immigrants to bring more of their dependents to the United States.

China is the only major source country for U.S. immigrants that has not experienced a relative decline in the importance of occupational preferences. The proportion of Chinese preference immigrants admitted under the occupational preferences actually increased from 16 percent during 1970–1974 to more than 18 percent during 1980–1984. Moreover, professionals have come to dominate the occupational preferences, whereas workers in short supply had been dominant throughout the 1970s.

ADJUSTMENT OF STATUS

There is a tendency to think of immigrants as persons arriving at American ports of entry loaded down with their possessions and ready to begin life in a new country. This characterization is inaccurate, however, since a substantial proportion of the persons officially counted as immigrants are not newly arrived but rather individuals already physically present in the United States who are "adjusted" to permanent resident status without leaving the country. Under U.S. law, aliens who are eligible to receive immigrant visas may apply to have their status adjusted to that of a permanent resident without having to obtain a visa from an American consulate in a foreign country.

In 1984, some 43 percent of all Asian immigrants were adjusted to permanent resident status after their arrival in the United States. Most of these adjustments of status were related to the large influx of Indochinese refugees who were permitted to become permanent residents after their arrival. In addition, more than 45,000 other Asians adjusted their status in 1984. Even excluding refugees, more Asians were adjusted to permanent resident status in 1984 than persons from any other region. Adjustment of status is particularly common for Asian immigrants who are admitted under the occupational preferences, more than half of whom were already living in the United States in 1984 at the time they attained immigrant status.

Persons who adjust their status originally entered the United States with nonimmigrant visas of various types (see Appendix Table 6.6). From 1970 to 1979, most Asian immigrants who adjusted their status originally entered the United States as either tourists or students. In 1982–1984, in contrast, nearly 70 percent of those who adjusted were refugees. Immigrants from China and India were particularly likely to have entered as students, whereas Filipinos were disproportionately likely to have come as tourists or to have arrived on temporary worker visas or exchange visitor visas.

It is not possible to determine from published INS data what proportion of nonimmigrants who enter in various visa categories eventually adjust their status and become permanent residents of the United States, but an examination of adjustments of status in relation to nonimmigrant admissions gives some indication of the most popular routes used to adjust status. More than 1 million Asians per year came to the United States on nonimmigrant visas during the 1970s, and this number expanded to over 2 million annually in 1982–1984 (see Appendix Table 6.7). More than 85 percent of them came as temporary visitors in 1982–1984, most as tourists but a substantial number for business. Clearly, the proportion of temporary visitors who stay on and are adjusted to permanent resident status is small, probably less than 1 percent (see Appendix Table 6.6).

The largest group of nonimmigrants (after temporary visitors) in 1982–1984 consisted of students and their dependents. In 1984, more than 70,000 Asian students were admitted to the United States as nonimmigrants—substantially more than the average of 42,471 Asian students who were admitted each year between 1970 and 1979. An average of 8,182 students per year were adjusted to permanent resident status in the 1970s, and that number rose to more than 10,000 annually in 1982–1984. Admission to the United States in student status is thus a popular route to eventual immigration. Persons classified by the INS as exchange visitors also have an unusually high propensity to adjust their status, as do temporary workers and trainees.

DISCUSSION

Despite the dominance of Asians in recent immigration flows to the United States, Asian immigration has not figured prominently in the current debate about reforming immigration policies. Perhaps this is because Asian immigrants are generally not perceived to be a "problem." Illegal immigration from Asia is not a conspicuous issue and its magnitude is relatively small. Moreover, Asians in the United States are considered a model minority in many respects. The only substantial issue concerning Asian immigrants is the flow of refugees since the beginning of the Indochinese Refugee Resettlement Program in 1975 (see Chapter 7). Other legislative initiatives, such as a proposal included in an early version of the Simpson–Mazzoli bill to eliminate fifth-preference immigration, would vitally affect Asian immigration, but few of these proposals were made with Asian immigration in mind. The major features of the Simpson–Rodino bill (employer sanctions and legalization of some undocumented immigrants), which was signed into law in late 1986, should have little effect on Asian immigration.

Currently a huge backlog exists of immigrant visa applications from Asia (952,290 active applicants registered at consular offices as of 1 January 1985),[4] and more Asians will become eligible for immigration as the pool of Asians in the United States continues to grow. Barring a major revision of the family reunification provisions of immigration law, immigration from Asia will remain strong.

The strength of the demand for immigration is a result of a confluence of several forces. Overall, the differences between the United States and Asia in level of economic development and opportunity structure are the dominant cause. Related to this differential is the sheer size of the population in Asia and the pressure of the population on the available land and resources (particularly in such countries as China and India). Asia contains well over half of the world's population and more than 70 percent of the population of the less developed countries. Moreover, the population density in Asia is more than six times as high as the density in the rest of the world.

While the pressures from poverty and density are very real, many countries in Asia are also undergoing dynamic economic and social development, with the result that aspirations are changing rapidly. For some upwardly mobile Asians, even in the newly industrializing countries like South Korea, opportunities at home seem too constricted. There is also a general awareness in Asia that Asian Americans are a highly successful group; for the potential immigrant with a relative in the United States, this awareness is augmented by a specific role model. The close family ties characteristic of Asian families further encourage migration under U.S. family reunification policies and help to provide the resources that are necessary for an international move.

Labor market factors also encourage immigration from some Asian countries, such as India, in which trained professionals cannot be absorbed by the local economy. Moreover, the entrepreneurial skills possessed by immigrants from some Asian countries, such as Taiwan and South Korea, are well rewarded in the United States. The close politi-

---

4. Based on unpublished tables from the Visa Office, Bureau of Consular Affairs, U.S. Department of State. The Asian figure constitutes 53.6 percent of the "registered demand" for immigrant visas worldwide. The backlog is primarily from the following countries: the Philippines (336,284); India (155,197); Korea (123,577); China, Mainland-born (107,448); Vietnam (79,097); China, Taiwan-born (59,541); and Pakistan (45,980). These figures do not include the backlog of adjustment of status cases being processed by the INS or visa applicants who are not subject to numerical limitation. The backlog in certain preference categories is particularly extreme—more than fifteen years for third-preference applicants in the Philippines, for example, and almost twelve years for fifth-preference applicants in Hong Kong.

cal and military ties between the United States and several of the major Asian sending countries are an important contributing factor. More generally, the influence of American mass culture, transmitted mainly by the media, is a signficant force, albeit difficult to quantify. Finally, Asian applicants for U.S. immigrant visas face few constraints imposed by the governments of their countries of origin. Although many of these forces are at work in the case of immigration from other regions, it is particularly in the case of Asia that they converge and reinforce one another.

Given the continuation of a strong demand for immigration from Asia and a favorable U.S. immigration policy that is based on considerations of family reunification, labor market needs, and refugee resettlement, what is the long-term prospect for future Asian immigration? Although large-scale immigration from Asia is likely to continue, the growth rates characteristic of Asian immigration over the last decade cannot continue unabated. Between 1975 and 1984, Asian immigration grew at an annual rate of 7.2 percent. If this rate of growth were to continue and if total U.S. immigration from all countries stabilized at 565,000 annually (the average amount of immigration in the period 1980–1984), then by 1996 all U.S. immigration would originate in Asia. Clearly, then, the growth rate of Asian immigration will have to decline unless the United States substantially liberalizes its immigration policy.

Already there are signs that overall Asian immigration to the United States has reached a plateau. In 1983 and 1984, immigration from Asia dropped substantially—entirely because of a slowdown in the admission of Vietnamese and Laotian refugees.[5] Aside from Indochinese refugees, Asian immigration increased slightly in 1983 and decreased slightly in 1984. If Asian immigration were to remain stable at its 1984 level of 240,000 per year, Bouvier and Agresta project that the post-1980 population of Asian immigrants and their descendants will swell to 5.7 million by the year 2000 and 15.6 million just thirty years later (see Chapter 12). Therefore, at the same time that the United States is turning increasingly toward Asia as the region of the future, Asians in the United States are figuring more prominently in this transition and in other aspects of American life.

5. Preliminary data for fiscal year 1985 indicate that immigration from Asia increased by about 9,000 persons between 1984 and 1985, despite a continuing decline in the number of immigrants from Vietnam.

Appendix Table 6.1. Asian Immigration to the United States: 1820–1984

Year	Asia	China[a]	Japan[b]	India	Philippines[b]	Korea[b]	Other Asia
1820–1853	198	88	—	95	—	—	15
1854	13,100	13,100	—	—	—	—	—
1855	3,540	3,526	—	6	—	—	8
1856	4,747	4,733	—	13	—	—	1
1857	5,945	5,944	—	1	—	—	—
1858	5,133	5,128	—	5	—	—	—
1859	3,461	3,457	—	2	—	—	2
1860	5,476	5,467	—	5	—	—	4
1861	7,528	7,518	1	6	—	—	3
1862	3,640	3,633	—	5	—	—	2
1863	7,216	7,214	—	1	—	—	1
1864	2,982	2,975	—	6	—	—	1
1865	2,947	2,942	—	5	—	—	—
1866	2,411	2,385	7	17	—	—	2
1867	3,961	3,863	67	2	—	—	29
1868	5,171	5,157	—	—	—	—	14
1869	12,947	12,874	63	3	—	—	7
1870	15,825	15,740	48	24	—	—	13
1871	7,236	7,135	78	14	—	—	9
1872	7,825	7,788	17	12	—	—	8
1873	20,322	20,292	9	15	—	—	6
1874	13,832	13,776	21	17	—	—	18
1875	16,498	16,437	3	19	—	—	39

Year						
1876	22,935	22,781	4	25	—	—	125
1877	10,637	10,594	7	17	—	—	19
1878	9,007	8,992	2	8	—	—	5
1879	9,629	9,604	4	15	—	—	6
1880	5,835	5,802	4	21	—	—	8
1881	11,977	11,890	11	33	—	—	43
1882	39,629	39,579	5	10	—	—	35
1883	8,113	8,031	27	9	—	—	46
1884	510	279	20	12	—	—	199
1885	198	22	49	34	—	—	93
1886	302	40	194	17	—	—	51
1887	407	10	229	32	—	—	136
1888	570	26	404	20	—	—	120
1889	1,132	118	640	59	—	—	315
1890	3,322	1,716	691	43	—	—	872
1891	5,190	2,836	1,136	42	—	—	1,176
1892	NA	NA	NA	NA	NA	NA	NA
1893	2,392	472	1,380	—	—	—	540
1894	4,690	1,170	1,931	—	—	—	1,589
1895	1,728	539	1,150	—	—	—	39
1896	2,625	1,441	1,110	—	—	—	74
1897	4,930	3,363	1,526	—	—	—	41
1898	4,362	2,071	2,230	—	—	—	61
1899	4,536	1,660	2,844	17	—	—	15

Appendix Table 6.1. (continued)

Year	Asia	China[a]	Japan[b]	India	Philippines[b]	Korea[b]	Other Asia
1900	13,984	1,247	12,635	9	—	—	93
1901	7,811	2,459	5,269	22	—	—	61
1902	16,048	1,649	14,270	93	—	—	36
1903	22,848	2,209	19,968	94	—	—	577
1904	20,951	4,309	14,264	261	—	—	2,117
1905	17,768	2,166	10,331	190	—	—	5,081
1906	15,946	1,544	13,835	216	—	—	351
1907	32,471	961	30,226	898	—	—	386
1908	18,612	1,397	15,803	1,040	—	—	372
1909	5,398	1,943	3,111	203	—	—	141
1910	8,321	1,968	2,720	1,696	—	—	1,937
1911	7,199	1,460	4,520	524	—	—	695
1912	8,661	1,765	6,114	175	—	—	607
1913	11,403	2,105	8,281	179	—	—	838
1914	12,557	2,502	8,929	221	—	—	905
1915	11,668	2,660	8,613	161	—	—	234
1916	11,534	2,460	8,680	112	—	—	282
1917	12,363	2,237	8,991	109	—	—	1,026
1918	12,658	1,795	10,213	130	—	—	520
1919	12,655	1,964	10,064	171	—	—	456
1920	12,472	2,330	9,432	300	—	—	410
1921	13,299	4,009	7,878	511	—	—	901
1922	12,265	4,406	6,716	360	—	—	783

1923	11,522	4,986	5,809	257	—	—	470
1924	19,245	6,992	8,801	183	—	—	3,269
1925	3,527	1,937	723	65	—	—	802
1926	3,376	1,751	654	93	—	—	878
1927	3,596	1,471	723	102	—	—	1,300
1928	3,300	1,320	550	102	—	—	1,328
1929	3,688	1,446	771	103	—	—	1,368
1930	4,417	1,589	837	110	—	—	1,881
1931	3,206	1,150	653	123	—	—	1,280
1932	1,888	750	526	87	—	—	525
1933	525	148	75	44	—	—	258
1934	575	187	86	28	—	—	274
1935	651	229	88	32	—	—	302
1936	773	273	91	13	72	—	324
1937	1,136	293	132	47	84	—	580
1938	2,481	613	93	34	116	—	1,625
1939	2,266	642	102	36	119	—	1,367
1940	2,043	643	102	52	137	—	1,109
1941	1,955	1,003	289	94	170	—	399
1942	584	179	44	36	51	—	274
1943	306	65	20	71	8	—	142
1944	216	50	4	41	4	—	117
1945	448	71	1	103	19	—	254
1946	2,092	252	14	425	475	—	926
1947	6,711	3,191	131	432	910	—	2,047
1948	11,891	7,203	423	263	1,168	44	2,790
1949	7,555	3,415	529	175	1,157	39	2,240

Appendix Table 6.1. *(continued)*

Year	Asia	China[a]	Japan[b]	India	Philippines[b]	Korea[b]	Other Asia
1950	4,495	1,280	100	121	729	24	2,241
1951	7,146	335	271	109	3,228	21	3,182
1952	9,316	263	3,814	123	1,179	47	3,890
1953	8,218	528	2,579	104	1,074	75	3,858
1954	9,937	254	3,846	144	1,234	175	4,284
1955	10,881	568	4,150	194	1,598	263	4,108
1956	17,279	1,386	5,967	185	1,792	579	7,370
1957	19,931	2,098	6,829	196	1,874	577	8,357
1958	20,673	1,143	6,847	323	2,034	1,470	8,856
1959	25,030	1,702	6,248	351	2,503	1,614	12,612
1960	20,685	3,681	5,471	391	2,954	1,507	6,681
1961	18,432	3,213	4,313	421	2,738	1,534	6,213
1962	19,064	4,017	3,897	545	3,437	1,538	5,630
1963	20,436	4,658	4,056	1,173	3,618	2,580	4,351
1964	18,007	5,009	3,680	634	3,006	2,362	3,316
1965	17,080	4,057	3,180	582	3,130	2,165	3,966
1966	35,807	13,736	3,394	2,458	6,093	2,492	7,634
1967	53,403	19,741	3,946	4,642	10,865	3,956	10,253
1968	50,841	12,738	3,613	4,682	16,731	3,811	9,266
1969	65,111	15,440	3,957	5,963	20,744	6,045	12,962
1970	83,468	14,093	4,485	10,114	31,203	9,314	14,259
1971	92,165	14,417	5,326	14,317	28,471	14,297	15,337
1972	108,208	17,339	5,777	16,929	29,376	18,876	19,911

Year						
1973	111,927	17,297	5,676	13,128	30,799	22,930	22,097
1974	117,023	18,056	4,917	12,795	32,857	28,028	20,370
1975	118,952	18,536	4,293	15,785	31,751	28,362	20,225
1976	133,486	18,824	4,275	17,500	37,281	30,803	24,803
1976 TQ[c]	34,052	5,034	1,142	4,572	9,738	6,887	6,679
1977	138,771	19,765	4,192	18,636	39,111	30,917	26,150
1978	232,141	21,331	4,028	20,772	37,216	29,288	119,506
1979	170,851	24,272	4,063	19,717	41,300	29,248	52,251
1980	217,353	27,651	4,225	22,607	42,316	32,320	88,234
1981	244,075	25,803	3,896	21,522	43,772	32,663	116,419
1982	293,872	36,984	3,903	21,738	45,102	31,724	154,421
1983	261,132	42,475	4,092	25,451	41,546	33,339	114,229
1984	239,722	35,841	4,043	24,964	42,768	33,042	99,064

Sources: U.S. Bureau of the Census (1975:series C 89–119); INS (1969, 1970:table 14; 1980, 1981:table 13; 1982–1984:table IMM 1.3). Years ending 30 June except 1977–1984 (years ending 30 September); 1854–1867 (years ending 31 December); 1868 (six months ending 30 June).

Note: Immigrants are classified according to country of birth from 1960 to 1984 and country of last permanent residence from 1906 to 1959. According to the U.S. Bureau of the Census (1975:98), "prior to 1906, data cover countries from which aliens came."

[a]In this table and subsequent tables, China includes Taiwan beginning in 1957. Under the International Security and Development Cooperation Act of 1981, Taiwan and Mainland China were given separate annual limitations of 20,000 visas starting in 1982. The number of visas issued for Taiwan alone was 9,884 in 1982, 16,729 in 1983, and 12,478 in 1984.

[b]Data for the Philippines are unavailable prior to 1936. There is no record of data for Korea prior to 1948 or for Japan prior to 1861. The U.S. Immigration and Naturalization Service makes no distinction between North and South Korea as a country of origin in its published statistics on immigrants.

[c]Transition quarter (TQ) covers the three-month period, July–September 1976.

Appendix Table 6.2. Immigration to the United States, by Region of Birth: 1960–1984

Year	All Countries	Asia	North/Central America	Europe	South America	Africa	Oceania	Other Countries
				(Number)				
1960	265,398	20,685	85,075	139,670	13,048	2,319	1,179	3,422
1961	271,344	18,432	103,388	127,749	15,470	1,980	1,204	3,121
1962	283,763	19,064	121,226	119,692	17,592	1,931	1,203	3,055
1963	306,260	20,436	129,705	125,939	22,919	2,639	1,289	3,333
1964	292,248	18,007	112,973	123,064	31,102	2,887	1,325	2,890
1965	296,697	17,080	126,729	114,329	30,962	3,383	1,512	2,702
1966	323,040	35,807	127,340	125,023	25,836	3,137	1,820	4,077
1967	361,972	53,403	140,138	139,514	16,517	4,236	2,328	5,836
1968	454,448	50,841	228,060	139,514	21,976	5,078	2,588	6,391
1969	358,579	65,111	132,426	120,086	23,928	5,876	2,639	8,513
1970	373,326	83,468	129,114	118,106	21,973	8,115	3,198	9,352
1971	370,478	92,165	140,126	96,498	20,702	6,772	2,919	11,296
1972	384,685	108,208	144,377	89,993	19,359	6,612	3,284	12,852
1973	400,063	111,927	152,788	92,870	20,335	6,655	3,255	12,233
1974	394,861	117,023	151,445	81,212	22,307	6,182	3,051	13,641
1975	386,194	118,974	146,669	73,996	22,984	6,729	3,346	13,496
1976	398,613	133,506	142,307	72,411	22,699	7,723	3,591	16,376
1976 TQ[a]	103,676	34,055	36,807	18,166	6,209	2,322	988	5,129
1977	462,315	138,782	187,346	70,010	32,954	10,155	4,091	18,977
1978	601,442	232,158	220,784	73,198	41,764	11,524	4,396	17,618
1979	460,348	170,862	157,579	60,845	35,344	12,838	4,449	18,431

Year								
1980	530,639	217,366	164,772	72,121	39,717	13,981	3,951	18,731
1981	596,600	244,106	210,427	66,695	35,913	15,029	4,187	20,243
1982	594,131	293,872	158,057	69,174	35,448	14,314	3,833	19,433
1983	559,763	261,132	168,487	58,867	36,087	15,084	3,511	16,595
1984	543,903	239,722	166,706	64,076	37,460	15,540	3,817	16,582

(Percentage)[b]

Year								
1960	100.0	7.8	32.1	52.6	4.9	0.9	0.4	1.3
1961	100.0	6.8	38.1	47.1	5.7	0.7	0.4	1.2
1962	100.0	6.7	42.7	42.2	6.2	0.7	0.4	1.1
1963	100.0	6.7	42.4	41.1	7.5	0.9	0.4	1.1
1964	100.0	6.2	38.7	42.1	10.6	1.0	0.5	1.0
1965	100.0	5.8	42.7	38.5	10.4	1.1	0.5	0.9
1966	100.0	11.1	39.4	38.7	8.0	1.0	0.6	1.3
1967	100.0	14.8	38.7	38.5	4.6	1.2	0.6	1.6
1968	100.0	11.2	50.2	30.7	4.8	1.1	0.6	1.4
1969	100.0	18.2	36.9	33.5	6.7	1.6	0.7	2.4
1970	100.0	22.4	34.6	31.6	5.9	2.2	0.9	2.5
1971	100.0	24.9	37.8	26.1	5.6	1.8	0.8	3.1
1972	100.0	28.1	37.5	23.4	5.0	1.7	0.9	3.3
1973	100.0	28.0	38.2	23.2	5.1	1.7	0.8	3.1
1974	100.0	29.6	38.4	20.6	5.7	1.6	0.8	3.5
1975	100.0	30.8	38.0	19.2	6.0	1.7	0.9	3.5
1976	100.0	33.5	35.7	18.2	5.7	1.9	0.9	4.1
1976 TQ[a]	100.0	32.8	35.5	17.5	6.0	2.2	1.0	4.9
1977	100.0	30.0	40.5	15.1	7.1	2.2	0.9	4.1
1978	100.0	38.6	36.7	12.2	6.9	1.9	0.7	2.9
1979	100.0	37.1	34.2	13.2	7.7	2.8	1.0	4.0

Appendix Table 6.2. (continued)

Year	All Countries	Asia	North/Central America	Europe	South America	Africa	Oceania	Other Countries
1980	100.0	41.0	31.1	13.6	7.5	2.6	0.7	3.5
1981	100.0	40.9	35.3	11.2	6.0	2.5	0.7	3.4
1982	100.0	49.5	26.6	11.6	6.0	2.4	0.6	3.3
1983	100.0	46.7	30.1	10.5	6.4	2.7	0.6	3.0
1984	100.0	44.1	30.6	11.8	6.9	2.9	0.7	3.0

Sources: INS (1969, 1970:table 14; 1980, 1981:table 13; 1982-1984:table IMM 1.3). Years ending 30 June through 1976 and 30 September after 1976 (in this table and subsequent tables).

[a]Transition quarter (TQ) covers the three-month period July-September 1976.
[b]In this table and subsequent tables not all percentages add to 100.0 due to rounding.

Appendix Table 6.3. Asian Immigration to the United States, by Country of Birth: 1960-1984

Country of Birth	1960-1984	1960-1964	1965-1969	1970-1974	1975-1979	1980-1984	1984
			(Number)				
Asia	2,916,192	96,624	222,242	512,791	828,337	1,256,198	239,722
Philippines	637,923	15,753	57,563	152,706	196,397	215,504	42,768
Vietnam	387,278	603	2,564	14,661	122,987	246,463	37,236
China	444,008	20,578	65,712	81,202	107,762	168,754	35,841
Korea	440,028	9,521	18,469	93,445	155,505	163,088	33,042
India	302,038	3,164	18,327	67,283	96,982	116,282	24,964
Iran	103,261	2,960	5,935	12,901	24,666	56,799	13,807
Laos	110,840[a]	NA	NA	166[b]	8,430	102,244	12,279

Kampuchea	64,589[a]	NA	NA	166[b]	5,459	58,964	11,856
Pakistan	56,432	813	2,704	11,228	17,282	24,405	5,509
Hong Kong	93,995	3,103	19,088	20,446	27,059	24,299	5,465
Thailand	70,459	703	2,748	18,740	23,026	25,242	4,885
Japan[c]	112,930	23,327	20,649	26,802	21,993	20,159	4,043
Afghanistan	11,287[a]	NA	NA	398[b]	929	9,960	3,222
Indonesia	27,380	13,261	2,541	2,910	3,426	5,242	1,113
Malaysia	8,383[a]	NA	NA	1,307[b]	2,471	4,605	879
Bangladesh	6,859[a]	NA	NA	301[b]	3,021	3,537	823
Burma	13,194[a]	NA	NA	3,080[b]	5,558	4,556	719
Sri Lanka	5,786[a]	NA	NA	1,320[b]	2,090	2,376	554
Singapore	3,953[a]	NA	NA	635[b]	1,459	1,859	377
Macau	3,225[a]	NA	NA	595[b]	1,358	1,272	260
Nepal	977[a]	NA	NA	168[b]	351	458	75
Brunei	164[a]	NA	NA	NA	84	80	5
Bhutan	90[a]	NA	NA	9[b]	36	45	—
Maldives	12[a]	NA	NA	1[b]	6	5	—
Other Asia	11,101	2,838	5,942	2,321	—	—	—

(Percentage)

Asia	100.0	100.0	100.0	100.0	100.0	100.0	100.0
Philippines	21.9	16.3	25.9	29.8	23.7	17.2	17.8
Vietnam	13.3	0.6	1.2	2.9	14.8	19.6	15.5
China	15.2	21.3	29.6	15.8	13.0	13.4	15.0
Korea	15.1	9.9	8.3	18.2	18.8	13.0	13.8
India	10.4	3.3	8.3	13.1	11.7	9.3	10.4
Iran	3.5	3.1	2.7	2.5	3.0	4.5	5.8
Laos	3.8[a]	NA	NA	b,d	1.0	8.1	5.1

Appendix Table 6.3. (continued)

Country of Birth	1960–1984	1960–1964	1965–1969	1970–1974	1975–1979	1980–1984	1984
Kampuchea	2.2[a]	NA	NA	b,d	0.7	4.7	5.0
Pakistan	1.9	0.8	1.2	2.2	2.1	1.9	2.3
Hong Kong	3.2	3.2	8.6	4.0	3.3	1.9	2.3
Thailand	2.4	0.7	1.2	3.7	2.8	2.0	2.0
Japan[c]	3.9	24.1	9.3	5.2	2.7	1.6	1.7
Afghanistan	0.4[a]	NA	NA	0.1[b]	0.1	0.8	1.3
Indonesia	0.9	13.7	1.1	0.6	0.4	0.4	0.5
Malaysia	0.3[a]	NA	NA	0.3[b]	0.3	0.4	0.4
Bangladesh	0.2[a]	NA	NA	0.1[b]	0.4	0.3	0.3
Burma	0.5[a]	NA	NA	0.6[b]	0.7	0.4	0.3
Sri Lanka	0.2[a]	NA	NA	0.3[b]	0.3	0.2	0.2
Singapore	0.1[a]	NA	NA	0.1[b]	0.2	0.2	0.2
Macao	0.1[a]	NA	NA	0.1[b]	0.2	0.1	0.1
Nepal	a,d	NA	NA	b,d	d	d	d
Brunei	a,d	NA	NA	NA	d	d	d
Bhutan	a,d	NA	NA	b,d	d	d	—
Maldives	a,d	NA	NA	b,d	d	d	—
Other Asia	0.4	2.9	2.7	0.5	—	—	—

Sources: INS (1969, 1970:table 14; 1980, 1981:table 13; 1982–1984:table IMM 1.3).

Note: In this table and subsequent tables, the period 1975–1979 covers a five and one-quarter-year period because the fiscal year was changed in 1976 and a transition quarter was added in that year.

[a]Data for 1971–1984.
[b]Data for 1971–1974.
[c]Including the Ryukyu Islands.
[d]Less than 0.05 percent.

Appendix Table 6.4. Asian Immigration to the United States, by Class under the Immigration Laws, and Region or Country of Birth: 1960–1984

Region or Country of Birth	1960–1984	1960–1964	1965–1969	1970–1974	1975–1979	1980–1984	1984
		Subject to Numerical Limitation[a]					
Asia	1,525,227	11,519	145,341	362,203	483,724	522,440	108,253
Philippines	340,551	341	38,447	100,988	103,192	97,583	19,957
Vietnam[b]	30,005	NA	549	1,561	13,713	14,182	3,642
China	320,767	1,820	46,828	65,657	82,160	124,302	27,493
Korea	267,899	523	6,820	62,442	100,974	97,140	18,992
India	262,374	1,116	16,211	63,458	88,967	92,622	18,492
Iran	54,263	1,127	3,443	8,805	14,920	25,968	5,217
Laos[b]	543	NA	NA	NA	NA	543	143
Pakistan[b]	22,761	NA	2,138	3,324[c]	NA	17,299	3,590
Hong Kong	73,904	486	16,580	17,859	22,294	16,685	3,877
Thailand[b]	25,079	NA	809[d]	6,144	9,266	8,860	1,597
Japan[e]	36,912	964	5,108	9,950	10,853	10,037	2,063
Indonesia	10,382	937	2,081	2,294	2,270	2,800	553
Other Asia	79,787	4,205	6,327	19,721	35,115	14,419	2,637
North America	1,761,891	9,773	125,350	528,755	566,706	531,307	92,606
Europe	1,693,827	453,279	490,093	359,024	251,798	139,633	23,175
South America	344,080	893	23,206	79,315	117,754	122,912	22,218
Africa	120,022	7,417	15,785	26,867	36,525	33,428	5,928
Oceania	44,296	3,811	7,117	9,519	13,352	10,497	1,926

Appendix Table 6.4. (continued)

Region or Country of Birth	1960–1984	1960–1964	1965–1969	1970–1974	1975–1979	1980–1984	1984
		Not Subject to Numerical Limitation[f]					
Asia	1,405,362	86,551	78,013	155,896	351,144	733,758	131,469
Philippines	297,370	15,412	19,116	51,718	93,203	117,921	22,811
Vietnam[b]	356,444	NA	1,789	13,100	109,274	232,281	33,594
China	123,215	18,758	18,884	15,545	25,576	44,452	8,348
Korea	172,129	8,998	11,649	31,003	54,531	65,948	14,050
India	39,555	2,048	2,116	3,795	7,936	23,660	6,472
Iran	48,802	1,636	2,492	4,096	9,747	30,831	8,590
Laos[b]	101,701	NA	NA	NA	NA	101,701	12,136
Pakistan[b]	7,814	NA	379	329[c]	NA	7,106	1,919
Hong Kong	20,092	2,617	2,508	2,588	4,765	7,614	1,588
Thailand[b]	43,824	NA	1,086[d]	12,596	13,760	16,382	3,288
Japan[e]	75,070	21,991	15,097	16,784	11,076	10,122	1,980
Indonesia	16,934	12,324	460	607	1,101	2,442	560
Other Asia	102,412	2,767	2,437	3,735	20,175	73,298	16,133
North America	2,022,937	542,594	629,343	189,080	324,778	337,142	74,100
Europe	758,999	182,835	148,373	119,663	116,828	191,300	40,901
South America	326,523	99,238	96,013	25,359	44,200	61,713	15,242
Africa	73,417	4,737	5,925	7,469	14,766	40,520	9,612
Oceania	28,673	2,389	3,770	6,195	7,517	8,802	1,891

Percentage Not Subject to Numerical Limitation

Asia	48.0	88.2	34.9	30.1	42.1	58.4	54.8
Philippines	46.6	97.8	33.2	33.9	47.5	54.7	53.3
Vietnam[b]	92.2	NA	76.5	89.4	88.9	94.2	90.2
China	27.8	91.2	28.7	19.1	23.7	26.3	23.3
Korea	39.1	94.5	63.1	33.2	35.1	40.4	42.5
India	13.1	64.7	11.6	5.6	8.2	20.4	25.9
Iran	47.4	59.2	42.0	31.8	39.5	54.3	62.2
Laos[b]	99.5	NA	NA	NA	NA	99.5	98.8
Pakistan[b]	25.6	NA	15.1	9.0[c]	NA	29.1	34.8
Hong Kong	21.4	84.3	13.1	12.7	17.6	31.3	29.1
Thailand[b]	63.6	NA	57.3[d]	67.2	59.8	64.9	67.3
Japan[e]	67.0	95.8	74.7	62.8	50.5	50.2	49.0
Indonesia	62.0	92.9	18.1	20.9	32.7	46.6	50.3
Other Asia	56.2	39.7	27.8	15.9	36.5	83.6	86.0
North America	53.4	98.2	83.4	26.3	36.4	38.8	44.4
Europe	30.9	28.7	23.2	25.0	31.7	57.8	63.8
South America	48.7	99.1	80.5	24.2	27.3	33.4	40.7
Africa	38.0	39.0	27.3	21.8	28.8	54.8	61.8
Oceania	39.3	38.5	34.6	39.4	36.0	45.6	49.5

Sources: INS (1960–1981:table 6; 1982–1984:table IMM 2.2).

[a] For 1960–1965 these are quota immigrants.

[b] Data not available for every year from 1960 to 1984.

[c] Data for 1970–1971 only.

[d] Data for 1968–1969 only.

[e] Including the Ryukyu Islands.

[f] For 1960–1965 these are nonquota immigrants.

Appendix Table 6.5.   Immigrants (Subject to Limitation) Admitted to ability: 1970–1984

| | | Family Preferences | | | |
| | | | 1st Prefer- ence | 2nd Prefer- ence | 4th Prefer- ence | 5th Prefer- ence |
Geographic Area of Chargeability[a] and Period	Total Immigrants	Total Family Preferences	Unmarried Sons and Daughters of U.S. Citizens[b]	Spouses, Unmarried Sons and Daughters of Resident Aliens[b]	Married Sons and Daughters of U.S. Citizens[c]	Brothers and Sisters of U.S. Citizens[c]
Asia						
1970–1974	353,614	148,763	2,505	89,086	5,802	51,370
1975–1979	477,482	335,455	3,591	157,875	11,854	162,135
1980–1984	515,069	417,523	11,123	189,023	31,097	186,280
1984	107,335	87,220	3,056	33,742	6,996	43,426
Philippines						
1970–1974	100,770	47,742	1,810	39,503	1,853	4,576
1975–1979	102,656	74,243	2,325	58,538	3,917	9,463
1980–1984	97,036	81,847	8,706	46,265	7,835	19,041
1984	19,844	15,927	2,494	6,444	1,949	5,040
Vietnam						
1970–1974	1,555	564	4	311	4	245
1975–1979	13,985	4,705	26	1,363	42	3,274
1980–1984	14,603	11,517	251	7,125	541	3,600
1984	3,779	3,692	148	2,011	235	1,298
China						
1970–1974	79,264	38,301	400	16,655	3,315	17,931
1975–1979	101,917	78,266	813	30,490	6,141	40,822
1980–1984	133,487	108,673	1,337	43,101	18,097	46,138
1984	30,250	25,815	176	7,710	3,603	14,326
Korea						
1970–1974	62,485	28,329	66	10,849	197	17,217
1975–1979	99,606	80,370	100	24,533	627	55,110
1980–1984	96,332	85,956	313	42,271	2,247	41,125
1984	18,833	15,922	105	8,082	581	7,154
India						
1970–1974	63,961	16,224	15	12,617	88	3,504
1975–1979	89,841	53,055	51	23,765	305	28,934
1980–1984	92,460	75,685	97	26,654	912	48,022
1984	18,388	15,457	28	5,241	306	9,882

the United States, by Preference Category and Geographic Area of Charge-

| Total Occupational Preferences | Occupational Preferences | | | | Refugees | | | Nonpreference Immigrants and Others[d] |
| | 3rd Preference | | 6th Preference | | | 7th Preference | | |
	Immigrants in Professions	Dependents	Other Workers	Dependents	Total Refugees	Admitted	Adjusted	
(Number)								
104,480	42,503	39,233	12,455	10,289	8,543	7,760	783	91,828
90,084	28,607	32,128	15,794	13,555	14,732	14,439	293	37,211
93,691	25,449	28,895	18,190	21,157	3,466	3,275	191	389
20,080	5,142	6,483	3,719	4,736	—	—	—	35
52,885	26,690	26,151	22	22	—	—	—	143
27,575	10,314	14,024	1,949	1,288	1	1	—	837
15,107	2,075	5,507	3,728	3,797	—	—	—	82
3,901	633	1,415	886	967	—	—	—	16
331	64	55	137	75	2	1	1	658
926	215	429	117	165	7,406	7,332	74	948
412	81	102	92	137	2,599	2,500	99	75
87	21	23	17	26	—	—	—	—
12,728	3,048	2,284	3,997	3,399	8,408	7,681	727	19,827
13,488	2,889	2,738	3,898	3,963	6,263	6,121	142	3,900
24,171	7,717	7,050	3,844	5,560	523	480	43	120
4,422	1,671	1,631	401	719	—	—	—	13
13,119	3,116	3,746	2,904	3,353	2	—	2	21,035
15,616	4,811	5,704	1,983	3,118	2	1	1	3,618
10,368	1,696	3,074	1,865	3,733	—	—	—	8
2,911	359	763	557	1,232	—	—	—	—
16,789	7,066	5,385	2,505	1,833	9	5	4	30,939
21,815	8,190	7,352	3,914	2,359	25	20	5	14,946
16,752	7,248	6,898	1,416	1,190	1	—	1	22
2,930	963	1,160	395	412	—	—	—	1

138

Appendix Table 6.5. *(continued)*

Geographic Area of Chargeability[a] and Period	Total Immigrants	Total Family Preferences	1st Preference Unmarried Sons and Daughters of U.S. Citizens[b]	2nd Preference Spouses, Unmarried Sons and Daughters of Resident Aliens[b]	4th Preference Married Sons and Daughters of U.S. Citizens[c]	5th Preference Brothers and Sisters of U.S. Citizens[c]
Europe						
1970–1974	385,283	252,267	2,077	78,059	17,871	154,260
1975–1979	274,821	174,539	1,912	56,259	11,497	104,871
1980–1984	157,495	96,183	2,667	38,716	11,566	43,234
1984	24,792	13,189	529	4,895	1,978	5,787
Africa						
1970–1974	25,602	7,014	45	4,091	165	2,713
1975–1979	32,230	18,260	101	7,030	478	10,651
1980–1984	33,408	22,655	240	10,781	853	10,781
1984	6,001	4,039	53	1,899	185	1,902
Oceania						
1970–1974	8,902	5,193	44	2,255	156	2,738
1975–1979	12,840	9,580	60	3,995	360	5,165
1980–1984	10,383	7,364	119	3,170	555	3,520
1984	1,886	1,332	31	520	77	704
North America[e]						
1980–1984	452,717	395,512	16,616	256,900	30,212	91,784
1984	91,697	82,380	3,506	59,270	3,666	15,938
South America[e]						
1980–1984	117,467	99,662	1,285	52,236	5,177	40,964
1984	22,404	18,742	306	10,092	1,311	7,033
Independent Western Hemisphere[e]						
1980–1984	73,600	—	—	—	—	—

| | Occupational Preferences | | | | Refugees | | | |
| | 3rd Preference | | 6th Preference | | 7th Preference | | | |
Total Occupational Preferences	Immigrants in Professions	Dependents	Other Workers	Dependents	Total Refugees	Admitted	Adjusted	Nonpreference Immigrants and Others[d]
41,996	1,874	1,610	20,678	17,834	33,173	28,604	4,569	57,847
34,891	2,894	3,686	13,585	14,726	32,068	29,774	2,294	33,323
57,357	13,064	17,412	12,637	14,244	3,516	2,961	555	439
11,589	2,937	4,087	2,188	2,377	—	—	—	14
4,610	1,465	1,334	1,014	797	1,411	1,376	35	12,567
6,239	1,237	1,555	1,545	1,902	975	756	219	6,756
10,332	2,728	3,130	1,990	2,484	358	238	120	63
1,950	515	621	364	450	—	—	—	12
1,546	132	106	653	655	2	2	—	2,161
1,969	241	293	599	836	—	—	—	1,291
3,012	821	1,066	533	592	1	1	—	6
554	162	205	85	102	—	—	—	—
50,096	5,746	9,061	17,232	18,057	4,038	4,032	6	3,071
9,219	1,175	1,706	3,132	3,206	—	—	—	98
16,888	1,502	2,150	6,448	6,788	32	3	29	885
3,652	356	540	1,328	1,428	—	—	—	10
—	—	—	—	—	—	—	—	73,600

Appendix Table 6.5. (*continued*)

Geographic Area of Chargeability[a] and Period	Total Immigrants	Family Preferences				
		Total Family Preferences	1st Preference	2nd Preference	4th Preference	5th Preference
			Unmarried Sons and Daughters of U.S. Citizens[b]	Spouses, Unmarried Sons and Daughters of Resident Aliens[b]	Married Sons and Daughters of U.S. Citizens[c]	Brothers and Sisters of U.S. Citizens[c]
Asia						
1970–1974	100.0	42.1	0.7	25.2	1.6	14.5
1975–1979	100.0	70.3	0.8	33.1	2.5	34.0
1980–1984	100.0	81.1	2.2	36.7	6.0	36.2
1984	100.0	81.3	2.8	31.4	6.5	40.5
Philippines						
1970–1974	100.0	47.4	1.8	39.2	1.8	4.5
1975–1979	100.0	72.3	2.3	57.0	3.8	9.2
1980–1984	100.0	84.3	9.0	47.7	8.1	19.6
1984	100.0	80.3	12.6	32.5	9.8	25.4
Vietnam						
1970–1974	100.0	36.3	0.3	20.0	0.3	15.8
1975–1979	100.0	33.6	0.2	9.8	0.3	23.4
1980–1984	100.0	78.9	1.7	48.8	3.7	24.7
1984	100.0	97.7	3.9	53.2	6.2	34.3
China						
1970–1974	100.0	48.3	0.5	21.0	4.2	22.6
1975–1979	100.0	76.8	0.8	29.9	6.0	40.1
1980–1984	100.0	81.4	1.0	32.3	13.6	34.6
1984	100.0	85.3	0.6	25.5	11.9	47.4
Korea						
1970–1974	100.0	45.3	0.1	17.4	0.3	27.6
1975–1979	100.0	80.7	0.1	24.6	0.6	55.3
1980–1984	100.0	89.2	0.3	43.9	2.3	42.7
1984	100.0	84.5	0.6	42.9	3.1	38.0
India						
1970–1974	100.0	25.4	f	19.7	0.1	5.5
1975–1979	100.0	59.1	0.1	26.5	0.3	32.2
1980–1984	100.0	81.9	0.1	28.8	1.0	51.9
1984	100.0	84.1	0.2	28.5	1.7	53.7

| Total Occupational Preferences | Occupational Preferences | | | | Refugees | | | Nonpreference Immigrants and Others[d] |
| | 3rd Preference | | 6th Preference | | 7th Preference | | | |
	Immigrants in Professions	Dependents	Other Workers	Dependents	Total Refugees	Admitted	Adjusted	
(Percentage)								
29.6	12.0	11.1	3.5	2.9	2.4	2.2	0.2	26.0
18.9	6.0	6.7	3.3	2.8	3.1	3.0	0.1	7.8
18.2	5.0	5.6	3.5	4.1	0.7	0.6	f	0.1
18.7	4.8	6.0	3.5	4.4	—	—	—	f
52.5	26.5	26.0	f	f	—	—	—	0.1
26.9	10.1	13.7	1.9	1.3	f	f	—	0.8
15.6	2.1	5.7	3.8	3.9	—	—	—	0.1
19.7	3.2	7.1	4.5	4.9	—	—	—	0.1
21.3	4.1	3.5	8.8	4.8	0.1	0.1	0.1	42.3
6.6	1.5	3.1	0.8	1.2	53.0	52.4	0.5	6.8
2.8	0.6	0.7	0.6	0.9	17.8	17.1	0.7	0.5
2.3	0.6	0.6	0.4	0.7	—	—	—	—
16.1	3.9	2.9	5.0	4.3	10.6	9.7	0.9	25.0
13.2	2.8	2.7	3.8	3.9	6.2	6.0	0.1	3.8
18.1	5.8	5.3	2.9	4.2	0.4	0.4	f	0.1
14.6	5.5	5.4	1.3	2.4	—	—	—	f
21.0	5.0	6.0	4.7	5.4	f	—	f	33.7
15.7	4.8	5.7	2.0	3.1	f	f	f	3.6
10.8	1.8	3.2	1.9	3.9	—	—	—	f
15.5	1.9	4.1	3.0	6.5	—	—	—	—
26.3	11.1	8.4	3.9	2.9	f	f	f	48.4
24.3	9.1	8.2	4.4	2.6	f	f	f	16.6
18.1	7.8	7.5	1.5	1.3	f	—	f	f
15.9	5.2	6.3	2.1	2.2	—	—	—	f

Appendix Table 6.5. (*continued*)

Geographic Area of Chargeability[a] and Period	Total Immigrants	Total Family Preferences	1st Preference — Unmarried Sons and Daughters of U.S. Citizens[b]	2nd Preference — Spouses, Unmarried Sons and Daughters of Resident Aliens[b]	4th Preference — Married Sons and Daughters of U.S. Citizens[c]	5th Preference — Brothers and Sisters of U.S. Citizens[c]
Europe						
1970–1974	100.0	65.5	0.5	20.3	4.6	40.0
1975–1979	100.0	63.5	0.7	20.5	4.2	38.2
1980–1984	100.0	61.1	1.7	24.6	7.3	27.5
1984	100.0	53.2	2.1	19.7	8.0	23.3
Africa						
1970–1974	100.0	27.4	0.2	16.0	0.6	10.6
1975–1979	100.0	56.7	0.3	21.8	1.5	33.1
1980–1984	100.0	67.8	0.7	32.3	2.5	32.3
1984	100.0	67.3	0.9	31.6	3.1	31.7
Oceania						
1970–1974	100.0	58.3	0.5	25.3	1.8	30.8
1975–1979	100.0	74.6	0.5	31.1	2.8	40.2
1980–1984	100.0	70.9	1.1	30.5	5.3	33.9
1984	100.0	70.6	1.6	27.6	4.1	37.3
North America[e]						
1980–1984	100.0	87.4	3.7	56.7	6.7	20.3
1984	100.0	89.8	3.8	64.6	4.0	17.4
South America[e]						
1980–1984	100.0	84.8	1.1	44.5	4.4	34.9
1984	100.0	83.7	1.4	45.0	5.9	31.4
Independent Western Hemisphere[e]						
1980–1984	100.0	—	—	—	—	—

Source: INS (1970–1979:table 7A; 1980, 1981:table 5; 1982, 1983, 1984:table IMM 2.1).

[a]In defining geographic area of chargeability, we have used the INS convention of placing dependencies under their metropolitan countries. Thus, for example, in certain years Hong Kong, Macao, and Brunei are included under Europe rather than under Asia.

[b]Includes children of this group.

[c]Includes spouses and children of this group.

| | Occupational Preferences | | | | Refugees | | | |
| | 3rd Preference | | 6th Preference | | | 7th Preference | | |
Total Occupational Preferences	Immigrants in Professions	Dependents	Other Workers	Dependents	Total Refugees	Admitted	Adjusted	Nonpreference Immigrants and Others[d]
10.9	0.5	0.4	5.4	4.6	8.6	7.4	1.2	15.0
12.7	1.1	1.3	4.9	5.4	11.7	10.8	0.8	12.1
36.4	8.3	11.1	8.0	9.0	2.2	1.9	0.4	0.3
46.7	11.8	16.5	8.8	9.6	—	—	—	0.1
18.0	5.7	5.2	4.0	3.1	5.5	5.4	0.1	49.1
19.4	3.8	4.8	4.8	5.9	3.0	2.4	0.7	21.0
30.9	8.2	9.4	6.0	7.4	1.1	0.7	0.4	0.2
32.5	8.6	10.3	6.1	7.5	—	—	—	0.2
17.4	1.5	1.2	7.3	7.4	f	f	—	24.3
15.3	1.9	2.3	4.7	6.5	—	—	—	10.1
29.0	7.9	10.3	5.1	5.7	f	f	—	0.1
29.4	8.6	10.9	4.5	5.4	—	—	—	—
11.1	1.3	2.0	3.8	4.0	0.9	0.9	f	0.7
10.1	1.3	1.9	3.4	3.5	—	—	—	0.1
14.4	1.3	1.8	5.5	5.8	f	f	f	0.8
16.3	1.6	2.4	5.9	6.4	—	—	—	f
—	—	—	—	—	—	—	—	100.0

[d]For 1980–1984, includes nonpreference immigrants, recaptured Cuban number (Silva) immigrants, and those suspension of deportation adjustments and foreign governmental official adjustments that are subject to numerical limitation.

[e]Data not available for the years 1970–1976 because prior to 1977 Western Hemisphere countries were not subject to numerical limitation. There were no Independent Western Hemisphere admissions in 1984.

[f]Less than 0.05 percent.

Appendix Table 6.6. Aliens Adjusted to Permanent Resident Status,

Country of Birth and Period	Total Adjusted	Temporary Visitors (Business)	Temporary Visitors (Pleasure)	Treaty Traders and Investors	Students
Asia					
1970–1974	134,717	3,900	47,051	2,327	42,201
1975–1979	127,300	3,931	45,989	2,971	39,622
1982–1984	397,790	3,731	50,282	4,431	30,192
Philippines					
1970–1974	26,084	575	16,973	81	1,444
1975–1979	26,307	617	13,230	140	1,066
1982–1984	27,551	946	11,530	152	654
Vietnam					
1970–1974	1,379	23	570	7	380
1975–1979	6,430	38	665	15	427
1982–1984	137,229	17	1,843	6	89
China					
1970–1974	32,136	970	10,056	419	13,557
1975–1979	22,832	916	7,949	478	9,569
1982–1984	28,284	707	7,616	1,569	8,073
Korea					
1970–1974	16,497	1,171	4,639	1,000	4,479
1975–1979	8,845	874	3,021	801	1,973
1982–1984	12,397	793	4,758	1,328	1,319
India					
1970–1974	26,625	282	3,301	88	11,142
1975–1979	19,910	365	4,748	46	8,527
1982–1984	11,414	286	4,159	32	2,502
Asia					
1970–1974	100.0	2.9	34.9	1.7	31.3
1975–1979	100.0	3.1	36.1	2.3	31.1
1982–1984	100.0	0.9	12.6	1.1	7.6
Philippines					
1970–1974	100.0	2.2	65.1	0.3	5.5
1975–1979	100.0	2.4	50.3	0.5	4.1
1982–1984	100.0	3.4	41.8	0.6	2.4
Vietnam					
1970–1974	100.0	1.7	41.3	0.5	27.6
1975–1979	100.0	0.6	10.3	0.2	6.6
1982–1984	100.0	a	1.3	a	0.1

by Status at Entry and Country of Birth: 1970–1984

Spouses and Children of Students	Temporary Workers and Trainees	Exchange Visitors	Spouses and Children of Exchange Visitors	Parolees and Refugees	All Others
(Number)					
7,317	2,457	14,865	7,025	3,403	4,171
5,513	5,072	6,732	2,952	8,863	5,655
3,889	7,372	2,569	1,621	271,843	21,860
122	1,010	3,469	438	1,044	928
83	3,902	3,390	783	1,683	1,413
27	3,394	1,442	747	1,851	6,808
12	85	66	38	32	166
21	13	52	16	5,052	131
3	33	6	—	134,886	346
2,049	176	1,735	1,102	924	1,148
1,603	161	459	354	427	916
1,841	1,024	175	135	3,226	3,918
1,044	444	1,814	1,138	163	605
599	325	155	84	171	842
565	387	47	36	138	3,026
3,193	337	4,285	2,777	709	511
2,130	300	1,462	1,091	467	774
506	1,264	461	428	136	1,640
(Percentage)					
5.4	1.8	11.0	5.2	2.5	3.1
4.3	4.0	5.3	2.3	7.0	4.4
1.0	1.9	0.6	0.4	68.3	5.5
0.5	3.9	13.3	1.7	4.0	3.6
0.3	14.8	12.9	3.0	6.4	5.4
0.1	12.3	5.2	2.7	6.7	24.7
0.9	6.2	4.8	2.8	2.3	12.0
0.3	0.2	0.8	0.3	78.6	2.0
a	a	a	—	98.3	0.3

Appendix Table 6.6. *(continued)*

Country of Birth and Period	Total Adjusted	Temporary Visitors (Business)	Temporary Visitors (Pleasure)	Treaty Traders and Investors	Students
China					
1970–1974	100.0	3.0	31.3	1.3	42.2
1975–1979	100.0	4.0	34.8	2.1	41.9
1982–1984	100.0	2.5	26.9	5.5	28.5
Korea					
1970–1974	100.0	7.1	28.1	6.1	27.2
1975–1979	100.0	9.9	34.2	9.1	22.3
1982–1984	100.0	6.4	38.4	10.7	10.6
India					
1970–1974	100.0	1.1	12.4	0.3	41.9
1975–1979	100.0	1.8	23.9	0.2	42.8
1982–1984	100.0	2.5	36.4	0.3	21.9

Sources: INS (1970–1979:table 6C; 1982–1984:table IMM 3.2).

Note: Data not available for 1980 and 1981.

[a]Less than 0.05 percent.

Spouses and Children of Students	Temporary Workers and Trainees	Exchange Visitors	Spouses and Children of Exchange Visitors	Parolees and Refugees	All Others
6.4	0.6	5.4	3.4	2.9	3.6
7.0	0.7	2.0	1.6	1.9	4.0
6.5	3.6	0.6	0.5	11.4	13.9
6.3	2.7	11.0	6.9	1.0	3.7
6.8	3.7	1.8	1.0	1.9	9.5
4.6	3.1	0.4	0.3	1.1	24.4
12.0	1.3	16.1	10.4	2.7	1.9
10.7	1.5	7.3	5.5	2.4	3.9
4.4	11.1	4.0	3.7	1.2	14.4

Appendix Table 6.7. Nonimmigrants Admitted under the U.S. Immi-

Country of Birth and Period[a]	Total Number Admitted[b]	Foreign Government Officials	Temporary Visitors (Business)	Temporary Visitors (Pleasure)	Transit Aliens
Asia					
1970–1974	3,511,509	73,377	497,679	2,093,354	176,444
1975–1979	6,786,492	77,934	765,806	4,460,070	272,733
1982–1983	4,293,675	28,749	550,078	3,201,892	105,265
1984	2,304,688	15,600	315,074	1,637,827	65,959
Philippines					
1970–1974	264,035	4,042	18,193	119,959	20,876
1975–1979	429,933	5,158	35,550	161,072	42,593
1982–1983	207,000	3,563	31,209	119,418	22,701
1984	120,210	2,059	18,045	71,484	14,828
Vietnam					
1970–1974	32,400	10,998	2,568	5,913	653
1975–1979	22,437	366	1,610	13,045	794
1982–1983	8,850	272	631	4,056	590
1984	26,261	—	81	2,138	508
China					
1970–1974	233,886	5,200	28,347	95,576	27,379
1975–1979	408,336	5,441	60,262	172,880	39,737
1982–1983	279,061	968	55,603	146,295	16,233
1984	166,012	839	36,343	86,291	10,059
Korea					
1970–1974	107,673	5,320	16,832	25,677	12,298
1975–1979	219,639	5,093	42,528	46,618	31,313
1982–1983	178,890	3,132	52,249	59,557	20,255
1984	102,363	1,859	26,852	36,399	13,645
India					
1970–1974	245,363	3,053	23,472	90,387	21,262
1975–1979	431,409	2,716	40,925	180,195	37,135
1982–1983	171,765	1,572	29,733	106,326	7,639
1984	103,783	1,096	19,933	63,362	4,123
Japan					
1970–1974	2,210,813	15,543	376,841	1,584,802	63,687
1975–1979	4,270,411	21,367	502,731	3,389,477	65,917
1982–1983	2,863,845	11,094	300,807	2,402,578	16,125
1984	1,467,063	5,182	172,922	1,200,237	11,191

gration Laws, by Status at Entry and Country of Birth: 1970–1984

Treaty Traders and Investors	Students	Spouses and Children of Students	International Representatives	Temporary Workers and Trainees	Spouses and Children of Temporary Workers and Trainees
73,462	155,898	15,190	20,259	28,496	3,787
111,536	268,809	25,349	29,038	29,883	2,916
70,568	149,300	19,443	12,766	15,662	2,420
43,136	73,247	11,208	8,926	7,967	1,567
1,418	4,272	345	2,588	14,210	2,208
2,037	4,715	337	4,086	15,463	611
1,378	4,251	162	2,341	6,837	194
1,018	1,787	100	1,537	2,825	212
67	2,547	95	311	154	10
46	1,021	41	399	28	13
6	18	57	141	23	13
—	16	2	51	3	2
3,353	22,518	2,862	1,965	1,252	143
6,126	23,081	3,604	1,937	1,578	184
9,200	21,752	4,520	1,013	937	271
3,915	10,381	2,616	788	578	188
4,162	5,985	1,266	698	3,884	177
9,131	6,344	1,932	951	3,214	219
6,902	15,018	6,262	414	733	301
3,572	8,428	3,825	248	416	95
1,041	24,126	4,645	5,230	1,337	332
635	14,385	2,275	7,286	1,650	530
81	10,595	1,266	2,837	1,629	596
25	6,104	648	2,201	966	351
60,402	20,225	1,978	2,571	6,010	691
89,150	59,339	4,579	3,914	5,900	849
50,048	32,636	2,236	1,417	3,920	576
33,140	14,542	1,164	1,059	2,205	371

(continued)

Appendix Table 6.7. *(continued)*

Country of Birth and Period	Exchange Visitors	Spouses and Children of Exchange Visitors	Returning Resident Aliens	All Others
Asia				
1970–1974	50,921	21,393	272,807	28,442
1975–1979	41,803	23,199	635,057	42,359
1982–1983	33,582	15,722	NA	88,228
1984	17,987	8,187	NA	98,003
Philippines				
1970–1974	7,430	1,602	63,955	2,937
1975–1979	3,966	834	148,031	5,480
1982–1983	1,623	219	NA	13,104
1984	708	122	NA	5,485
Vietnam				
1970–1974	2,052	92	2,536	4,404
1975–1979	367	36	4,285	386
1982–1983	146	53	NA	2,844
1984	15	1	NA	23,444
China				
1970–1974	3,477	1,464	39,140	1,210
1975–1979	2,863	888	87,348	2,407
1982–1983	8,876	1,026	NA	12,367
1984	4,847	622	NA	8,545
Korea				
1970–1974	2,308	918	21,259	6,889
1975–1979	2,142	690	63,254	6,210
1982–1983	2,213	2,143	NA	9,711
1984	1,307	1,229	NA	4,488
India				
1970–1974	9,580	4,680	55,370	848
1975–1979	5,943	2,724	133,164	1,846
1982–1983	3,058	1,435	NA	4,998
1984	1,764	743	NA	2,467
Japan				
1970–1974	10,544	8,394	50,289	8,836
1975–1979	12,734	12,920	81,650	19,884
1982–1983	10,900	8,493	NA	23,015
1984	5,640	4,273	NA	15,137

Sources: INS (1970–1979:table 16; 1982, 1983:table NIM 1; 1984:table NIM 1.1).

[a]Data not available for 1980 and 1981. For 1982 and 1983, nonimmigrants are tabulated by country of last residence, and for 1984 nonimmigrants are tabulated by country of citizenship. For 1983, data are for the calendar year rather than the fiscal year.

[b]Total does not include returning resident aliens for 1982-1984.

REFERENCES

Brown, C. L., and C. W. Pannell

    1985   "The Chinese in America." In J. O. McKee (ed.), *Ethnicity in America: A Geographical Appraisal.* Dubuque, Iowa: Kendall/Hunt.

Cafferty, P. S. J., B. Chiswick, A. M. Greeley, and T. A. Sullivan

    1983   *The Dilemma of American Immigration: Beyond the Golden Door.* New Brunswick, N.J.: Transaction Books.

Chandrasekhar, S.

    1981   "A History of United States Legislation with Respect to Immigration from India." *Population Review,* 25(1–2):11–28.

Hill, K.

    1985   "Illegal Aliens: An Assessment." In D. B. Levine et al. (eds.), *Immigration Statistics: A Story of Neglect.* Washington, D.C.: National Academy Press.

Immigration and Naturalization Service (INS)

    1960–   *Annual Report: Immigration and Naturalization Service.* Washington,
    1977   D.C.: Government Printing Office.

————— .

    1978–   *Statistical Yearbook of the Immigration and Naturalization Service.* Washing-
    1984   ton, D.C.: Government Printing Office.

————— .

    1986   *Immigration Statistics: Fiscal Year 1985, Advance Report.* Washington, D.C.: Government Printing Office.

Jasso, G., and M. R. Rosenzweig

    1982   "Estimating the Emigration Rates of Legal Immigrants Using Administrative and Survey Data: 1971 Cohort of Immigrants to the United States." *Demography,* 19(3):279–290.

Nishi, M.

    1985   "Japanese Americans." In J. O. McKee (ed.), *Ethnicity in America: A Geographical Appraisal.* Dubuque, Iowa: Kendall/Hunt.

Pido, A. J. A.

    1985   *The Pilipinos in America: MacroMicro Dimensions of Immigration and Integration.* New York: Center for Migration Studies.

Select Committee on Population

    1978   *Legal and Illegal Immigration to the United States.* U.S. House of Representatives, 95th Cong., 2nd Sess., Serial C. Washington D.C.: Government Printing Office.

Slater, C.

  1985   "The Illegals." *American Demographics*, 7(1):26–29. January.

U.S. Bureau of the Census

  1975   *Historical Statistics of the United States: Colonial Times to 1970.* Pt. 1. Washington, D.C.: Department of Commerce.

Warren, R., and E. P. Kraly

  1985   *The Elusive Exodus: Emigration from the United States.* Population Trends and Current Policy, No. 8. Washington, D.C.: Population Reference Bureau.

7

Southeast Asian Refugee Migration to the United States

Linda W. Gordon

This work traces the history of migration from three Southeast Asian nations to the United States. In 1975, when the governments of Vietnam, Laos, and Cambodia (Kampuchea) fell to communist forces, the first refugees from these nations arrived in the United States. This first wave of refugees greatly outnumbered the earlier immigrants from these countries, and it was dwarfed in turn by the second wave, which peaked in 1980 following renewed turmoil in Southeast Asia. Although a few people from other Southeast Asian countries have been given refugee status since 1975, they constitute less than one-half of 1 percent of the total, so that these three nations are the usual focus of discussion of Southeast Asian refugees. The 761,000 refugees resettled in the United States are 51 percent of the worldwide total; Australia, Canada, and France have each accepted more than 100,000 refugees.

Throughout this discussion, the terms *refugee* and *immigrant* are used according to their definitions in immigration law. Specifically, refugees from Southeast Asia are persons who arrived under the Indochina

This chapter originated as a background paper prepared for the Conference on Asia–Pacific Immigration to the United States. My study has benefited greatly from suggestions by Philip Holman, David Howell, and conference participants. I am responsible for whatever limitations remain. The points of view expressed are my own and do not necessarily represent the policy of the Office of Refugee Resettlement.

Table 7.1.   Immigrants Admitted from Kampuchea, Laos, and Vietnam:
            1955–1974

| Federal | Country of Birth | | | |
Fiscal Year	Kampuchea	Laos	Vietnam	Total
1970–1974	188	196	14,661	15,045
1965–1969	75	56	2,564	2,695
1960–1964	23	13	603	639
1955–1959	4	1	174	179
Total	290	266	18,002	18,558
(Percentage)	(1.6)	(1.4)	(97.0)	(100.0)

Sources: INS annual reports and unpublished data.

Migration and Refugee Assistance Act of 1975 or under the Refugee Act
of 1980. Immigrants are persons admitted with permanent resident alien
status. Only those who arrive in refugee status are eligible for federal
refugee program benefits, although the mode of departure from the
country of origin is not directly related to the determination of immigration status.

MIGRANT FLOWS FROM SOUTHEAST ASIA

Before 1975: Early Migrations

The history of immigration from Vietnam, Laos, and Kampuchea to the
United States is brief compared with immigration from other Asian nations. Through the 1940s, only a few immigrants born in these three
countries had appeared in Immigration and Naturalization Service (INS)
statistics since record keeping began in 1819. Annual immigrant admissions totaled no more than 55 during the 1950s, increased gradually
during the 1960s from 100 to 1,000 by the end of the decade, and ranged
from 1,500 to 4,700 during 1970–1974. Vietnamese comprised 97 percent
of this flow. From 1955 through 1974, fewer than 300 immigrants were
admitted from Laos, a similar number from Kampuchea, and roughly
18,000 from Vietnam (see Table 7.1).

This numerical history reflects the history of American involvement
in Indochina, as well as the legal restrictions on Asian immigration that
were in effect until the mid-1960s. A significant portion of the Vietnamese immigration from the 1960s through 1974 can be attributed to
spouses of Americans who had been stationed in Vietnam. Moreover,
in the 1960s Vietnamese began coming to the United States on student
visas, often under U.S. government sponsorship. Some of them later
obtained immigrant status, at which time they would have appeared
in the statistics of Table 7.1.

Therefore, through 1974 the number of Vietnamese living in the United States was small compared with other Asian groups. They were likely to be students or married to Americans, which was conducive to their wide dispersal about the country. In January 1975, some 18 percent of the 12,867 Vietnamese who registered under the INS Alien Address Report Program were living in California, 7 percent were in Texas, and the rest were widely scattered (unpublished INS data). A Vietnamese presence was not discernible in American communities, and the numbers of Kampucheans and Lao at that time were negligible. Hence there was an insufficient basis for the formation of ethnic communities, and the earliest immigrants were not well equipped to help the refugees who began arriving in 1975.

1975 to 1984: Two Refugee Waves

The evacuation of Americans and Vietnamese from Saigon in April 1975 remains a vivid memory for people who lived through that time, but the history of the Southeast Asian refugee movement to the United States in subsequent years is less well known. In 1975, the United States resettled approximately 130,000 Southeast Asian refugees, of whom more than 95 percent were Vietnamese and almost all the rest Kampuchean. When the U.S. resettlement camps closed in December 1975 with all the refugees placed in communities around the country, the arrival phase of the refugee story was thought to have ended.

During the next few years, several small programs were announced to admit refugees from Southeast Asia under the attorney general's "parole" authority. Exact flow figures during the 1976–1977 period are difficult to reconstruct; Table 7.2 represents a set of best estimates. During 1976–1977, about 17,000 refugees were resettled. Beginning in 1978, the refugees were accepted under a series of Indochinese Parole Programs. The period of 1978 through 1980 saw the exodus of several hundred thousand "boat people" from Vietnam, as well as large numbers of refugees fleeing Kampuchea and Laos overland. In early 1979, the United States committed itself to accept 7,000 refugees monthly, and this figure was doubled by that summer in response to desperate conditions in the refugee camps. Yearly arrivals of refugees in the United States increased almost exponentially: 20,400 in 1978, 80,700 in 1979, 166,700 in 1980.

In several ways, 1980 was a watershed year for the refugee program. The Refugee Act of 1980 took effect on 1 April; it was the peak year for Soviet as well as Southeast Asian refugee arrivals; and 125,000 Cubans as well as thousands of Haitians arrived outside the purview of the new act. Refugees were a major news story. The sheer numbers of arriving refugees posed great difficulties for the institutions attempt-

Table 7.2. Southeast Asian Refugee and Immigrant Arrivals: 1975–1985

Federal Fiscal Year	Refugee Arrivals, by Country of Nationality[a]				New Arrival Immigrants, by Country of Birth[b]			
	Kampuchea	Laos	Vietnam	Total Refugees	Kampuchea	Laos	Vietnam	Total Immigrants
1985	19,200	5,300	25,400	49,900	147	148	4,661	4,956
1984	19,900	7,200	24,900	52,000	170	161	4,878	5,209
1983	13,200	2,900	23,000	39,100	123	108	2,790	3,021
1982	20,100	9,400	42,600	72,100	69	80	2,452	2,601
1981	27,100	19,300	86,100	132,500	73	41	1,714	1,828
1980	16,000	55,500	95,200	166,700	120	114	4,104	4,338
1979	6,000	30,200	44,500	80,700	162	124	6,365	6,651
1978	1,300	8,000	11,100	20,400	71	123	1,890	2,084
1977	300	400	1,900	2,600	126	237	4,629	4,992
1976[c]	1,100	10,200	3,200	14,500	126	163	4,230	4,519
1975	4,600	800	125,000	130,400	98	96	3,039	3,233
Total	128,800	149,200[d]	482,900	760,900	1,285	1,395	40,752	43,432

[a]These refugee arrival figures were compiled from mostly unpublished records maintained by the State Department, the Immigration and Naturalization Service, the Office of Refugee Resettlement, and its predecessor the Indochina Refugee Assistance Program. Exact monthly flow figures have been compiled since 1978 for the refugees as a group and since 1982 by nationality; earlier figures are estimates. All figures are rounded to the nearest hundred.

[b]For 1975–1977, total immigrants admitted. For 1978–1985, calculated by subtracting persons adjusting status from total immigrants admitted to avoid double counting, since 1978 was the first year in which the refugees were eligible to adjust their status. Source: INS.

[c]Includes transition quarter.

[d]The State Department reports that 56,685 of the refugees from Laos were Hmong or other highland peoples.

ing to serve them, as the number of Southeast Asians ever admitted to the United States rose by 63 percent in a single year.

Beginning with 1981, new consultation procedures under the Refugee Act to set yearly arrival ceilings for refugees at the beginning of each year came into play. For FY 1981 the Asian portion of the ceiling was 168,000, but the number who actually arrived was 132,500. A similar pattern characterized the next two years: In 1982 the Asian ceiling was 100,000, whereas 72,100 arrived; in 1983 the Asian ceiling was 64,000, whereas 39,100 arrived. In each year, for various reasons, fewer refugees were admitted to the United States than had been contemplated.

When 1984 refugee admission levels were being established, congressional sentiment was voiced that the ceilings set during the consultation process should reflect expected arrivals more accurately than had been the case in 1981–1983. A ceiling of 50,000 was set for 1984, which was later adjusted to 52,000. Actual 1984 arrivals reached the 52,000 level. The 1985 ceiling was set at 50,000, and admissions came close to that figure.

By midsummer of 1984, 700,000 refugees from Southeast Asia had arrived in the United States. Refugees now make up a substantial minority of Asian Americans, more than one out of five. As arrival flows appear to be stabilizing, the history of Southeast Asian refugee migration to the United States can be viewed from the mid-1980s as two major waves, with peaks in 1975 and 1980, seen clearly in Figure 7.1.

Immigrants in the Refugee Flow

Although almost all of the people who came to the United States after fleeing Southeast Asia in 1975 and subsequently were refugees under American law as well as in common parlance, significant numbers have arrived in other immigration statuses. As such, they may count against regular immigration quotas but not against the annual refugee program ceilings. Spouses of American citizens usually enter as immigrants; children of American citizens may enter as immigrants or occasionally as American citizens; long-term employees of the U.S. government abroad may qualify as "special immigrants"; fiancés of American citizens may arrive as "nonimmigrants"; and the immigration laws provide still other options. From 1975 to about 1980, little distinction was made among these immigration statuses in refugee program statistics: Most Southeast Asians became "refugees" in State Department and Office of Refugee Resettlement (ORR) reports. INS statistics preserve the legal distinctions but fail to distinguish immigrants who enter from refugee camps from immigrants who arrive independently. Thus it is difficult to reconstruct exactly the number of immigrants from Southeast Asia who arrived from 1975 to 1981 in addition to those already counted in the

158

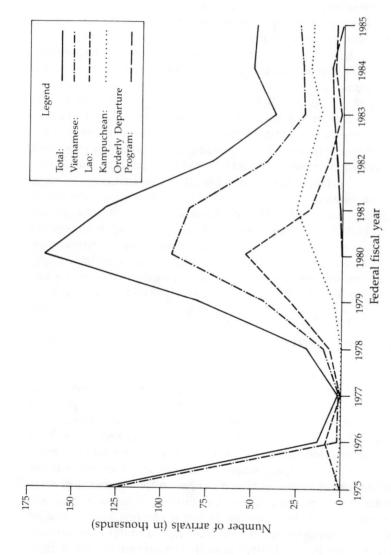

Figure 7.1. Refugee Flow from Southeast Asia to the United States, 1975–1985, by Nationality

Source: Table 7.2.

refugee flow, although the "new arrival immigrants" data in Table 7.2 represent a reasonable estimate of that flow. For the years 1978 through 1985, that data series shows the official INS count of persons admitted to immigrant status (born in Kampuchea, Laos, or Vietnam), excluding persons who had adjusted from some other immigration status (usually refugee) in that year. Before 1978, this group of refugees was not eligible to adjust to immigrant status. From 1975 through 1985, immigrant admissions from these three countries ranged from fewer than 2,000 to more than 6,000 yearly in addition to refugee admissions, for an eleven-year total of more than 43,000.

Beginning in 1980, the ORR and the State Department have maintained counts of Southeast Asian immigrants arriving as part of the refugee flow. While the two data series do not agree exactly, both show a clear trend toward increasing numbers of immigrants. Roughly 12,500 of the 43,000 immigrants have traveled in the refugee flow, nearly two-thirds of them arriving in 1984 and 1985. The primary mechanism for this increase in immigrants has been the launching of the Orderly Departure Program from Vietnam in 1980, together with the fact that many among the 1975 wave of refugees are now able to bring in close relatives. In the absence of regular diplomatic relations between the United States and Vietnam, the Orderly Departure Program facilitates migration from Vietnam to the United States in order to discourage dangerous escapes by boat. Before it was established, few of the Southeast Asians in the refugee flow are thought to have arrived in other than refugee status. Therefore the immigrants shown in the "new arrival immigrants" column of Table 7.2 for 1975 through 1985 appear to have arrived, for the most part, outside the refugee program flow. Almost all of these immigrants have been from Vietnam.

Variations in Ethnic Composition

Although people often speak of refugees from Southeast Asia as a single group for the sake of convenience, the reality is much more complex. I have referred above to the three nations from which these refugees come, each with at least one distinct language and culture. Most official U.S. government statistics classify the refugees into these three categories according to country of birth or citizenship. Finer distinctions are possible but are usually not made because the needed records are not available. Many observers find it useful to distinguish between lowland Lao and tribal people from the highlands of Laos, of whom the best known are the Hmong, but smaller groups have also entered. The State Department's official refugee figures make this distinction, and from this source we know that the number of "highland Lao" who had entered the United States was nearly 57,000 at the close of 1985—38 percent of the refugees from Laos. Another distinction of interest is the number of ethnic Chinese in the Southeast Asian refugee population. Although this statistic is not available in any U.S. government sources, a substantial number of ethnic Chinese are known to have arrived among the second wave of Vietnamese refugees, and they exist among the other refugee nationalities as well. Owing to the lack of data, this discussion is limited primarily to the three groups defined by country of origin. We shall have to ignore the finer ethnic distinctions.

From the estimates presented in Table 7.2, it is clear that the arrival of each of the three nationalities followed a different time sequence. The greatest number of Vietnamese, 125,000, arrived in 1975 and was followed by a second larger wave centered around 1980 but never again approaching the 1975 level in a single year. During 1983–1985, Vietnamese refugee arrivals leveled off at 23,000 to 25,000 each year (to which must be added several thousand immigrants). More than 482,000 Vietnamese had arrived in the United States as refugees through 1985, and at least 58,000 others have been admitted as immigrants since the early 1950s.

Legislation including persons from Laos in the Indochina Refugee Program did not take effect until 1 July 1976. Nevertheless, a few hundred refugees from Laos were admitted under the parole authority in late 1975 and early 1976. Then, in 1976–1977, the majority of those admitted were from Laos, most of them highland Lao. In the next few years the arrival of refugees from Laos paralleled that of the Vietnamese, peaking at 55,500 in 1980 and declining subsequently. The exact mix of highland and lowland Lao arrivals each year during 1978–1980 is not known, but lowland Lao held nearly a 2-to-1 majority during that time. Fewer than 3,000 refugees arrived from Laos in 1983, but the total in 1984 reached 7,200. In 1981–1985, the ratio of lowland to highland Lao arrivals was approximately 2.5 to 1. By the end of 1985, some 149,200 refugees from Laos had entered the United States; the inclusion of immigrants adds only about 1,400 to this figure.

Refugees from Kampuchea did not begin to arrive in significant numbers until 1979, after the initial group of about 4,600 who came in 1975. · Arrivals from Kampuchea peaked in 1981–1982, later than Vietnamese or Lao arrivals. A policy dispute in 1983 centered about whether persons who had fled Kampuchea should be required to prove they had reason to fear persecution as individuals. This debate contributed to a decline in Kampuchean arrivals, but in 1984 significant numbers were again approved and arrivals reached nearly 20,000. Nearly 129,000 Kampuchean refugees had arrived as of late 1985; another 1,300 had entered as immigrants.

SOUTHEAST ASIAN REFUGEES IN THE UNITED STATES

Age–Sex Composition

The structure of the Southeast Asian refugee population is unusual by comparison with the U.S. population and with immigrants generally. The refugees are young. The median age of the Vietnamese at the time of arrival has been 19 or 20 in each year since 1975. In recent years, the median age of the arriving Kampucheans and Lao has been 17 or 18. As of late 1985, the median age of the resident population of the refugees who had arrived since 1975 was estimated as 24.6 (excluding children born in the United States). The school-age population (6–17) was about 28 percent of the total, and 55 percent were aged 18 to 44. About 2.8 percent were 65 years old or older (HHS, 1986:89).

In 1975, the arriving refugee population contained almost equal numbers of males and females. In every year since, however, males have outnumbered females; the proportions have been remarkably constant at about 58 to 42 percent. The excess of males is greatest among the Vietnamese; recent arrivals from Kampuchea and Laos have been more evenly divided between the sexes.

The preponderance of males is greatest among persons aged 15 to 24; in 1981, for example, 162.4 men arrived for every 100 women in that age category (Gordon, 1982a). The refugees' sex ratios resemble those of the U.S. population only among persons under 5 years old and those over 50. The dangers inherent in becoming a refugee—a question of who attempts to escape and who reaches the refugee camps—no doubt are partly responsible for the excess of young males in the refugee population.

Fertility

The high sex ratio among persons in the prime years of family formation would provide more than enough potential mates for every woman of childbearing age if marriage were to take place only within each nationality group. In fact, the sex ratio indicates that a large number of Southeast Asian refugee men, particularly the Vietnamese, will either remain single, marry younger women as the next generation approaches adulthood, or find wives outside their own group (Gordon, 1982a).

The prospect of a mate for every woman and the young age structure of the Southeast Asian refugee population imply a potential for high fertility. As with any small population subgroup, however, exact data on their fertility are not available from standard vital registration systems. Anecdotal evidence suggests a large number of births to refugee women in the United States. Certainly refugee cash assistance cases in states with large refugee populations have been observed to contain many American-born children. The annual rate of natural increase can be estimated at 3 to 4 percent from this data base, which is probably biased toward including the larger families. Among the groups, the Vietnamese appear to be at the lower end of this range and the highland Lao at the higher end.

In a pilot study of data being tabulated by the ORR, I analyzed information on numbers of living children borne by a small sample of Vietnamese and Lao refugee women (Gordon, 1982a). Using assumptions that tend to underestimate fertility, I derived a crude birthrate of 28 per 1,000 population for these combined refugee populations during their first few years in the country. This sample also contained a significant number of children who had been born in refugee camps.

A study of refugee fertility in San Diego (Rumbaut and Weeks, 1986) confirms and elaborates this picture of high fertility. A random sample of 355 refugee households was interviewed, representing four major ethnic groups: Vietnamese, ethnic Chinese from Vietnam, Kampucheans, and Hmong. Ever-married women of ages 18 to 49 were queried about their fertility histories. All refugee groups manifested higher fertility on several measures than the U.S. population, with the Hmong showing extremely high fertility. Rumbaut and Weeks concluded that the observed ethnic differentials could be explained by the influence of background variables, however, including length of time in the United States, premigration social background, migration history, and economic and cultural adaptation.

Thus the available evidence, though incomplete, points consistently to high fertility in this refugee population, at least during the first several years in the United States. Some of this fertility can certainly be attributed to the age structure. Long-term patterns of childbearing among Southeast Asian Americans deserve continued attention by researchers.

Mortality and Emigration

Data on mortality among Southeast Asian refugees in the United States are almost nonexistent. As with fertility statistics, they are too rare to be identified in standard U.S. vital records systems. Moreover, the same young age structure that contributes to a high birth rate among the refugee population also implies few deaths from natural causes. Occasional reports of accidental deaths are received.

The one aspect of refugee mortality in the United States that has received research attention is the phenomenon of sudden nocturnal deaths occurring to young, previously healthy, male refugees (Baron et al., 1983). The Centers for Disease Control (CDC) in March 1983 completed an epidemiological study of fifty-one sudden death cases and made note of an additional twenty-eight cases. Of these, thirty-nine cases (49 percent) involved Hmong, twenty-one (27 percent) involved lowland Lao, and the rest were almost evenly split between Kampucheans and Vietnamese. Thus refugees from Laos have been disproportionately affected. The median age at time of death was 33, and only one victim was female. No cause for these deaths could be established by the CDC, and nationwide monitoring of these cases ended in April 1984.

No direct data on the emigration of Southeast Asian refugees have been collected. The circumstances of the refugees' flight and the situations in the countries of origin make return migration improbable, and emigration by Southeast Asian refugees is thought to be rare. Nevertheless, occasional anecdotes of refugees returning to fight for the liberation of their homelands are heard. In summary, the growth of this refugee community in the United States to date has been nearly unchecked by mortality or emigration.

Geographic Distribution

Residence patterns. The placement of Southeast Asian refugees in American communities has received considerable attention from federal policymakers. This response stands in contrast to the absence of any control over the placement of immigrants in the United States and indeed to the general freedom of persons in this country to reside where they wish. However, the history of efforts to control the residence patterns of refugees dates back to 1945 (Forbes, 1984) and thus is not limited to Southeast Asians, although recent efforts have focused on them as the largest refugee group.

Federal policy promotes dispersal of refugees about the country. This policy is thought to speed their assimilation into American society and to lessen the impact on American communities of large groups arriving at one time. In the case of the Southeast Asian refugees who arrived in 1975, the policy of dispersal resulted in an initial pattern of settlement much closer to that of the U.S. population at large than to that of earlier refugee groups or other immigrants (Forbes, 1984). The largest number were placed in California, which received nearly 21 percent of the newcomers. Every state except Alaska received at least one hundred persons. Moreover, the refugees were placed in fairly small groups across the fifty states (Baker and North, 1984:55–58).

Significant redistribution of the 1975 arrivals occurred during the late 1970s, so that they were less widely spread when the second wave began to arrive. Many persons in the second wave had ties to those in the first wave and therefore were placed near them. From 1979 through 1981, about 30 percent of the arriving Southeast Asian refugees were placed in California, but in 1982 implementation of tighter controls on refugee placement dropped this figure to 25 percent. At the same time, continuing migration to California has resulted in steady growth of that state's share of the Southeast Asian refugee population, now estimated at 40 percent. Another 34 percent reside in nine additional states, with 7.5 percent in Texas and 4.5 percent in Washington state. Nevertheless, the refugees from Southeast Asia remain more dispersed than other immigrant populations. Detailed statistics on their placement and geographic distribution may be found in the *Report to the Congress: Refugee Resettlement Program* (published annually; see HHS, 1986) and some of my earlier work (Gordon, 1980, 1982b).

Of the three major refugee nationality groups, residential concentration in California is most characteristic of the Vietnamese. Other places with particularly large concentrations of Vietnamese are Texas, Washington state, Pennsylvania, New York, Louisiana, and the Washington, D.C., area. Refugees from Laos, including the Hmong, have also settled in large numbers in California, and significant concentrations of refugees from Laos have developed in Minnesota and Wisconsin, Rhode Island, Illinois, Texas, Washington state, and Oregon.

In the late 1970s, the residence patterns of the Kampucheans closely resembled those of the Vietnamese (Gordon, 1980). They were present in largest numbers in California, Washington state, Texas, and Pennsylvania. By 1981 when arrivals from Kampuchea were reaching their highest level (Figure 7.1), the large number of 1980 arrivals had aroused calls for renewed emphasis on dispersal of refugees. Most of the arriving refugees from Vietnam and Laos were being reunited with relatives already in the United States, so that their destinations were predetermined. Since Kampucheans were arriving in large numbers for the first time, few were joining family members and most were available for placement anywhere.

Through a project developed in 1980, about 8,000 Kampucheans who arrived between January 1981 and March 1982 were placed in twelve selected communities around the country. These sites were considered to be not already overburdened by refugees and to offer good opportunities for employment. Each site was to receive between 300 and 1,200 refugees in hopes of establishing a nucleus for the formation of a viable ethnic community. They were located in nine states: Arizona, Florida, Georgia, Illinois, Massachusetts, New York, Ohio, Texas, and Virginia. As expected, these sites have continued to attract more Kampucheans. The planned cluster resettlement approach is considered desirable by refugee program officials and was continued in 1983. That year saw the development of two new sites for Kampucheans in North Carolina as well as two sites for Vietnamese in Arizona.

In summary, then, although California is the most common residence for each nationality, their geographic distribution varies among the other states. Residence patterns have been shaped in part by policy, in part by the timing of arrivals within each group, and in part by the preferences of the refugees themselves.

Secondary migration. When refugees leave the communities in which they were placed upon arrival in the United States, the change of residence is called *secondary migration* in the refugee program context. Because federal policy is to influence the geographic distribution of refugees in order to divert resettlements from areas having limited opportunities, and because the provision of resettlement services is geared to placement activity, secondary migration is viewed by many as problematic. Because of substantial political interest, the most current information on secondary migration is always reviewed in the ORR's annual *Report to the Congress* (HHS, 1986:93–97), and Forbes (1984) has summarized the state of knowledge on the topic.

All available sources of information confirm that the 1975 refugees, almost all of them Vietnamese, were very likely to relocate during their first few years in the United States. Baker and North (1984:59) found that 45 percent had moved to a different state by 1980. Refugees tended to prefer urban places with a warm climate and an existing Asian population, and they were especially likely to move if their resettlement locations did not fit this description or if they were not placed where they had requested. Movement tended to be toward the South and West, particularly into California. As ethnic communities began to form, secondary migration led to greater concentrations of refugees.

The picture regarding the second wave of Southeast Asian refugees is more complex. The second wave was ethnically more diverse than the first, and the migration of Kampucheans, Lao, and Hmong may be influenced by considerations different from those of the Vietnamese. Urban centers in the East and Midwest, such as Boston, Providence, and St. Paul, have become magnets for refugees from Laos and Kampuchea. Hmong refugees have been especially mobile, sometimes arriving in large numbers in new communities in response to suggestions by their leaders. Less information is available about the second wave than was true for the 1975 wave, but California is still the most popular destination for secondary migrants. The volume of secondary migration among Southeast Asian refugees continues to be high by comparison with other U.S. residents (Gordon, 1984). The residence patterns of the first refugee wave stabilized after the initial period of substantial movement, however, and the second wave is expected to exhibit greater geographic stability in future years as well. The establishment of employment and social ties in local communities should bring refugee migration patterns more into line with those of other residents (Forbes, 1984).

Adjustment and Adaptation to American Life

Employment and Earnings. The definitive assessment of Southeast Asian refugee adjustment to the United States will not be written for a generation or more. Nevertheless, efforts to monitor their adjustment continue in the U.S. refugee program. Data on labor force participation, employment, and use of public services are collected in an annual telephone survey of a random nationwide sample of Southeast Asian refugees, since the Refugee Act of 1980 places special emphasis on these questions. Findings are reported annually in the ORR's *Report to the Congress.* Several local studies of refugee adjustment have been carried out under private auspices (see HHS, 1981). Baker and North (1984) linked administrative record systems for an analysis of labor force participation and earnings of the 1975 arrivals. One three-site survey examined the social, psychological, and economic adaptation of the Vietnamese who arrived between 1975 and 1979 (Dunning, 1982). North (1984) has summarized available knowledge on refugee earnings and use of assistance programs. A major study, funded by the ORR, of the process by which refugees achieve self-sufficiency in the United States was recently released (Caplan et al., 1985).

All these sources indicate that in time the refugees approach comparability with the resident population in labor force participation and other economic indicators; the question is at what speed and by what paths. The ORR's annual survey in 1984 found that the labor force participation rates of refugees who had arrived from 1975 to 1978 surpassed those of the U.S. population; however, the unemployment rates of all refugee cohorts were still higher than the national averages (HHS, 1985:91). In October 1984, overall refugee labor force participation was 55 percent, compared with 64 percent for the U.S. population; the refugee unemployment rate was 14.6 percent, compared with 7.0 percent (unadjusted). These surveys have shown consistently that refugees in their first year of residence manifest low labor force participation, high unemployment, low wages among those who are employed, and high use of cash assistance; but in time all these indicators move toward the national rates, with the most rapid improvement taking place during the first few years in the country. Indications are that refugees have particular difficulty finding and retaining jobs during periods of constriction in the American economy (HHS, 1985:88–102).

The studies that examine refugee experiences in depth shed more light on refugee adjustment during the first few years of residence. Baker and North (1984) found that the 1975 arrivals moved rather quickly into the labor force; by 1980 their employment-to-population ratio had reached that of the total U.S. population. The Dunning (1982) survey also showed good progress by the first-wave Vietnamese in the economic arena, indicating that participation in the labor force led to employment, upward job mobility, and movement away from dependency on cash assistance. Questions about the quality of life in America, however, elicited a sense of deterioration in their lives that seemed to go beyond downward occupational mobility to a deeper malaise associated with their experience of being refugees. The refugees interviewed by Caplan et al. (1985) were moving more slowly toward self-sufficiency; they arrived later (1978–1981), and the sample included a higher proportion of ethnic Chinese as well as lowland Lao. The refugees in the five-site Caplan study were less likely to experience upward occupational mobility than those in the Dunning survey; their most common strategy for economic achievement was to have several wage earners in a household. The key point at which these households became self-sufficient was when the second family member in the household obtained employment. Accordingly, the size and composition of the refugee household became a key predictor of that household's ability to be self-supporting. This finding is confirmed by the ORR's annual survey results (HHS, 1985). In 1984, for example, refugee households receiving cash assistance had a mean size of 5.1 persons, of whom 48.0 percent were under 16 years old, and a mean of 1.2 persons holding a job. Households receiving no cash assistance contained a mean of 3.8 persons, of whom 34.4 percent were under 16 years old, and 1.9 persons on average held a job. On a more discouraging note, Bach (1984) and North (1984) believe there is a movement by some refugees into the underground economy.

Certain aspects of the aggregate earnings of refugees who arrived from 1975 through 1979 have been compiled from tax records. Between 1980 and 1983, the number of tax returns reporting self-employment income grew, as did the amount of self-employment income. Moreover, income from interest and dividends increased. By 1983, the median adjusted gross income of tax-filing units headed by 1975 arrivals was within $1,000 of the median for all U.S. taxpayers (HHS, 1986:113–116). These figures support the picture of steady improvement in refugee incomes, although incomes remain below the average for American citizens.

Occupational patterns. Information on the occupations entered by refugees in the United States has been summarized by Bach (1984). Like most other immigrant groups, refugees commonly experience a decline in their former occupational status. The ORR's annual survey of refugees in 1984 showed that 57 percent of the employed adults sampled had held white-collar jobs in their countries of origin, whereas only 30 percent held white-collar jobs at the time of the survey (HHS, 1985:92).

One reason advanced by Bach for downward occupational mobility is the general pattern of insertion of refugees (and other recent immigrants) into the economy. They have concentrated disproportionately in the manufacturing sector at a time when American workers have withdrawn from that sector. In the 1983 annual survey, 41 percent of the employed adults worked in manufacturing, 24 percent in retail trade, and 15 percent in professional and related activities (Bach, 1984:76-79). Examination of the specific jobs held showed that, except for the professionals, refugees were employed at relatively low-skilled jobs across a wide range of occupational sectors.

Immigrant status and citizenship. In October 1977, legislation was enacted to enable the first wave of Southeast Asian refugees to adjust their immigration status to that of permanent resident alien after two years' residence in the United States. This legislation covered all Southeast Asians admitted as refugees prior to the Refugee Act of 1980, which contains a waiting period of one year. Permanent resident ("immigrant") status is significant because it is the first step toward obtaining citizenship; it confers eligibility for certain types of employment; and it may symbolize movement toward integration into American society.

The first wave of refugees responded with enthusiasm to the opportunity to adjust their status. By the end of the first year (1978) that this benefit was available, 116,680, or 90 percent of those eligible, had applied. By the end of 1984, more than two-thirds of the refugees who arrived before the 1980 Refugee Act had become permanent resident aliens. The more recent arrivals have also adjusted to immigrant status in large numbers, generally during their second year of residence, but exact data by nationality are not available.

The minimum waiting period for immigrants to apply for citizenship is five years after arrival in the United States. Therefore the 1975 cohort of refugees first became eligible in 1980. From 1980 through 1984, the most recent year for which data are available, approximately 47,000 Southeast Asian refugees became American citizens. This number represents about 19 percent of those eligible, indicating that refugees are much slower to naturalize than they were to obtain immigrant status. A Vietnamese psychiatrist interviewed on the subject of assimilation (*Washington Post*, 18 April 1985) observed that refugees cling to memories of life in Vietnam. Many still think of the United States as a temporary refuge and regard obtaining citizenship as a form of sell-ing out. The propensity of these refugees not to become American citizens has implications for the future of immigration from Southeast Asia.

Impact on American communities. The issue of the refugees' impact on American communities is central in the refugee program. One study has focused on the impact of Southeast Asian refugees in five communities (Finnan and Cooperstein, 1983). These sites were distributed across the country and selected to vary in the size and characteristics of the local refugee community, characteristics of the locality, and other factors. None had experienced violent conflicts between refugees and other residents, as happened in Denver and on the Texas Gulf Coast, but one (New Orleans) had seen significant tensions between blacks and Vietnamese over allegations that the refugees were receiving preference for jobs and housing.

The study considered the effects of refugees on many dimensions of community life: housing, employment, public assistance, educational services, adult educational and employment services, and medical and mental health services. Perceptions as well as objective effects were assessed. The major short-term effects were increased demand for public services and changes in community relations caused by the arrival of the new ethnic groups. The researchers concluded that refugees are most likely to have a negative impact on American communities when they arrive in large numbers in a short period of time and no established ethnic enclaves are in place to receive them. This combination of factors describes the early situation of the Southeast Asian refugees particularly well. Other things being equal, a strong local economy and an existing Asian population of any kind have helped to ameliorate the impact of Asian refugees on communities. Negative effects of refugees were felt to be largely short-term effects. Over a longer time frame, refugees need fewer special services; they find jobs, pay taxes, start businesses, and gain acceptance as established subgroups within the community.

Assessment of the long-term impact must await future developments, but with new refugee arrivals at current levels, little public concern is being expressed. The process by which refugees are placed in significant numbers in communities, which now includes consultation with local officials, may be more important than the actual results to community perceptions of impact. Even so, the large-scale movement of refugees outside official channels continues to cause difficulties because advance preparations to provide special services for them cannot be made. Therefore secondary migration is more likely than initial placements to lead to the feeling that refugee resettlement brings trouble (Forbes, 1984).

PROSPECTS FOR THE FUTURE

The Refugee Program

For the next few years, arrivals under the refugee program will continue to dominate the picture of immigration from Southeast Asia. For 1986, the refugee ceiling figure was 45,500, reduced by about 10 percent from the two previous years. No comparable planning figures are available yet for later years. As of September 1985, however, approximately 152,000 refugees were still in first asylum camps in Southeast Asia, down from 158,000 one year earlier. (At their peak in early 1980, the first asylum camps held more than 400,000 refugees.) Many persons in first asylum have applied and been found ineligible for admission to the United States. New arrivals seeking asylum in Southeast Asia have averaged 40,000 to 45,000 yearly from 1983 to 1985 (excluding the Orderly Departure Program). The United States historically has taken more than half the refugees from the countries of first asylum. These figures thus suggest an impending decline in refugee arrivals from the camps, barring new upheavals in Southeast Asia.

The Orderly Departure Program

In contrast with the refugee program, the Orderly Departure Program (ODP) from Vietnam is expected to grow. During FY 1985, some 1,200 refugees and 3,700 immigrants came to the United States through this program. (Another 12,900 persons went to other countries.) The program currently operates under quotas of 1,000 departures per month to the United States and 1,000 monthly to other countries. In late 1984 the State Department had more than 104,000 active ODP cases, including nearly 500,000 persons for processing. The Vietnamese official in charge of the program was quoted as saying that Vietnam stood ready to release 4,000 people or more each month to the United States (*Washington Post*, 26 June 1984). There is no indication of willingness on the American side to accept this level of admissions, but clearly the potential exists for expansion of current program levels.

The subject of Amerasian migration out of Vietnam has recently gained public attention. Amerasians are the children of American personnel and Vietnamese women who were left behind when the U.S. presence in Vietnam ended. Their outcast status in Vietnam is symbolized by the Vietnamese term for them: the "dust of life." The Vietnamese official quoted above urged in the same statement that the United States accept "5,000 or even 10,000" Amerasians each month through the Orderly Departure Program. Often Amerasians are accompanied by their Asian mothers and half-siblings, so a "case" may in fact include several persons. While this statement seems to imply a very large potential for Amerasian migration from Vietnam, the existence of such a potential has not been documented and is viewed officially with skepticism. Through the end of 1985, about 3,500 Amerasians had migrated through the ODP in various immigration statuses. It seems clear that the volume of orderly migration from Vietnam to the United States will be determined in the near future more by relations between the two governments than by the wishes of individuals.

CONCLUSION AND IMPLICATIONS

During the next decade—and in the absence of new political upheavals—the prospect is for migration from Southeast Asia to shift from refugee camps in first asylum countries to a more regularized movement like that provided by the Orderly Departure Program. In theory, this development implies a related shift away from the use of the refugee status, with its implications of politically motivated migration, toward the use of the immigrant status.

In late 1985, the secretary of state commissioned an Indochinese Refugee Panel to review the refugee situation and U.S. policies and options for responding to it. The panel concluded that the situation in Southeast Asia continues to warrant special relief efforts, but it also recommended a restructuring of the refugee program to place more emphasis on immigrant visas (U.S. Department of State, 1986).

As the Southeast Asians now in the United States gain citizenship, they will also gain the right under U.S. immigration law to bring in immediate relatives as immigrants outside the quota system and other categories of close relatives in high-preference classes. As with immigration from other nations, a potential exists for substantial chain migration of relatives. Many Vietnamese now living in the United States are trying to reunify their families, and the major obstacle seems to be obtaining permission to leave Vietnam. For migrants from Kampuchea and Laos, no program comparable to the ODP exists and the future of migration is more difficult to foresee.

With more than 500,000 arrivals in the past ten years and a high rate of natural increase, the Vietnamese are almost certainly the fourth largest of the Asian American groups at mid-decade. The Kampuchean, Hmong, and Lao groups are smaller but of significant size and growing rapidly. The arrival and establishment of these groups over the short span of ten years has not only diversified the Asian component of the American population but heightened public awareness of Asian immigration as well.

REFERENCES

Bach, R. L.

1984   "Labor Force Participation and Employment of Southeast Asian Refugees in the United States." Paper presented at the Refugee Policy Forum, Wingspread Conference Center, 6–8 February, Racine, Wisconsin.

Baker, R. P., and D. S. North

1984   *The 1975 Refugees: Their First Five Years in America.* Washington, D.C.: New TransCentury Foundation.

Baron, R. C., S. B. Thacker, L. Gorelkin, A. A. Vernon, W. R. Taylor, and K. Choi

1983   "Sudden Death Among Southeast Asian Refugees: An Unexplained Nocturnal Phenomenon." *Journal of the American Medical Association,* 250(21):2947–2951.

Caplan, N., J. K. Whitmore, and Q. L. Bui

1985   *Southeast Asian Refugee Self-Sufficiency Study.* Institute for Social Research, University of Michigan. Washington, D.C.: Office of Refugee Resettlement.

Dunning, B. B.

1982   *Survey of the Social, Psychological and Economic Adaptation of Vietnamese Refugees in the U.S., 1975–1979.* Bureau of Social Science Research, Inc. Washington, D.C.: Social Security Administration.

Finnan, C. R., and R. A. Cooperstein

1983   *Southeast Asian Refugee Resettlement at the Local Level: The Role of the Ethnic Community and the Nature of Refugee Impact.* Menlo Park, Calif.: SRI International.

Forbes, S. S.

1984   "Residency Patterns and Secondary Migration of Refugees." Paper presented at the Refugee Policy Forum, Wingspread Conference Center, 6–8 February, Racine, Wisconsin.

Gordon, L. W.

1980   "Settlement Patterns of Indochinese Refugees in the United States." *INS Reporter,* 28(3):6–10. Spring.

————————.

1982a   "New Data on the Fertility of Southeast Asian Refugees in the United States." Paper presented at the annual meeting of the Population Association of America, 29 April–1 May, San Diego.

————————.

1982b   "Southeast Asian Refugees in the United States: Dispersal and Concentration." Paper presented at the annual meetings of the Southwest Social Science Association, 17–20 March, San Antonio, Texas.

1984   "Migration of Refugees Within the United States: New Data Sources and Findings." Paper presented at the annual meetings of the Association of American Geographers, 23 April, Washington, D.C.

North, D. S.

1984   "Refugee Earnings and Utilization of Financial Assistance Programs." Paper presented at the Refugee Policy Forum, Wingspread Conference Center, 6–8 February, Racine, Wisconsin.

Rumbaut, R. G., and J. R. Weeks

1986   "Fertility and Adaptation: Indochinese Refugees in the United States." *International Migration Review,* 20 (Special Issue). Summer.

U.S. Department of Health and Human Services (HHS)

1981   *Refugee Resettlement in the United States: An Annotated Bibliography on the Adjustment of Cuban, Soviet and Southeast Asian Refugees.* Washington, D.C.: Office of Refugee Resettlement.

1985   *Report to the Congress: Refugee Resettlement Program.* Washington, D.C.: Office of Refugee Resettlement.

1986   *Report to the Congress: Refugee Resettlement Program.* Washington, D.C.: Office of Refugee Resettlement.

U.S. Department of State

1986   *Report of the Indochinese Refugee Panel.* Washington, D.C.: Bureau for Refugee Programs.

8

The Asian
and Pacific Island
Peoples of Australia

Charles A. Price

The history of immigration from Asian and Pacific countries into the four main English-speaking countries of the region—the United States, Canada, Australia, and New Zealand—has been remarkably uniform. Substantial migration began in the mid-nineteenth century with Chinese diggers flocking to the goldfields of California, British Columbia, the west coast of New Zealand, and the east coast of Australia. Their numbers were sufficient to provoke much white agitation, eventually resulting in restrictions on Chinese immigration and controls on Chinese settlement affecting occupation, ownership of property, areas of residence, and so on. By the late 1880s these restrictions had become severe in all four countries. During the next two decades, by which time other non-European peoples were migrating in appreciable numbers, white restrictionists worked hard to extend Chinese-type controls to all Asians and Pacific Islanders, succeeding in all four countries between 1897 and 1924. These restrictions, which remained in force until the 1950s and 1960s, caused a drastic reduction in numbers as immigrants returned to their homes or else slowly died out; the Japanese of Hawaii, California, and British Columbia, with their pattern of family migration, were the exception. Since the removal of most restrictions in the 1960s, numbers have increased markedly and today Asian and Pacific populations are an appreciable element in all four countries.

HISTORICAL BACKGROUND: "WHITE AUSTRALIA"

The principal Asian and Pacific peoples involved in the Australian story are listed in the statistical tables, Table 8.1 giving numbers over time by birth place, Table 8.2 giving numbers by race, Table 8.3 giving region of settlement, and Table 8.4 showing occupations. In Table 8.1 the 1901 column reveals the numerical position that had developed during the nineteenth century; later columns show numerical changes between 1901 and 1981. The columns headed SR (sex ratio) reveal how few women came with their menfolk during the nineteenth century and how most groups had achieved a better balance by 1981.

In nineteenth-century Australia the Chinese, mainly from Kwangtung province in the south, remained the major Asian–Pacific group. Reaching a peak of 38,500 in the 1880s, and still numbering over 29,000 in 1901, they were settled in every colony, gradually abandoning gold-digging for bush-clearing, vegetable gardening, carpentry, and trade; and in Sydney and Melbourne they were establishing small but noticeable Chinatowns. Next in number were the Pacific Islanders, recruited in the 1860s for general work on farms and sheep stations but in the 1880s and 1890s concentrating in the sugar plantations of northern Queensland. Drawn mainly from the New Hebrides (Vanuatu) and Solomon Islands, they totaled more than 10,000 in 1901, mostly in Queensland, but with a thousand or more in New South Wales and a thin scattering elsewhere. Then came the Indians, fewer than the birthplace statistics suggest since many Indian-born persons in Australia were children of British military and civil service families; but there were a few Gujarati, Sind, and Bengali traders and a noticeable number of Sikhs and Muslims from the Punjab. Some of these people worked as tropical laborers in northern Queensland, some were in sugar and then bananas in northern New South Wales, others spent their time hawking goods about the country towns; in all, by 1901, they totaled just under 5,000.

A small but famous subgroup from the Indian region were the Pathan camelmen from Afghanistan, Baluchistan, and the northwest provinces of India, popularly known as "Afghans" or "Ghans." Recruited with their camels in the 1860s to develop the arid interior, they provided a major service in opening up the outback, carrying not only domestic supplies but also pumps and pipes for wells, rails and sleepers for railway lines, and ore from the early desert mines. Though they dominated outback transport until the advent of the motor truck in the 1920s, they never numbered more than 600 or so at any one time. Their main legacy are the camels: Australia now has one of the largest wild camel populations in the world and a small but flourishing camel export trade.

Next in importance were the Japanese, partly in tropical labor in Queensland but also engaging in pearling off the coasts of Queensland, Western Australia, and the Northern Territory; in 1901 they totaled more than 3,500. Also important in tropical labor and pearling were Malay peoples from British Malay territories and the Dutch East Indies (over 1,500 in 1901) and Filipinos (about 1,000). Pearl shell and trepang (bêche-de-mer) had sometimes attracted seamen from Macassar and Bone in Sulawesi, but European pearling captains, when developing their businesses from the 1860s onward, preferred to recruit divers from the well-known pearling areas of Ceylon, the Malacca Straits, the Sulu Islands off the Philippines, the Solor-Alor Islands north of Timor, and the Aru Islands east toward New Guinea. Later the Japanese entered the business, first as divers and then as captains and owners; in the 1920s and 1930s they dominated Australian pearling and received special exemption from immigration restrictions so long as they stayed in that business.

Other Asian–Pacific peoples numbered a few hundred only. This group, of course, excludes the Arab peoples of western Asia, mainly because Arabic speakers are as much part of Africa as Asia, are very different from Asian peoples farther east, and in their migration history are similar to southern Europeans. The term Asian–Pacific, as used here, also excludes immigrants from the Pacific shores of the Americas. One should not forget that American immigrants have been influential in Australia since the 1850s—numbering 12,500 by 1901 and 100,000 at present—and that in Australian eyes the Pacific includes that ocean's eastern rim as well as its western edge and oceanic islands. Nor does the term Asian–Pacific here include the 180,000 New Zealanders in Australia—largely Anglo–Celtic in origin—though one should note the 10,000 or more Maoris now in Australia, beneficiaries of a long-standing arrangement whereby Australia and New Zealand agree to allow each others' citizens to move freely across the Tasman Sea.

Severe immigration restrictions, imposed between 1897 and 1902 and progressively dismantled between 1949 and 1973, were popularly known as the White Australia policy; these drastically reduced the number of Asian–Pacific peoples in Australia, except for those engaged in exempt occupations such as pearling. Not that the new restrictions involved deportation of residents, unless we include some 7,000 or so Pacific Islanders who had entered Queensland under short-term contracts with guarantees of free return home and who were repatriated in 1906. The main reason was that nineteenth century Asian–Pacific men brought few women with them—see the sex ratios for 1901 in Table 8.1—and after 1902 found it impossible to do so even if they had wished. Many therefore returned to their original homes, though a few stayed on to

Table 8.1. Asian–Pacific Immigrants in Australia: 1901–1981

Birthplace[a]	1981 No.	1981 SR	1976 No.	1976 SR	1971 No.	1971 SR
South Asia	64,067	100.6	54,726	103.1	39,977	109.0
Afghanistan	21	—	18	—	16	—
India	42,930	100.2	37,589	102.8	29,212	107.4
Pakistan	2,611	111.3	1,798	135.0	1,658	147.8
Bangladesh	1,008	128.3	454	149.5		
Sri Lanka	17,497	98.8	14,867	99.3	9,091	108.1
Southeast Asia	141,582	97.8	57,398	103.9	37,661	120.5
Burma	7,593	93.6	6,329	93.8	4,932	95.0
Thailand	3,475	59.2	1,665	71.8	1,004	97.2
Malaysia	32,916	101.8	19,881	112.5	14,945	134.7
Singapore	12,428	92.4	8,990	105.0	5,532	124.1
Indonesia	12,962	113.1	9,358	123.4	7,981	125.3
East Timor	3,849	101.2	1,834	88.5	NA	NA
Philippines	16,060	53.8	5,962	75.0	2,550	87.0
Kampuchea	3,745	109.7	496	126.5		
Laos	5,579	103.1	454	124.8	717	143.9
Vietnam	42,975	118.2	2,429	96.7		
East Asia	57,012	101.6	36,507	109.8	28,581	121.0
China	26,321	100.3	19,542	108.6	17,601	116.9
Taiwan	1,272	82.4	431	125.7		
Hong Kong	16,362	106.7	8,820	114.4	5,583	136.2
Japan	8,356	92.0	6,254	91.8	4,929	114.7
Korea	4,701	114.0	1,460	210.0	468	196.2
Other Asia[b]	1,404	113.0	2,858	112.2	1,550	337.9
Christmas Island[c]	979	113.7	416	122.5	246	101.6
Cocos and Keelings[c]	516	106.6	254	141.9	99	196.0
Total Asia	265,560	99.5	152,159	105.1	108,114	117.7
Pacific Islands	37,473	95.0	25,602	97.0	16,285	101.2
Nauru	448	106.7	378	102.1	496	97.6
Papua New Guinea	19,564	96.3	15,560	99.0	8,903	107.4
Solomons	754	85.4	427	95.0	322	84.0
Vanuatu (N.H.)	678	88.4	480	92.0	421	102.4
New Caledonia	933	68.6	782	65.3	900	66.7
Fiji	9,771	97.5	5,976	100.1	4,015	102.8
Tonga	2,795	102.9	893	100.2	448	87.4
Cook Islands	685	76.7	126	63.6		
Western Samoa	799	92.5	259	85.0		
Kiribati and Tuvalu	156	57.1	132	97.0	562	97.9
Other British Pacific	890	84.9	363	92.1		
Other Pacific			226	58.0	218	77.2

1961		1947		1901	
No.	SR	No.	SR	No.	SR
18,805	134.4	8,184	180.9	8,765	411.4
14	—	22	—	394	—
14,167	130.1				
1,191	346.1	7,468	180.0	7,760	389.9
3,433	115.5	694	181.0	611	370.0
17,183	160.4	3,123	154.1	2,887	1,403.6
1,492	94.0	120	275.0	40	300.0
371	174.8	25	212.5	37	311.1
5,793	206.0				
2,759	171.0	1,768	141.9	932	1,126.3
6,018	143.8	1,006	154.0	1,044	1,238.5
NA	NA	35	775.0	NA	NA
430	129.9	141	187.8	823	5,386.7
320	150.0	28	211.1	11	175.0
20,539	171.7	7,504	322.8	33,678	3,862.1
14,488	171.0	6,404	404.6	29,907	7,490.6
3,544	230.9	762	112.3	167	475.9
2,306	114.3	330	129.2	3,602	743.6
201	204.5	8	166.7	2	—
1,993	144.5	641	214.2	140	600.0
21	90.9	10	NA	NA	NA
10	233.3	4	NA	NA	NA
58,551	154.5	19,466	217.7	45,470	1,538.0
7,994	101.0	4,409	94.9	10,271	981.2
103	139.5	34	88.9	NA	NA
3,361	108.6	1,238	98.1	40	300.0
160	92.8	117	200.0	3,628	1,498.2
290	92.7	290	108.6	5,457	1,454.0
764	66.4	801	71.2	98	1,125.0
2,674	106.3	1,509	97.0	586	110.8
201	93.3	123	112.1	148	270.0
				46	666.7
				89	709.1
279	92.4	192	100.0	25	1,150.0
				60	400.0
162	90.6	105	98.1	94	1,780.0

Table 8.1. *(continued)*

	1981		1976		1971	
Birthplace[a]	No.	SR	No.	SR	No.	SR
Total Asia–Pacific	303,033	98.9	177,761	103.9	124,399	115.4
% of Foreign-Born	9.8		6.5		4.8	
All Foreign-Born	3,102,582	107.3	2,718,832	109.5	2,579,318	114.3
Australian-Born	11,752,279	97.2	10,829,616	97.8	10,176,320	98.0
Grand Total	14,854,861	99.4	13,548,448	100.0	12,755,638	101.1

Sources: Tables are based on Australian censuses with occasional estimation to take Afghanistan out of "Other Asia" or the Solomons and Vanuatu out of "Other Pacific." For 1901 the Queensland category "Pacific Islands" (8,760 in all) was distributed with the aid of Queensland shipping records giving islands of origin. In Tables 8.1 and 8.2 the 1981 statistics have been raised to allow for an officially recognized census undercount averaging 1.9 percent.

Note: SR = sex ratio = males per 100 females; a dash signifies no females.

marry white women. Others developed a strange kind of commuter life, spending a few years in Australia, then a year or two at home starting a family, then two or three more years in Australia, then two years at home, and so on; some Chinese vegetable gardeners and carpenters developed this pattern as a permanent way of life. A few more fortunate men—usually traders with businesses of value to the Australian economy—received permission to bring wives and children and achieved a de facto permanent status by receiving a fresh temporary permit every five years. Alternatively, the Australian government allowed replacement; for instance, a Chinese vegetable gardener wanting to return permanently to China could send his nephew as a substitute, but the nephew could not bring his own family. Australia also allowed in students and ministers of religion, again on temporary permits.

The result of these restrictions and procedures was the continuation of the old Asian–Pacific population but at a much lower level. This foreign-born population, having increased from 42,000 in 1861 to 56,500 in 1891, fell to less than 24,000 in 1947—that is, from 3.64 percent of the total population in 1861 to 1.78 percent in 1891 and 0.33 percent in 1947. Because of all the British persons born in Asia, the Asian–Pacific racial total was smaller still; even when those born in Australia are included, it was barely 21,000 in 1947, with another 6,500 of mixed racial origin.

LIFTING OF RESTRICTIONS AFTER WORLD WAR II

These groups, though small, had much to do with the revival of Asian–Pacific immigration once the restrictions were eased—first for refugees

1961		1947		1901	
No.	SR	No.	SR	No.	SR
66,545	146.6	23,875	184.6	55,741	1,396.0
3.7		3.2		6.5	
1,778,780	124.7	744,187	127.5	859,804	151.3
8,729,406	98.2	6,835,171	97.8	2,913,997	100.4
10,508,186	102.2	7,579,358	100.4	3,773,801	110.1

[a]Asian countries exclude Asiatic Russia and countries west of Afghanistan. The Pacific excludes New Zealand and American countries bordering the Pacific.

[b]"Other Asia" covers the census category "Other Asia" or "Asia not elsewhere indicated." This category includes countries such as Sikkim, Brunei, and Mongolia and is difficult to distribute among major subregions of Asia.

[c]These islands are located in the Indian Ocean.

(1949), including Chinese temporarily in Australia when the Communists defeated Chiang Kai-shek, then for persons who had lived in Australia on temporary permits for fifteen years (1956), then for Anglo Asians (1964), then for persons with professional and technical skills (1966), and, finally, with the introduction of completely nondiscriminatory policies from 1973 onward, for everyone. Survivors of earlier settler families took the chance, especially after 1956, of sponsoring relatives and friends and in this way strengthened their little Cantonese, Sikh, Malay, or other communities. The jump in Asian–Pacific-born population—from 23,875 in 1947 to 66,545 in 1961 (Table 8.1)—owes much to this sponsoring.

Exceptional here were the Afghan camelmen. Having brought almost no women before 1900, most had gone home when the camel business faded during the 1930s. A few had stayed, married white or Aboriginal Australians, and had children; but these had few links with the homelands and did little sponsoring. Even allowing for a few Afghan refugees from the Russian invasion, there are probably no more than 900 or so Afghan-born persons in the country today. Also an exception are the old Pacific Islanders, descendants of the 3,000 or so islanders staying in Australia when the others were repatriated in 1904–1906; by the 1950s they had lost touch with their ancestral islands and, calling themselves "South Sea Islanders," have had little to do with new immigrants from the Pacific. They claim to number 20,000, but census statistics suggest a maximum of 10,000.

Some of the rise in Asian–Pacific birthplace numbers between 1947 and 1961 came not from ethnic Asians but from Europeans or part-

Europeans born in Asian and Pacific countries. Notable here are "Burgher" immigrants from Sri Lanka (persons of mixed Dutch, Portuguese, British, and Singhalese ancestry), ethnic Dutch persons born in Indonesia, ethnic French folk born in New Caledonia, and ethnic Russians born in China to parents who had come from Russia to build the northern railway system or to avoid the Communist takeover of 1917. More numerous still were ethnic Britons born in Asian and Pacific parts of the British Commonwealth, while a growing number of persons born in Papua New Guinea were children of Australian servicemen, planters, and administrators temporarily settled there. Table 8.2, giving the racial composition of the various birthplace categories in 1976, illustrates the point clearly. (Incidentally, this is the last race analysis available because, after 1976, antiracist liberal humanitarians succeeded in having the race question removed from the census on the grounds that it was an invasion of privacy and could lead to racist discrimination.) Analysis of census language questions (1976, 1981) show the same thing: 60 to 85 percent of persons born in India, Sri Lanka, Burma, Singapore, and Papua New Guinea used English as their only language, indicating that many of them were of British or Australian descent.

The rise of the Asian–Pacific-born population, from 66,500 in 1961 to 124,400 in 1971, reflects further concessions to persons of mixed ancestry; much of the increase in the Burma-born population was Anglo Burman and some of the Indian-born increase was Anglo Indian (see Tables 8.1 and 8.2). But the rise also reflects the 1966 concessions to persons with professional and technical skills; these brought in many Indians, Sri Lankans, Malaysians (Chinese as well as Malay), Chinese from Hong Kong and Singapore, Indians from Fiji, and so on. These persons, having trained in local or other universities using British curricula and standards, found their qualifications immediately accepted in Australia because most Australian professional societies and institutions recognized the qualifications of institutions that recognized theirs. (Things were harder for graduates from European institutions, which, being outside the British Commonwealth, did not automatically accept Australian qualifications.) Moreover, ability to speak English fluently was a major factor in obtaining both an immigration permit and a job; here Indians, Singhalese, Malaysians, and other persons from British Commonwealth countries had a considerable advantage.

The increase at this time also reflects Australia's greater willingness to accept non-European students for temporary residence and training. Many of them then stayed on, either by marrying Australian citizens or by finding employers willing to sponsor them with the Department of Immigration. In the mid-1960s, Australia was training well over 10,000 non-European students at any one time.

Table 8.2. Asian–Pacific Immigrants in Australia, by Race: 1976

Birthplace[a]	Euro-pean (%)	Chinese (%)	Pacific Islander (%)	Other (%)	Total (%)	Number (Excluding Not Stated)
India	70.1	0.2	0.0	29.7	100.0	36,128
Pakistan	59.7	0.5	0.0	39.8	100.0	1,721
Bangladesh	34.0	0.0	0.0	66.0	100.0	397
Sri Lanka	59.7	0.1	0.0	40.2	100.0	14,324
Burma	52.8	2.8	0.0	44.4	100.0	6,154
Thailand	24.3	7.7	0.0	68.0	100.0	1,598
Malaysia	39.3	37.5	0.0	23.2	100.0	19,356
Singapore	62.0	23.5	0.0	14.5	100.0	8,534
Indonesia	65.3	9.9	0.0	24.8	100.0	9,047
East Timor	24.4	34.2	0.0	41.4	100.0	1,760
Philippines	27.8	1.6	0.0	70.6	100.0	5,586
Kampuchea	8.2	16.1	0.0	75.7	100.0	485
Laos	3.6	2.7	0.0	93.7	100.0	442
Vietnam[b]	13.7	3.2	0.0	83.1	100.0	2,304
China	44.2	41.6	0.0	14.2	100.0	18,698
Taiwan	19.9	80.1	0.0	0.0	100.0	367
Hong Kong	29.8	54.0	0.0	16.2	100.0	8,452
Japan	17.3	0.7	0.0	82.0	100.0	5,707
Korea	12.1	0.3	0.0	87.6	100.0	1,272
Other Asia[c]	74.6	7.8	0.0	17.6	100.0	2,762
Christmas Island	26.4	32.8	0.0	40.8	100.0	412
Cocos Islands	22.4	0.9	0.0	76.7	100.0	228
Nauru	61.3	2.2	36.5	0.0	100.0	367
Papua New Guinea	77.2	8.7	11.7	2.4	100.0	15,016
Solomon Islands	65.0	24.3	10.7	0.0	100.0	403
Vanuatu	78.8	6.1	15.1	0.0	100.0	462
New Caledonia	94.6	0.5	4.9	0.0	100.0	734
Fiji	52.8	4.3	20.7	22.2	100.0	5,669
Tonga	18.5	0.0	81.5	0.0	100.0	813
Cook Islands	36.5	0.0	63.5	0.0	100.0	115
Western Samoa	45.4	0.0	54.6	0.0	100.0	251
Kiribati and Tuvalu	47.5	4.9	47.6	0.0	100.0	122
Other Pacific	56.7	8.7	24.5	10.1	100.0	564

Source: See Table 8.1 sources.

[a]Asian countries exclude western Asia (countries west of Afghanistan) and Asiatic Russia. Pacific countries exclude New Zealand and American countries bordering the Pacific.

[b]In 1976 there were in Australia few Vietnamese-born persons of ethnic Chinese origin. These increased greatly in the years 1977–1983, and estimates suggest the racial proportions in 1984 were European 0.7%, Chinese 31.7%, and Vietnamese 67.6% (total numbers about 55,000). The 1976 race question (not asked in 1981) was based on self-identification.

[c]"Other Asia" covers the census category "Other Asia" or "Asia not elsewhere indicated." This category includes countries such as Sikkim, Brunei, and Mongolia and is difficult to distribute between major divisions of South, East, and Southeast Asia.

Asian–Pacific immigration to Australia continued to increase in much the same way between 1971 and 1976. In birthplace terms the total rose to 178,000 (Table 8.1) and in ethnic terms to 83,000—more if we include Chinese immigrants born in Europe, America, and Africa, or Indian and similar immigrants born in Britain, maybe 89,000 all told (deducting Western Asian, African, and Amerindian elements in the "Other" column of Table 8.2). But this increase was not nearly so marked as that from 1976 to 1981—to 303,000 in birthplace terms and some 200,000 in ethnic terms.

Nondiscrimination and Refugees

The reasons for the marked rise in Asian–Pacific immigration to Australia are various. First was the declaration of the Whitlam Labor government, when it attained office in late 1972, that Australian immigration policy would be completely free of any discrimination on grounds of race, skin color, or nationality—statements repeated, in slightly more elegant terms, by the Fraser Liberal-National government of 1975–1983 and the Hawke Labor government of 1983 onward. Since 1973, therefore, there has been little or no discrimination on ethnic grounds against those seeking entry under any one of the four main immigration categories: refugee and special humanitarian; family reunion; general eligibility (for those possessing skills, business enterprise, or capital much needed in Australia); and special eligibility (for foreign-born children of Australian citizens, New Zealanders, and the like). In recent years Asians and Pacific Islanders have been entering under all these categories.

Second, there has been a distinct change in Australia's position as a country of refugee settlement. Before 1973 Australia not only accepted numerous refugees—more than 385,000 in the period 1947–1972—but also assisted them with passage and accommodation costs and in matters of employment and welfare; this help was mainly governmental, but some came from voluntary societies. The refugees were almost all European, however. Even as late as 1972 the Liberal government was most reluctant to help Asian refugees such as those Indians striving to escape from the repression of Idi Amin's Uganda; in fact, it issued only 200 permits to those Indians (in contrast to Canada's immediate offer to accept 2,500)—and only because those 200 happened to meet the somewhat restrictive entry criteria then prevailing.

The Whitlam government, with its much publicized nondiscriminatory policy, issued a few more entry permits for Ugandan Indians but then became entangled in political issues that markedly decreased its ability to respond quickly and generously to refugee situations nearer at hand. Most reluctant to upset Indonesia over the Timor crisis of 1975, the government avoided supporting the Fretilin independence movement; when 1,700 Timorese refugees arrived in northern Australia by small ship or plane, they were permitted to stay but with temporary permits only. Similarly, Prime Minister Whitlam's dislike of U.S. policies in Vietnam made him reluctant to accept Vietnamese refugees from American spheres of influence. Eventually, in late 1975, he agreed to accept 500 from Hong Kong and Singapore.

The Fraser government, taking office in December 1975, decided to tidy up the muddle. Australia gave permanent residence to the Timorese, agreed to accept at least 4,000 Vietnamese, and in May 1978 officially announced that "Australia fully recognizes its humanitarian commitment and responsibility to admit refugees for resettlement." But it soon found itself in difficulties with the Indochinese, mainly because a few small boats containing refugees successfully sailed all the way from Vietnam to the north coast of Australia. Moreover, Indonesia and Malaysia made it clear that if Australia did not accept a reasonable number of the boat refugees landing on their shores, they would refuel new refugee boats and send them direct to northern Australia.

The Australian government, preferring to keep some control over intake through its own selection officers and procedures, raised its agreed intake to 9,000 per year in May 1978 and again, after the Geneva Convention of July 1979, to 14,000 per year. The generous intake permitted by Canada and the massive intake undertaken by the United States had some influence, though there was also a genuine Australian desire to help solve a major refugee problem—particularly one that was in Australia's own region and had to some extent arisen from military action in which Australian forces had been engaged alongside those of the United States.

By the time the Hawke Labor government took office in March 1983, the major crisis was over and the refugee camps of Malaysia and Indonesia were much less crowded. Though the refugee population in Thailand was still high, the Fraser government had already felt able to reduce the Indochinese refugee inflow from a peak of 15,000 in 1980–1981 to 12,500 in 1982–1983. The Hawke government, therefore, irrespective of how much of Whitlam's views it may or may not have inherited, believed it could quite properly reduce intake further—to 10,000 in 1983–1984 and a proposed 6,000 in 1985–1986. This decline, however, was somewhat counterbalanced by an increase in the number of family reunion cases direct from Vietnam. It took the Fraser government several years to negotiate this "orderly departure" program with Vietnam—each side wanting more control over the operation than the other would concede—but with the help of the United Nations High Commissioner for Refugees (UNHCR) a compromise was reached in

March 1982, and family sponsorship by Indochinese refugees settled in Australia got under way. Nearly 600 arrived in 1982–1983, more than 2,500 in 1983–1984, and 6,000 proposed for 1985–1986. (The Australian financial and immigration year runs from 1 July to 30 June.)

All in all, by June 1984 Australia had accepted more than 88,000 Indochinese refugees and over 2,500 relatives direct from Vietnam—about 91,000 in all. This number is marginally less than those accepted by France and Canada, and much less than the more than 700,000 resettled by the United States. In terms of total population, though, the Australian intake is greater than that of any other country, except countries of first asylum such as Hong Kong. Moreover, numbers of Vietnamese refugees resettled by New Zealand, anxious to join relations and friends in the larger Vietnamese communities in Australia, are acquiring New Zealand citizenship and then taking advantage of the Australian–New Zealand migration agreement to move permanently to Australia.

Family Reunion

The third reason for the marked rise in recent Asian–Pacific migration to Australia is that immigrants from this region have been making greater use of the family reunion program than others. Liberalization of the program in 1981—extending the categories from spouses, dependent children, and aged parents to working parents, older children, and siblings—arose mainly from pressure exerted by the large Mediterranean groups in Australia: Italians, Greeks, Maltese, and others. These peoples have used the wider categories relatively little, however, enabling Asian–Pacific families to occupy more of the family reunion quota. In the two years 1982–1984, Asian peoples took about 30 percent of this quota, compared with continental Europe's less than 18 percent and the United Kingdom's and Eire's 30 percent.

The general category—skill, enterprise, and capital—was much used by Indians and others in the 1960s and 1970s but not so much as by British, European, and American immigrants. That is still the situation: Asians took 10.7 percent of this quota in 1982–1984, compared with the 20.4 percent taken by Europeans and 34.5 percent taken by Britons. When the quota for the category was large, this small Asian proportion did not matter; enough Asians could come in, establish themselves, and then use the family reunion program to keep migration going. But lately the general category has been cut because of continued recession and unemployment—from 75,000 in 1981–1982 to 12,100 in 1983–1984—so that new migration is down and future family reunion handicapped. This situation affects Asians rather than Pacific Islanders; the latter, lacking surplus skill and enterprise except perhaps in Fiji, have trouble getting migration going—which is one reason why Pacific

Island numbers have increased quite slowly (see Table 8.1) and why there is talk of making special arrangements for recruiting unskilled Pacific Island labor.

To summarize recent events, then, three main factors—emphasis on family reunion, a nondiscriminatory admission policy, and acceptance of responsibility for refugees generally—have worked together to produce a substantial increase in Asian–Pacific immigration to Australia. Taking 80 percent of the refugee quota (the other 20 percent are East Europeans, western Asians, and a few Africans and Latin Americans), plus nearly 30 percent of the family reunion quota and over 10 percent of the general category, Asian–Pacific persons made up well over one-third of new settler movement in 1983–1984. Moreover, because settler loss is much lower for Asian–Pacific peoples than for many others, their proportion in net intake has risen to more than 40 percent. (Settler loss has averaged 21 percent in the period 1947–1983—about 23 percent for British, 27 percent for Italians and Greeks, 30 percent for Dutch and Germans, and over 40 percent for North Americans. The Asian–Pacific loss has been less than 10 percent, the Indochinese being only 2 percent so far.)

A MILD WHITE BACKLASH

At first this increase bothered few. Anglo–Celtic Australians and the newer European arrivals accepted Asian–Pacific immigrants quite peaceably—much to the surprise of observers who had thought that old White Australia principles were too deeply ingrained tᴐ accept a large non-European immigration. Publication of the 1982–1984 proportions, however, has caused some upheaval, not just from the small minority of racist neo-Fascists and a solid group of White Australia conservatives entrenched in Returned Soldiers clubs and the like, but also among moderate Australians who are happy to have some Asian–Pacific immigrants but feel it is happening too quickly and on too large a scale. Led by a well-known Melbourne historian, Professor Geoffrey Blainey, these moderates are discussing the whole question quite openly, criticizing extreme "antiracists" for trying to muzzle them, and influencing members of the Liberal-National coalition to make the question political. For a while it seemed that Australia's bipartisan immigration policy—which with minor ups and downs has dominated Australian thinking on immigration since 1945—was in real jeopardy. But all political parties eventually decided to downplay the issue during the election campaign of late 1984 and things gradually settled down again, though perhaps only temporarily.

In the heat of political debate, sound statistical work tends to be overlooked. The government, adamant that nondiscrimination will remain the basis of Australia's immigration policy, quoted birthplace statistics showing that Asians in mid-1984 represented less than 2 percent of the total population and at present trends will constitute only 4 percent in the year 2000. Their opponents, with loud cries of "Asianization," concentrate on the high proportion of Asians in recent net migration, point to Gallup polls suggesting most Australians want less Asian immigration, and draw attention to strong anti-Asian feelings in parts of the country. The middle view is less often heard: In ethnic terms—that is, excluding Europeans born in Asia but including ethnic Asians born in Australia—the Asian proportion is now a little over 2.5 percent of the total population, and at present trends it will reach 7 percent or so by A.D. 2000. Although this increase is certainly not Asianization on a national scale, it is very unevenly distributed, causing much unrest in areas of Asian concentration.

GEOGRAPHICAL DISTRIBUTION

Table 8.3 presents the geographical distribution as it actually was in the 1981 census; the statistics are given by states because regional details are too voluminous for compact presentation. Certain concentrations are at once visible. Western Australia, particularly its capital city of Perth, has a disproportionate share of Indians, Singapore Chinese, Malays, and, above all, Anglo Burmans; this explains why anti-Asian feeling has been rumbling in Perth for more than twenty years. (The abnormally high proportions of Christmas and Cocos Islanders in Perth involve too few persons to arouse much reaction.) The Northern Territory has only one real concentration—the East Timorese, still there in numbers after arriving there as refugees in 1975. More of them, however, are now in Melbourne, Victoria, and a lesser number in Sydney, New South Wales. Both South Australia and Tasmania have less than a proportionate share of Asian–Pacific settlers—though, because of an active voluntary society, South Australia has taken more than 4,000 Vietnamese. Queensland's share is more equivocal: With a lower than expected share of all Asian groups except Indonesians, it has a disproportionately high share of some Pacific Islanders, notably those from Vanuatu and the Solomons; these, however, are newcomers, mostly unconnected with Queensland's Solomon and New Hebridean settlers of the last century.

New South Wales and Victoria, the two major states of the Australian Commonwealth, have attracted most of the Asian–Pacific immigrants, though not evenly. Kampucheans are equally divided between the two, but Laotians and Vietnamese are disproportionately strong in Sydney— which is one reason why anti-Indochinese feeling is strong there. Indonesians, Filipinos, Chinese, and Koreans are also heavily concentrated in Sydney, as are certain Pacific Island groups, notably New Caledonians, Fijians, Tongans, and Samoans. Some people, certain church welfare workers, for instance, say these numbers should be even larger because hundreds of Pacific Islanders have entered illegally via small boats and become "lost" in major metropolitan concentrations; but firm details here are lacking. The one thing certain is that the distribution of Asian–Pacific settlers was very different in 1981 from what it was in 1891; the spread in agricultural, pastoral, and fishing areas has gone, replaced by concentration in a few major cities.

It is worth noting here that though Australia has other illegal entrants besides Pacific Islanders—as far back as the 1870s Australian colonies were complaining about Chinese smuggling themselves ashore at night—the total number does not seem to be very great. Australia's position as an island continent, with wide sea boundaries, puts it in a situation very different from that of the United States. The major problem is the 50,000 or so illegal overstayers—persons who enter legally as short-term visitors but then vanish and try to stay permanently. Three amnesties since 1973 have reduced the problem somewhat but by no means solved it. Despite the number of overstayers, there is little evidence to suggest that Asian–Pacific immigrants are noticeably worse than others in staying on illegally.

OCCUPATIONAL DISTRIBUTION

Table 8.4 gives the 1981 occupational distribution, confirming that few Asian–Pacific settlers, except for a handful of Christmas and Cocos Island miners, are now in farming, fishing, or mining. The much higher proportions of South and East Asians in the professional and technical category, both men and women, also of most Southeast Asian groups except the Indochinese and Timorese, reflect the highly qualified and skilled migration of the 1960s and 1970s; many of the men are doctors, architects, draftsmen, and teachers, whereas the women are largely teachers and nurses. High Chinese proportions in the executive and service categories arise from Chinese traders, restaurant keepers, and their assistants, continuing this prewar tradition. The slight lift in the Vietnamese proportion in service occupations (5.3 percent) indicates a solid move into Vietnamese restaurants.

Concentration of Indochinese and Timorese in both the unemployed and the production and processing categories (the latter covers a wide range of factory work from highly skilled to completely unskilled) illustrates that these refugee peoples take whatever jobs they can find but, being recent arrivals with little English, often have trouble finding them. Moreover, because government aid to refugees covers free passage to Australia and afterward standard social security benefits includ-

Table 8.3. Distribution of Asian–Pacific Immigrants in Australia: 1981

Birthplace[a]	New South Wales (%)	Victoria (%)	Queensland (%)	South Australia (%)	Western Australia (%)	Tasmania (%)	Northern Territory (%)	ACT[b] (%)	Total (%)	Number
India	29.4	29.9	7.0	6.1	24.2	1.0	0.7	1.7	100.0	42,930
Pakistan	41.1	21.1	7.6	4.7	19.4	0.8	1.8	3.5	100.0	2,611
Bangladesh	40.4	22.2	8.0	4.3	15.0	3.7	0.2	6.2	100.0	1,008
Sri Lanka	21.6	56.3	7.4	3.8	7.6	0.5	0.7	2.1	100.0	17,497
Burma	18.1	11.7	4.8	1.7	60.7	0.5	0.3	2.2	100.0	7,590
Thailand	39.9	21.3	8.5	5.9	13.2	1.2	3.6	6.4	100.0	3,472
Malaysia	30.3	31.4	9.4	6.2	17.3	1.3	1.3	2.8	100.0	32,916
Singapore	31.0	20.3	9.6	5.6	28.0	1.1	1.9	2.9	100.0	12,428
Indonesia	44.4	18.3	16.9	5.1	9.6	0.9	2.1	2.7	100.0	12,962
East Timor	28.2	34.1	0.8	1.7	6.3	0.0	28.8	0.1	100.0	3,849
Philippines	54.4	22.4	9.1	3.9	5.4	0.8	2.4	1.6	100.0	16,060
Kampuchea	44.1	41.2	2.6	8.8	1.4	0.0	0.2	1.7	100.0	3,745
Laos	64.6	20.6	2.1	3.1	1.5	0.5	0.3	7.3	100.0	5,579
Vietnam	41.2	31.2	8.5	9.4	6.8	0.5	0.5	1.9	100.0	42,975
China	56.7	21.3	10.7	4.4	3.6	0.9	0.6	1.8	100.0	26,321
Taiwan	44.8	25.7	14.6	4.2	4.5	1.0	0.9	4.3	100.0	1,272
Hong Kong	55.9	22.2	7.4	3.1	7.3	1.0	0.7	2.4	100.0	16,362
Japan	51.5	23.9	7.7	3.5	9.1	0.9	0.7	2.7	100.0	8,356
Korea	74.2	8.6	5.0	2.0	6.6	0.7	0.6	2.3	100.0	4,701
Other Asia[c]	49.6	22.0	7.6	4.0	10.4	1.3	1.9	3.2	100.0	1,390
Christmas Island	5.4	4.3	1.5	0.7	86.8	0.0	0.3	1.0	100.0	979
Cocos Islands	2.8	2.2	1.2	0.6	92.2	0.0	0.8	0.2	100.0	516

Nauru	21.2	50.9	14.8	2.5	5.8	3.2	0.7	0.9	100.0	448
Papua New Guinea	29.0	10.8	42.3	4.6	4.6	1.7	3.3	3.7	100.0	19,564
Solomon Islands	56.3	9.4	24.4	1.9	4.4	1.7	0.8	1.1	100.0	747
Vanuatu	57.4	13.8	19.0	2.6	4.0	0.0	0.8	2.4	100.0	675
New Caledonia	73.7	6.0	14.6	2.0	2.9	0.0	0.3	0.5	100.0	922
Fiji	59.8	14.2	14.5	3.5	3.3	2.3	0.8	1.6	100.0	9,771
Tonga	68.3	12.0	9.9	0.8	1.8	0.7	4.1	2.4	100.0	2,773
Cook Islands	54.9	20.5	10.6	2.9	8.2	1.1	0.9	0.9	100.0	679
Western Samoa	52.7	14.9	17.3	2.1	5.7	2.0	2.6	2.7	100.0	792
Kiribati and Tuvalu	36.4	30.8	17.5	2.8	8.4	0.0	2.7	1.4	100.0	156
Other Pacific	49.7	15.2	15.7	2.5	14.1	0.6	1.4	0.8	100.0	890
Foreign-born	34.7	28.8	11.4	9.6	11.4	1.5	0.9	1.7	100.0	3,102,582
Australian-born	35.3	25.6	17.0	8.6	8.0	3.2	0.8	1.5	100.0	11,752,279
Total Population	35.2	26.3	15.8	8.8	8.7	2.9	0.8	1.5	100.0	14,854,861

Source: See Table 8.1 sources.

Note: In all states except Queensland and Tasmania, the great majority of Asian–Pacific immigrants were in the capital cities: Sydney in New South Wales, Melbourne in Victoria, Adelaide in South Australia, Perth in Western Australia, Darwin in the Northern Territory, and Canberra in the Australian Captial Territory.

[a] Asian countries exclude western Asia (countries west of Afghanistan) and Asiatic Russia. Pacific countries exclude New Zealand and American countries bordering the Pacific Ocean.

[b] Australian Capital Territory (in New South Wales).

[c] "Other Asia" covers the census category "Other Asia" or "Asia not elsewhere indicated." This category includes countries such as Sikkim, Brunei, and Mongolia and is difficult to distribute between major divisions of South, East, and Southeast Asia.

Table 8.4.   Occupations of Asian–Pacific Immigrants Aged 15 and Over

Birthplace[a]	Profes- sional, Technical	Admin, Executive	Clerical	Sales	Farming, Fishing, Mining
India	18.3	6.0	11.2	5.0	1.8
Pakistan	19.4	7.2	9.1	5.6	0.5
Bangladesh	15.6	3.5	7.2	2.8	0.9
Sri Lanka	18.2	4.8	21.5	4.9	0.5
Burma	12.6	3.8	10.0	3.8	1.5
Thailand	13.5	2.6	7.4	3.5	1.1
Malaysia	28.5	4.1	6.0	2.7	0.8
Singapore	22.4	5.7	8.7	6.0	1.2
Indonesia	16.3	6.0	6.2	3.8	2.1
East Timor	1.3	1.1	1.2	2.3	1.2
Philippines	17.2	2.0	11.3	3.8	0.6
Kampuchea	3.0	0.2	1.8	0.4	0.7
Laos	4.0	0.2	2.8	0.8	0.4
Vietnam	3.0	0.3	1.0	0.5	0.6
China	12.6	10.9	3.2	4.2	1.7
Taiwan	12.6	5.1	3.8	0.9	0.0
Hong Kong	19.6	7.2	6.0	3.4	0.7
Japan	12.9	19.3	6.1	4.9	1.3
Korea	5.1	2.9	2.3	1.9	0.9
Other Asia[b]	19.6	4.0	7.6	4.3	1.4
Christmas Island	5.9	0.5	2.4	2.4	7.1
Cocos Islands	2.2	0.0	1.3	0.9	12.9
Nauru	9.3	2.8	8.6	3.6	0.7
Papua New Guinea	9.8	3.2	7.3	5.3	2.9
Solomon Islands	12.1	2.9	4.2	6.3	2.1
Vanuatu	11.7	4.2	4.2	4.2	4.2
New Caledonia	6.2	5.3	3.7	5.9	1.5
Fiji	11.9	4.6	7.0	4.0	2.0
Tonga	4.7	0.5	1.7	0.6	1.0
Cook Islands	5.0	0.0	3.5	2.7	0.4
Western Samoa	8.6	2.1	4.1	1.8	1.2
Kiribati and Tuvalu	12.5	2.1	8.3	4.2	0.0
Other Pacific	5.6	2.1	4.2	1.5	3.9
All Foreign	8.1	5.1	4.4	4.6	2.7
Australia	8.7	5.5	6.8	5.1	7.6

Source: Australian census, 1981.

Note: In this table numbers are not adjusted for census undercount. These major occupa- tional categories are too broad to show minor concentrations, e.g., of medical doctors from India, Sri Lanka, Singapore, and Hong Kong, or of architects from India, Malaysia,

(Percentage Distribution): 1981

Males					
Produc-tion Processing	Service, Recrea-tion	Other	Unem-ployed	Not in Labor Force	Total Number
23.4	3.6	7.7	3.2	19.8	19,388
22.0	3.8	6.2	4.1	22.1	1,149
28.1	4.0	8.6	3.0	26.3	430
18.6	2.8	7.1	2.8	18.8	7,644
31.8	4.9	7.1	4.9	19.6	3,195
16.7	9.9	5.0	4.3	36.0	808
9.6	6.5	4.9	3.8	33.1	13,018
15.9	5.4	6.2	4.3	24.2	4,280
25.3	6.3	7.0	3.8	23.2	6,133
42.1	8.8	7.3	9.7	25.0	1,366
31.0	3.7	7.8	3.9	18.7	4,004
41.1	3.3	4.2	15.8	29.5	1,320
50.4	3.1	5.5	10.1	22.7	1,871
38.7	5.3	5.2	17.9	27.5	15,855
15.8	19.6	4.2	4.5	23.3	12,631
11.4	7.0	5.1	3.5	50.6	316
8.0	21.1	4.1	3.2	26.7	6,722
10.3	5.2	4.5	2.3	33.2	3,088
33.1	8.3	5.5	3.3	36.7	1,996
14.8	12.8	5.9	4.2	25.4	647
50.4	2.8	4.3	6.9	17.3	421
61.3	2.2	2.3	2.2	14.7	225
17.2	5.0	7.1	3.6	42.1	140
23.0	3.9	9.6	5.1	29.9	5,176
22.2	3.3	8.8	1.3	36.8	239
21.3	5.9	4.6	3.3	36.4	239
18.9	5.0	4.1	5.9	43.5	322
32.9	3.9	7.4	4.1	22.2	3,911
55.4	2.8	9.5	5.4	18.4	11,011
44.4	4.6	18.4	10.7	10.3	261
44.1	3.2	10.1	11.5	13.3	338
6.2	8.3	6.3	8.3	43.8	48
41.7	2.7	7.1	5.9	25.3	336
33.4	4.4	10.4	4.6	22.3	1,514,210
27.0	3.6	8.8	4.1	22.8	3,880,725

(*continued*)

Indonesia, Japan, and Other Asia. The "Other" category includes the major categories of Transport and Communication, Armed Services (low proportions except for Singapore, Papua New Guinea, and the Solomons), and Inadequately Described (high for Cook Islands and Samoa).

Table 8.4. (*continued*)

| Birthplace[a] | Females (Selected Occupations) | | | | |
	Profes-sional Technical	Produc-tion, Processing	Unem-ployed	Not in Labor Force	Total Number
India	11.5	4.0	3.2	47.1	19,489
Pakistan	10.0	4.2	4.3	48.8	1,037
Bangladesh	4.9	10.9	6.3	50.5	303
Sri Lanka	9.1	6.3	2.7	42.9	7,721
Burma	7.6	4.0	3.9	49.4	3,468
Thailand	7.4	5.9	4.7	54.5	1,608
Malaysia	22.4	2.0	3.2	47.5	12,875
Singapore	15.5	2.6	3.7	43.6	4,814
Indonesia	9.7	4.9	3.0	55.1	5,364
East Timor	1.4	21.4	10.0	46.3	1,337
Philippines	13.7	6.5	5.8	44.2	8,706
Kampuchea	1.6	20.3	15.6	55.5	1,248
Laos	2.1	29.6	11.3	47.1	1,819
Vietnam	2.7	27.0	16.4	43.5	13,075
China	6.2	5.5	2.9	56.4	12,593
Taiwan	7.9	7.1	5.2	53.9	367
Hong Kong	11.2	4.2	2.5	44.9	6,283
Japan	5.9	2.5	1.7	67.7	345
Korea	3.3	18.6	4.1	51.7	1,578
Other Asia[b]	15.1	5.7	2.8	47.6	542
Christmas Island	4.6	5.1	12.5	46.7	351
Cocos Islands	0.9	14.8	4.8	70.8	209
Nauru	9.8	1.3	1.3	61.5	153
Papua New Guinea	10.8	1.9	4.8	49.3	5,543
Solomon Islands	8.8	3.3	4.0	52.5	274
Vanuatu	9.7	2.5	4.0	54.1	279
New Caledonia	2.7	4.5	3.3	67.9	485
Fiji	9.5	6.4	4.0	49.0	4,018
Tonga	7.8	15.5	5.1	51.9	1,111
Cook Islands	2.7	19.1	10.8	42.8	334
Western Samoa	11.0	8.8	6.9	46.0	363
Kiribati and Tuvalu	12.4	3.4	2.2	62.9	89
Other Pacific	7.7	9.6	5.3	48.8	418
All Foreign	5.9	7.6	3.4	54.1	1,399,824
Australia	7.6	2.6	3.0	54.5	4,124,666

[a]Asian countries exclude western Asia (countries west of Afghanistan) and Asiatic Russia, Pacific countries exclude New Zealand and American countries bordering the Pacific.

[b]"Other Asia" covers the census category "Other Asia" or "Asia not elsewhere indicated." This category indicates countries such as Sikkim, Brunei, and Mongolia and is difficult to distribute between major divisions of South, East, and Southeast Asia.

ing unemployment allowances, it is worthwhile for both husbands and wives to seek jobs and, if unsuccessful, accept unemployment benefits; in fact wives often find jobs more easily than husbands.

It is not clear why some groups have lower than average proportions, and others higher, in the category "not in labor force." Plainly, though, such differences are not always associated with age; the proportion aged 15 to 19 and 65+ for Malaysia, for example, is much lower than the proportion of men not in the labor force. Maybe some of the differences can be explained by the presence of visitors; many Japanese, for instance, visit Australia for business as well as pleasure but, if counted in the census, are not considered part of the Australian labor force. (Table 8.4 excludes those younger than 15.)

Apart from a few small groups, the proportion of Asian–Pacific women in the "not in labor force" category (which includes housewives) is about average. One must remember that some Asian–Pacific groups have a marked predominance of women over men, nearly 2 to 1 for Filipinos and Thais (see the 1981 sex ratios in Table 8.1). In part this ratio reflects the immigration of women for teaching, nursing, and domestic jobs, but it also reflects the large number of Australian men who, when working abroad, marry Asian or Pacific Island women. Filipino women, for example, have won such a high reputation as capable and considerate wives and mothers that there have sprung up marriage marts to put Filipino women in touch with lonely Australian men in the outback—a modern version of the "picture bride" operation common with Californian Japanese and others in earlier days.

MULTICULTURALISM AND THE ETHNIC MIX

Much more could be said about Asian–Pacific immigrants in Australia and their contribution to the new multicultural society that is emerging; Australia has now almost as many ethnic and language groups as the United States, and non-Anglo–Celtic elements make up at least one quarter of the total population. Certainly Asian groups have their share of representation in Ethnic Communities Councils and on governmental advisory bodies; they also have their share of programs on the government-provided ethnic radio and television networks. A few take advantage of government subsidies for ethnic schools. Pacific Islanders, partly because they are much less numerous, make much less use of such facilities, though the organization representing the old South Sea Islander population is actively pressing the government for concessions in housing and education. (They were for so long lumped in with Australian Aborigines that they do not see why they should not share in the benefits now going to Aborigines.)

What does the future hold? Indochinese groups show signs of developing fairly solid communities. Reinforced by their refugee migration and fairly concentrated settlement, they may go the way of other solid groups, notably Italians, Greeks, Yugoslavs, and Lebanese; though even with these Mediterranean peoples out-marriage rates, low in the first generation, have risen to something between 50 and 90 percent with the second generation. Other Asian–Pacific groups show high out-marriage rates because of their high educational level; some have achieved permanent residence only because they married Australians when visiting as students or after meeting Australians working in their own country. Even as late as 1979, when many of the Asian–Pacific populations of Australia had become large enough to provide adequate numbers of brides and grooms, the out-marriage rates were still quite high, even for women, who are usually less likely to out-marry than men. Among marriages occurring within Australia, the 1975–1979 out-marriage proportions for women born in Asian–Pacific countries were: India, 66.9 percent; Pakistan, 77.7; Sri Lanka, 57.1; Malaysia, 65.0; Singapore, 88.2; Indonesia, 78.9; Philippines, 71.2; China, 55.2; Hong Kong, 67.9; Fiji, 81.0; other Commonwealth Pacific, 69.4; and other Pacific, 94.9 percent. The equivalent proportions for Mediterranean peoples in Australia were (1974–1978): Italy, 34.4; Greece, 17.9; Yugoslavia, 20.6; Lebanon, 19.3; and Malta, 55.3 percent. In short, at present Asian–Pacific groups are experiencing out-marriage very much more than most Mediterranean immigrants, even in the first generation, and most of these out-marriages are with native Australians.

The outcome, then, is not so much the perpetuation of large solid Asian–Pacific communities, except perhaps among the Indochinese, but the appearance of numerous Australians, widely scattered through Australian society, of mixed Asian–Pacific and other origins. Asians and Pacific Islanders are contributing, therefore, less to the perpetuation of a pluralist multicultural society than to the emergence of a new ethnically mixed society, reminiscent more of the American melting pot than of Swiss cantonal pluralism.

REFERENCES

Palfreeman, A. C.

   1967   *The Administration of the White Australia Policy.* Melbourne: Melbourne University Press.

Price, C. A.

   1970   "Overseas Migration to Australia, 1947–1970." In C. A. Price (ed.), *Australian Immigration Bibliography and Digest.* No. 2. Canberra: Australian National University, Department of Geography.

————— .

    1974   *The Great White Walls Are Built.* Canberra: Australian National University Press.

————— .

    1975   "Australian Immigration: The Whitlam Government 1972–75." In C. A. Price (ed.), *Australian Immigration Bibliography and Digest.* No. 3. Canberra: Australian National University, Department of Geography.

————— .

    1979   "Immigration and Population Policy: The Fraser Government." In C. A. Price (ed.), *Australian Immigration Bibliography and Digest.* No. 4. Canberra: Australian National University, Department of Geography.

Willard, M.

    1923   *History of the White Australia Policy to 1920.* Melbourne: Melbourne University Press. Reprinted Melbourne: Frank Cass, 1967.

Yarwood, A. T.

    1964   *Asian Migration to Australia.* Melbourne: Melbourne University Press.

9

New Zealand's Admission of Asians and Pacific Islanders

Andrew D. Trlin

Given its status as a developed country characterized by high levels of social and economic development attained under conditions of political stability, New Zealand is obviously attractive to potential migrants in less advantaged populations throughout Asia and the Pacific. New Zealand recognizes, however, that it has attendant internal and external responsibilities with respect to the volume and types of immigration that it can effectively manage—responsibilities that directly affect the admission of Asians and Pacific Islanders.

The general aim of this chapter is to examine the manner in which New Zealand exercises these responsibilities in its immigration policies and to indicate some consequent outcomes. The chapter is divided into three parts: a review of restrictive immigration legislation and policies relating to the admission of Asians and Pacific Islanders; an examination of New Zealand's current immigration policies with specific reference, where appropriate, to the entry of Asian and Pacific migrants; and, finally, to indicate policy outcomes, a review of the size and characteristics of Asian and Pacific populations in New Zealand using published results from the 1981 census.

RESTRICTIVE IMMIGRATION: 1881–1977

By 1865 the peak period of the Otago gold rush had ended and European miners were deserting the area in large numbers. To replace them, and thereby to sustain economic buoyancy, the Dunedin Chamber of Commerce brought over the first group of twelve Chinese gold diggers from the goldfields of Victoria, Australia. The Chinese population thereafter grew quickly—rising from 1,219 in 1867 to 4,217 in 1871—and just as quickly gave rise to a public clamor seeking restrictive immigration. It was a familiar sequence of events as evidenced by responses to Chinese immigration in California, Canada, and Australia (see Price, 1974).

According to Roy (1970:16), four general factors lay behind the demand for restrictive immigration. First and foremost, in the context of a primary producing economy dependent on fluctuating prices offered by world markets, was a working-class fear of cheap labor depressing an already uncertain income level. Second were similar middle-class fears of competition in the sphere of retail business—fears reinforced by a perceived threat posed by non-Europeans to middle-class respectability. Third were the politicians with strong racist attitudes who were prepared to make political capital of public fears. Finally there were the hostile stereotypes of persons not of British origin—stereotypes often adopted uncritically from British immigrants who had acquired their attitudes in India, China, Australia, and elsewhere. Over the period 1871–1920 these four factors promoted the introduction of restrictive legislation controlling immigration on racial or ethnic criteria.

In 1881 the first Chinese Immigrants Act was passed. It restricted the number of Chinese carried by any ship bound for New Zealand to one for every 10 tons weight of the ship and levied a poll tax of £10 per Chinese. These measures were subsequently made more severe by amendments to the Chinese Immigrants Act in 1888 and 1896 that raised the ratio of Chinese to ship's tonnage first to one to 100 tons and then to one to 200 tons while the poll tax increased tenfold to £100. The flow of arrivals was reduced but not before some 6,500 Chinese, the majority from Australia, had gained entry between 1874 and 1896.

While one "menace" was being checked another was being detected, namely, Indian hawkers. In 1896 the Indian population in New Zealand, consisting mainly of peddlers, hawkers, and domestics, was only forty-six persons. Nevertheless, the call was now for blanket legislation extending the restrictions on Chinese to all "Asiatics." Thus in 1895 an Asiatic and Other Immigration Bill was introduced, but it was defeated by the Legislative Council. In 1896 the bill was again put forward, this time amended to exclude British subjects (that is, Indians) from its operation, but failed to receive Royal Assent. The main problem was that Britain was seeking closer relations with Japan and wished to avoid causing offense. An alternative that would both protect New Zealand's interests and avoid embarrassment for Britain was clearly necessary.

The alternative recommended by Britain's prime minister, Joseph Chamberlain, was legislation of the kind already tried out in Natal; it imposed an educational test on would-be immigrants and evaded the question of race as a criterion of admission, but was rigged to exclude any unwanted candidates.

Chamberlain's suggestion was taken up. In 1899 an Immigration Restriction Act was passed that prescribed a language test. Unlike the Natal model, however, which involved a test "in any European language," the 1899 Bill had appended a schedule that set a prescribed test in English. Thus it was possible for a candidate to cram for the test, a fact that Indian immigrants (particularly from Fiji) quickly recognized and exploited. A decade passed before the Immigration Restriction Amendment Act of 1910 changed the fixed form of the literacy test in order to defeat crammers. The same act also attempted to close another loophole by imposing a £100 bond on transit passengers, tourists, businessmen, and students who would otherwise have been prohibited immigrants. If a Chinese "visitor" came into this category, he was required to post a bond of £200.

By 1916 there were only 2,147 Chinese and 181 Indians resident in New Zealand, a situation reflecting in part the temporary nature of Asian immigration but primarily the restrictions imposed between 1881 and 1910. Immediately after World War I, however, the numbers of Chinese and Indians seeking entry rose sharply; international travel was once again feasible, families separated by the war sought to be reunited, and there were also the fiancés and fiancées of New Zealand residents whose marriages had been delayed by the war. Thus, by the time of the 1921 census, the Chinese and Indian populations had quickly increased to 3,266 and 671, respectively. Inevitably, even as their numbers were growing, the demands for restrictive legislation were renewed, reinforced now by two influential sections of the population who felt that their interests were threatened. The Returned Serviceman's Association was concerned that nothing should impede the rehabilitation of its members; the trade unions, exercising their increasing power, took the orthodox view that the "Asian influx" was an attempt by capitalists to recruit cheap labor and depress the wages of native-born workers (see O'Connor, 1968:53–55). The outcome was new legislation in the form of the Immigration Restriction Amendment Act of 1920.

Under the act of 1920 an important principle was established and remained in effect until the early 1970s. This principle was to allow free entry of all persons of exclusively British (including Irish) birth and descent, to require all persons of non-British origin to obtain entry permits by application, and to invest the Minister of Customs (later the

Minister of Labor and Immigration) with sole discretionary power to approve or disallow such applications and hence entry to New Zealand. It was an important principle for at least three reasons. First, it concluded a long search for an instrument acceptable to Britain and to a world increasingly ready to condemn *overt* displays of racial prejudice. Second, it established what was, if not literally a White New Zealand policy, "at least one which was carefully designed to prevent the settlement of Asians" (O'Connor, 1968:41). And finally, it gave the government a more flexible instrument for immigration control than any that had previously been fashioned in New Zealand.

The flexibility and effectiveness of the Immigration Restriction Amendment Act was readily apparent during the 1920s and 1930s. In 1921, for example, it was decided to allow entry only to the wives and minor children of Indians who were permanent residents in New Zealand, but in 1926 provision was also made for the fiancés and fiancées of New Zealand-born Indians in recognition of a tradition of arranged matches and the fact that partners could not always be found among the prospective spouses locally available. Chinese immigration, on the other hand, was initially controlled by authorizing only one hundred entry permits a year; but in 1926, under renewed public pressure, the decision was taken to allow entry only to the wives and fiancées of New Zealand-born Chinese. Later there was a detectable softening in attitudes and policy; the poll tax on Chinese arrivals, abolished by the Finance Act of 1944, was not in fact levied after September 1934, and in 1937 the decision was made to admit as refugees the wives and children of Chinese who were not New Zealand-born. (The right of permanent residence was eventually granted to these refugees in 1947.)

During the years 1921 to 1945, no more than 1,870 Chinese and 1,113 Indians arrived intending permanent residence—a record that indicates (even if allowance is made for the effects of the 1930s depression and World War II) that Asian immigration had been effectively curbed by restrictive legislation and policy. Over the same period the total Asian population of New Zealand (Chinese, Indians, and others, including those born in New Zealand) increased from about 4,600 in 1921 to almost 7,900 in 1945.

Since 1945 the Asian population in New Zealand has continued to increase. By 1976 there were 14,860 Chinese (accounting for 0.47 percent of the total population compared with 0.29 percent in 1945) and 9,247 Indians (0.29 percent of the total population compared with about 0.09 percent in 1945). Part of this increase was due to a more liberal immigration policy that permitted the entry of refugees, persons of Eurasian origin from countries gaining independence after World War II, and numerous Asian students. Nevertheless, as recently as 1970 the permanent entry of Chinese and Indians was still, with few exceptions, limited "to the wives and legitimate or legitimated, unmarried infant children of males resident in New Zealand and to the wives, husbands, and fiancé(e)s of New Zealand citizens" (Department of Labour, 1970:6). Obviously natural increase accounted for a substantial part of the population growth. Indeed, in 1971 New Zealand-born members accounted respectively for 51.6 and 44.1 percent of the Chinese and Indian populations.

According to the Department of Labour (1970:5), the continuation of restraints upon Asian immigration during the 1950s and 1960s was in part based upon the perceived problems of assimilation posed by Asian immigrants but in part also a response to large-scale immigration from the South Pacific. Including the New Zealand-born, the 1976 census revealed a total of about 27,900 Samoans, 18,600 Cook Islanders, 5,700 Niueans, 4,000 Tongans, and 1,700 Tokelauans resident in the country. Overall these Pacific Island Polynesians accounted for almost 2 percent of the total population compared with 0.12 percent in 1945.

Effectively beginning during World War II, the immigration of Pacific Island Polynesians gathered pace during the 1950s and burst into full flood during the 1960s and early 1970s. Not all of these islanders have enjoyed equal rights of entry. Cook Islanders, Niueans, and Tokelauans had the benefit of New Zealand citizenship and hence unrestricted entry. For Tokelauans, moreover, the New Zealand government embarked upon a resettlement scheme whereby migrants were assisted to move to prearranged employment and accommodation in New Zealand. Prompted by recognition of problems arising from rapid population growth in atoll environments with severely limited resources, this resettlement scheme involved about 500 migrants during the period 1966–1975. Immigration from Western Samoa, Tonga, and Fiji, however, was to varying degrees restricted.

A quota system has existed for the permanent entry of Western Samoan citizens since 1962, when New Zealand signed the Treaty of Friendship on the declaration of Samoan independence. Quota applicants have been required to meet normal immigration requirements (concerning age, family size, health, and character) and to be in possession of acceptable guarantees of accommodation and employment. In 1970 the quota for Western Samoans was 1,500 persons per year—a figure that, in turn, was perceived to require restraints upon the entry of unskilled migrants from Tonga and Fiji. Accordingly, with few exceptions on humanitarian or occupational grounds, permanent entry of Tongans and Fijians was restricted to the fiancés, fiancées, husbands, wives, and children of New Zealand residents (Department of Labour,

1970:5). Provision was made for temporary migrant workers, however, as a form of aid by New Zealand to assist in the development of both Fiji and Tonga.

For Fijians, a scheme was set up during the 1960s (when local labor was scarce under conditions of full employment) whereby farmers could apply through the Department of Labour to obtain temporary workers for rural activities such as scrub cutting, tussock eradication, market gardening, and tobacco picking. A rather different scheme for Tongans was established in 1966, whereby they could enter New Zealand for a period of up to three months if they could produce evidence of means of support or, alternatively, if they could obtain a letter of guarantee signed by a New Zealand resident covering accommodation and maintenance. This scheme was not widely used until the early 1970s, when the number of Tongan arrivals increased in response to the availability of jobs.

The restrictions upon Fijians, Tongans, and even Western Samoans inevitably invited attempts to beat the system and deliberate noncompliance with the conditions of entry. There were cases, for example, where Fijian Indians on visitor or student permits contrived to marry in New Zealand and then pleaded compassionate grounds to gain permanent residence and citizenship. Rather more serious was the question of "overstaying." With the exception of a requirement applicable to Fijians there was, prior to 1978, no legal prohibition on visitors taking up employment. Until the early 1970s, control over the number of temporary migrants was also lax and no systematic efforts were made to trace or prosecute persons who overstayed their entry permits. These conditions appear to have engendered a feeling among Tongans, Western Samoans, and some Fijians that they could enter New Zealand as visitors, find employment, and become de facto permanent residents. It was undoubtedly a situation that also suited many New Zealand employers confronted by shortages of unskilled and semiskilled labor.

Government concern regarding overstayers, as well as high rates of permanent immigration from the United Kingdom, emerged as the economic climate deteriorated after 1972. It was feared that large immigration gains could not be absorbed without straining public services and jeopardizing employment opportunities for New Zealanders. The Labour government (1972–1975) responded with a major immigration policy review that drastically changed regulations governing permanent entry. In particular, the era of free entry for persons of exclusively British and Irish birth and descent, which had existed since the Immigration Restriction Amendment Act of 1920, came to an end in April 1974. At the same time steps were taken to deal with overstayers.

Much has been written about the overstayer issue (see De Bres and Campbell, 1976; Macdonald, 1977; Chan, 1981; NZCTD, 1982:41–44), and therefore only the more important details need be repeated here. In March 1974 police made "dawn raids" on Auckland houses where illegal immigrants were suspected of staying. Public feeling was aroused by reports of the insensitive treatment meted out to often innocent persons, and a more restrained procedure was subsequently adopted. In April 1974, a stay of proceedings for Tongan illegal immigrants was announced with the aim of getting as many as possible to register themselves voluntarily with the Department of Labour by 31 May in exchange for immunity from prosecution. More than 3,000 Tongans registered; of these the permits of 2,000 were extended to varying dates until December 1974 in order to give New Zealand employers a chance to replace key workers.

Moves to regulate Pacific immigration, initiated by the Labour government, were continued by the National Party administration elected in November 1975. Dawn raids were resumed, public calls for an amnesty for overstayers mounted, and another stay of proceedings was announced in April 1976—this time for persons of any nationality who had remained in the country after the expiry of their permits. By 1 July 1976, a total of 4,647 overstayers had registered, a figure well short of the numbers the Minister of Immigration believed to be in New Zealand. In October 1976, further controversy was sparked off by press reports, later confirmed, of random checks carried out by the police on Polynesians in the streets of Auckland. Savoring of police-state tactics, the practice infringed civil liberties, aroused hostility among Pacific Islanders, upset already strained relations with island governments, and gave rise to large public demonstrations. The minister responded by agreeing to reopen the amnesty register from 20 December 1976 to 31 January 1977. Final figures for the register showed 5,381 overstayers: 2,507 Tongans, 2,464 Western Samoans, 336 Fijians, and 74 people of other nationalities. Of those, 3,657 Pacific Islanders and 55 others were eventually granted permanent residence (Gill, 1977:71–72).

CURRENT IMMIGRATION POLICIES

To understand the government's current policies, it is necessary to know the considerations or responsibilities that have led to them. The first responsibility of government is management of the domestic economy. In view of New Zealand's small population (3.14 million in 1981) and its heavy reliance upon vulnerable primary exports to finance a broad spectrum of essential imports, the findings of studies on the economic effects of immigration are of special significance. In his assessment of the effects of British, Australian, North American, and Pacific Island migrants, McGill (1981:17) concluded:

Allowing more highly skilled immigrants into the country (assuming they have low fertility) does maximize the internal gain to New Zealand but produces a heavy strain on the level of imports. With Australian and North American immigrants in particular, both the potential gains (in production) and losses (in terms of the balance of payments) are large.

Pacific Island immigrants have a markedly different pattern of income and expenditure flows . . . due to their high fertility level as well as the low level of skills. However, the effects overall are more moderate than for the other groups examined.

Such conclusions have far-reaching policy implications. The immigration of skilled workers is undoubtedly in the national interest where the establishment of new industries requires skills unavailable in New Zealand, where it is impractical or uneconomic to develop domestic sources of certain specialist skills, and where it is necessary to replace skilled New Zealanders who have emigrated. The selection and entry of these and other migrants must, of course, be controlled to ensure that their numbers do not exceed the country's capacity to provide employment, housing, and various services.

Domestic considerations of the population's ethnic and racial composition, the maintenance of social cohesion, and harmonious intergroup relations may also be important. The "great question of assimilation and integration" was cited in 1970 as being second only to economic considerations in policy formulation and hence restrictions on entry. Past experience, it was claimed, indicated that "the greater and more obvious the differences between the immigrant and the average New Zealander, the longer and more difficult the period of assimilation and [the] greater the tendency of immigrants to hive off into little colonies which become self-sufficient and resistant to the process of assimilation" (Department of Labour, 1970:3).

Asians (along with Southern and Eastern Europeans) were among those cited as presenting "more difficult problems of assimilation." Accordingly, policy provisions were intended to limit the immigration of such groups to numbers that experience suggested could be absorbed without detriment to the "racial balance" of the country and its harmonious intergroup relationships. By 1970 this limitation was achieved for Asians (and others) by admitting only those migrants related in specific ways to nationals already permanently resident in New Zealand. Outside this range of relationships, individuals were considered if they could bring to New Zealand some needed skill or quality. Fernando (1975:354), for example, estimated that 150 Sri Lankan doctors took up positions in New Zealand between 1970 and 1974.

It must be emphasized that neither considerations of assimilation, integration, and racial harmony nor *specific* consequent limitations on the permanent entry of Asians (or others) have appeared in any official statements of policy since at least October 1978 (see Department of Labour, 1978, 1979, 1983a). Their absence may reflect an evolving perception of New Zealand as a multicultural society and sensitivity to issues of racism in international relations. Nevertheless, current provisions—in both their actual and potential operation—are such that the outcomes for Asian immigration may be little different from those of previous decades.

Finally, external considerations, to varying degrees political in nature, reflect New Zealand's foreign policy aims. As a member of the United Nations, New Zealand has long accepted its humanitarian responsibility to assist in the resettlement of refugees when so requested by the United Nations High Commissioner for Refugees (UNHCR)—for example, the admission of Indochinese refugees. New Zealand also continues to acknowledge a special responsibility toward the social and economic development of South Pacific countries that it formerly administered (Western Samoa) or that are British Commonwealth members (Tonga and Fiji). Recognition of this responsibility is manifested in special entry provisions of various types. Furthermore, as a developed country New Zealand provides assistance to its developing neighbors in the Pacific and Asia. Here immigration provisions are geared to the admission of overseas students, with the primary aim of training them "to a stage where they can be of value in the development programs of their own countries" (Department of Labour, 1983a:11–12).

Entry Permits

Under the Immigration Act of 1964, persons other than New Zealand citizens (including persons born in the Cook Islands, Niue, or Tokelau Islands) who seek either permanent or temporary residence in New Zealand are required to obtain an entry permit. Exempted from this requirement are Australian citizens, and other British Commonwealth citizens and citizens of the Republic of Ireland who have been granted the right to reside indefinitely without restriction in Australia. These exemptions are part of a special reciprocal arrangement between New Zealand and Australia that has facilitated trans-Tasman labor mobility of massive proportions, by local standards. During the three-year period ending 31 March 1979, for example, the net loss of permanent and long-term migrants to Australia accounted for 75.2 percent of New Zealand's total net loss of such migrants (−85,980); see Trlin and Spoonley (1980:A150–A153) and Pool (1980). More recently, for the year ending 31 March 1984, Australia was declared the country of last permanent residence by 38.7 percent of the 40,700 permanent and long-term arrivals recorded in New Zealand—a percentage well ahead of that for former residents of the United Kingdom (18.7 percent), United States (5.2 percent), Canada (2.4 percent), Western Samoa (2.6 percent), or the Cook Islands and Niue (1.37 percent). Freedom of movement between Australia and New Zealand, irrespective of their geographic proximity, is obviously a key factor in New Zealand's pattern of international migration.

Permanent Entry Policies

Setting aside such matters as specific criteria for permanent entry (health, character, age, prearranged accommodation, and the like), the important point is that permanent entry policies are selective. Three main categories exist for the granting of permits: occupational grounds, family reunification grounds, and humanitarian grounds.

Entry on occupational grounds. Prior to February 1986, preference was given to persons from "traditional source countries" who had qualifications and skills not only relevant to New Zealand but also in sufficient demand in New Zealand to warrant recruitment overseas (Department of Labour, 1983a:2).

The range of relevant skills—called the Occupational Priority List (OPL)—varies according to levels of employment and vacancies for particular skills (see Department of Labour, 1982:16–17, 1983b:5). Applicants with skills other than those on the current OPL may be considered if prospective employers can demonstrate that they have been unable to find a suitable New Zealand resident for the position. Aside from the question of skills, however, the preference expressed for prospective migrants from traditional source countries (United Kingdom, Netherlands, and others) represented an important restriction upon the admission of Asians and certain Pacific Islanders. In fact, skilled persons from developing countries were specifically excluded from consideration on occupational grounds unless their skills were needed in New Zealand, were not in demand in the country of origin, and could not be obtained from a developed country. This aspect of policy was based upon the perceived actual or potential need for skilled persons in developing countries and sought to avoid the depletion of such skills.

The removal in February 1986 of the traditional source-countries preference, together with the ending of the embargo upon recruitment of skilled workers from developing countries, is obviously a major policy change in relation to permanent entry on occupational grounds. Taken at face value, it may be perceived as an important dismantling of the last props of the old White New Zealand immigration policy, and also as a change facilitating the increased entry of suitably qualified Asians and Pacific Islanders. Whether or not the latter occurs, however, will depend upon at least two factors: first, the standards or criteria set for assessment of OPL skills and qualifications held by Asians and Pacific Islanders; and, second, the establishment of recruitment procedures and facilities matching those currently existing for the United Kingdom and other Western European nations.

Entry on family reunification grounds. Application categories for family reunification with New Zealand citizens or permanent residents include: spouses and dependent children; parents who have no children living in their own country; brothers and sisters and independent children if they are single, have no children or other dependents, and are alone in their country of residence; and other cases involving special circumstances, such as "a high degree of financial or emotional dependence on the New Zealand citizen or permanent resident." Though somewhat austere, these application categories are nevertheless more liberal than those applied to Chinese and Indians as recently as 1970.

Fiancés and fiancées are not covered by categories relating to close family ties. Such persons are normally considered under temporary entry policy as visitors who may subsequently apply to have their status changed to that of permanent resident. Current policy makes it clear, however, that "there is no automatic right to permanent status simply by virtue of a marriage" to a New Zealand citizen or permanent resident (Department of Labour, 1983a:7). This aspect of policy may be perceived as a warning to temporary migrants who resort to marriage as a device to attain permanent resident status for which they would not normally be qualified. Prior experience with marriages of convenience on the part of some Fijian Indians, Tongans, and Asian students has apparently resulted in a tightening of immigration policy.

Entry on humanitarian grounds. Humanitarian grounds apply to refugees, but others who have some family connection with New Zealand may qualify if it can be shown that their circumstances "are significantly worse than those of others in their community." Refugee schemes are considered by the government in response to UNHCR requests and after consultation with New Zealand voluntary agencies exercising the function of refugee sponsorship. The refugee selection process places emphasis upon the humanitarian circumstances of each case, but it is usual to look for people who can be expected to adapt readily to New Zealand society. Account is taken also of any previous association with New Zealand and of links with friends or relatives in the country. For Indochinese refugees, priority has been given in recent years to those with immediate family members already resident in New Zealand; once

established, refugee settlers may sponsor the entry of relatives under
normal family reunification policy.

The number of refugees accepted at any one time depends primarily on the availability of both long-term resettlement resources (accommodation, employment, and so forth) and suitable sponsors. Political
considerations and public opinion, however, may be also influential as
evidenced by the admission of Indochinese refugees. Having officially
recognized Hanoi in 1973, the Labour government was determined to
avoid offending North Vietnam, which had objected to the evacuation
of orphans and refugees during the last days of the Saigon government
(Binzegger, 1980:60–61). This stance, coupled with increasing domestic economic difficulties in the mid-1970s, produced a situation in which
New Zealand's participation at the time of "Operation Babylift" (April
1975) was limited to the admission of three orphan babies, and only
535 Indochinese refugees were resettled prior to March 1979. Political
and economic considerations might have been less influential had public
opinion in favor of refugee admission been more in evidence. Such was
not the case until the plight of refugees eventually captured the public
eye in late 1978 (see Bowie, 1981). During the five years prior to March
1984, about 5,000 Indochinese were resettled.

Entry on other grounds. Beyond the three grounds described above are
other, less common, means by which persons may qualify for permanent entry. The Minister of Immigration, for example, may approve applications by persons who have distinguished themselves in the arts,
sciences, or public life overseas and by those who have been actively
promoting or protecting New Zealand's interests overseas. There are
also provisions relating to entrepreneurs and Western Samoan citizens
that warrant more detailed attention.

Entrepreneurs of proven ability wishing to invest capital or establish businesses in New Zealand, whatever their country of origin and
irrespective of their skills or age, may be considered for entry if it can
be determined that they meet other immigration criteria and will bring
capital and skills that will benefit the country. "Passive" investments
(as in real estate) are not acceptable under this policy. Thus far the number of successful applications has been very small and has included
a mere handful of Asians. Nevertheless, the provision has a significant
long-term potential in relation to the admission of entrepreneurs from
Hong Kong, Taiwan, Japan, and other Asian countries.

As noted earlier in this chapter, a quota system for permanent entry
of Western Samoans has operated since 1962. The quota level, currently
set over and above the numbers qualifying for entry under normal immigration policy (specifically family reunification), has been subject to

some variation. During the term of the third Labour government (1972–1975), the quota was increased from 1,500 to 1,650 per year and then reduced to 1,100 in January 1976 (a level at which it has remained) by the newly elected National government as part of a general restraint on immigration. There have been allegations that the quota, undeniably a form of favorable treatment, was not filled during the late 1970s owing to New Zealand restrictions (unspecified) that produced delays of three or four years before entry was attained (see NZCTD, 1982:37). In 1982, as a result of a Privy Council decision in favor of a Samoan overstayer who claimed that she was not liable for conviction or deportation because she was a New Zealand citizen (under the terms of legislation passed in 1928 and 1948), the legality of the quota and other restrictions on Samoan migrants was put in doubt. Full details of the case are available elsewhere (Ministry of Foreign Affairs, 1983), but one major implication of the Privy Council's decision was that about 100,000 people—more than three-fifths of the total population of Western Samoa—were eligible for unrestricted entry to New Zealand. Discussions between New Zealand and Western Samoa produced a remedy in the form of a protocol to the 1962 Treaty of Friendship between the two countries. To give effect to the protocol, and hence to maintain the status quo with regard to Samoan immigration, New Zealand passed the Citizenship (Western Samoa) Act, which became law on 14 September 1982.

Temporary Entry Policies

Excluding policies relating to nonworking visitors and tourists, there are three sets of policies that directly or indirectly govern the temporary immigration of Pacific Islanders and Asians. The details of these policies, as set out by the Department of Labour (1983a:10–12), are discussed in the following paragraphs.

Entry of managerial and other skilled overseas staff. Provision is made for the entry of employees and their dependents brought in by an employing company in New Zealand or by overseas companies that have tendered successfully for major work contracts in New Zealand. The employing company must give an undertaking that the applicant possesses a specialist skill and will be filling a position for which it has not been possible to recruit a suitably qualified New Zealand resident. This provision for managerial and skilled staff is of special interest because it accounts for a high proportion of the Japanese migrants resident in New Zealand at any one time.

Entry of South Pacific workers. The scheme introduced in the 1960s for the recruitment of Fijians to be employed in rural work still functions and is designed to be self-regulating in relation to job opportunities. Workers, in the main selected by the Fiji government, obtain permits initially for four months, with the option of a two-month extension. To spread the employment opportunities among as many people as possible, each worker is required to spend twelve months in Fiji before reentering New Zealand.

The first official urban work permit scheme was introduced for Tongans in January 1975; the period of employment was four months, which could be extended to six months. Similar schemes were introduced in February and June 1976 for Fiji and Western Samoa, respectively. In November 1976, these three schemes were reviewed and amalgamated. At present the urban scheme provides for migrant worker recruitment where local labor is not available and the period of employment is eleven months. Responsibility for the selection of workers and for ensuring that a period of twelve months elapses before any worker reenters New Zealand has rested with the governments of Fiji, Tonga, and Western Samoa (Department of Labour, 1983c).

The urban work scheme—distinguished by rigorous entry and departure provisions—was introduced in response to the overstayer problems of the mid-1970s. It was for this reason also that, under agreements with the respective governments, the maximum duration of other temporary permits normally issued to Tongans, Fijians, and Western Samoans was set at a level (currently three months except for parents wishing to visit adult children) below that applying to other nonworking visitors (currently six months). The Department of Labour (1983a:9) states that "this limit operates to protect the official Work Permit Scheme . . . and make it less economic for visitors to come to New Zealand on the off-chance of finding work." Furthermore, it is an offense now for any person (irrespective of nationality) on a temporary permit to take employment while in New Zealand without having specific authority to do so. Clearly, the overstayer issue (a problem still evident among Tongan, Fijian, and Samoan immigrants) produced a tightening of immigration regulations.

Entry of overseas students. The admission of overseas students is perceived primarily as an important contribution to the development of their homelands. Preference is given first to students from the South Pacific, then to those from Southeast Asia, and finally to others "from countries with which New Zealand has close political and trade links" (Department of Labour, 1983a:11–12). Students seeking entry are subject to normal immigration requirements, to restrictions upon employment and the courses of study that may be undertaken, and to minimum English language ability requirements.

The susceptibility of foreign students to learning problems and other difficulties of adjustment, commonly related to competence in the host language, has been documented in a growing body of international literature. Overseas students in New Zealand appear to be no exception (see Furneaux, 1973; Leo, 1973; Koh, 1980), and thus the English language ability requirement can be readily defended. Nevertheless, there is inevitably scope for debate regarding the instruments and standards adopted for the assessment of this requirement. It is sufficient here simply to note that the development and implementation since the early 1970s of Language Achievement Tests for Overseas Students (LATOS) have been the subject of a heated controversy in New Zealand that has also caused political and diplomatic embarrassment abroad (see St. George, 1981).

Policy Implications for Pacific and Asian Immigration

The policies discussed above indicate that Pacific Islanders have clear advantages over Asians (and most others apart from citizens and certain permanent residents of Australia) with respect to immigration to New Zealand. These advantages include the New Zealand citizenship and hence unrestricted entry of Cook Islanders, Niueans, and Tokelauans; the Western Samoan quota; the temporary work schemes for Fijians, Tongans, and Western Samoans; and the preference given to South Pacific students. While the first of these advantages may be dismissed as a colonial legacy, the remainder can be interpreted as conscious responses to what New Zealand regards as its external responsibilities. It must be acknowledged, however, that the discharge of responsibilities in the form of immigration policies is colored by self-interest, and the effects upon Pacific Island societies are far from being uniformly beneficial.

For the Pacific Islands, emigration has reduced population growth rates, relieved pressure on available land, provided employment and educational opportunities, and generated income in the form of remittances. But emigration has also depleted the young portion of the labor force, produced shortages of skilled labor (see Macpherson, 1983), and often resulted in high levels of dependency upon remittances (NZCTD, 1982:22–24). Economic recessions in New Zealand, by depressing immigrant employment opportunities and hence remittances, may therefore have a devastating effect on small Pacific Island economies.

For New Zealand, the immigration of Pacific Islanders has distinct economic advantages that are enhanced by requiring an employment guarantee for Samoan quota applicants and by gearing temporary permits to current employment opportunities. Thus guest workers from the Pacific may, as Miles (1984) put it, be summoned by New Zealand capital when required and similarly dispensed with. As unemployment levels have increased since the mid-1970s, the number of Fijians, Tongans, and Samoans approved for entry under the work permit scheme has declined—dropping from 906 for the year ending 31 March 1978 to a level of only 288 for the year ending 31 March 1984 (Department of Labour, 1984a). The impact of New Zealand's economic recession was not, of course, confined to temporary migrants alone; Bedford's (1983:20–23) analysis of South Pacific arrivals and departures revealed a net gain of 7,050 for the period 1976–1981, compared with 23,520 for the years 1971–1976. Concentrated in semiskilled and unskilled urban-based manufacturing occupations, heavily concentrated in the state rental and low-cost housing areas of Auckland and other cities (Trlin, 1984), and prominent among discrimination complainants (Trlin, 1982:177), Pacific Islanders in New Zealand form part of what has been described as an emergent "eth-class" (Macpherson, 1977) or "Polynesian proletariat" (NZCTD, 1982:51–54). Nevertheless, they continue to seek entry for the attainment of goals that remain elusive in their homelands.

The embargo on recruitment of skilled workers from developing countries has until recently precluded, with few exceptions, the permanent entry of Asian immigrants on occupational grounds. But what about skilled migrants from Japan or perhaps Singapore and Hong Kong? Such applicants have been handicapped, if not excluded, by the preference expressed for "people from traditional source countries"— that is, the United Kingdom, Netherlands, and other West European countries. A few have qualified as entrepreneurs and much larger numbers for temporary residence as company employees (notably Japanese) and especially students. In general, therefore, the vast majority of Asian migrants seeking permanent entry to New Zealand have been restricted to qualification for entry on family reunification or humanitarian grounds. Indeed, for the year ending 31 March 1984, only 403 permanent entry applications were approved for applicants from twenty-one Asian nations; of these, 9.7 percent were approved on occupational grounds, 50.4 percent on family reunification grounds, and 39.9 percent on humanitarian grounds. (The last were almost exclusively refugees from Kampuchea, Vietnam, and Laos.) During the same period, 1,087 applications from United Kingdom and Northern Ireland citizens were approved for permanent entry—39.8 percent on occupational grounds, 58.5 percent for family reunification, and 1.6 percent on humanitarian grounds. It is still too early to determine what effects, if any, the policy change of February 1986 has had upon the permanent entry of Asians, but it seems reasonable to anticipate an increase in the number of entry applications approved on occupational grounds and hence some shift in the relative importance of family and humanitarian grounds.

Despite restrictions on entry, Asian immigration has increased since the early 1970s. Most of this increase is accounted for by refugees— ranging from 42 Chinese refugees from Indonesia in 1970–1971 to 5,549 Indochinese refugees accepted between 1975 and March 1984 (Department of Labour, 1984b). Humanitarian considerations have therefore proved to be of more than token importance. As for the growth and resilience of immigrant communities, however, the admission of refugees is less important than approval of applications for family reunification and marriage. Where durable cultural values continue to favor in-group marriage, an appropriate policy provision becomes quite significant. Kasanji (1980:228) notes that among Indians in New Zealand, for example, "marriage within one's own subcaste is still the custom" and that if such a marriage cannot be arranged in New Zealand, then parents and their adult sons and daughters will travel abroad to find a suitable partner. Pressure for in-group marriage may also arise from prejudice among members of the host population. A survey in Auckland, employing the Bogardus Social Distance Scale, found that in 1970 fewer than 15 percent of the New Zealand-born respondents were prepared to accept immigrants from China, India, or Japan to close kinship by marriage (Trlin, 1971:146). Under conditions such as these, a policy provision for marriage will continue to facilitate an inflow of brides, grooms, fiancés, and fiancées.

Immigrants arriving for reasons of marriage, together with wives and dependent children admitted for family reunification, are characteristics of the chain migration process. Today it is a process enforced by immigration policy. Chain migration has long been recognized as the key feature of New Zealand's Chinese and Indian communities (see Taher, 1970; Zodgekar, 1980), as a prime determinant of their settlement patterns, and, ironically, as a process that hampers progress along the social and economic dimensions of assimilation.

NEW ZEALAND'S PACIFIC AND ASIAN POPULATIONS

Results from the 1981 census (Department of Statistics, 1983a, 1983b) indicate the size and characteristics of New Zealand's Pacific and Asian populations defined in terms of birthplace and ethnic origin. Though of interest in themselves, the demographic configurations of these population groups have in some cases a particular value as indicators of the effects of New Zealand's past and present immigration policies.

Birthplace Data

In 1981 the foreign-born accounted for 14.8 percent of the 3.14 million people usually resident in New Zealand. Immigrants from the United Kingdom, Australia, continental Europe, and North America were predominant, accounting for 76.2 percent of the foreign-born. Most of the remainder were from thirty Asian and Pacific birthplaces, of which only thirteen had in excess of 1,000 members (Table 9.1). If Cook Islanders, Niueans, and Tokelauans are set aside, on the grounds of New Zealand citizenship and hence unrestricted entry, then the number of groups with more than 1,000 members falls to ten. Exclude also those immigrants of "European" ethnic origin—the offspring or descendants of Dutch settlers in Indonesia and those of British, Australian, and New Zealand citizens (serving as administrators, company managers, and the like) in Fiji, Hong Kong, India, Malaysia, Singapore, and Sri Lanka—and the significance of Pacific and Asian birthplaces is further reduced. The inescapable conclusion arising from these points is that New Zealand's immigration policies have over a long period success-fully restricted Pacific and especially Asian immigration in favor of migrants from traditional European sources.

Duration of residence data indicate the recency of immigration; for eleven of the thirty birthplaces listed in Table 9.1, at least 65 percent of the immigrants arrived during the nine years preceding the 1981 census. Prominent among these new arrivals are Tongans, Malaysians, Singaporeans, and Indochinese refugees (Vietnamese, Kampucheans, and Laotians), the last providing stark evidence of the humanitarian component in immigration policy. Other policy provisions are suggested by new arrivals from Japan and the Philippines. The temporary entry and turnover of company employees explains why more than half of the Japanese are in the 0–4 years residence category, while almost all the longer-term residents (10 years plus) are the wives of New Zealand servicemen (members of either J-Force, in the allied occupation of Japan, or K-Force during the Korean War). Entry on the grounds of marriage to a New Zealand resident is also the key factor underlying the recency and female domination of immigration from the Philippines.

To complete the picture of recency in immigration, it may be noted that for another eight birthplaces about 40 to 59 percent of migrants had been resident for less than ten years. In terms of population numbers, the most important origins in this category were Hong Kong, Fiji, Cook Islands, Samoa, and Niue—the majority in the four latter groups arriving since the early 1960s. There were only three major birthplaces wherein the percentage resident for twenty years or more exceeded 50 percent: Indonesia (Dutch nationals arriving during the late 1940s and 1950s), China, and India.

The sex composition, age, residential distribution, and employment status of the various birthplace groups (Table 9.1) may be summarized as follows. First, contrary to the masculinity typical of long-distance international migration, the proportions of males and females were generally well balanced, although there were three cases (French Polynesia, Japan, and the Philippines) of female domination. Reflecting perhaps a liberal admission policy for wives and fiancées, this feature may be related to the relative proximity of South Pacific birthplaces. Second, consistent with the age selectivity (both natural and enforced by policy) and recency of international migration, the age compositions were noticeably youthful. Third, with four minor exceptions, at least 80 percent of each birthplace group was located in the twenty-three main urban areas of New Zealand, and Auckland was the prime location for Pacific migrants. Entry requirements concerning guarantees of employment and accommodation, along with kin-based sponsorship of arrivals, are probably the main determinants of this settlement pattern.

As expected, given the youthfulness of the migrants, the percentage employed full-time in the labor force was typically above the national average of 58 percent. Where the percentage in full-time employment was low, the explanation was almost invariably to be found in an exceptionally high percentage of full-time students as illustrated by the example of migrants from Papua New Guinea, Malaysia, Singapore, and Thailand. Obviously, the provision for the temporary entry of overseas students has a profound effect upon the size and age composition of some birthplace groups, as well as their urban concentration and duration of residence characteristics.

The preference given to overseas students from the South Pacific and Southeast Asia is confirmed in annual statistics published by the Department of Education. In 1981, Pacific and Asian students (2,896 in number) accounted for 86.4 percent of all overseas students in New Zealand. The major countries of origin were Malaysia, Fiji, Samoa, Singapore, Tonga, and the Cook Islands; Malaysians accounted for about 37 percent of all Pacific and Asian students at that time. While the majority of students were enrolled in universities and other tertiary education institutions (67.6 percent), secondary school enrollments were also significant, especially for Pacific Islanders as compared with Asians (Department of Education, 1982).

Ethnic Origin Data

In terms of the size and hence significance of immigrant ethnic groups, a major drawback of simple birthplace statistics is the invisibility of New Zealand-born generations. Another drawback is the phenomenon of birthplace fragmentation, which conceals the cultural affinity and eth-

Table 9.1. Pacific and Asian Birthplace Groups in New Zealand: Selected Characteristics, 1981

Birthplace	Usually Resident Population, 1981[a]	Ethnic Origin (% European)[b]	Sex Composition (% Male)	Age Group % 0-14	Age Group % 15-44	Residential Distribution % Urban[c]	Residential Distribution % Auckland[d]	Employment Status[e] (% Full-time) In Labor Force	Employment Status[e] (% Full-time) Student	Duration of Residence in N.Z.[f] (Years) % 0-4	Duration of Residence in N.Z.[f] (Years) % 5-9
Pacific Islands											
American Samoa	123	NA	43.9	24.4	61.0	97.6	63.4	66.7	10.0	12.2	17.1
Cook Islands	13,848	2.4	50.3	16.6	64.2	87.5	63.9	70.0	4.1	17.0	28.5
Fiji	6,372	45.1	52.3	11.6	66.2	84.0	53.9	62.7	12.1	23.7	20.5
French Polynesia	216	NA	36.1	18.0	41.7	88.9	68.0	41.7	6.7	18.0	20.8
Kiribati	120	NA	45.0	22.5	60.0	82.5	50.0	57.6	18.2	25.0	20.0
Niue	5,091	2.0	50.0	15.7	59.9	95.7	85.5	67.0	4.5	15.8	23.6
Norfolk Island	177	NA	52.5	18.6	39.0	78.0	40.7	62.5	2.1	18.6	13.6
Papua New Guinea	636	NA	50.9	49.5	45.3	76.4	32.1	48.6	29.0	37.0	31.3
Pitcairn Island	117	NA	48.7	7.7	43.6	97.4	33.3	64.9	8.1	7.5	10.0
Samoa	24,141	4.4	49.6	11.0	75.2	96.5	64.3	69.9	4.8	14.9	27.6
Solomon Islands	201	NA	55.2	29.8	58.2	74.6	32.8	55.6	28.9	34.8	19.7
Tokelau Islands	1,281	0.5	51.7	10.8	67.9	90.9	19.2	60.3	9.7	11.5	18.7
Tonga	5,232	6.4	51.6	14.9	66.7	95.3	82.2	65.8	7.9	26.9	38.8
Tuvalu	123	NA	51.2	14.6	53.7	82.9	48.8	57.1	11.4	29.3	19.5
Vanuatu	120	NA	57.5	27.5	57.5	60.0	32.5	40.1	37.0	27.5	25.0
Asia											
Burma	369	NA	47.1	1.6	34.1	81.3	46.3	54.5	1.6	9.0	9.8
China (including Taiwan)	4,269	8.5	49.6	2.1	40.2	83.9	33.4	63.2	2.2	15.4	7.9
Hong Kong	1,290	30.0	48.1	19.1	63.7	90.0	44.4	62.9	15.8	27.7	22.8
India	6,018	40.3	51.7	3.2	53.9	84.1	42.8	63.9	3.4	12.1	14.6
Indonesia	1,695	74.9	54.7	5.8	41.9	83.5	39.3	62.8	5.8	15.9	11.1

Japan	744	13.3	38.3	19.3	60.1	92.7	43.1	50.0	10.5	53.2	16.9
Kampuchea	729	NA	51.4	25.5	65.0	86.8	24.3	69.1	11.0	86.8	3.3
Laos	213	NA	57.7	29.6	62.0	93.0	50.7	60.0	10.0	84.3	2.9
Malaysia	3,330	22.2	57.5	9.5	83.6	89.4	29.2	48.1	38.4	39.6	25.5
Pakistan	384	NA	53.9	3.9	43.7	82.0	41.4	60.2	4.9	11.7	15.6
Philippines	405	NA	28.8	14.1	77.8	84.4	34.8	50.0	9.5	70.1	16.4
Singapore	1,884	55.7	45.7	37.2	56.4	80.1	35.7	49.4	27.0	38.4	27.1
Sri Lanka	936	23.4	52.2	14.4	57.0	80.1	24.7	63.2	18.4	17.9	52.9
Thailand	303	21.8	35.6	32.7	59.4	87.1	30.7	37.7	31.9	59.4	14.8
Vietnam	2,406	0.9	55.8	30.0	63.2	87.0	31.5	71.1	12.1	85.3	4.4
N.Z. Total Population	3,143,307	85.8	49.7	26.9	44.9	67.5	24.3	58.0	6.5	—	—

Source: Department of Statistics (1983a).

^a*Usually resident population* includes the population present at the place of enumeration on census night but excludes persons whose usual residence is overseas (e.g., tourists, ships' crews). For example, for the birthplace Japan, the de facto population present on census night (1981) was 1,767, compared with the usually resident population of 744. Only usually resident population statistics have been employed for calculations in this table.

^b*Ethnic origin* refers to blood mixture of races within a person and is calculated by adding one-half of mother's ethnic origin to one-half of father's ethnic origin. Half or more origin is the general criterion for inclusion in an ethnic group, and cases of half origins are currently assigned to one particular ethnic classification according to a predetermined priority order, with "European" as the category of lowest priority. For example, a person who is half-Samoan and half-European is counted as a Samoan.

^c*Percentage resident in urban areas* refers here to the percentage of the population that resided in the twenty-three main urban areas. A main urban area is defined as being centered on a major city or borough, includes neighboring territory regarded as suburban, and had a 1981 census population of 30,000 or more.

^d*Percentage resident in Auckland* refers to the percentage of the population that resided in the four combined main urban areas of Northern Auckland, Western Auckland, Central Auckland, and Southern Auckland.

^eEmployment status percentages refer only to the population of ages 15 years and over. The official minimum school-leaving age in New Zealand is 15 years.

^fDuration of residence percentages have been calculated on the basis of the complete usually-resident population (including those persons who did not specify duration of residence). In some cases persons in the "not specified" category account for a substantial share of the birthplace group (Samoa, 16.5 percent); thus caution is required, and the percentage might best be regarded as a conservative indicator of recency of immigration.

nic group membership of migrants from diverse birthplaces. To some extent both problems may be resolved via the use of ethnic origin data from the 1981 census. Even on this criterion, however, of the eleven largest Pacific and Asian ethnic origin groups, only Samoans accounted for more than 1 percent of New Zealand's usually resident population (Table 9.2). On the other hand, for the Pacific ethnic origin groups, the numbers resident in New Zealand become more significant when expressed as a percentage of the population back home. Tongans in New Zealand equaled about 7 percent of the mid-1981 population of Tonga, but the percentages for Samoans, Cook Islanders, and Niueans were 26.6, 132.6, and 269.0 percent, respectively.

The contribution of New Zealand-born generations to the population size of these groups varied considerably, reflecting the influence of such factors as the recency and type of migration (permanent versus temporary) and the presence of "other" foreign-born. Thus the New Zealand-born were of little importance to the Vietnamese population (recent refugee arrivals) but accounted for about 30 percent of the Japanese, Tongan, and Fijian groups (which include high proportions of temporary migrants) and for more than 40 percent of established groups such as the Samoans, Cook Islanders, Chinese, and Indians. Included among the "other" foreign-born Chinese and Indians, and constituting the majority of persons in these categories, are students from Malaysia, Singapore, Hong Kong, and Fiji.

Where data were available, it was found that the dependency ratios were low and that the young (0–14 years) accounted for most of the dependents (Table 9.2). The dependency load of youth, in part the predictable outcome of recent arrival and age selectivity in migration (reinforced by entry requirements for persons other than Cook Islanders, Niueans, and Tokelauans), is related to fertility patterns. For ever-married Pacific Island Polynesian women of ages 25–29 and 30–34, the mean number of children born alive was 2.11 and 2.99, respectively, compared with 1.04 and 1.90 for Chinese women and 1.28 and 2.04 for Indian women in the same age groups (Department of Statistics, 1983a:89). It is not surprising, therefore, that the Chinese and Indian youth loads were well below those for the Samoan, Cook Islander, and Tokelauan populations.

The dependency ratio is assumed to measure the number of dependents each hundred persons in the working-age years (15–59, defined by the official school-leaving age and eligibility for National Superannuation in New Zealand) must support. In its conventional form, however, the ratio fails to account for students 15–24 years of age, for persons 60 years of age and above who remain in the labor force, and for the social roles that restrict female labor force participation. A more

Table 9.2. Pacific and Asian Ethnic Origin Groups in New Zealand: Selected Characteristics, 1981

Ethnic Origin[a]	Usually Resident Population, 1981[a]		Birthplace			Dependency Ratio (DR)[c]			Economic Dependency Ratio[d]
	Number	% of N.Z. Population	% Homeland-Born[b]	% N.Z.-Born	% Other	Young	Old	Total	
Pacific Island									
Cook Island Maori	23,880	0.76	54.5	43.1	2.4	64.6	5.0	69.6	128.7
Fijian	1,836	0.06	68.1	28.6	3.3	43.3	3.8	47.1	96.8
Niuean	8,079	0.26	58.4	38.1	3.5	58.7	9.0	67.7	123.3
Samoan	42,078	1.34	51.8	46.3	1.9	77.1	2.8	79.9	149.5
Tokelauan	2,274	0.07	52.8	39.3	7.9	80.9	7.2	88.1	187.1
Tongan	6,900	0.22	64.7	31.5	3.8	60.1	6.9	67.0	126.4
Asia									
Chinese	18,480	0.59	20.9	48.7	30.4	42.1	11.1	53.2	113.3
Indian	11,244	0.36	30.8	45.9	23.3	47.7	6.1	53.8	112.8
Japanese	1,026	0.03	61.7	31.3	7.0	NA	NA	NA	NA
Sri Lankan	933	0.03	73.6	15.1	11.3	NA	NA	NA	NA
Vietnamese	1,371	0.04	86.0	9.2	4.8	NA	NA	NA	NA

Sources: Department of Statistics (1983a; 1983b).

[a]See Table 9.1 for explanations of usually resident population and ethnic origin.

[b]This category is limited to persons of a particular ethnic origin who were born in the country commonly associated with that ethnic origin— e.g., Indians born in India, Chinese born in China and Taiwan.

[c]$DR\ Young = \dfrac{\text{usually resident pop. 0–14 years}}{\text{usually resident pop. 15–59 years}} \times 100;$ $DR\ Old = \dfrac{\text{usually resident pop. 60 years and over}}{\text{usually resident pop. 15–59 years}} \times 100;$

DR Total = sum of DR Young and DR Old.

[d]Economic dependency ratio = $\dfrac{\text{usually resident pop. 0–14 years} + \text{usually resident pop. 15 years and over not working}}{\text{usually resident pop. 15 years and over in labor force (full-time and part-time)}} \times 100.$

refined economic dependency ratio was therefore calculated that produced results approximately double those derived from the conventional measure (Table 9.2). Most of the increase was accounted for by women (presumably engaged in childrearing) in the case of the Pacific ethnic origin groups, but full-time overseas students were a key artificial component in the Chinese and Indian dependency loads.

CONCLUSION

The immigration of Asians and Pacific Islanders (other than Cook Islanders, Niueans, and Tokelauans) is subject to a formidable array of restrictions. These controls not only determine the number and types of migrants granted admission, but also shape the demographic and social character of immigrant populations within New Zealand. To some outside observers, it may seem that the current situation, for Asians in particular, is little different from that produced by a combination of legislation and policy in the 1920s. In one sense this is true, given the continuing importance of family reunification as a justification for permanent entry. But it may also be argued that a change has occurred in the form of a transition from restrictions motivated by prejudice, racism, and fear to restrictions framed in accord with perceived responsibilities both at home and abroad.

Chief among the responsibilities underlying current immigration policies are management of the domestic economy, the provision of assistance toward the social and economic development of less-advantaged Pacific and Asian neighbors, and the humanitarian resettlement of refugees and family reunification. These responsibilities, manifest in specific policies for either permanent or temporary entry, have facilitated a more liberal and diverse immigration of Asians than most New Zealanders would have considered desirable three decades ago. They have also regulated, with some success, the more recent pressures for entry exerted by Pacific Islanders. Yet even now, despite the recent change in policy for permanent entry on occupational grounds, many Asians might regard New Zealand's policies with suspicion. This skepticism is understandable: The admission of refugees is ephemeral, as is the presence of students and temporary workers; and whereas the embargo on the admission of skilled workers may have been in the interests of developing countries, it may also have conveniently appeased sectional interests within New Zealand characterized by long-standing fears, prejudices, and racism. To such a view there is no convincing practical answer beyond a plea for trust in New Zealand's goodwill.

What are the future prospects for Asian and Pacific immigration? The answer to this question probably depends upon the successful handling of difficulties that have plagued the New Zealand economy since the early 1970s. If balanced growth is restored to the economy and inflation and unemployment are reduced, it may be expected that New Zealand will renew and expand commitments to the social and economic development of its South Pacific neighbors. The Samoan quota could be raised; temporary work permit schemes could be expanded; and even family reunification policies could be liberalized in the case of Fijians, Tongans, and Samoans. Such actions might be motivated by a desire to restore relationships strained and disrupted by the overstayer issue in the mid-1970s and the more recent Samoan citizenship crisis. Of course, the flow of South Pacific immigrants could be substantially reduced by more effective assistance in the development of island industries, tourism, and educational opportunities. Examples elsewhere in the world, however, offer little hope of such an outcome in the immediate future.

For Asians, it is frankly difficult to envisage the New Zealand government being able to offer, or New Zealanders tolerating, much more than minor modifications to current immigration policies. One important variable is the present Labour government's expressed desire to restore badly shaken relationships with Black African nations—a desire that may involve the commitment of resources and opportunities to temporary student migrants from that region. Whether or not this commitment will affect the preference for Asian students remains to be seen. On a more positive note, however, the experience with Indochinese refugees has demonstrated the existence of previously underestimated levels of community goodwill and tolerance.

Given the appropriate resources and sponsors, the resettlement of Indochinese refugees may be expected to continue and could even be expanded to other Asian refugees when the need arises. One obvious long-term example concerns the future of Hong Kong after 1997, irrespective of agreements already announced. New Zealanders are aware also of the confrontations involving Tamils in Sri Lanka, Sikhs in India, Muslims in the Philippines, and the uncertain future of Taiwan. Another case, admittedly less obvious, is that of Chinese Malaysians. Should members of this group come to find that their circumstances are "significantly worse than those of others in their community" (Department of Labour, 1983a:4), New Zealand would be hard put to deny them favorable treatment. After all, hundreds of Chinese Malaysians have availed themselves of educational opportunities in New Zealand, are thus familiar with the environment and working conditions, and have formed contacts with friends, families, and potential employers. Inasmuch as opportunities for overseas students have been defined in New Zealand's immigration policy as a form of aid to developing countries, it would seem that under certain circumstances the

consequences of such aid could prove to be more complex than was
initially envisaged.

REFERENCES

Bedford, R.

    1983   "Net Migration and Polynesian Population Growth in New Zealand,
              1971–1981." *New Zealand Population Review,* 9(2):18–46.

Binzegger, A.

    1980   *New Zealand's Policy on Refugees.* Wellington: New Zealand Institute
              of International Affairs.

Bowie, A.

    1981   "Some Room at the Inn." *New Zealand International Review,* 6(1):29–31.

Chan, Y.

    1981   "Overstaying—Challenge Followed by Change." *Victoria University of
              Wellington Law Review,* 11:211–232.

De Bres, J., and R. Campbell

    1976   *The Overstayers: Illegal Migration from the Pacific to New Zealand.* Auck-
              land: Auckland Resource Centre for World Development.

Department of Education

    1982   *Education Statistics of New Zealand 1981.* Wellington: Department of
              Education.

Department of Labour

    1970   "A Look at New Zealand's Immigration Policy." Wellington: Depart-
              ment of Labour, Immigration Division. Mimeographed.

    ——————.

    1978   *Immigration and New Zealand: A Statement of Current Immigration Pol-
              icy.* 1st ed. Wellington: Department of Labour, Immigration Division.

    ——————.

    1979   *Immigration and New Zealand: A Statement of Current Immigration Pol-
              icy.* 2nd ed. Wellington: Department of Labour, Immigration Division.

    ——————.

    1982   "The Occupational Priority List (OPL)." *Labour and Employment Gazette,*
              32(2):16–17.

    ——————.

    1983a   *Immigration and New Zealand: A Statement of Current Immigration Pol-
              icy.* 3rd ed. Wellington: Department of Labour, Immigration Division.

1983b "Revision of the Occupational Priority List." *Labour and Employment Gazette,* 33(3):5.

1983c "Entry to New Zealand from the South Pacific: Work Permit Scheme." Wellington: Department of Labour, Immigration Division. Mimeographed.

1984a "Temporary Entry from the South Pacific: Numbers of Persons Approved for Temporary Entry to New Zealand Under the Work Permit Scheme, 1 April 1977 to 31 March 1984." Wellington: Department of Labour, Immigration Division. Mimeographed.

1984b "Acceptance of Refugees as Settlers in New Zealand." Wellington: Department of Labour, Immigration Division. Mimeographed.

Department of Statistics
1983a *New Zealand Census of Population and Dwellings 1981.* Vol. 7, *Birthplaces and Ethnic Origin.* Wellington: Government Printer.

1983b *New Zealand Census of Population and Dwellings 1981,* Vol. 8B, *Pacific Island Polynesian Population and Dwellings.* Wellington: Government Printer.

Fernando, G. P. S.
1975 "Sri Lankan Doctors in New Zealand." *New Zealand Medical Journal,* 82(552):354–355.

Furneaux, M.
1973 "Pacific Island Students at Auckland University: An Exploratory Survey of the Problems of Learning and Adjustment of Undergraduates from Tonga, Cook Islands and Western Samoa." M.A. thesis, University of Auckland.

Gill, T. F.
1977 "Outcome of Overstayer Review." *New Zealand Foreign Affairs Review,* 27(2):71-72.

Kasanji, L.
1980 "Food, Marriage and Festivals: A Comparative Study of Indians in Gujarat and Indians in New Zealand." In K. N. Tiwari (ed.), *Indians in New Zealand: Studies in a Sub-Culture.* Wellington: Price Milburn for New Zealand Indian Central Association.

Koh, K. K. C.

  1980   "An Investigation of Some Perceived Problems of Situational Adjust-
          ment Encountered by the Malaysian Chinese Students at the Univer-
          sity of Waikato." M.A. thesis, University of Waikato, Hamilton.

Leo, A. M.

  1973   "Itinerant Migrants: A Case Study of the Characteristics and Adjust-
          ment of Malaysian Students in New Zealand." M.A. thesis, Massey
          University, Palmerston North.

Macdonald, B. K.

  1977   "Pacific Immigration and the Politicians." *Comment* (New Series),
          1(1):11–14.

Macpherson, C.

  1977   "Polynesians in New Zealand: An Emerging Eth-Class." In D. Pitt
          (ed.), *Social Class in New Zealand*. Auckland: Longman Paul.

————.

  1983   "The Skills Transfer Debate: Great Promise or Faint Hope for Western
          Samoa?" *New Zealand Population Review*, 9(2):47–76.

McGill, J. F.

  1981   *Immigration and the New Zealand Economy.* Research Paper No. 26. Wel-
          lington: New Zealand Institute of Economic Research.

Miles, R.

  1984   "Summoned by Capital: The Political Economy of Labour Migration."
          In P. Spoonley et al. (eds.), *Tauiwi: Racism and Ethnicity in New Zealand*.
          Palmerston North: Dunmore Press.

Ministry of Foreign Affairs

  1983   *New Zealand Citizenship and Western Samoans.* Information Bulletin No.
          4. Wellington: Ministry of Foreign Affairs.

New Zealand Coalition for Trade and Development (NZCTD)

  1982   *The Ebbing Tide: The Impact of Migration on Pacific Island Societies.* Wel-
          lington: New Zealand Coalition for Trade and Development.

O'Connor, P. S.

  1968   "Keeping New Zealand White 1908–1920." *New Zealand Journal of His-
          tory*, 2(1):41–65.

Pool, I. (ed.)

  1980   *Trans-Tasman Migration: Proceedings of a Workshop on Population Flows
          Between Australia and New Zealand or Vice-Versa.* Hamilton: Population
          Studies Centre, University of Waikato.

Price, C. A.

    1974   *The Great White Walls Are Built: Restrictive Immigration to North America and Australasia, 1836–1888.* Canberra: Australian Institute of International Affairs and Australian National University Press.

Roy, W. T.

    1970   "Immigration Policy and Legislation." In K. W. Thomson and A. D. Trlin (eds.), *Immigrants in New Zealand.* Palmerston North: Massey University.

St. George, R.

    1981   "The Language Achievement Tests for Overseas Students—LATOS: A Kiwi Controversy." *New Zealand Journal of Educational Studies,* 16(2):111–127.

Taher, M.

    1970   "The Asians." In K. W. Thomson and A. D. Trlin (eds.), *Immigrants in New Zealand.* Palmerston North: Massey University.

Trlin, A. D.

    1971   "Social Distance and Assimilation Orientation: A Survey of Attitudes Towards Immigrants in New Zealand." *Pacific Viewpoint,* 12(2):141–162.

————.

    1982   "The New Zealand Race Relations Act: Conciliators, Conciliation and Complaints (1972–1981)." *Political Science,* 34(2):170–193.

————.

    1984   "Changing Ethnic Residential Distribution and Segregation in Auckland." In P. Spoonley et al. (eds.), *Tauiwi: Racism and Ethnicity in New Zealand.* Palmerston North: Dunmore Press.

Trlin, A. D., and P. Spoonley

    1980   "Goodbye New Zealand: Net External Migration Losses in the 1960s and 1970s." In C. A. Price (ed.), *Australian Immigration: A Bibliography and Digest.* No. 4. Canberra: Department of Demography, Australian National University.

Zodgekar, A. V.

    1980   "Demographic Aspects of Indians in New Zealand." In K. N. Tiwari (ed.), *Indians in New Zealand: Studies in a Sub-Culture.* Wellington: Price Milburn for New Zealand Indian Central Association.

10
Asian Immigrants
to Canada

Daniel Kubat

Before World War I, rural immigrants from Europe were encouraged to settle the vast areas of the Canadian prairies. Between 1871 and 1931 Canada's total population increased from 3.6 million to some 10.3 million, a considerable growth considering that during the same period about 5 million people are presumed to have emigrated, mostly to the United States. Among these vast numbers of immigrants, Asians were but a small trickle, settling mainly in British Columbia. Most Asians came from their home countries, primarily China, but among the early gold seekers from the United States there were Chinese also.

Since the end of World War II, Canada has become a haven to immigrants, whose numbers continue to be impressive in terms of net gain—close to 2 million through the 1971 census. Since then, the total number of arrivals has generally continued at well over 100,000 annually. Among the new arrivals, Asians have gained numerical prominence.

The inflow of immigrants after World War II can be divided into two phases separated by the year 1967. Between 1946 and 1967, immigrants from Europe and the British Isles accounted for close to 80 percent of all immigrants to Canada. Countries of Asia and the Pacific contributed only 3.9 percent of all immigrants and Oceania and other Pacific islands only 0.4 percent (Table 10.1). The largest proportion of Asians immigrating to Canada before 1967 were Chinese, Japanese, and East

Table 10.1. Percentage Distribution of Immigrants to Canada, by Country or Region of Last Permanent Residence: 1946–1983

Origin	1946–1967[a]	1968–1976[a]	1977	1978	1979	1980	1981	1982	1983
United Kingdom	22.5	16.0	15.7	13.7	11.5	12.8	16.4	13.6	6.4
Other European countries	55.9	29.3	19.8	21.2	17.8	16.0	19.6	24.5	20.8
Africa	1.0	4.0	5.6	4.9	3.5	3.0	3.5	3.7	4.1
Asia and the Pacific	3.9	20.0	27.3	27.8	45.1[b]	50.0[b]	38.0	34.4	41.6
Australia	1.4	2.0	1.3	1.4	1.2	1.1	1.0	0.8	0.4
United States	6.6	13.2	11.2	11.5	8.6	6.9	8.2	7.7	8.3
Other North and Central American and Caribbean countries	3.2	10.3	11.5	10.8	6.3	5.7	7.5	8.5	12.2
South America	1.1	4.6	6.8	7.9	5.3	3.8	4.8	5.6	5.4
Oceania and other islands	0.4	0.7	0.8	0.8	0.6	0.7	0.7	1.0	0.8
All origins[c]	96.0	100.1	100.0	100.0	99.9	100.0	99.7	99.8	100.0
Number (000s)	132.8	164.1	114.9	86.3	112.1	143.1	128.6	121.1	89.2

Sources: Department of Manpower and Immigration, annual statistical reports; Employment and Immigration, Canada, immigration statistics, annual; Annual Report to Parliament on Immigration Levels, annual, since 1979.

[a] Annual average.

[b] Includes about 60,000 Vietnamese refugees during 1979–1980.

[c] Percentages may not sum to 100.0 because of rounding or the omission of unspecified-origin immigrants.

Indian laborers who settled at first in British Columbia. After 1967, however, immigration to Canada began to shift away from Europe and toward the countries of the Third World; Asia and the Pacific contributed 20 percent of all immigrants to Canada between 1968 and 1976.

The year 1976 was another milestone in Canadian immigration history. With the passage of the 1976 Immigration Act, Canada institutionalized fair admission practices and also encouraged family reunification and admission of refugees. The legislation removed any remnants of discrimination by race or ethnic origin. It also proved especially generous to those from Asia with relatives in Canada and those from Southeast Asia who were seeking refuge from political and racial persecution and the ravages of war, many of whom chose Canada as their country of resettlement. Their intake explains the large proportion of Asians in the immigration figures for 1979 and 1980.

HISTORICAL LANDMARKS

Immigration to Canada was not subject to regulation until the immigration of Asians, primarily Chinese, to the West Coast began to be seen as a threat. The first Immigration Act, such as it was, was passed in 1868 and dealt primarily with matters of transportation and settlement. The second Immigration Act, which was not passed until 1910, consolidated a great array of preceding legislation and orders-in-council. The significance of the 1910 legislation lies in its explicitness about "prohibited classes" of immigrants and its stipulation that "persons [are] prohibited from entry who do not fulfill, meet or comply with the conditions and requirements of any regulations which for the time being are in force and applicable to such persons under Sections 37 and 38 of this Act" (Statutes of Canada, chap. 27, sec. 3:i). The most significant provision of the 1910 act was the discretion given to immigration officers, a feature of Canadian immigration administration lasting well past World War II (Hawkins, 1972:102).

Early Restrictions on Asian Immigrants

Two distinct periods in immigration by Asians to Canada reflect the overall development of Canada's immigration policies. The first—before World War II—was a period of increasing control over immigration from the Orient, encouraged by the provincial government of British Columbia, which viewed the Chinese, Japanese, and East Indian immigrants as a threat to the financial stability and cultural identity of the province.

Immigration of Chinese. Chinese immigration to Canada was essentially the immigration to British Columbia of workers needed to complete the Canadian Pacific Railway (Belanger, 1968). Until the end of

1885, the year the railway was completed, immigration of Chinese to Canada was unrestricted. Although no reliable statistics were kept on the inflow of what was deemed to be contract labor, census data from 1881 did include 4,383 Chinese; the next census in 1891 showed a doubling of the Chinese population (Kubat and Thornton, 1974:10). Even though a fair proportion of Chinese moved eventually to other provinces, their initial arrival through the ports of British Columbia greatly increased their visibility to the population.

Finally, succumbing to pressure by the citizens of British Columbia to check the immigration of Chinese, the federal government in 1886 imposed a head tax of $50 on all Chinese arrivals. Although the head tax was periodically adjusted upward, it did not stem the flow of Chinese immigrants over the long run. Head tax figures indicate a gradual increase of Chinese arrivals from 212 in 1886, to 1,166 in 1890, to 4,847 in 1904. In 1905, the number of arrivals dropped to 77 with the raising of the head tax to $500 (Nord, 1976:143). By 1908, however, immigration of Chinese had again reached more than 2,000 per year, and it increased shortly thereafter to an annual figure of about 6,000 until World War I.

The Chinese were viewed as a threat to small merchants, the trades, and organized labor mainly because of their diligence and work ethos and only secondarily because of their racial visibility.[1] The focus of immigration at this time was on agriculture. Canada wanted agriculturists from the British Isles or northwestern Europe and, failing that, from eastern and central Europe (Sifton, 1922). Immigrants to the cities were discouraged. Hence it was because the Chinese came to British Columbia to work as laborers or in trades and services in the cities, and for that reason alone, that they were to be discouraged from immigrating.

The legislative response to the immigration of Asians reflected the prevailing philosophy of race. The anthropological wisdom of the day held that races are essentially dissimilar and that consequently the customs and practices of each race are only manifestations of the underlying dissimilarity. To translate racial dissimilarity into an impossibility of assimilation was only the next logical step in viewing the issue of immigration. One would not be far from the truth to see in the selective immigration policy of the day an effort to drown out, as it were, the unassimilable minorities by enlarging the population with immigrants understood to be more compatible. Whereas the government of the United States imposed quotas on immigration to control for eth-

---

1. Actually, their "clannishness" meant that they posed no threat of exogamy. Their unbalanced sex ratio in favor of males promised only a modest reproduction rate, moreover, and their sojourner status seemed to promise their eventual return to China.

Table 10.2. Ethnic Origins of Population in Canada Classified as Asian: Census Years 1881–1981

| Census Year | Asian Ethnic Origin[a] | | |
	Chinese	Japanese	Others[b]
1881	4,383	NA[c]	NA[c]
1891[d]	9,192	NA[c]	NA[c]
1901	17,312	4,738	1,681
1911	27,831	9,067	6,315
1921	39,587	15,868	10,459
1931	46,519	23,342	14,687
1941	34,627	22,149	16,288
1951	32,528	21,663	18,636
1961	58,197	29,157	34,399
1971	118,815	37,263	129,465
1981	289,245	40,995	344,095

Sources: Kubat and Thornton (1974:10); Nord (1976); Census of Canada (1981:Cat. 92–911, vol. 1, app.).

[a]Prior to 1951, classification was by "racial origin." In 1891, the classification was English, French, and Other. Chinese, Japanese, and East Indians were defined by color. Other "races" were defined by territory or culture. In 1951, descent was traced through the father's lineage. After 1971, ethnic origin was based on either parent's lineage.

[b]Primarily East Indians until 1961.

[c]Not available or numerically negligible.

[d]Data from Nord (1976:142).

nicity, the Canadian government continued to promote immigration from favored nations in order to populate the country with the "right" stock. The Chinese Exclusionary Act of 1923 was the culmination of Canadian restrictionist policies on immigration of Asians. For the time being, it completely stopped the immigration of Chinese to Canada.

Immigration of Japanese. Although the restrictive policies on Asian immigration were directed mainly toward the Chinese, the Japanese arrivals were not welcomed either, especially in British Columbia. By the 1901 census, 4,738 Japanese were living in Canada, nearly all of them in British Columbia (Table 10.2). Unlike the Chinese, many of whom were brought to Canada as contract laborers, the Japanese were mainly voluntary migrants. The residents of British Columbia viewed the Japanese as an even greater threat than the Chinese; the Japanese were believed to be more clannish, to be willing to work even harder, to have a higher birthrate, and to be more aggressive than the Chinese.

The Anti-Asiatic League formed in British Columbia in 1907 was a culmination of efforts, mostly on the part of organized labor, to thwart the immigration of the Japanese to British Columbia.[2] In response to the sudden influx of Japanese to British Columbia, the federal government saw itself forced to negotiate directly with Japan. The gentlemen's agreement that was reached limited the emigration of Japanese to Canada to 400 annually, not including returning migrants and their wives and children. This quota was revised downward to 150 in 1923; and beginning in 1928, wives and children of returning migrants were included in the quota of 150.

Immigration from Japan ceased, understandably, in 1941. By then, 22,000 Japanese were living in Canada. Those Japanese, who were classified as enemy aliens, were relocated into the interior of the country; after the war some were repatriated to Japan. Their relocation and dispersal under the War Measure Act invoked in January 1942 abruptly ended the first phase in the history of Japanese immigration to Canada (Tsuji, 1975).

The effectiveness of the dispersal of the Japanese can be seen from the percentage distribution of all Japanese in Canada residing in British Columbia. Until 1941, about 95 percent of all Japanese in Canada lived in British Columbia, where they represented some 2.7 percent of all residents. After World War II, the proportion of Japanese Canadians living in British Columbia declined to about 33 percent, but it is now increasing slightly. Still, the Japanese represent only about 0.6 percent of all British Columbian residents (Daniels, 1977:73). The issue of compensating the Japanese Canadians for their property losses during the war, as well as the matter of acknowledging the wrongdoing to the Canadian citizens of Japanese ancestry, has yet to be fully resolved.

Immigration of East Indians. The arrival of several thousand East Indians in 1906–1908 tested the ingenuity of Canadian immigration authorities in determining how best to discourage the immigration of British subjects who were normally eligible for landing but presumed "unassimilable." Most of the arriving Sikhs were contract laborers who soon displaced the Chinese and Japanese in the lumber mills of British Columbia. After a series of anti-Asian riots in 1907, the federal government began to develop measures to ban all Asians from immigrating. The government was unable, however, to secure a Gentlemen's Agreement with India similar to that with Japan, nor was it in a posi-

---

2. Some sources estimated Japanese immigration at more than 10,000 for the years 1906–1908 and at more than 15,000 total by the year 1915 (Adachi, 1976:1).

tion to impose a direct ban on immigration of British subjects. The only help Canada was able to receive from the government in New Delhi was the invoking of the Indian statute of 1883 that limited emigration of contract labor from India (Nord, 1976:65). Eventually Canada responded by requiring as of 1908 that immigrants from India have $200 cash on hand upon landing. All immigrants also became subject to the "continuous journey" clause in the 1908 Immigration Regulations—that is, all immigrants were to arrive in Canada "by continuous journey and on through tickets from the country of their citizenship or birth" (Andracki, 1978:99). Combined with the wide powers that the Immigration Act of 1910 gave to immigration officials at the border, such provisions were bound to curb the arrival in Canada of persons deemed unassimilable. The start of World War I, however, soon shifted the interests of Canadians to other matters, and the issue of Asian immigration was laid to rest for the next four years.

Postwar Policy Reversals

Thus immigration of Asians was virtually stopped during the interwar period, especially after the Chinese exclusionary legislation. The Great Depression, during which net immigration to Canada from all countries was negative, left the question of immigration of Asians fairly dormant.

The postwar euphoria of goodwill toward China, the repeal of the Chinese exclusionary legislation in the United States in 1943, and Canada's membership in the new United Nations resulted in a policy reversal toward Asian immigrants in the late 1940s (Andracki, 1978:185). The key to the reversal of Canada's immigration policy is to be found in a much-cited 1947 speech by then Prime Minister Mackenzie King. The message was that Canada would continue to accept immigrants up to its "absorptive capacity." Immigrants from the British Isles, northwestern Europe, and the United States would stay on the preferred list, and the range of admissible next of kin was broadened. Still, immigration to Canada was to remain a privilege because "the people of Canada do not wish, as a result of mass immigration, to make fundamental alteration to the character of [Canada's] population" (CIPS, 1974a:206). Despite this change in policy, immigration of Asians remained at a low level.

In 1952, with land settlement in Canada fairly complete, the focus of new immigration legislation shifted from agriculture to nonagricultural sectors of the economy. Regulations in 1962—in their focus on education, training, and skills—reflected the new concerns of a rapidly industrializing country seeking to expand its professional work force. The 1966 White Paper on Immigration was explicit as to Canada's new orientation: "We do not have a frontier open to new agricultural settlement. Despite its low population density, Canada has become a highly complex industrialized and urbanized society. And such a society is increasingly demanding of the quality of its work force" (Department of Manpower and Immigration, 1966:8).

The Immigration Regulations of 1967 provided for a system of admission that was nondiscriminatory but selective regarding educational attainment, skills, and financial resources (Keely and Ewell, 1981). The system was based on a point scheme designed to minimize personal bias in the admissions procedure. Immigration officers awarded points within a given range for education, occupational and language skills, presence of next of kin in Canada, willingness to locate in areas of need, and adaptability to Canada. The regulations of 1967 established essentially three classes of immigrants: variously defined family members of permanent Canadian residents, immigrants seeking a new livelihood in the country, and immigrants needing a refuge.

The 1976–1978 Immigration Legislation

The present immigration legislation is universalistic and compassionate to both the physically and the politically disadvantaged. At the same time, the new policy is keyed to the demographic and specifically the labor market needs of the country (Passaris, 1984).

The 1976 Immigration Act, the Immigration Regulations of 1978, and the ministerial guidelines—like the 1967 regulations—recognize three basic classes of immigrants: family class, selected workers class, and refugees. Family class includes the proximate kin of Canadian residents, including children, parents, and other close relatives. Family class admissions have represented about one-half of all immigration to Canada since the legislation went into effect. The selected workers class consists of persons who were previously deemed "independent" immigrants—that is, their entry into the country is governed simply by the desire to settle in Canada rather than elsewhere. This class has been greatly restricted during the last few years, numbering perhaps only 10 percent of all admissions. Specifically, the admissions of "selected workers" as independent immigrants declined from 18,143 in 1982 to 6,558 in 1984. The new revisions of the selection criteria and the projected increase for intake of "selected workers" to between 12,000 and 15,000 in 1986 are in compliance with the immigration philosophy, wherein immigration is seen as an instrument to effect demographic change in the country (Employment and Immigration, 1985). In the same class but tabulated separately are entrepreneurs (now actively sought by Canada), pensioners, and others who bring their own means of subsistence. The refugee class consists of convention refugees, as defined by the United Nations, and of designated classes—namely, persons whom Canada deems to be in a refugee-like situation. Refugee class admissions are numerous during years characterized by international emergencies. Refugees are evaluated primarily as independent immigrants, except that a measure of compassion favors their admission to Canada for resettlement. During recent years, the intake of refugees has been about 12,000 annually; each year a similar number is designated as a target figure for admission. Among the Asian refugees admitted during the last decade were 228 Tibetans (1970), about 5,000 Ugandan Asians (1972–1973), and almost 60,000 Southeast Asians, primarily Vietnamese (1979–1980).

CHARACTERISTICS OF IMMIGRANTS FROM ASIA

Between 1946 and 1981, the total number of immigrants from Asia was about 424,000; the 1981 census identified about 674,000 as ethnic Asians, including those who were foreign-born and those who identified themselves as Asians (Table 10.2). The number of ethnic Asians in Canada more than doubled between 1971 and 1981, with an immigration total during that period of about 277,000—almost as many as were listed in the 1971 census (285,000). An analysis by place of birth (Table 10.3) shows that the largest number of Asian foreign-born enumerated in 1981 came from East Asia. They were followed, in order, by persons from Southeast Asia, South Asia, and Western Asia.

The two major considerations that influence the size of Canada's immigrant intake are labor market demands and Canada's demographic outlook. While the employment situation is not likely to encourage the federal government to invite many immigrants, concerns have been voiced recently that the present-day natural increase of the Canadian population cannot guarantee any growth into the twenty-first century. Thus an increased intake of immigrants has been proposed by the Minister of Employment and Immigration in response to demands for a yet wider interpretation of the family class admission (MacDonald, 1985).

Distribution by Type of Admission

Since the Asian immigrants to Canada are the most recent, they are the most likely to be the source of additional immigration through family class admissions. Of all immigrants admitted to Canada in 1981, 1982, 1983, and 1984, family class admissions represented 40, 41, 55, and 50 percent, respectively, or about 50,000 persons each year. Assisted relatives admissions for the four years accounted for 14 percent (or 17,000) of all admissions in 1981, 10 percent (12,000) in 1982, 6 percent (5,000) in 1983, and 9 percent (8,100) in 1984 (Employment and Immigration,

Table 10.3.   Population Born in Asia, by Region and Coun-
             try, as Enumerated in the 1981 Canadian Census

Place of Birth	Population
All Asia	543,495
Males	274,630
Females	268,860
East Asia	196,740
Hong Kong	58,980
China (Taiwan)	54,320
China (People's Republic)	52,395
Japan	11,910
South Korea	10,165
Other East Asia	8,975
South Asia	130,625
India	109,665
Pakistan	15,140
Sri Lanka	4,195
Other South Asia	1,630
Southeast Asia	152,585
Philippines	66,450
Vietnam	50,710
Laos	8,855
Kampuchea	5,595
Other Southeast Asia	20,965
Western Asia	63,545
Lebanon	22,595
Israel	11,205
Turkey	8,805
Other Western Asia	20,940

Source: Census of Canada (1981:Population, table 1B).

1985). The dramatic decline in admission of assisted relatives resulted
from the sharp reduction in the selected workers category for which
employment had to be secured in advance (Employment and Immigration, Canada, 1984:10). Nonetheless, assisted relatives from Asia and
the Pacific constituted 48 percent of all assisted relatives in 1981, 43 percent in 1982, and 47 percent in 1983.

In 1983, family class admissions from Asia represented 45 percent
of all family landings that year. In 1980 and 1981 family class admissions from Asia and the Pacific had been 45 percent and 44 percent,
respectively. Family class admissions from Vietnam during 1980 and
1981 were only a small fraction of the total immigration from that country; most immigrants from Vietnam were admitted in the refugee class.

As the Vietnamese become established and are permitted to bring over their relatives, however, the family class immigration levels for the Vietnamese is expected to increase.

It may be safely concluded, then, that immigrants from Asia and the Pacific are likely to continue arriving in Canada under the family class provisions. There have been enough new admissions, particularly of refugees, to generate future family class admissions even if immigration to Canada should become curtailed again.

Geographic Distribution

Whereas Asians arriving in Canada before the exclusionist legislation of 1923 tended to settle in British Columbia, the postexclusionist immigration of Asians has concentrated in central Canada, mainly in Ontario. The pattern for 1980 is fairly typical of the recent distribution pattern of Asians in Canada. Of the 71,600 Asians admitted to Canada in 1980, about 30 percent declared Ontario as their province of intended destination; 20 percent chose British Columbia. Those whose last country of permanent residence was India went primarily to Ontario (about 45 percent) and British Columbia (about 39 percent). Of the 637 Fijians (mostly of East Indian origin) arriving in 1980, however, 485 went to British Columbia and 94 to adjoining Alberta. The province of Quebec proved to be hospitable to French-speaking Southeast Asians arriving either from Vietnam or from what is now Kampuchea.

The 1981 census enumerated nearly 45 percent of all Canadian residents born in Asia as living in Ontario and slightly more than 25 percent in British Columbia (Census of Canada, 1981, Cat. N92–913, table 1B). In 1983, nearly 45 percent of all immigrants went to Ontario, about 18 percent to Quebec, and 16 percent to British Columbia. Of the Asian refugees admitted during 1983, some 37 percent of the Indochinese moved to Ontario, 18 percent to Quebec, 14 percent to British Columbia, and 19 percent to Alberta (Policy and Program Development, 1984).

The favoring of Ontario by Asian immigrants is a pattern that is likely to prevail. Ever since the post–World War II immigration policy began to encourage immigration by urban professionals, immigrants from Asia have been gravitating to the largest cities, primarily Toronto. Several factors are responsible for this attraction. The early immigrants to British Columbia, mostly Chinese, did not establish strong communities, primarily because of their unfavorable sex ratio. The Japanese were resettled away from Vancouver early during World War II, and their immigration numbers after the war were not sufficient to make British Columbia a province of concentration. In contrast, central Canada not only had more to offer but also lacked the residual emnity toward Asians that

Table 10.4.   Percentage Distribution of Immigrants from Three Major
             Source Countries, by Intended Occupation: 1971

Intended Occupation	Hong Kong	India	Philippines
Managerial	6.2	3.3	2.9
Professional/Technical	35.2	34.5	22.1
Clerical	20.8	10.1	37.8
Commercial/Financial	2.5	4.9	5.6
Other	34.8	47.0	31.3
All occupations[a]	99.5	99.8	98.9

Source: Indra (1980).

[a]Percentages do not sum to 100.0 because of rounding.

still exists in British Columbia. Primarily, though, the attraction of Ontario is occupational.

Occupational Patterns

Canada is the land of first choice for most immigrants who ultimately
enter the country, mainly because of the occupational success they expect to enjoy. Whereas Asian immigrants of the past came mainly as
laborers, Asian immigrants after World War II came to Canada intending to work in jobs near the top of the occupational scale (Table 10.4).
Occupational success was dictated as much by the condition of their
admissibility as by the occupational mix of potential immigrants.

The selection criteria for immigration to Canada changed after World
War II to accept urban immigrants suitable to an industrial society. Asian
countries, particularly India, trained a far greater number of skilled
professionals than their economies were able to absorb. Therefore, while
many Asian immigrants do not enjoy high occupational ranking—in
particular those brought to Canada under the family reunification program and those coming as Southeast Asian, mostly Vietnamese,
refugees—Asians generally fare better occupationally than other immigrants.

Apart from the skilled professions, another avenue for Asian immigrants is the proprietorship of small businesses—for example, cafes
and stores where family organization and willingness to work long
hours make it possible to stay in business. The early discriminatory policies against Asians—those barring them from work in state-supported
enterprises in British Columbia, as well as a host of subtle employment
policies—turned many Asian immigrants to entrepreneurship (Chan
and Hogan, 1982:64). Ultimately, therefore, the profile of the Asians

in Canada may be explained by history combined with the initial selection of immigrants in response to legislative provisions.

ADJUSTMENT AND ASSIMILATION OF ASIANS IN CANADA

The early concerns of Canadian immigration legislation were directed primarily to the question of assimilability. Inasmuch as the formal provisions barring Asians from full socioeconomic, and particularly political, integration proved a de facto deterrent to assimilation, the proponents of racial unassimilability seem to have been vindicated (Buchignani, 1979). Asians were forced into occupations that were independent of the state bureaucracy or professions. Thus they were also dependent on each other, giving evidence to the observed traits of clannishness. Moreover, the chain migration that even now characterizes immigration patterns from Southeast Asia fueled Asian immigration to Canada (Buchignani, 1979:58).

Formal conditions for political integration today are offered to all immigrants, especially since the revision of the Citizenship Act in 1978, which shortened the waiting period for acquisition of Canadian citizenship to three years of permanent residence. Asian immigrants are taking advantage of the citizenship provisions much more readily than immigrants from Europe or the United States. Of all the foreign-born who immigrated to Canada between 1970 and 1977, some 54 percent were Canadian citizens by the time of the 1981 census. For immigrants from Asia, the proportion is usually much higher. From among the immigrating cohorts entering Canada between 1970 and 1977, the proportions of those who became naturalized by the time of the 1981 census were about 80 percent for persons from Hong Kong, Pakistan, Taiwan, Vietnam, and China; about 70 percent for persons from the Philippines, India, and Korea; and only 41 percent for persons from Japan (Census of Canada 1981:table 5).

Thus all the legal barriers to integration into Canadian society have been removed. The cultural differences remain, however, for the cultural mosaic of Canada has its roots in history and Asians are part of that mosaic. Although the great majority of Asians coming to Canada during the laissez-faire period of immigration were simply transported to Canada and may not have immigrated on their own volition, this was also true of other large groups of immigrants—for example, those from eastern and central Europe who were transported to Canada en masse to settle the lands.

The pronounced multiculturalism of Canada today can traced to the collective immigration by large ethnic groups who sponsor, in turn, a chain migration of relatives and friends. Such migration has always been common. It explains, for instance, immigration to Canada around the turn of the century and again after World War II.

Studies of social mobility suggest there is a difference between upward social mobility as experienced by individuals and as experienced by upwardly mobile groups. Upwardly mobile individuals accept readily the rules of conduct of the social stratum they are moving into. But entire groups who experience upward mobility by being displaced upward by in-migrating lower-status populations are likely to retain modes of personal conduct unbecoming to their new status. Similarly, the immigration of nationals in groups produces ethnic ghettos, but it also reinforces ethnic or racial identity. This process allows us to understand both the charges of "clannishness" that were leveled against the Asian immigrants in British Columbia at the beginning of this century and the unassimilability thesis that undergirded Canadian immigration policies until some twenty years ago.

No multicultural society can exist without some type of recognized pecking order in which certain ethnic groups are at a disadvantage. Why, then, would a person go to all the trouble of migrating only to be faced with such deprivation? The answer is exemplified by the circumstances of the initial migration of Chinese workers to Canada. In their case, as in the case of indentured East Indian workers to the West Indies or to Fiji, it was likely understood that the stay in Canada was temporary and that, despite all the deprivation, the dividend on the hard work would be a return home with some capital, however small. In this respect, the Chinese migrants to Canada in the 1880s resembled the Italian workers in Montreal in the 1880s. The new refugees from Asia face an analogous situation, although under economic conditions much improved.

Deprivation is tolerated essentially under two conditions: a prospect of hope for oneself or a certainty of succor in one's community. Certainly the prospect of returning home has been a driving force in the minds of many immigrants; just as certainly, the social isolation of newcomers has made the dependence on one's community only greater. Nor should it be forgotten that the obviously lower standard of living shared by the Asian minority in British Columbia is mostly in the eyes of the beholder. Enduring poverty and discrimination for a purpose, then, taxes one's patience somewhat less than where there is no hope at all.

REFERENCES

Adachi, K.

1976   *The Enemy That Never Was: A History of Japanese Canadians.* Toronto: McClelland and Stewart.

Andracki, S.

1978   *Immigration of Orientals into Canada with Special Reference to Chinese.*
New York: Arno Press.

Basavarajappa, K. G., and S. S. Halli

n.d.   "Migration History of Persons of Indian Origin in Canada." London:
Department of Sociology, University of Western Ontario.

Belanger, P. W.

1968   "Problems and Prospects of Increased Japanese Emigration to Can-
ada: A Case Study of the Attitudes of a Selected Sample of Japanese
Canadians to Immigration from Japan." Master's thesis, Carleton
University, Ottawa.

Buchignani, N.

1977   "A Review of the Historical and Sociological Literature on East Indians in Canada." *Canadian Ethnic Studies,* 7(1):86–108.

1979   "South Asian Canadians and the Ethnic Mosaic: An Overview." *Canadian Ethnic Studies,* 9(1):48–68.

Canadian Immigration and Population Study (CIPS)

1974a   The *Immigration Program.* Vol. 2. Ottawa: Department of Manpower
and Immigration.

1974b   *Immigration and Population Statistics.* Vol. 3. Ottawa: Department of
Manpower and Immigration.

Census of Canada

1981   *Volume 1. Ottawa: Statistics Canada.* Cat. No. 92–913. Ottawa: Statistics Canada.

Chan, J., and J. Hogan

1982   *Law and the Chinese in Canada.* Toronto: University of Toronto, Centre
in Criminology.

Corbett, D. C.

1957   *Canada's Immigration Policy: A Critique.* Toronto: University of Toronto Press.

Daniels, R.

1977   "The Japanese Experience in North America: An Essay in Comparative Racism." *Canadian Ethnic Studies,* 7(2):41–100.

Department of Manpower and Immigration

1966   *Canadian Immigration Policy (The White Paper).* Ottawa: Queen's Printer.

Employment and Immigration, Canada

   1983   *Background Paper on Future Immigration Levels.* MP–22-7. Ottawa:
           Minister of Supply and Services.

   1984   *Background Paper on Future Immigration Levels.* WH–5–066B. Ottawa:
           Minister of Supply and Services.

   1985   *Annual Report to Parliament on Future Immigration Levels.* MP22–2/1985.
           Ottawa: Minister of Supply and Services.

Hawkins, F.

   1972   *Canada and Immigration: Public Policy and Public Concern.* Montreal and
           London: McGill–Queen's University Press.

Indra, D. M.

   1980   "Changes in Canadian Immigration Patterns." In K. V. Ujimoto and
           G. Hirabashi (eds.), *Visible Minorities and Multiculturalism: Asians in
           Canada.* Toronto: Butterworths.

Keely, C. B., and P. J. Ewell

   1981   "International Migration: Canada and the United States." In M. M.
           Kritz et al. (eds.), *Global Trends in Migration: Theory and Research on
           International Population Movements.* New York: Center for Migration
           Studies.

Kubat, D.

   1979   "Canada." In D. Kubat (ed.), *The Politics of Migration Policies: The First
           World in the 1970s.* New York: Center for Migration Studies.

Kubat, D., and D. Thornton

   1974   *A Statistical Profile of Canadian Society.* Toronto: McGraw-Hill Ryerson

Lanphier, C. M.

   1981   "Canada's Response to Refugees." *International Migration Review,*
           15:113–130.

MacDonald, F.

   1985   *Report to Parliament on the Review of Future Directions for Immigration
           Levels.* WH–5–067/6/85. Ottawa: Department of Employment and Im-
           migration.

MacInnes, T.

   1927   *Oriental Occupational of British Columbia.* Vancouver: Sun Publishing
           Company.

Neuwirth, G., and L. Clark

    1981   "Indochinese Refugees in Canada: Sponsorship and Adjustment."
           International Migration Review, 15:131–140.

Nord, D. C.

    1976   "Strangers unto Our World: Asian Immigration and the Evolution
           of Canadian Immigration Policies." Master's thesis, Duke University.

Palmer, H., ed.

    1975   *Immigration and the Rise of Multiculturalism.* Toronto: Copp Clark.

Passaris, C.

    1984   "The Economic Determinants of Canada's Multicultural Immigration."
           International Migration, 22(2):90–100.

Policy and Program Development

    1984   "Immigration Levels, 1985–1987: Analytical Considerations." Ottawa:
           Department of Employment and Immigration.

Royal Commission on Bilingualism and Biculturalism

    1969   *The Cultural Contribution of the Other Ethnic Groups.* Report, Book 6.
           Ottawa: Queen's Printer.

Sifton, Sir C.

    1922   "Immigrants Canada Wants." *Maclean's Magazine,* 1 April. Reprinted
           in H. Palmer (ed.), *Immigration and the Rise of Multiculturalism.* To-
           ronto: Copp Clark, 1975.

Siu, B.

    1980   "Employment of Indochinese Refugees." In I. Chu et al. (eds.), *Liv-
           ing and Growing in Canada: A Chinese Perspective.* Toronto: Council of
           Chinese Canadians.

Tsuji, M.

    1975   "Redefining the Japanese-Canadian." In H. Palmer (ed.), *Immigra-
           tion and the Rise of Multiculturalism.* Toronto: Copp Clark.

Ujimoto, V. K.

    1979   "Postwar Japanese Immigrants in British Columbia: Japanese Cul-
           ture and Job Transferability." In J. L. Elliott (ed.), *Two Nations, Many
           Cultures.* Scarborough, Ontario: Prentice-Hall.

Woodsworths, J. S.

    1909   *Strangers Within Our Gates or Coming Canadians.* Toronto: Missionary
           Society of the Methodist Church.

PART III. ASIANS IN THE UNITED STATES

11

Asian Americans: Growth and Change in the 1970s

Peter S. Xenos,
Robert W. Gardner,
Herbert R. Barringer,
and Michael J. Levin

Asian Americans—people living in the United States who classify themselves as Asian—make up a small but growing percentage of the national population. Residentially concentrated in certain parts of the country, they receive publicity far out of proportion to their numbers. The Asian American population is composed of both native-born and foreign-born, and, with continuing high rates of immigration, its composition is changing rapidly. With differing historical backgrounds, Asian Americans form not a monolithic group but a variegated collection of ethnic communities with different demographic and socioeconomic characteristics. This chapter draws upon censuses and other

This chapter was prepared initially for the 1984 Conference on Asia–Pacific Immigration to the United States. Revised versions were presented at the 1985 annual meeting of the Population Association of America, Boston, and at the 1985 annual meeting of the Association for Asian Studies, Philadelphia. Some of the material presented herein has appeared in different form in Gardner et al. (1985). The research was supported by a grant from the Russell Sage Foundation for the preparation of a monograph on Asian and Pacific Americans for the 1980 U.S. census monograph series. Significant support has also come from the East–West Population Institute and the Department of Sociology, University of Hawaii. The cooperation of the U.S. Bureau of the Census is also acknowledged. This chapter could not have been prepared without the tireless efforts of Shanta Danaraj, Jerald Plett, and Macrina Abenoja. Naomi Higa is also due thanks for her excellent assistance with data processing.

sources to highlight recent growth and change and the resulting heterogeneity in today's Asian American population.

There is a voluminous literature on the Asian American experience. Much of the best of that literature considers one ethnic group in depth and draws on a range of evidence to describe and interpret its unique immigration and adaptation history. Frequently, the description is based on analysis of detailed data collected in a region or major city (Kim and Condon, 1975; Bonacich et al., 1977; Hurh et al., 1980; Kim, 1981; Yanagisako, 1985). In this respect the literature on Asian Americans parallels in richness and insight the material that chronicles the great European migrations of the nineteenth and twentieth centuries. (See, for example, Thomas and Znaniecki, 1918–1920.)

Analysis of Asian Americans based on national statistical sources, such as the decennial census and the major national surveys of households, is less adequate. Several factors account for this inadequacy, among them the inadequate manner in which persons of Asian ethnicity have been tabulated in the censuses and the relatively small size (at least until recently) of many Asian population groups. The former characteristic has limited the value of the censuses,[1] while the latter has rendered most general-purpose household surveys useless.[2] Even the U.S. census public-use samples offer somewhat limited opportunities for analysis.[3]

Nevertheless, some important statistical work has appeared. The Bureau of the Census itself has published detailed tabulations for the major races. The 1910 census reported separately on Chinese, Japanese, Filipinos, Koreans, and Asian Indians. The 1950 and 1960 censuses resulted in reports on "nonwhite races" that covered Japanese, Chinese, and Filipinos (U.S. Bureau of the Census, 1953, 1963), and the 1970 census produced a special report on the same groups (U.S. Bureau of the Census, 1973). Relevant data in other censuses were scattered and usually less detailed.

Analysis based on the 1970 data includes a study sponsored by the U.S. Commission on Civil Rights (1980), another focused on labor force

---

1. The Japanese and Chinese "races" have been distinguished since 1870 and 1860, respectively. The Filipino and Korean races were distinguished as early as the 1910 census, but Koreans were shown only intermittently thereafter. As recently as 1960 Koreans were not distinguished.
2. We have looked at such nongovernmental data sources as the General Social Survey and the High School and Beyond data set. Some government-sponsored surveys are proving useful, however. They include the Survey of Income and Education (SIE), which comprises 4,373 Asian Americans, and certain recent rounds of the Current Population Survey (CPS).
3. For example, the 1970 public-use sample (combined 15 percent and 5 percent) includes the following frequencies: Japanese 589, Chinese 403, Filipino 336, Korean 105.

issues (Wilber et al., 1975), and a series of analyses by Charles Hirschman and Morrison Wong compared 1960 and 1970 census data as well
as the 1976 Survey of Income and Education (Hirschman and Wong,
1981, 1983, 1984). These analyses of the 1970 census data do not, of
course, reflect the enormous immigration by persons of Asian origin
that has occurred since 1970. In 1980, no fewer than 3.5 million Asians
were enumerated in the census—133 percent more than the 1.5 million
enumerated in 1970 (a slight exaggeration of the actual growth, since
some groups were counted separately in 1980 but not in 1970). Nearly
half of this 1980 Asian population reported themselves to have been
immigrants in the intercensal period.

The 1980 census offers much more detail on Asian Americans than
has been available in the past. For the 1980 round, the categories "Asian
Indian" and "Vietnamese" were added to the 1970 questionnaire's
precoded categories for the question on race—"Japanese," "Chinese,"
"Filipino," and "Korean." Moreover, the 1980 census has generated data
on many smaller groups based upon write-in responses to the question on race. Other useful questionnaire items that were continued in
1980 include place of birth and U.S. citizenship. The 1970 item on mother
tongue was dropped in 1980 in favor of a three-part question measur-
ing current language and ability to speak English. Finally, the 1980 census introduced a question on ancestry that was meant to elicit a
self-identification on the basis of cultural and geographic origins to
replace information in the earlier censuses on parents' birthplace—from
which came the valuable first- and second-generation ("foreign stock")
data. (See, for example, Hutchinson, 1956.) Although the ancestry item
provides an interesting new perspective on many groups in the U.S.
population,[4] it adds little to our understanding of Asian Americans because among Asians there is a high degree of consistency between
responses on race and ancestry. The contrast between Asians and many
other racial groups in this regard is notable. The loss of any means of
distinguishing immigrant generations and the "foreign stock" in the
1980 census data clearly limits our ability to frame discussion against
the background of earlier European immigrations.

Our initial strategy for analysis has been to focus on the race question from the 1980 census and produce tables for each of the six largest
Asian American populations. We have disaggregated the national population for each race when possible to show data separately for each
region and for each of the five states with major concentrations of Asian

---

4. See the analysis in Levin and Farley (1982), McKenney et al. (1983), and the 1980 census monograph now in preparation by Stanley Lieberson.

Table 11.1.   Population of the United States, by Race: Census Years

Population	1900 (1 June)	1910 (15 April)[a]	1920 (1 Jan.)	1930 (1 April)[b]
U.S. total	76,212,168	92,228,531	106,021,568	123,202,660
White	66,868,508	81,812,405	94,903,540	110,395,753
Black	8,834,395	9,828,667	10,463,607	11,891,842
American Indian	237,196	276,927[c]	244,437	343,352[c]
Asian Americans	204,462[d]	257,480[d]	341,108[d]	500,788[d]
Japanese	85,716	152,745	220,596	278,743
Chinese	118,746	94,414	85,202	102,159
Filipino[f]	NA	2,767	26,634	108,424
Korean	NA	5,008	6,181	8,332
Asian Indian	NA	2,546	2,495	3,130
Vietnamese	NA	NA	NA	NA

Sources: Most of the data are from U.S. Bureau of the Census (1984, PC80–1–B1, table 40) with the following exceptions: 1980 data: PC80–S1–12 and PC80–1–C1 (tables 74, 75, 77, 161, and 167); 1970 data for Koreans are from PC(1)–D1 (table 270); 1950 data for Koreans are from U.S. Bureau of the Census (1953, PC(2)–C52, table A); 1940 data for Koreans are from the 1940 census, Nonwhite Population, text table, p. 2, and Population Characteristics, Second Series, text table, p. 1, and table A; 1930 data for Koreans are from the 1930 census, chapter 2, table 8, footnote 2; chapter 3, table 1; chapter 10, table 15; and Outlying Territories and Possessions, Hawaii, tables 3 and 4, and Alaska, table 2, footnote 1; 1920 data for Koreans are from the 1920 census, PC(3), text table, p.11, and PC(3), Hawaii, tables 2 and 11; 1910 data on Koreans are from the 1920 census, PC(2), chapter II, table 1, and the 1910 census, PC(3), Hawaii, tables 6 and 10, and Alaska, table 5, footnote 3.

Note: United States includes Hawaii and Alaska for all years except where noted. Data may not agree with those in other tables because of differences in the sources.

[a]In Alaska, the census was taken on 31 December 1909.

Americans: California, Hawaii, New York, Illinois, and Texas.[5] In this chapter, however, we focus almost exclusively on the national level. In keeping with the broad theme of this book, we also present at the end of the chapter a brief profile of Pacific Islanders in the United States, drawing upon 1980 census data for the two largest migrant groups, Samoans and Guamanians.

POPULATION GROWTH AND ITS SOURCES

The census collects and presents data for ethnic groups that are numerically rather large, combining the remaining ethnic groups into an "Other" category. Thus, a group first appears in the census when it

5. The states examined separately are those with 125,000 or more Asian Americans. They contained 2.5 million Asian Americans in 1980, about two-thirds of the Asian American total.

1900–1980

1940 (1 April)[b]	1950 (1 April)	1960 (1 April)	1970 (1 April)	1980 (1 April)
132,165,129	151,325,798	179,323,175	203,211,926	226,545,805
118,357,831	135,149,629	158,831,732	177,748,975	188,371,622
12,865,914	15,044,937	18,871,831	22,580,289	26,495,025
345,252	357,499	523,591	792,730	1,364,033
500,957[d]	606,121[d]	877,934[d]	1,439,562[d]	3,466,421[e]
285,115	326,379	464,332	591,290	716,331
106,334	150,005	237,292	436,062	812,178
98,535	122,707	176,310	343,060	781,894
8,568	7,030[g]	NA	69,150[h]	354,593
2,405	NA	NA	NA	361,531
NA	NA	NA	NA	245,025

[b]In Alaska, the census was taken on 1 October of the preceding year.

[c]Special efforts were made to secure a complete enumeration of persons with any perceptable amount of American Indian ancestry.

[d]Represents the sum of the groups listed only.

[e]Includes 166,377 other Asian Americans. Data in the present table are from a sample and do not exactly agree with the 100 percent tabulations found in PC80-1-B1. Figures from the 100 percent tabulations are as follows: Japanese, 700,794; Chinese, 806,040; Filipinos, 774,652; Koreans, 354,593; Asian Indians, 361,531; Vietnamese, 261,729. See discussion in PC80-S1-12, p. 1.

[f]Included with "other races" for the United States in 1900 and for Alaska in 1920 and 1950.

[g]Data are for Hawaii only.

[h]Excludes Koreans in Alaska.

grows from numerical insignificance to appreciable size.

In 1900, the first year for which data are shown in Table 11.1, only Chinese and Japanese appeared separately. In the following decennial census, Filipinos, Asian Indians, and Koreans appeared. Vietnamese and several others appeared for the first time only in 1980. Some groups (such as the Vietnamese) have arrived as immigrants only recently, but others (for example, Asian Indians) have been established in small numbers in the United States for some time.

The size and growth of a population are determined by the combined action of births, deaths, immigration, and emigration. The size and growth of the various Asian American populations have been strongly affected by their immigration (and, to a lesser extent, emigration) histories, beginning with the fact that these groups all originated as immigrants in the nineteenth or twentieth centuries.

The Chinese and Japanese came first, and by 1900 both these groups numbered around 100,000.[6] The Japanese population had grown substantially by 1920 in spite of the Gentlemen's Agreement between Japan and the United States to limit Japanese immigration; but the Chinese population had declined somewhat by then, actually showing a net emigration in the period before 1920 (and during the 1920s as well). A new group, the Filipinos, first appeared on the scene about 1906 and grew rapidly, while another new group, the Koreans, showed little growth by 1920.

All four of these groups increased, although at varying rates, during the 1920-1930 decade, but their growth then nearly ceased or even turned negative owing to the effective closing in 1924 of the Golden Door to anyone from Asia. (Data on growth rates are found in Table 11.2.) Most of the 1940-1950 growth, which averaged about 2 percent, probably occurred in the second half of the decade after the wartime turmoil had abated.

Numbers and growth rates increased from 1950 to 1960 for all three groups for which we have 1960 data. The great watershed, however, occurred in the late 1960s and afterward, when the effects of the new immigration law began to be felt. Filipino and Chinese numbers, reflecting the rapid growth in immigration detailed in the sections that follow, began to rise rapidly. This rise continued through the 1970s, and the Koreans, enumerated again in 1970, joined in. Japanese, alone of the major Asian groups, were not immigrating in especially large numbers and showed only slight rates of increase.

By 1980, Chinese, who had ranked first in 1900 but never again since then, once more had become the most numerous Asian American group, followed closely by the rapidly growing Filipinos and the slowly growing Japanese. Asian Indians and Koreans stood next, followed by Vietnamese, another group showing high levels of immigration in the 1970s.

On the basis of immigration data and certain assumptions about continuation of recent fertility and mortality levels, we have estimated the population of Asian Americans as of 30 September 1985. The results (Table 11.3) indicate that the Chinese are still the most numerous but are about to be overtaken by Filipinos. The Vietnamese have moved into fourth place and the Koreans have overtaken Asian Indians. Two predominantly refugee groups from Southeast Asia—Laotians and Kampucheans—have also shown significant gains.

---

6. In this discussion, we deal with U.S. boundary changes by considering the country to include all states of the union in 1980. Thus, when available, data for Alaska and particularly for Hawaii have been added to the data for the United States as defined before 1960.

Table 11.2. Intercensal Percentage Growth Rates, U.S. Total and Asian Americans: 1900–1910 to 1970–1980

Population	1900–1910	1910–1920	1920–1930	1930–1940	1940–1950	1950–1960	1960–1970	1970–1980	1900–1980
U.S. total	1.93	1.44	1.47	0.70	1.35	1.70	1.25	1.09	1.36
Asian Americans									
Japanese	5.85	3.78	2.28	0.23	1.35	3.53	2.42	1.92	2.65
Chinese	-2.32	-1.06	1.77	0.40	3.44	4.59	6.06	6.22	2.40
Filipino	NA	23.31	13.70	-0.96	2.19	3.62	6.66	8.24	8.06[a]
Korean	NA	2.13	2.91	0.28	NA	NA	NA	16.43	6.12[a]
Asian Indian	NA	-0.20	2.27	-2.63	NA	NA	NA	NA	NA

Source: Table 1.

Note: Not calculated for other Asian American groups because data were not available. Figures for total Asian Americans not calculated because of changing composition. Calculated according to the formula $r = (ln[P_t/P_0])/t$, t = intercensal time interval in years.

[a] 1910–1980.

Table 11.3.   Estimated Population of Asian Americans as
               of 30 September 1985

Ethnicity	Number	Percentage
All Asian Americans	5,147,900	100.0
Chinese	1,079,400	21.0
Filipinos	1,051,600	20.4
Japanese	766,300	14.9
Vietnamese	634,300	12.3
Koreans	542,400	10.5
Asian Indians	525,600	10.2
Laotians	218,400	4.2
Kampucheans	160,800	3.1
All others	169,200	3.3

Source: See text.

DEMOGRAPHIC PROFILE

Each of the six largest Asian American groups in 1980 was substantially affected by the timing and demographic composition of its recent immigration. As Table 11.4 shows, the immigrant proportion is well above one-half for all but the Japanese and exceeds two-thirds among Koreans, Asian Indians, and Vietnamese. Moreover, from nearly half to virtually all the immigrants in each group arrived in the 1970s. These recent immigrants make up more than one-third of the 1980 population of every group except the Japanese, and they comprise more than half of the Korean, Asian Indian, and Vietnamese populations.

Table 11.4.   Immigrants in the Asian American Population, by Race:
               1980

Ethnicity	Percentage of Total Population Who Were Immigrants	Percentage of Immigrants Who Arrived during 1970–1980	Percentage of Total Population Who Were Recent Immigrants
Japanese	28.4	47.5	13.5
Chinese	63.3	60.4	38.1
Filipinos	64.7	64.1	41.5
Koreans	81.9	84.6	69.3
Asian Indians	70.4	78.5	55.3
Vietnamese	90.5	98.1	88.8

Source: U.S. Bureau of the Census, unpublished tabulations.

Note: Immigrant is defined here as foreign-born of non-U.S. parents.

Table 11.5. Percentage Distribution of Asian Americans,
by Age and Ethnicity: 1980

Ethnicity	Broad Age Group (%)		
	0–14	15–44	45 +
Japanese	8.8	53.0	38.1
Chinese	9.4	60.4	30.3
Filipinos	11.3	60.6	28.1
Koreans	23.5	59.5	14.0
Asian Indians	15.2	72.0	12.8
Vietnamese	30.6	59.3	10.1

Source: U.S. Bureau of the Census (1984, tabulation ENS–1, sequence 10).

Thus both the long-time Asian American groups and the newer groups are now composed mostly of immigrants, and the recently established groups are made up substantially of immigrants who arrived in the 1970s. In fact, the only community that can be characterized as being of long standing and made up primarily of native-born Americans is the Japanese. The ethnic mix of Asian Americans is undergoing dramatic change as new immigrants arrive. In 1960 Japanese, Chinese, and Filipinos made up 90 percent of all Asians, but by 1980 that share had dropped to 65 percent with the immigration of Koreans, Vietnamese, and Asian Indians. While Chinese and Filipinos maintained their shares with immigration of their own, the Japanese share plummeted from 47 to 20 percent.

Asian American age composition varies substantially across the races. The most important differences are summarized in Table 11.5. The long-standing Asian communities, especially the Japanese, have high proportions in the older ages, while the more recently established communities have higher proportions in the younger ages. Asian Indians, mostly immigrants, have by far the highest proportion of their population in the working ages.

The 1980 sex composition of immigrants by age group (data not shown) indicates the preponderance of females among Korean and recent Filipino immigrants and the preponderance of males among Asian Indian and Vietnamese immigrants. The Filipino and Japanese data show clearly the changes over time in the sex composition of immigrants. The first wave of now-aged Filipino males is visible, as is the postwar influx of Japanese females.

Table 11.6 shows the 1970 and 1980 geographic distributions of the total U.S. population and of Chinese, Japanese, Filipinos, and Koreans together and separately. Compared with the total U.S. population, the Asian American population in 1970 was heavily concentrated in the

Table 11.6. Total and Asian American Population of the United States and Intercensal Growth Rates, by Region and Ethnicity: 1970 and 1980

Year and Region	United States	Asian Americans	Chinese	Japanese	Filipinos	Koreans
1970 population						
United States	203,210,158	1,427,565	433,469	586,675	336,823	70,598
Northeast	49,044,015	200,031	116,519	39,035	30,492	13,985
North Central	56,564,917	120,782	37,791	42,492	27,080	13,419
South	62,792,882	101,975	32,710	28,350	28,891	12,024
West	34,808,344	1,004,777	246,449	476,798	250,360	31,170
1970 percentage						
United States	100.0	100.0	100.0	100.0	100.0	100.0
Northeast	24.1	14.0	26.9	6.7	9.1	19.8
North Central	27.8	8.5	8.7	7.2	8.0	19.0
South	30.9	7.1	7.5	4.8	8.6	17.0
West	17.1	70.4	56.9	81.3	74.3	44.2
1980 population						
United States	226,545,805	2,667,796	812,178	716,331	781,894	357,393
Northeast	49,135,283	409,945	217,624	46,913	77,051	68,357
North Central	58,865,670	266,699	74,944	46,254	80,928	64,573
South	75,372,362	295,671	91,415	47,631	85,626	70,999
West	43,172,490	1,695,481	428,195	575,533	538,289	153,464

1980 percentage						
United States	100.0	100.0	100.0	100.0	100.0	100.0
Northeast	21.7	15.4	26.8	6.5	9.9	19.1
North Central	26.0	10.0	9.2	6.5	10.4	18.1
South	33.3	11.1	11.3	6.6	11.0	19.9
West	19.1	63.6	52.7	80.3	68.8	42.9
Average annual growth rate (%)						
United States	1.1	6.3	6.3	2.0	8.4	16.2
Northeast	—[a]	7.2	6.2	1.8	9.3	15.9
North Central	0.4	7.9	6.8	0.8	10.9	15.7
South	1.8	10.6	10.3	5.2	10.9	17.8
West	2.2	5.2	5.5	1.9	7.7	15.9

Sources: U.S. 1970: U.S. Bureau of the Census (1973, PC(1)–C1, table 140); U.S. 1980: U.S. Bureau of the Census (1984. PC80–S1–12, table 1); Asian Americans 1970, 1980: sum of columns; Chinese, Filipinos, Japanese, Koreans 1980: U.S. Bureau of the Census (1984, PC80–S1–12, table 1); Chinese, Japanese, and Filipinos 1970: U.S. Bureau of the Census (1973, PC(1)–D1, table 270).

Note: Asian American here includes only Chinese, Japanese, Filipino, and Korean. Data do not agree exactly with those in Table 11.1 because of differences in the underlying census source volumes.

[a]Less than 0.05 percent.

Western region of the country, where over 70 percent of all Asian Americans lived. All three other regions showed fewer Asian Americans.

Among the Asian American groups, however, the regional distribution in 1970 varied considerably. Chinese, for instance, were actually slightly more concentrated in the Northeast than was the total population, although they were still found predominantly in the West. Filipinos and Japanese, on the other hand, were even more concentrated in the West than Asian Americans as a whole, and they showed low percentages in the other three regions. Koreans showed the most even distribution.

Data for 1980 indicate that substantial changes had taken place. The total U.S. population grew at an annual rate of 1.1 percent during the decade, showing almost no growth in the Northeast and North Central regions and growth rates of about 2 percent in the South and West. In contrast, the Asian American population grew by more than 6 percent during the decade. The fastest growth (an annual rate of more than 10 percent) took place in the South, home of the fewest Asian Americans in 1970, and the slowest growth took place in the West, home of the most Asian Americans in 1970 (and still in 1980).

Korean growth rates during the decade were higher than the rates for all Asian Americans for every region and were highest (17.8 percent) in the South. Japanese rates, on the other hand, were lower than Asian American rates for every region and were only 2 percent overall. Filipino and Chinese growth rates were intermediate.

These differential growth rates, of course, resulted in a changed distribution of the population in 1980. For the U.S. population as a whole, the proportion of the population living in the Northeast and North Central regions fell, whereas it rose for the South and West: The South in 1980 was home to exactly one-third of the total U.S. population.

The changes in percentage distribution for Asian Americans were not the same at all. The percentage living in the West fell from 70.4 in 1970 to 63.6 in 1980, while the share for all other regions rose, especially in the South. Among the various ethnicities, different patterns obtained. The Chinese shifted slightly from the West to the South and even more slightly to the North Central region. Filipino patterns somewhat paralleled those of all Asian Americans, with the West losing part of its share and all other regions gaining. The South gained in proportion for Japanese and Koreans at the expense of the other three regions. Thus, in 1980, we see that the distribution of all Asian Americans and that of the individual groups had come slightly closer to the distribution of the total population.

From Table 11.7, which presents a region-by-region matrix of 1975 and 1980 residence for Asian Americans, can be calculated both gross and

Table 11.7. Asian and Pacific Americans, by Region of Residence: 1975 and 1980

1980 Residence (Persons Aged 5+)	Total	Same State	1975 Residence						
			Total	Different State					Abroad
				North-east	North Central	South	West		
All persons	3,389,293	2,180,117	319,792	82,191	60,384	74,725	102,492		889,384
Northeast	538,781	329,360	50,921	26,850	7,705	8,760	7,606		158,500
North Central	381,751	206,902	43,319	9,699	13,119	9,723	10,778		131,150
South	461,881	200,661	88,860	22,686	16,396	30,150	19,628		172,360
West	2,006,880	1,443,194	136,692	22,956	23,164	26,092	64,480		426,994

Source: U.S. Bureau of the Census (1984, PC80–S1-16, table 1).

Note: This table of necessity refers to all Asian and Pacific Americans 5 years old and older in 1980, not just the Asian groups enumerated separately in 1970 as in Table 11.4.

net flows of Asian Americans among the four regions. A similar table for the total U.S. population (data not shown) indicates that between 1975 and 1980 there was a general movement of the population toward the South and West. The Northeast lost to all other regions, the North Central region gained only from the Northeast, the South lost only to the West, and the West gained from net migration flows from all other regions.

The pattern of Asian American net internal migration was the same, indicating a general movement from the northern and central parts of the country toward the South and West. The largest streams numerically were all toward the West, and the next largest were toward the South. Because the Asian American population in the West is so much larger than that of the South, however, the impact of internal migration was far greater on the South than on the West. The largest single stream in 1975 was that from the South to the West, accounting for 9.5 percent of the 1975 Asian American population of the South.

The data and observations just presented allow us to paint a broad picture of the patterns and recent changes of Asian American regional distribution in the United States. Internal migration flows are toward the South and West, but differences probably exist among the different ethnicities that our data do not show. Immigration patterns are also toward the South and West but not necessarily in proportion to the numbers of the ethnic groups already living there. Overall, the dominance of the West as a home for Asian Americans continues, but the Asian American distribution seems to be shifting slowly toward that of the total U.S. population. The different Asian American groups are not similarly distributed, as the Chinese and the Asian Indians show a definite preference for the Northeastern region.

SOCIAL CONDITIONS AND ECONOMIC STANDING

Most Asian Americans are faring relatively well in economic and social terms—a fact widely reported by the media—but it is important to recognize that the various Asian American groups differ a great deal. Collectively they certainly do not fit the model of a disadvantaged minority population, but the popular notion that they are highly successful applies much more to some Asian American groups than to others. Significant poverty exists in some Asian American communities, and the adjustment problems of recent arrivals from Asia are often severe. To elaborate on these statements, the following discussion considers living arrangements, education, work-force patterns, and incomes.

Families and Households

It is unwise to generalize about the family life and living arrangements of Asian Americans. Judging from the 1980 census, the Asian American ethnic groups vary considerably in their living arrangements (Table 11.8)—not only because they have distinct cultural backgrounds, but also because they differ dramatically in their histories of immigration and adaptation.

Japanese American households are small—identical in average size to white households at 2.7 persons. Japanese American couples have few children; moreover, their households include few persons outside the immediate family. Chinese households are similar in their small size and simple composition. But in Chinese households nearly one person in eight (almost 12 percent) is a relative outside the immediate family or a person unrelated to the householder. The households of Asian Indians are also small. Korean households are somewhat larger, mainly because they contain more children. Filipino households are larger still; more relatives of the householder are present, as well as more children. Finally, Vietnamese households are the largest because they commonly contain other relatives beyond the immediate family and the number of children per householder is high.

In these census data, a *household* comprises the persons who share distinct living quarters, which means that they live and eat separately from others and have direct access to their quarters from the outside. A *family household* comprises a householder and those in the household who are related to him or her by birth, marriage, or adoption. A person living alone makes up a *nonfamily household*, as do combinations of unrelated persons who share living arrangements.

For whites in 1980, the average household comprised 2.7 persons and the average family 3.2 persons. Household size can be smaller than family size because, by definition, families must contain at least two people. Many white households were small in 1980, and some did not contain families. Among whites in 1980, only three of four households had a householder who was also a member of a family within the household. The remaining one-fourth were, frequently, persons living alone.

Census data on household size and composition reveal much about how different groups live in America—not only their childbearing behavior but also their life-styles and the circumstances that affect their living conditions. Much of the variation in household composition among Asian Americans results from choices they have made about whether two unrelated families will pool resources to rent or buy a sin-

Table 11.8. Indicators of Household and Family Composition and Living Arrangements, by Ethnicity: 1980

Household or Family Indicator	Whites	Blacks	Spanish Origin	Japanese	Chinese	Filipinos	Koreans	Asian Indians	Vietnamese
Household type									
Family households with male householders (%)	63.4	42.7	63.4	60.7	68.0	70.9	72.0	66.7	69.5
Family households with female householders (%)	10.1	29.8	18.1	10.1	11.1	12.3	11.2	6.4	14.2
Nonfamily households (%)	26.5	27.5	18.5	29.2	20.9	16.8	16.8	26.9	16.3
Household members, by relationship to householder									
Householder (%)	37.4	32.8	28.0	34.0	31.8	26.4	23.2	35.0	21.0
Spouse (%)	23.6	13.2	17.5	27.6	21.9	21.1	26.4	23.7	16.5
Child (%)	33.1	41.1	43.9	30.0	34.7	37.3	42.0	32.5	42.2
Other relative (%)	3.3	9.5	7.2	4.8	7.9	11.6	6.2	6.5	14.3
Not related (%)	2.6	3.4	3.4	3.6	3.7	3.6	2.2	2.3	6.0
Persons per household	2.7	3.1	3.4	2.7	3.1	3.6	3.4	2.9	4.4
Persons per family	3.2	3.7	3.9	3.2	3.6	4.1	3.8	3.5	4.6
Percentage of persons under 18 living with two parents	82.9	45.4	70.9	87.3	88.2	84.5	89.4	92.7	74.1
Percentage of persons not living in households	2.4	3.1	1.9	2.7	3.0	2.2	1.8	1.4	1.8

Sources: U.S. Bureau of the Census (1984, PC80-1-01-A, tables 121, 160, 161, 164; tabulation ENS-1, table 10).

gle dwelling, whether a family will take in other family members or boarders, when young adults will form new households, and so on.

The 1980 census identified all persons in households by their relationships to the *householder*, who was usually the person in whose name the living quarters were owned or rented. For whites in 1980, some 37 percent of all household members were householders. Another 24 percent were spouses of householders, 33 percent were children of householders, and the few remaining household members were other relatives of the householder (3.3 percent) or unrelated to the householder (2.6 percent). Both blacks and Hispanics had larger households and larger families than whites, in part because of the presence of other relatives and unrelated persons. Black and Hispanic families were also larger than white families owing to higher levels of childbearing. Both blacks and Hispanics had greater proportions of female householders, in many cases because husbands were not present.

It is noteworthy that a greater share of the children in each Asian American community live with both their parents than is true for Hispanics, blacks, or even whites. Only among the Vietnamese is this share below that of the white population. For Asian Indians, this share is more than double that of the black population. Nearly 93 percent of Asian Indian children under 18 live as members of two-parent families, compared with just 45 percent of blacks. Eighty-nine percent of Korean children, 88 percent of Chinese children, and 87 percent of Japanese children live with both parents.

To the extent that the proportion of all households containing people living alone or with unrelated individuals rather than families is an indication, the fragmentation of the family has not touched some Asian groups to the degree it has affected whites and blacks in America. Whereas 28 percent of black households and 27 percent of white households are nonfamily households, only 16 percent of Vietnamese households, 17 percent of Korean and Filipino households, and 21 percent of Chinese households are not composed of a householder and his or her family.

Japanese and Asian Indian households have a different experience; their shares of nonfamily households are somewhat above the average for whites. In the case of the Japanese, this fact probably reflects the presence of many older people now living alone as widows or widowers, whereas for Asian Indians it may reflect working-age people who have come to the United States without their families.

Households of Recent Immigrants

The living arrangements of recent immigrants of the different Asian American racial groups reflect both cultural preferences and the difficulties they face in making the economic adjustment to the United States. When recent immigrants are compared with the total population, a striking contrast in household size and composition appears, for each Asian race, between recent immigrants and earlier arrivals. The differences are much larger than any of the differences in household composition among the races.

In recent immigrant households, "other relatives" make up a significant proportion of all households—28 percent among the Japanese, 41 percent among the Asian Indians, 46 percent for Chinese, 49 percent for Koreans, and about 55 percent for Filipinos and Vietnamese. This statistic explains why the households of recent immigrants are so much larger than in the Asian American population as a whole or among Americans in general. Another feature of immigrant households is that they are built around young couples who are at such an early stage of childbearing that they have from one-half to nearly one full child less than Asian American households in general.

The households of recent immigrants appear to function as economic units.[7] One indication of this is that they are much more likely than other households to contain additional workers. Among Koreans as a whole, for example, 92 percent of households contain only the immediate family—the householder, spouse, and children—and only 6 percent also contain other relatives. But among Korean immigrants to America between 1975 and 1980, other relatives beyond the immediate family are present in 49 percent of the households. Only half of all Korean immigrant households contain just the immediate family members.

The pattern is much the same for other Asian American groups. More than half of Filipino immigrant households contain other relatives beyond the immediate family, versus just 12 percent among Filipino households as a whole. For Chinese, the difference is 46 percent versus 8 percent. In almost every case, recent immigrant households contain more persons per family; usually these people are members of extended families functioning as economic units that enable the new arrivals to make a living.[8]

7. It is not really possible to prove this point using census data alone. In-depth studies of various Asian American communities make the point consistently, however, and offer a range of evidence to back it up. (See Hurh et al., 1980, on Koreans in Chicago; Kuo and Lin, 1977, on the Chinese in Washington, D.C.; Caces, 1985, on Filipinos in Honolulu; U.S. Department of Health and Human Services, 1985, on Indochinese in several large cities.)

8. The economic benefits of these living arrangements include sharing of such fixed costs as rents or mortgages, easy provision of child care services, and security against loss of employment by one member of the household. Of course, there are costs as well, such as the crowded living arrangements and loss of privacy.

Education

Perhaps the most remarkable—and surely the most publicized—characteristic of Asian Americans is their exceptional performance in the nation's schools. Newspapers and magazines frequently report on the educational accomplishments of Asian Americans: their disproportionate representation at elite colleges and universities, their high scores on achievement tests of various kinds, and in general their extraordinary commitment to economic advancement through education.

One simple and useful index of the educational achievement of a group is the percentage completing high school (Table 11.9). Examining this indicator in different age groups across the U.S. population in 1980 documents the educational progress that has been achieved over the course of the twentieth century. Americans born in the early 1950s contrast sharply in high school completion with an older group born in the 1920s and 1930s, both for men and for women. Among whites, 69 percent of the older group completed high school, whereas 87 percent of the younger group did so. Only 43 percent of older black males completed high school, compared with 74 percent of the younger group.

Asian Americans as a whole were already at high school completion levels close to those of whites in the past, and recently they have reached levels well above those of whites. Among the Japanese, for example, 88 percent of the older men completed high school, and for the younger group the level was even higher. For men, every Asian group except the Vietnamese enjoys a higher rate of high school completion than do white men, in both the older and the younger ages. For Korean and Asian Indian men aged 25 to 29 in 1980, more than 93 percent of each group had completed high school, and 90 percent of Chinese and 89 percent of Filipinos had done so.

Another dramatic change can be found in the pattern of gender differentials. Substantial educational inequity favoring males still exists among Koreans and Vietnamese, but the gender gap has closed impressively for each of the other groups. The gender gap in high school completion rates has narrowed for Chinese from an 11 percentage point difference for those aged 45 to 54 to only 2.8 points for those aged 25 to 29 in 1980. Among Japanese, the gap has narrowed from 5.6 percentage points to virtually nil. And the gap has been cut by more than half for Filipinos—from an 8.3 percentage point gap between men and women aged 45 to 54 to a 3.8 point gap for those aged 25 to 29 in 1980.

A wide range of high school completion rates exists within the different Asian groups according to whether a person was born in the United States or abroad. Chinese born in the United States are much more likely to have completed high school than Chinese immigrants. For

Table 11.9. Rates of High School Completion, by Ethnicity and Sex, for Two Age Groups: 1980

Ethnicity	Male (%)			Female (%)			Sex Difference (%)	
	25-29	45-54	Difference	25-29	45-54	Difference	25-29	45-54
Whites	87.0	68.7	18.3	87.2	70.1	17.1	-0.2	-1.4
Blacks	73.8	42.9	30.9	76.5	45.9	30.6	-2.7	-3.0
Japanese	96.4	88.1	8.3	96.3	82.5	13.8	0.1	5.6
Chinese	90.2	68.7	21.5	87.4	57.7	29.7	2.8	11.0
Filipinos	88.8	79.6	9.2	85.0	71.3	13.7	3.8	8.3
Koreans	93.5	90.4	3.1	79.0	68.5	10.5	14.5	21.9
Asian Indians	93.5	86.1	7.4	87.9	62.0	25.9	5.6	24.1
Vietnamese	75.5	63.6	11.9	63.4	41.4	22.0	12.1	22.2

Sources: U.S. Bureau of the Census (1984, PC80-1-D1-A, table 262; tabulation ENS-1, table 6).

Asian Indians the pattern is just the reverse. For other groups, however, there is little difference.

Except for the Japanese and Vietnamese, there is little difference in high school completion rates according to whether or not members of the group were living in the United States or abroad in 1975. For Japanese, those living abroad in 1975 had higher rates of high school completion than those living in the United States. Education is now widespread in Japan, whereas the figures for Japanese living in the United States in 1975 include many older Japanese who came to this country as uneducated laborers earlier in the century. Vietnamese living abroad in 1975 were less educated than those living in the United States, however, because educational opportunity in Vietnam in 1975 was far behind that in the United States and most Vietnamese Americans are recent arrivals.

Many Asian Americans are of course immigrants who received their schooling before they came to the United States. Others immigrated to this country with further schooling as an objective. It is impossible to distinguish the educational performance of Asian Americans born in the United States from the performance of those born abroad who completed their education in the United States or from the educational experiences of those who were both born and educated abroad.

Nevertheless, it is possible to trace the major patterns by combining information taken from censuses in both the United States and the countries of origin. We have done this for two of the main immigrant groups, Filipinos and Koreans (Table 11.10). For both these groups, we have data on persons aged 25 to 29 in 1980 enumerated in censuses in both the country of origin and the United States. For those enumerated in the United States in 1980, we also present a rough breakdown by period of immigration. Most of those in this age group who immigrated to the United States between 1975 and 1980 completed high school before immigrating. Those who immigrated before 1960 were 10 years old or less at the time; if they completed high school, then they probably did so in the United States.

A notable pattern emerges. As expected, those who migrated from the Philippines or Korea to the United States were much better educated than those in the same age group who remained behind. Remarkably, however, those who left at age 20 or older, after their high school years, had nearly as high a proportion completing high school as did the comparable U.S. population.

There is thus an extraordinary selectivity of high school graduates among those leaving the Philippines and Korea for the United States. Those who left home at an early age and presumably received their high school education in the United States are no more and no less

Table 11.10.   Rates of High School Completion, by Birthplace and
Period (Age) of Immigration: Filipinos and Koreans, 1980

Population	Males (%)	Females (%)
Population of Philippines still in Philippines in 1980	27.1	23.9
Filipinos in U.S. in 1980		
Born in U.S.	89.7	90.0
Born in Philippines[a]		
Immigrated 1975–1980 at ages 20–30	84.9	84.9
Immigrated 1960 or before at ages <10	87.5	87.1
Population of Korea still in Korea in 1980	53.7	36.1
Koreans in U.S. in 1980		
Born in U.S.	93.3	80.2
Born in Korea[a]		
Immigrated 1975–1980 at ages 20–30	93.6	70.6
Immigrated 1960 or before at ages <10	99.9	92.9

Sources: U.S. data: Bureau of the Census (1984, special tabulation of the foreign-born by country of birth; tabulation ENS–l, table 10). Philippines and Korea data: 1980 census national summary tables.

[a]Persons born in third countries are excluded.

educated than those who left later and must have received their high school education at home before immigrating.

To the extent that this pattern holds among other recent immigrants to the United States, this country is receiving the best-educated people of the sending countries, and their inclusion in the total U.S. population will bring up our own educational levels. This pattern is the opposite of that for Hispanics and for the European immigrants of the past, whose education lagged behind that of U.S. residents.

Asian Americans at Work

In some ways, the labor force experience of Asian Americans closely parallels that of Americans in general. In other ways, important differences arise from the fact that a high proportion of Asian Americans are recent immigrants.

The men in each of the six major Asian American groups except the Vietnamese participate in the labor force about as much as white Americans or more so. Asian American women, too, participate in the labor force at rates equal to, or above, those of the white population. It is among Asian American women that patterns of labor market adjustment are most prominent (Table 11.11).

The 1980 census found 49 percent of white women aged 16 or over working or looking for work, a statistic that includes retired people. Asian Indians and Vietnamese women were a percentage point or two below this level, while 55 percent of Korean women, 58 percent of Chinese, and 59 percent of Japanese women were in the labor force. Filipino women were especially likely to be employed or looking for employment; 68 percent were in the labor force.

Asian American women's labor force experience varies somewhat according to their family situation, although a majority in most categories are in the labor force. Those who are wives living with their husbands have labor force participation rates that are somewhat lower than those who live in situations in which no husband is present. Like American women in general, Asian American women are active in the labor force even when they have childbearing responsibilities. Filipino women are by far the most likely group to be in the labor force regardless of their family situation. It is likely, as subsequent discussion will support, that this finding reflects greater economic need among Filipino families.

Some differences exist in labor force participation rates between those Asian American women who were born abroad and those born in this country. In general, recent arrivals—those who immigrated to the United States after 1975—have lower labor force participation rates than either the native-born or those who immigrated earlier. But the patterns differ by race.

Native-born Asian American women are more likely to be working or looking for work than those born abroad, except among Asian Indians and Filipinos. Many Asian Indian and Filipino women may have come to this country to find work, or expecting that it would be necessary to take a job, whereas proportionally more of the Japanese, Chinese, and Koreans have come as nonworking wives. They have not yet attained the high labor force participation levels of native-born American women. The low labor force participation rate of Vietnamese women reflects their relative lack of preparation for the American labor market. For example, about 34 percent report that they speak English "not well" or "not at all."

For Asian Indian women, the difference between immigrants and the native-born is striking: Whereas 54 percent of foreign-born women are in the labor force, this is true of just 29 percent of those born in America. For Japanese, however, the situation is the reverse: A high 68 percent of Japanese American women born in this country are in the labor force versus only 43 percent of those born abroad.

Table 11.11. Female Labor Force Participation Rates for Various Population Subgroups of Asian Americans, by Ethnicity: 1980

Population Subgroup	Japanese	Chinese	Filipinos	Koreans	Asian Indians	Viet-namese	Whites	Blacks	Hispanics
Family householders	72.5	70.3	79.0	71.1	58.2	56.0	39.0	41.0	68.5
Spouses	55.9	61.2	71.9	56.2	51.9	52.7	NA	NA	NA
Persons in families with own children <18	76.6	75.4	78.3	71.2	73.1	53.5	NA	NA	NA
Households with no husband present	72.7	69.8	78.5	72.9	57.3	57.6	NA	NA	NA
Households with no husband present and own children <18	77.8	76.3	77.2	73.6	74.9	56.6	NA	NA	NA
Native-born	68.3	65.0	64.5	59.1	29.4	56.1	NA	NA	NA
Foreign-born	42.7	56.0	68.8	54.8	53.6	48.7	NA	NA	NA
Foreign-born abroad in 1975	26.0	46.9	60.5	50.9	51.6	44.1	NA	NA	NA
Speaks only English at home	71.8	67.8	67.3	59.7	36.0	56.0	NA	NA	NA
Speaks another language at home	48.2	57.9	70.3	55.8	53.6	50.2	NA	NA	NA
Speaks English "not well" or "not at all"	26.8	48.5	32.2	50.5	30.9	34.1	NA	NA	NA

Source: U.S. Bureau of the Census of Population, 1984 (PC80-1-C1, tables 124, 134, 162, 164).

The greatest differences in labor force participation reflect English-language ability. As we might expect, Asian Americans with a poor command of English are much less likely to be in the labor market than those with a better command. This difference is true of both men and women, although men's rates are much higher than women's for both groups. For those Japanese women who speak only English at home, for example, 72 percent are in the labor force versus only 27 percent of those who responded to the 1980 census that they speak English "not well" or "not at all." The differences for women of other Asian groups are not so great as for the Japanese, but the substantial gaps suggest that not being able to communicate in English is among the greatest obstacles to labor force participation for Asian American immigrants and their descendants, as it has been for other groups in the past.

Occupations

Occupational roles are harder to quantify than is education, labor force participation, or unemployment, but data on occupations yield useful information about the status of an individual or a group. It is difficult to summarize occupational distributions, but several measures may be used to examine Table 11.12. The most prestigious and best paid occupational categories are clearly the first two listed: executive, administrative, and managerial on the one hand, and professional speciality on the other. Just over 23 percent of U.S. males are in these two categories. By contrast, more than 56 percent of Asian Indian males are in these occupations; and Chinese, Japanese, and Korean males are also concentrated there, whereas barely 15 percent of Vietnamese males are in these two occupations. Females show a similar pattern, although percentages in the first two listed occupations are lower than they are for males for all groups except Filipinos. Vietnamese are found concentrated among the last two categories listed: precision production, crafts, and repairs; and operators, fabricators, and laborers. Koreans also show high proportions in these occupations.

Incomes and Poverty

It has been reported widely that Asian American incomes exceed not only those of other minorities but also those of whites. These reports are true as overall averages, but it is important to recognize that not all the Asian American groups enjoy these high incomes, nor do all subgroups within each Asian American community. Within each Asian American group the foreign-born, and particularly the recent immigrants, have lower incomes (Table 11.13).

Table 11.12. Occupations of Employed Civilians, by Sex and Ethnicity: United States, 1980

Occupation	All Ethnicities	Caucasians	Blacks	Japanese	Chinese	Filipinos	Koreans	Asian Indians	Vietnamese
Total employed males 16+	56,004,690	48,843,987	4,674,871	199,016	225,100	170,417	67,185	111,172	47,174
Executive, administrative, managerial (%)	12.6	13.5	5.7	17.0	15.0	9.3	14.5	14.9	4.7
Professional speciality (%)	11.0	11.5	5.9	16.5	23.6	13.2	18.5	41.7	10.1
Technical (%)	3.0	3.1	2.0	5.5	6.7	5.9	5.1	8.0	10.5
Sales (%)	9.1	9.8	3.9	9.3	7.7	4.8	14.4	6.4	4.2
Administrative support (%)	6.9	6.6	9.3	8.6	7.8	14.1	5.2	7.1	7.9
Service (%)	9.2	8.3	17.0	8.8	22.2	16.3	9.5	5.0	13.4
Farming, forestry, fishing (%)	4.3	4.3	3.4	7.2	0.6	4.6	1.2	1.2	1.1
Precision production, craft, repair (%)	20.7	21.4	15.5	15.8	7.8	13.8	15.0	7.0	10.5
Operators, fabricators, laborers (%)	23.2	21.6	37.2	11.3	8.5	18.0	16.5	8.8	29.6

	41,634,665	35,183,388	4,659,177	183,518	174,864	191,052	73,563	59,683	33,541
Total employed females 16+									
Executive, administrative, managerial (%)	7.4	7.8	4.7	8.3	10.4	6.4	5.7	6.4	4.3
Professional speciality (%)	14.1	14.6	11.8	14.7	14.5	21.0	11.7	27.1	7.0
Technical (%)	3.1	3.1	3.3	3.1	5.9	6.1	2.5	7.0	4.6
Sales (%)	11.2	12.0	6.1	11.3	9.7	6.6	12.5	8.1	7.5
Administrative support (%)	31.2	32.2	25.8	31.6	24.7	28.2	14.8	25.1	20.2
Service (%)	17.9	16.3	29.3	17.2	13.8	16.7	22.9	13.0	17.9
Farming, forestry, fishing (%)	1.0	1.0	0.5	1.3	0.3	1.2	0.7	0.4	0.6
Precision production, craft, repair (%)	2.3	2.3	2.3	3.7	2.6	3.3	5.2	1.9	8.9
Operators, fabricators, laborers (%)	11.7	10.8	16.1	8.8	18.2	10.5	24.0	11.0	29.0

Source: U.S. Bureau of the Census (1984, PC80-1-C], tables 104, 125, 161).

Note: Data are estimates based on a sample.

Table 11.13. Indicators of Income and Poverty among Asian Americans, by Ethnicity and Immigrant Status: 1980

Ethnicity/Country of Birth and Indicator	All Asian Americans	Foreign-Born			
		Total	1975–1980	1970–1974	Before 1970
Japanese/Japan					
Median income ($) of full-time worker	16,829	9,937	9,444	9,946	9,986
% of families below poverty level	4.2	5.6	10.1	6.2	4.3
Chinese/China (Taiwan)					
Median income ($) of full-time worker	15,753	11,818	9,676	12,392	13,692
% of families below poverty level	10.5	11.8	22.8	6.1	2.8
Filipinos/Philippines					
Median income ($) of full-time worker	13,690	12,715	10,069	13,110	14,037
% of families below poverty level	6.2	5.3	8.8	3.8	4.6
Koreans/Korea					
Median income ($) of full-time worker	14,224	9,589	8,250	9,814	11,698
% of families below poverty level	13.1	7.9	11.1	6.6	4.0
Asian Indians/India					
Median income ($) of full-time worker	18,707	13,138	10,968	14,140	10,015
% of families below poverty level	7.4	5.0	10.7	3.2	2.2

Vietnamese/Vietnam					
Median income ($) of full-time worker	11,641	9,256	9,179	8,866	12,120
% of families below poverty level	35.1	30.3	35.7	8.7	6.8
Median income ($) of full-time worker					
White	15,572	NA	NA	NA	NA
Black	11,327	NA	NA	NA	NA
Hispanic	11,650	NA	NA	NA	NA
% of families below poverty level					
White	7.0	NA	NA	NA	NA
Black	26.5	NA	NA	NA	NA
Hispanic	21.3	NA	NA	NA	NA

Source: U.S. Bureau of the Census, unpublished tabulations.

The median annual incomes of full-time workers range from a high of $18,707 for Asian Indians to a low of $11,641 for Vietnamese. Only the Asian Indians, Japanese, and Chinese have full-time incomes above the level for whites; Filipinos, Koreans, and Vietnamese are below.

When foreign-born Asian Americans are considered separately by how recently they arrived in the United States, it is apparent that recent immigrants earn lower incomes than both native-born Asian Americans and immigrants who arrived earlier and have had time to adjust to the American economy. In most groups, however, the incomes of long-term immigrants never reach the levels of the native-born. The one significant exception to this pattern is Filipinos. Native-born Filipinos do relatively poorly, and Filipino immigrants who arrived before 1960 do relatively well.

The importance of family and household living arrangements for the economic adjustment of Asian Americans becomes clear when we consider the percentages of families with incomes below the poverty level. On this measure the pattern with individual incomes is reversed: The foreign-born do well relative to the native-born. This family-level indicator reflects not only the incomes of individual workers but also the ways in which families mobilize themselves in their living arrangements and labor force participation (and thus numbers of workers per family). Larger numbers of members of working age and higher labor force participation rates are the means by which foreign-born Asian American families raise their family income.

These strategies are effective to a degree, but they are not sufficient to deal with the problems of labor market adjustment experienced by many recent immigrants. For these groups, family poverty is severe. The most serious problems of poverty are found among recent immigrants from Taiwan and Vietnam, and in quantitative terms the poverty of many recently arrived Vietnamese and other Indochinese is a problem of national significance.

In fact, the 1980 census data we are considering here understate considerably the seriousness of the problem of economic and social adjustment currently being faced by recent Indochinese refugees. A large number of Indochinese have arrived since the 1980 census enumeration, and in comparison with the earliest group of refugees these most recent arrivals (the "boat people") are less well prepared for adjustment to American society—less proficient in English, less educated, less experienced at holding formal jobs in urban occupations, and, in general, less familiar with Western culture. Combined with the extreme disruption to persons and families they experienced in getting here, the social and economic implications are considerable.

Table 11.14.   Indicators of Reliance on Public Assistance or Social Security for Income, by Ethnicity: 1980

Ethnicity	Percentage of Households			Ratio of Aggregate Income from Specified Source to Aggregate Increase from Earnings	
	With No Income	With Aggregate Income from			
		Public Assistance	Social Security	Public Assistance	Social Security
White	18.4	5.9	26.8	0.82	6.4
Black	23.4	22.3	23.1	4.9	6.5
Hispanic	15.7	15.9	14.6	3.3	3.5
Japanese	9.5	4.2	18.5	0.47	3.2
Chinese	10.2	6.6	13.9	0.87	2.3
Filipino	7.0	10.0	16.1	1.26	2.7
Korean	8.1	6.2	5.7	0.83	0.8
Asian Indian	16.3	4.5	16.9	0.48	2.8
Vietnamese	20.1	28.1	5.2	7.4	1.2

Source: U.S. Bureau of the Census (1984, PC80, tables 128, 138, 164).

One recent survey of Southeast Asian refugees[9] indicates that on arrival two-thirds of all Indochinese adults could speak no English and
only 17 percent had only "some proficiency." To make up for this han-
dicap, 40 percent of all adults were found to be attending classes in
English as a second language (ESL) and two-thirds of all adults had
had "substantial ESL instruction." The same survey reported that two-
thirds of all households were below the poverty level after one year
in the United States, a figure that declined with time but remained at
30 percent after four years.

Are They a Burden?

One of the most frequently raised questions about immigrants from
Asia concerns the burden they might be putting on public assistance
resources at the local and federal levels. The 1980 census provides an
interesting perspective on this issue (Table 11.14). It included questions
regarding sources of personal income, distinguishing wages and salaries, income from self-employment, income in the form of interest, dividends on rentals, and two kinds of transfer payments from the
government—social security income and income from public assistance
programs. Although these data do not permit us to look separately at

9. The survey was carried out in 1982 for the Office of Refugee Resettlement. Interviews
were conducted in 1,384 Indochinese households in five areas of the country.

recent immigrants, they do provide a useful comparison among the racial groups.

Keeping in mind that the patterns in Table 11.14 combine the effects of the age composition of households, economic need, and willingness to apply for public assistance, one cannot help but be struck by the low proportions of Asian households that have no earned income and the low proportions of Asian households receiving income from public assistance or social security. Asian households operate in the main on a pay-as-you-go basis. The contrast with the income sources of the black and Hispanic minorities is clear.

There are two important exceptions to this general statement, however. First, a few groups (particularly the Japanese, Asian Indians, and Filipinos) include substantial numbers of the elderly—many who are survivors of immigration earlier in the century and some who arrived more recently as dependents of their adult offspring. The former group of Asian elderly draw somewhat on the social security system. Though the Asian American share of income from social security is currently below the levels for whites and blacks, we can expect this Asian demand on the social security system to increase as more Asian Americans reach retirement age. Second, public assistance is a source of income for a high proportion of Vietnamese households, predominantly the households of recent immigrants who arrived under the most disadvantageous circumstances imaginable. Their reliance on public assistance exceeds even that of blacks.

Here, again, the 1980 census data do not offer a current picture of the situation among Indochinese refugees. As the previously cited report on Southeast Asian refugees states (U.S. Department of Health and Human Services, 1985:148), "Virtually all Southeast Asian refugees begin their American lives on welfare." Overall at the time of the survey in 1982, some 65 percent of Indochinese households were receiving public assistance; among those in the United States for forty months or more, the level was still at 50 percent. These levels are of course linked with poor language proficiency and the lack of appropriate work experience in Southeast Asia. The unemployment rate in the sample was 42 percent, and it was 55 percent among those who in Southeast Asia had been engaged in farming, fishing, or unskilled labor.

The economic struggle these refugees are facing is apparent in statistics by length of time in the United States. Their unemployment rate was 86 percent soon after arrival, a figure that remained at 30 percent by the end of four years in this country. Although this latter figure is still very high, the shift toward employment and the shift away from public assistance indicated by the survey show that the Indochinese are prepared to do whatever is required to achieve self-sufficiency. The central role of household units in this process is also evident. With length of time in the United States, the percentage of households with two or more employed workers increases, and among these households with two or more workers only 7 percent are below the poverty level.

A NOTE ON PACIFIC ISLANDERS

Until recently, little was known about Pacific Islanders in the United States, partly because they do not show up accurately in immigration statistics. The two largest groups of Pacific Islanders in the United States (apart from native-born Hawaiians) are Samoans and Guamanians, most of whom are not subject to immigration controls. Samoans from American Samoa are U.S. nationals and Guamanians are U.S. citizens. The third largest group, Tongans, is subject to immigration controls, and Tongans are included in Immigration and Naturalization Service statistics.

The 1980 census was the first actual count of Pacific Islanders in the United States identified by specific ethnic categories; it was also the first attempt to describe the demographic and socioeconomic characteristics of these groups. Analyses are still preliminary, but we present here a profile that can be refined in subsequent work. For simplicity, we focus on Samoans and Guamanians, who together comprise 80 percent of all Pacific Islanders enumerated in the 1980 census (excluding Hawaiians).

A brief historical note is in order. From 1900 to 1951, American Samoa was administered by the Department of the Navy, and during that period many Samoans were employed at the U.S. naval base at Pago Pago. Since 1951, American Samoa has been administered as an unincorporated territory by the U.S. Department of the Interior. There is fairly free movement between American Samoa and Western Samoa (which is not a U.S. territory), and apparently many Western Samoans manage to enter the United States by way of American Samoa.

Guam is a U.S. territory, and in 1950 the Organic Act of Guam gave U.S. citizenship to its inhabitants. Thus Guamanians have unrestricted entry into the United States (like American Samoans), as well as full political rights (which American Samoans, as U.S. nationals, do not have). Guam is also a major site for U.S. military installations in the Pacific.

Enlistment for U.S. military service is a favored option among young Samoans and Guamanians, offering as it does an opportunity for travel, training, and an income that is high by island standards. Higher education is another common route for entry into the United States, assisted by the federal Basic Education Opportunity Grant (or Pell Grant), for which Pacific Islanders are eligible.

In 1980 the number of ethnic Pacific Islanders in the United States (not counting Hawaiians) was 87,320. Of these, 39,520 (45 percent) were Samoan and 30,699 (35 percent) were Guamanian. The third largest group was Tongans, numbering 6,226 (7 percent). In comparison with Asians, Pacific Islanders are a small group—about half as numerous as Kampucheans, for example.

If the total U.S. population is used as a standard of comparison, Samoans are seen to be a particularly disadvantaged group, whereas Guamanians are in an intermediate position. For example, the per capita income for Samoans is only 49 percent of the national figure, while for Guamanians it is 76 percent. Similarly, 28 percent of Samoan families fell below the official poverty line in 1980, compared with 12 percent of Guamanians and 10 percent of the whole population. Labor force data show that Samoans are disproportionately represented in service jobs and as operators or laborers.

Educationally, Samoans and Guamanians fall close to the national norm in percentage of high school graduates, but they have only about half the national percentage of college graduates. In contrast, Pacific Islanders in the United States have a younger age structure than the national population, and, as already indicated, many are enrolled for higher education. Geographically, Pacific Islanders are concentrated in urban areas in the West Coast and Hawaii.

Circular migration between the home island and the United States has been a common pattern for Samoans and Guamanians in the past. There is increasing evidence, however, of a trend toward permanent settlement in the United States. Pacific Islanders are becoming more and more attached to the greater affluence that they can attain in the United States and are finding it difficult to return and readjust to the limited horizons of island life. Thus there is reason to expect that Pacific Islanders will become a more prominent part of the U.S. multicultural mosaic, especially in Hawaii, California, Washington State, and Oregon. Moreover, the pool of eligible Micronesian movers in the Pacific has been enlarged by the recently-passed Compacts of Free Association. For these reasons, more research and policy attention needs to be given to the growing Pacific Islander population of the United States.

REFERENCES

Bonacich, E., I. H. Light, and C. C. Wong
    1977   "Koreans in Business." Society, 14(6):54–59.

Caces, F.

   1985   "Personal Network and the Material Adaptation of Recent Im-
           migrants: A Study of Filipinos in Hawaii." Ph. D. dissertation, Univer-
           sity of Hawaii.

Gardner, R. W., B. Robey, and P. C. Smith

   1985   "Asian Americans: Growth, Change and Diversity." *Population Bulle-
           tin*, 40(4):1–44. October.

Hirschman, C., and M. Wong

   1981   "Trends in Socio-economic Achievement Among Immigrant and
           Native-Born Asian Americans, 1960–1976." *Sociological Quarterly*,
           22:495–513.

   ———.

   1983   "Immigration, Education and Asian Americans: A Cohort Analysis."
           Paper presented at the annual meetings of the American Sociologi-
           cal Association, Detroit, 31 August–4 September.

   ———.

   1984   "Socio-economic Gains of Asian Americans, Blacks, and Hispanics,
           1960–1976." *American Journal of Sociology*, 90:584–607.

Hurh, W. M., H. C. Kim, and K. C. Kim

   1980   *Cultural and Social Adjustment Patterns of Korean Immigrants in the Chi-
           cago Area*. New Brunswick, N.J.: Transaction Books.

Hutchinson, E. P.

   1956   *Immigrants and Their Children: 1850–1950*. New York: Wiley.

Kim, B.-L. C., and M. E. Condon

   1975   *A Study of Asian Americans in Chicago: Their Socio-economic Characteris-
           tics, Problems, and Service Needs*. Interim Report to National Institute
           of Mental Health, Department of HEW. Washington, D.C.: U.S.
           Government Printing Office.

Kim, I.

   1981   *New Urban Immigrants: The Korean Community in New York*. Prince-
           ton, N.J.: Princeton University Press.

Kuo, W. H., and N. Lin

   1977   "Assimilation of Chinese-Americans in Washington, D.C." *Sociologi-
           cal Quarterly*, 18(3):340–358.

Levin, M. J., and R. Farley

   1982   "Historical Comparability of Ethnic Designations in the United
           States." In *Proceedings of the American Statistical Association, Social Statis-
           tics Section*. Washington, D.C.: American Statistical Association.

McKenney, N. R., R. Farley, and M. J. Levin

1983 "Direct and Indirect Measures of Ethnicity: How Different Definitions Affect the Size and Characteristics of Various Ethnic Groups."
In *Proceedings of the American Statistical Association, Social Statistics Sec-*
tion. Washington, D.C.: American Statistical Association.

Thomas, W. L., and F. Znaniecki

1918– *The Polish Peasant in Europe and America*. 2 vols. Chicago: University
1920 of Chicago Press.

U.S. Bureau of the Census

1953 *U.S. Census of Population: 1950. Nonwhite Population by Race*. Vol. 4,
pt. 3B. Washington, D.C.: U.S. Government Printing Office.

———.

1963 *U.S. Census of Population: 1960. Subject Reports. Nonwhite Population*
by Race. Final Report PC(2)–1C. Washington, D.C.: U.S. Government
Printing Office.

———.

1973 *U.S. Census of Population: 1970. Subject Reports. Japanese, Chinese, and*
Filipinos in the U.S. Final Report PC(2)–1G. Washington, D.C.: U.S.
Government Printing Office.

———.

1984 *1980 Census of Population*. Vol. 1, *Characteristic of the Population*. Final
Report PC80–1–D1–A. Washington, D.C.: U.S. Government Printing
Office.

U.S. Commission on Civil Rights

1980 *Success of Asian Americans: Fact or Fiction?* Clearinghouse Publication
64. Washington, D.C.: U.S. Commission on Civil Rights.

U.S. Department of Health and Human Services

1985 *Southeast Asian Refugee Self-Sufficiency Study: Final Report*. Washington, D.C.: Office of Refugee Resettlement.

Wilber, G. L., D. E. Jaco, R. J. Haga, and A. C. del Fierro, Jr.

1975 "Measures of Occupational Achievement, Mobility and Dissimilarity." In *Orientals in the American Labor Market: Minorities in the Labor*
Market. Vol. 2. Lexington: Social Welfare Research Institute, University of Kentucky.

Yanagisako, S.

1985 *Transforming the Past: Tradition and Kinship among Japanese Americans*.
Stanford: Stanford University Press.

12

The Future
Asian Population
of the United States

Leon F. Bouvier
and Anthony J. Agresta

Recent increases in the level of immigration to the United States from Asian countries have been dramatic. Indeed, the 140 percent growth in the number of Asian Americans between 1970 and 1980 was by far the largest of any group. Gains were even greater for certain Asian ethnic groups. Koreans, for example, numbered 70,598 in 1970; by 1980, 357,398 were enumerated—an increase of more than 400 percent. On the other hand, the Japanese population (see Chapter 11) grew by only 20 percent.

Given the volatile situations in several Asian nations that have led to large numbers of refugees and given the desire on the part of many Asian immigrants to be reunited with their families, immigration levels will undoubtedly remain high for many years. A recent study (Rumbaut and Weeks, 1986) suggests that by late 1984 the Vietnamese population in the United States was possibly as high as 566,450, the Khmer population, 137,391, and the Lao and the Hmong populations, 118,858 and 79,554, respectively—all the result of very recent migration. These estimates suggest enormous increases over the numbers reported in the 1980 census. Furthermore, the Asian population in the United States will grow not only through immigration but also as a result of the fertility of these immigrants after settling in this country.

How many Asian Americans will there be in the year 2000? In 2030? What will be the ethnic composition of this population? How will the various ethnic groups be distributed across the nation? What proportion will they constitute of the total U.S. population? These are some of the questions addressed in this chapter.

Finding answers to these questions involves the preparation of population projections not only for Asians in general but for each of the major ethnic groups: Japanese, Chinese, Filipinos, Koreans, Indians, Vietnamese, Kampucheans, Laotians, and others. To develop such projections, one must make assumptions about the future demographic behavior of these new immigrants: their fertility, their mortality, and their migration patterns both across international borders and within the United States.

Projections are not to be confused with predictions. Predictions reflect what the writer thinks will occur in the future. Projections are simply the mathematical results that emanate from various assumptions about future demographic behavior. Given certain clearly stated assumptions about such behavior, the population size in any future year can be ascertained. Barring mathematical errors, the projection itself can never be incorrect. In the words of Peter Morrison (1977:3) "The purpose of projecting populations is not exclusively, or even primarily, to make accurate predictions. Rather, it is to identify and chart the likely effects of influences and contingencies that will determine future population size." In this chapter, our projections show what will take place under specifically stated assumptions about the future demographic behavior of Asian Americans. Our assumptions have been selected for their apparent reasonableness, but there is no assurance they will be accurate predictions of the future.

Not only will the Asian American population grow substantially in future years, but also a remarkable shift will occur in its ethnic distribution. The Filipino, Korean, and Vietnamese groups will increase more rapidly than the Chinese and the Japanese. The Kampucheans and Laotians, inconsequential in 1970, will increase even more dramatically. But the implications of such growth go well beyond sheer numbers. With the native-born population of the United States exhibiting fertility well below the level needed for replacement, its proportion is likely to fall in future years, while that of the newest immigrant groups—Hispanic as well as Asian—will increase. The social and cultural changes resulting from these shifts in demographic behavior will significantly alter the nature of American society.

THE DATA BASE

To develop population projections for the Asian residents in the United States, the group itself must be defined and its 1980 population determined. Defining and counting is not as simple as it might appear at first glance, however. The Bureau of the Census and the Immigration and Naturalization Service (INS) do not agree on terminology, nor should they. These two agencies are concerned with vastly different aspects of the population. The Bureau of the Census enumerates people living in the United States on a given date–in this case, 1 April 1980. The INS, on the other hand, counts the people who enter the country legally every year.

The Bureau of the Census categorizes the population on a given date into racial groups. In 1980, it asked the following question: "Is this person white, black or Negro, Japanese, Chinese, Filipino, Korean, Vietnamese, Indian, Asian-Indian, Hawaiian, Guamanian, Samoan, Eskimo, Aleut, other?" The Asian category includes persons who indicated their race as Japanese, Chinese, Filipino, Korean, Vietnamese, or Asian Indian. The category "Other" includes Asians as well as others not listed separately (for example, Kampucheans, Laotians, Hmongs, Pakistanis). The INS is concerned solely with country of birth or of origin. Asia includes all the countries on that continent; thus Israel, Syria, and Turkey are included in the Asian immigration total.

Since we are dealing here with the future size of the Asian population of the United States, we use the Bureau of the Census's concept, thereby eliminating from the analysis such obviously non-Asian groups as the Israelis and the Turks. Immigration data for the Asian-born are thus limited to the groups specifically included under this definition. To develop projections for Asian Americans, the base population of 1980 is taken from Bureau of the Census statistics. Immigration data by country of birth, however, are used to derive assumptions about future levels of immigration. Thus, while our concepts derive from the Bureau of the Census concepts, our data come from both that agency and the INS.

Projections must be made for two distinct groups: Asian residents in the United States as of 1 April 1980 who were enumerated in the decennial census, and post-1980 immigrants from Asian countries of birth. By keeping the analyses separate, it is possible to determine the proportion of future immigrants and their descendants in the population in specific years. The base population for the resident group is the 1980 census, which counted 3,466,421 Asians (U.S. Bureau of the Census, 1983). Since the immigrant group is defined as those entrants and descendants of entrants who came to the United States after 1 April 1980, their base population is zero.

THE ASSUMPTIONS

Assumptions must be made for three demographic variables: fertility, mortality, and migration. In this chapter, only one mortality assumption is used. Life expectancy at birth was 69 years for males and 76 for females in 1980, the starting date. By the year 2010 it is assumed that life expectancy will be 76 years for males and 82 for females, with no further changes thereafter. The 1980 figures are those for the total U.S. population and were selected because there is no evidence of lower life expectancy among Asian groups in the country. Furthermore, a substantial proportion of the immigrants come from countries where life expectancy is high.

Data on the fertility of the various Asian ethnic groups are extremely limited. The National Center for Health Statistics (NCHS) suggests that Asian fertility is quite similar to that of whites. Yet it comments that "in many ways, the major Asian . . . groups are different from one another as well as from other races" (NCHS, 1984:1). A more recent study (Gardner et al., 1984) examines the children-ever-born data from the 1980 census to arrive at standardized children-ever-born rates for Asian ethnic groups. Although this is not an ideal measure of current fertility, it does yield reasonable approximations. Of the six principal Asian ethnic groups in the United States, only the Vietnamese exhibit higher fertility than the national average. Indeed, the Chinese, Japanese, Filipino, and Indian groups have lower fertility than the white U.S. population, according to these data on children ever born. Gordon (1982:2) analyzed data for Southeast Asia refugees and concluded that they "have borne children at a rate above replacement level and have an age structure more conducive to high fertility than that of the total United States population."

In this analysis, we posit that United States fertility will not increase to any appreciable degree in future years. On the basis of the study by Gardner and colleagues, we assume the total fertility rate (TFR) for the resident Chinese, Filipino, Korean, and Indian groups to be 1.8 children per woman in 1980. That figure approximates the rate for the total population. Japanese fertility is significantly lower than that of whites. We assume their fertility to be 1.6 in 1980. In contrast, Vietnamese fertility (about 3.0) is considerably higher than that of the total population. We assume further that convergence toward the overall rate (1.8) will proceed in future years and be attained by the year 2010. Thus the Japanese TFR will increase slightly, while that for the Vietnamese will drop.

Fertility is set somewhat higher for post-1980 immigrants. The justification is based on the report of Gardner and colleagues, which indicates that, for four of the six ethnic groups, fertility is higher for the foreign than for the native-born. (Filipinos and Indians are the exceptions.) The TFR for Vietnamese immigrants is assumed to begin at 3.2 and that for Japanese at 1.8; for the other groups, the beginning TFR is 2.0. Again, convergence is set for the year 2010 at 1.8. It is not possible to trace each new group as it enters the country. Thus, after the year 2010, all immigrants and their descendants will exhibit the same fertility as that of the 1980 resident and descendant populations.

The emergence of Kampucheans and Laotians (including the Hmongs from northern Laos) as significant immigrant groups necessitates identifying them in the projections. Ascertaining their fertility or mortality is difficult. The evidence from the Rumbaut and Weeks (1986) study suggests that their fertility may well be higher than that of the Vietnamese. To get a tentative idea of prospective numbers of these Indochinese in future years, we assume that their fertility and mortality behavior is the same as the Vietnamese whether as residents or as immigrants.

Future levels of immigration remain problematical. Will the U.S. government change its immigration laws? Will the level of refugee movements subside at some time? Could as yet unforeseen political disturbances result in new refugee streams from different sources in Asia? Political forecasting has never been within the demographer's realm of expertise. Thus we must rely on what appear to be reasonable assumptions about future levels of immigration based mainly on the current situation.

In recent years, total immigration to the United States has averaged about 600,000 annually. While some 100,000 may leave in any given year, at least that many undocumented entries take place (Warren and Kraly, 1984). Thus 600,000 serves as an approximate indicator of annual net immigration to the United States. There is no apparent reason to anticipate significant changes in the future. The proportion of Asians has risen in recent years. In the late 1970s, some 35 percent of all immigrants were of Asian origin; their proportion rose to almost 50 percent in the early 1980s. We assume that Asians will constitute 40 percent of all immigrants in future years, or about 240,000 annually.

Recently there has been a significant shift in the origin of Asian immigrants (mostly refugees). In the period 1980–1984, almost 25 percent came from Vietnam, another 19 percent from the Philippines, 15 percent from Korea, 13 percent from China and Hong Kong, 9 percent from India, and only 1.7 percent from Japan (INS, 1980–1984). The greatest increases came from countries with very small 1980 populations in the United States, Kampuchea and Laos in particular. In 1980, 16,044 Kampucheans were enumerated in the census. In 1981 alone, 12,749 were admitted as legal immigrants or refugees. Laotians now represent 6.8 percent and Kampucheans 5.5 percent of all Asian immigrants. For our projection, we have distributed the estimated 240,000 Asian immigrants per year as follows:

Vietnamese: 22.5 percent (54,000)
Filipino: 20.0 percent (48,000)
Korean: 15.0 percent (36,000)
Chinese: 13.0 percent (31,200)
Indian: 10.0 percent (24,000)
Laotian: 7.0 percent (16,800)
Kampuchean: 6.0 percent (14,400)
Other: 5.0 percent (12,000)
Japanese: 1.5 percent (3,600)

On the basis of these many assumptions, we have developed separate projections for each ethnic group (in addition to a residual "other" category) for both 1980 residents and their descendants and post-1980 immigrants and their descendants. Many deviations from these projections will, no doubt, be noted in the future. Totally unforeseen changes—political, economic, social, demographic—could take place over the next fifty years. Nevertheless, as of 1986, the projections appear to be quite realistic and, if anything, may err on the conservative side.

POPULATION PROJECTIONS

The 1980 population of 3,466,421 Asian Americans will increase substantially in future years—to almost 10 million by the turn of the century and 20 million by the year 2030—based on the assumptions discussed above. (See Table 12.1.) This increase translates into a tripling of the population in the twenty years between 1980 and 2000 and a doubling over the following thirty years. Within fifty years, the Asian population in the United States will have grown sixfold—from 3.5 million to 20 million.[1]

The resident population and its descendants will grow by more than 26 percent, peaking in the year 2020 before beginning a long-term decline resulting from fertility below the rate of replacement. Consequently, the post-1980 immigrants and their descendants will become an ever larger proportion of the total Asian group. Within fifty years, close to 80 percent will consist of post-1980 immigrants and their descendants, compared with only 58 percent at the turn of the twenty-first century.

Future levels of immigration undoubtedly will vary from our assumptions. Should current immigration laws remain on the books, the num-

---

1. These projections of the Asian population in the United States vary from those we published in "The Fastest Growing Minority" (1985). At the time of that article's preparation, information was not yet available on the extent of the refugee movement from Southeast Asia, which became particularly intense in the early 1980s.

Table 12.1. Projections of the Asian Population in the United States:
1980–2030

Year	Total Asian Population in U.S.	1980 U.S. Residents and Descendants	Post-1980 Immigrants and Descendants	Post-1980 as % of Total Asian Population
1980	3,466,421	3,466,421	—	—
1990	6,533,621	3,860,306	2,673,302	40.9
2000	9,850,364	4,141,323	5,709,041	58.0
2010	13,223,494	4,323,619	8,899,875	67.3
2020	16,610,866	4,382,602	12,228,664	73.6
2030	19,934,813	4,299,517	15,635,296	78.4

ber of immigrants entering the country under the numerically unlimited category reserved for the immediate relatives of citizens could increase substantially. Refugee totals could go up, given certain political
situations; illegal movements might increase.

ETHNIC PROJECTIONS

The growing contribution of post-1980 immigrants to the total Asian
population will result in major changes in the ethnic composition of
the group. If our assumptions about fertility and immigration levels
for the ethnic groups are even remotely accurate, shifts in rank order
will soon be forthcoming (Table 12.2).

By 1990, Filipinos will have surpassed the Chinese and constitute
the largest Asian ethnic group in the United States. The Koreans and
the Vietnamese will have surpassed the Japanese, who as recently as
1970 were the largest Asian group in the nation. In fifty years, Filipinos will number almost 4 million, more than five times their current
number. The Vietnamese will exhibit the most rapid growth—from
245,000 in 1980 to 3.9 million in 2030—and be a close second, followed
by the Koreans and Chinese. The future growth of the Laotian (and
Hmong) and Kampuchean populations will be particularly marked, and
both will have surpassed the Japanese by 2030.

In 1980, the Japanese comprised 20.6 percent of all Asian Americans;
by 2030, they will represent but 4.7 percent. In contrast, the Vietnamese
could grow from 7.1 percent to 19.7 percent over the fifty-year period.
The proportion of Chinese will fall somewhat, whereas that of Koreans
will rise from 10.3 percent to almost 15 percent. The Indochinese (that
is, the combined total of Vietnamese, Laotian Hmong, and Kampuchean) will surpass all other groups, forming 31.7 percent of the Asian
population in the United States in the year 2030. All this is in marked

Table 12.2. Projections of the Asian Population in the United States, by Ethnicity: 1980–2030

Ethnicity	1980	1990	2000	2010	2020	2030
Chinese	812,178	1,259,038	1,683,537	2,084,509	2,457,046	2,779,127
	(23.4)	(19.3)	(17.1)	(15.8)	(14.8)	(13.9)
Filipino	781,894	1,405,146	2,070,571	2,717,330	3,353,990	3,963,710
	(22.6)	(21.5)	(21.0)	(20.5)	(20.2)	(20.0)
Indian	387,223	684,339	1,006,305	1,331,762	1,634,601	1,919,163
	(11.2)	(10.4)	(10.2)	(10.1)	(9.8)	(9.6)
Japanese	716,331	804,535	856,619	893,135	929,914	945,534
	(20.6)	(12.4)	(8.7)	(6.8)	(5.6)	(4.7)
Kampuchean	16,044	185,301	386,673	603,874	833,415	1,073,111
	(10.5)	(2.9)	(3.9)	(4.6)	(5.0)	(5.4)
Korean	357,393	814,495	1,320,759	1,853,003	2,394,602	2,946,986
	(10.3)	(12.4)	(13.4)	(14.0)	(14.4)	(14.8)
Laotian	52,887	259,674	502,599	762,398	1,035,273	1,317,353
	(1.5)	(4.0)	(5.1)	(5.8)	(6.2)	(6.6)
Vietnamese	245,025	859,638	1,574,385	2,331,827	3,122,591	3,934,661
	(7.1)	(13.1)	(16.0)	(17.6)	(18.8)	(19.7)
Other	95,873	261,442	448,919	645,656	849,434	1,055,168
	(2.8)	(4.0)	(4.6)	(4.8)	(5.2)	(5.3)
Total	3,466,421	6,533,608	9,850,364	13,223,494	16,610,866	19,934,813
	(100.0)	(100.0)	(100.0)	(100.0)	(100.0)	(100.0)

Note: Percentages are given in parentheses.

Table 12.3. Percentage Distribution of Asians in the United States, by Region: 1980

Ethnicity	Northeast	North Central	South	West	Total
Chinese	26.8	9.2	11.2	52.8	100.0
Filipino	9.8	10.4	11.0	68.8	100.0
Indian	34.3	23.1	23.4	19.2	100.0
Kampuchean	14.3	14.1	16.0	55.6	100.0
Korean	19.1	18.1	19.9	42.9	100.0
Japanese	6.6	6.5	6.5	80.4	100.0
Laotian	9.5	30.5	15.1	44.9	100.0
Vietnamese	9.0	13.4	31.4	46.2	100.0
Other	17.1	12.3	14.2	56.4	100.0

Source: U.S. Bureau of the Census (1983).

contrast to 1970, when about two-thirds of all Asian Americans were of either Chinese or Japanese ancestry.

REGIONAL PROJECTIONS

Asian Americans are not randomly distributed among the fifty states. According to the 1980 census, well over half live in the West and five states are home to two-thirds of all Asian Americans: California, Hawaii, New York, Illinois, and Washington. Although there was some tendency to disperse during the 1970s, immigrants entering the nation since 1980 have shown similar preferences. Intended place of residence of legal immigrants leads to the same generalization: Asians tend to locate in the states and regions where other Asians reside.

Refugees from Southeast Asia provide a good example. Through the policy of sponsorship established by the federal government, the refugees were initially dispersed throughout the country. Yet by 1980 most such groups were concentrated in areas with a sizable Asian population (U.S. Bureau of the Census, 1983). Data on the internal movements of Asians within the nation (that is, secondary migration) are scant and do not reflect the possible patterns of post-1980 immigrants when they in turn decide where to reside.

Given these difficulties, a different approach is taken to project the distribution of the Asian American population. For the 1980 residents and their descendants, the ethnic distribution observed in the 1980 census is assumed to remain constant in future years (Table 12.3). In 1980, some 69 percent of all Filipinos resided in the western United States. That proportion of the total Filipino 1980 resident and descendant population in future years will be assigned to the West. Of the 956,681 Fili-

Table 12.4.   Percentage Distribution of Asian Immigrants in the United
States, by Region: 1980–1984

Ethnicity	Northeast	North Central	South	West	Total
Chinese	27.7	9.0	13.7	49.6	100.0
Filipino	10.0	11.2	10.1	68.7	100.0
Indian	34.6	21.4	21.0	23.0	100.0
Kampuchean	10.4	14.8	15.7	59.1	100.0
Korean	18.7	16.4	19.0	45.9	100.0
Japanese	6.6	6.5	6.5	80.4	100.0
Laotian	11.2	33.9	15.3	39.6	100.0
Vietnamese	7.0	14.3	24.2	54.5	100.0

Sources: INS (1982:table 5.3; 1985, unpublished data).

pino residents and descendants projected for the year 2000, for example, 658,197 will be residing in the West.

For the post-1980 immigrants and their descendants, the most recent data available on place of residence after entering the United States will serve as the guideline for determining regional distribution in future years (Table 12.4). In 1980–1984, some 55 percent of all immigrants from Vietnam located in the West. The future population distribution of post-1980 Vietnamese immigrants and their descendants will reflect this proportion; that is, 55 percent will be assigned to that region.

The West is now home to more than 56 percent of all Asians. This proportion will not change much in future years. We project that by the year 2000, 53 percent, or 5.3 million Asians, will be residents of that region. In fifty years, the proportion will fall slightly, to 52 percent. The West will be home to 10.4 million Asians, compared with 3.2 million living in the Northeast, 3.0 in the North Central region, and 3.3 million in the South.

Table 12.5 shows the projected population of Asian ethnic groups by regional distribution. More than half of all the Chinese, Japanese, Filipino, Vietnamese, and Kampucheans will continue to reside in the western part of the nation. Almost that many of the Koreans and Laotians will do so. Only the Indians will be more widely distributed, with about one-third living in the Northeast. Indeed, over the next fifty years the Indian population in the Northeast is projected to grow from 133,000 to 662,000.

PROPORTIONAL RACIAL DISTRIBUTION

The Asian population of the United States will grow considerably over the next fifty to seventy years. Will it grow proportionately? That is to say, will the percentage of the total U.S. population that is Asian Ameri-

Table 12.5. Projections of the Asian Population of the United States, by Ethnicity and Region: 1980–2030

Ethnicity and Region	1980	1990	2000	2010	2020	2030
Total Asian						
Northeast	592,798	1,092,609	1,622,698	2,155,666	2,684,654	3,196,000
North Central	426,370	889,719	1,4004,403	1,927,349	2,463,292	2,997,359
South	492,232	1,004,668	1,567,610	2,147,400	2,735,677	3,320,642
West	1,955,061	3,546,625	5,259,653	6,993,079	8,727,243	10,420,812
Chinese						
Northeast	217,664	340,846	458,145	569,110	672,285	761,845
North Central	74,720	115,081	153,338	189,461	222,982	251,891
South	90,964	150,522	207,879	262,385	313,514	358,618
West	428,830	652,589	864,175	1,063,553	1,248,265	1,406,764
Filipino						
Northeast	76,626	138,765	205,143	269,711	333,329	394,315
North Central	81,317	144,517	211,998	277,483	341,859	403,419
South	86,008	155,624	229,991	302,319	373,576	441,879
West	537,943	966,210	1,423,439	1,867,817	2,305,226	2,724,097
Indian						
Northeast	132,818	235,513	346,812	459,338	564,129	662,642
North Central	89,449	152,591	220,917	289,830	353,362	412,740
South	90,610	154,905	224,485	294,674	359,419	419,954
West	74,346	141,330	214,091	287,920	357,691	423,827
Kampuchean						
Northeast	2,294	20,068	41,157	63,863	87,828	112,801
North Central	2,262	27,281	57,058	89,183	123,139	158,606
South	2,567	29,153	60,781	94,890	130,894	168,570
West	8,921	108,799	227,677	355,938	491,534	633,134

Table 12.5. (continued)

Ethnicity and Region	1980	1990	2000	2010	2020	2030
Korean						
Northeast	68,262	153,954	248,815	348,487	449,812	553,102
North Central	64,688	151,057	246,821	347,625	450,428	555,391
South	71,121	147,956	232,641	321,182	410,399	500,948
West	153,322	361,528	592,482	835,709	1,083,963	1,337,545
Japanese						
Northeast	47,277	53,099	56,587	58,947	61,374	62,398
North Central	46,562	52,295	55,681	58,054	60,445	61,453
South	46,562	52,295	55,680	58,054	60,445	61,453
West	575,930	646,846	688,721	718,080	747,650	760,130
Laotian						
Northeast	5,024	27,939	54,936	83,866	114,294	145,823
North Central	16,131	85,741	467,672	255,407	347,644	443,142
South	7,986	39,595	76,739	116,468	158,202	201,352
West	23,746	106,399	203,252	306,657	415,133	527,036
Vietnamese						
Northeast	22,052	66,377	117,529	171,420	227,444	284,627
North Central	32,833	120,137	221,842	329,765	442,542	558,516
South	76,938	230,361	407,362	593,792	787,574	985,311
West	113,202	442,763	827,652	1,236,850	1,665,031	2,106,207

can increase over time? How will that changing proportion of the total population compare with that of other racial or ethnic groups?

Bouvier and Davis (1982) have prepared projections for each racial or ethnic group in the United States. Although their report did not concentrate on Asian Americans, its overall projections serve as a base for this discussion. (The original calculations have been readjusted to take into account the new projections emanating from this analysis.)

Relying on assumptions that approximate the medium assumptions used by the Bureau of the Census in its most recent projections for the nation (U.S. Bureau of the Census, 1982), we project the U.S. population to continue to grow in future years. That growth will end by the year 2040, however, when the population will peak at about 300 million. Only continued net migration will keep the population from peaking sooner.

The proportion of Asian Americans in the total population will increase dramatically in future years. From 1.6 percent of the population in 1980, it could approach 4 percent by 2000 and 6 percent by 2030. Furthermore, that proportion will have vastly different components from those of 1980.

The ethnic or racial composition of the U.S. population also will change drastically in future years. Not only will the Asian American proportion increase, but that of the non-Hispanic white majority will fall, in large part owing to that group's low fertility and the declining immigration from Europe. A recent study suggests that almost as many persons of European ancestry emigrate from the United States as enter it in any given year (Warren and Kraly, 1984).

According to the 1980 census and the Bouvier and Davis report (1982), some 79.9 percent of the population were non-Hispanic whites; another 11.7 percent were black, 6.4 percent were Hispanic, and 1.6 percent were Asian. (The residual category includes Native Americans, Pacific Islanders, and racially unidentified persons.)

With total annual net immigration limited to 600,000 (of whom 240,000 are Asian), the non-Hispanic white group will decline proportionately in future years. By 2020, some 70 percent of the population will be in this category; by 2050, about 60 percent will be so included. After 2010, non-Hispanic whites will begin experiencing a numerical decrease and in 2050 will number 162 million, compared with 198 million in 1980. The black population will grow to 41 million by 2020 and 45 million by 2050, but its proportional contribution will not rise much higher than 16 percent. Hispanics will increase in numbers from 15 million in 1980 to 24 million in 2000 and 40 million by 2050. Their proportion too will increase—from 6.4 percent in 1980 to 15 percent by 2050. Asians, as has been noted, will see their numbers grow from 3.5 million in 1980 to

20 million in fifty years, and their proportion will increase from 1.6 percent to 6 percent. By 2050, their numbers could reach 25 or 30 million, representing some 9 to 10 percent of the population of that year.

Thus the population composition of the United States is undergoing considerable change. The non-Hispanic white proportion will decline in future years, of that we can be certain. Blacks will increase numerically but their proportion will grow only slightly. Hispanics and Asians will increase substantially, both numerically and proportionately. Population projections, however, tell only a small part of the story of the changing American scene. What about the cultural changes these projections imply?

FUTURE PATTERNS OF CULTURAL ADAPTATION

Major shifts in the composition of the U.S. population, especially when they are abrupt, may create problems. How will the newest immigrants adapt to American society? The question is not new; it has been asked whenever a new wave of immigrants has arrived on these shores.

Since colonial times, the racial and ethnic composition of the nation has resembled a continuously changing kaleidoscope, reflecting the varying sources of immigration as well as the fertility and mortality of both natives and immigrants. We may go even further back in history to pre-Columbian times and arrive at a similar observation. The makeup of the inhabitants has always been in a process of change—the result of variations in demographic behavior, having few or numerous children, dying at an earlier or later age, moving or not moving. Indeed, this region shifted from being overwhelmingly Native American to being white Anglo–Saxon Protestant (WASP) largely because of the high mortality of the former group and the high immigration and fertility of the latter. The period between 1880 and 1914 witnessed a massive shift in country of origin of immigrants. As a result, what had been an essentially WASP society with a black minority became much more heterogeneous. The proportions of blacks and WASPs fell as immigration levels of other groups reached new highs.

As some of the offspring of new immigrants shed their ancestral cultural and linguistic traits, the concept of a "melting pot" assimilation process gained popularity. It was held that Italians, Poles, Greeks, and others would gradually melt into American society while contributing to it some of their own culture. This idealistic vision of a new American society never came to total fruition, although it was applicable to certain groups and individuals, particularly those who had migrated earlier in the nineteenth century. Today the term "melting pot" is often replaced by another expression, "salad bowl," the implication of which is obvious.

Taking issue with the melting pot concept, advocates of cultural pluralism point out that immigrants do not always melt into American society; some groups prefer to preserve their own distinct ethnic identities. Moreover, there are the "unmeltable ethnics"—blacks, Chicanos, and American Indians. The source of their plight can be found in a history of internal colonialism, during which these groups have been confined to specific areas and made to work under uniquely unfavorable conditions.

Still another mode of adaptation has resulted in the voluntary development of ethnic enclaves. Certain first-generation groups are economically successful despite their evident lack of acculturation. These groups tend to preserve their cultural identity and internal solidarity. Their approach to adaptation contradicts the assimilation theory predictions that acculturation is necessary for economic mobility. For an ethnic enclave to emerge, there must be a substantial number of immigrants of that ethnic group, sufficient sources of capital, and sufficient labor. In such a milieu, new immigrants can move ahead economically despite little knowledge of the host culture and language. Knowledge of English is meager among enclave minorities, but this lack of facility has little effect on the average income levels of such groups. Two current examples of ethnic enclaves are those of Cubans and Koreans in certain large metropolitan areas. (This section is based on Alejandro Portes's observations in Chapter 3.)

From this discussion of various modes of adaptation to American society, it is clear that different groups follow different paths as they proceed through the process. Furthermore, it is likely that the newest immigrants will follow different and as yet unforeseen avenues requiring revisions in the current concepts of adaptation. Precisely how will Asians, particularly the newest Asians, adjust to American society? Will they eventually become assimilated, or simply integrated, into the mainstream, perhaps in the second or even third generation? Will they opt for some kind of separatism through cultural pluralism or the setting up of voluntary ethnic enclaves? It is far too early to offer even tentative answers to these questions. Future research should examine these trends very carefully.

In a broader sense, another question needs be asked: What kind of nation do the American people want as they prepare to enter the twenty-first century? Or, as Yale law professor Peter Schuck puts it: "What are we? What do we wish to become? And most fundamentally, which individuals consitute the 'we' who shall decide this question?" (1985:285–286). Some would prefer a "status quo" society: a continuation of the assimilationist approach and the present racial and ethnic composition, though strongly influenced by Anglo–Saxon norms. They hope the newest immigrants will gradually rid themselves of their cultural and linguistic origins and embrace the English language and American customs.

However, as the time approaches when there will be no racial or ethnic majority, perhaps the assimilationist theory will mean "assimilation among" the many groups rather than "assimilation into" the Anglo-conforming society. In such a society, the increased incidence and ease of interracial and interethnic marriages would contribute to the eventual emergence of a more mixed society. Although the racial and ethnic proportions projected here would remain appropriate, they would be far less meaningful than should these groups remain distinct from each other.

Others see future demographic changes as marking the onset of a new phase in the ever changing American society: a "multicultural" society. There would be several ethnic enclaves, and cultural pluralism would increase alongside the integration of certain individuals and groups. Some time after the turn of the century, the United States could become the first truly multiracial society on planet Earth in the sense that equal opportunity would be available to all who desired to advance. In such a society, English would still predominate but other languages as well as cultures would be tolerated and even encouraged.

What direction the nation will take depends not only on the intensity of demographic behavior but also on the mode of adaptation that will occur in future years—in the family, in the community, in the schools, in the factories, in the churches, indeed in all the social institutions. The nation's identity is at a crossroad. Decisions made now regarding immigration policy on the part of the American people through their government, and decisions made by the immigrants themselves as to their choice of adaptation, will have far-reaching effects on the nature of American society in future decades.

REFERENCES

Bouvier, L. F., and A. Agresta

   1985   "The Fastest Growing Minority." *American Demographics*, 7(5):31ff.

Bouvier, L. F., and C. B. Davis

   1982   *The Future Racial Composition of the United States.* Washington, D.C.: Population Reference Bureau.

Gardner, R. W., P. C. Smith, and H. R. Barringer

   1984   "The Demography of Asian Americans: Growth, Change, and Heterogeneity." Paper presented at the annual meeting of the Population Association of America, Boston.

Gordon, L. W.

1982 "New Data on the Fertility of Southeast Asian Refugees in the United States." Paper presented at the annual meeting of the Population Association of America, San Diego.

Immigration and Naturalization Service (INS)

1980– *Statistical Yearbook of the Immigration and Naturalization Service,*
1984 *1980–81–82.* Unpublished tables, 1983–1984. Washington, D.C.: Department of Justice.

Morrison, P.

1977 *Forecasting Population of Small Areas: An Overview.* Santa Monica: Rand Corporation.

National Center for Health Statistics (NCHS)

1984 *Characteristics of Asian Births: United States, 1980.* Monthly Vital Statistics Report. Washington, D.C.: Department of Health and Human Services.

Rumbaut, R. G., and J. R. Weeks

1986 "Fertility and Adaptation: Indochinese Refugees in the United States." *International Migration Review,* 20(2). Summer.

Schuck, P. H.

1985 "Immigration Law and the Problem of Community." In N. Glazer (ed.), *Clamor at the Gates: The New American Immigration.* San Francisco: ICS Press.

U.S. Bureau of the Census

1982 *Projections of the Population of the United States by Age, Sex, and Race: 1983 to 2080.* Current Population Reports, Series P-25, No. 952. Washington, D.C.: Department of Commerce.

———.

1983 *Asians and Pacific Islander Population by State: 1980. Supplementary Report.* PC 80-Sl-12. Washington, D.C.: Department of Commerce.

Warren, R., and E. P. Kraly

1984 *The Elusive Exodus: Emigration from the United States.* Population Trends and Public Policy, No. 8. Washington, D.C.: Population Reference Bureau.

PART IV. SENDING-COUNTRY PERSPECTIVES

13

The Philippines
and Southeast Asia:
Historical Roots
and Contemporary Linkages

Benjamin V. Cariño

The post-1969 growth of immigration to the United States from Asia in general, and Southeast Asia in particular, has drawn the attention of a number of social scientists. (See, for instance, Fawcett et al., 1985; Keely, 1973; Boyd, 1974; and Chapters 6 and 7 of this volume.) The effects of the 1965 immigration reform on countries of origin, however, has attracted less attention. The impact of the policy changes (which were designed to implement an essentially egalitarian quota system) on immigration trends and patterns has varied enormously for different sending countries in Asia.

Although changes in immigration policies do influence the patterns of immigration, they fail to account for significant variations among countries in the magnitude of the flows and, much less, for the diversity found in their composition. A major thesis of this chapter is that the effects of the changes in immigration policy differ substantially in various sending-country contexts. From a broad perspective, such factors as the historical, economic, and political relationships between the United States and the country of origin, as well as the social and economic conditions in the source country, have to be examined to explain the major differences in immigration streams. In turn, variations in the magnitude and composition of the flows produce distinctive social and economic consequences for the the sending societies.

The varying impact of changes in immigration policy is evident in the case of the countries of Southeast Asia,[1] partly because of the heterogeneous character of the region. Despite important similarities in traditional cultures and social structures, the colonial and postcolonial histories of Southeast Asian countries have produced substantially dissimilar contemporary situations. In the words of Kahin (1964:v), "politically as well as culturally, the states of modern Southeast Asia are at least as varied as those of Europe." As we shall see in the sections that follow, the U.S. immigration reform of 1965 has been particularly significant for the Philippines, a country with a long history of political and economic ties with the United States. By contrast, the immigration consequences of the policy changes for the other countries in the region have been more modest or even negligible.

Focusing on the Philippines as a major sending country, and with illustrative examples and comparative data from the other countries in Southeast Asia, this chapter examines the trends of emigration to the United States and the macrostructural factors that may have influenced them and, moreover, the consequences of these trends for the source areas. In comparing the Philippines with other countries in the region, important contrasts and similarities will be highlighted.

TRENDS AND DETERMINANTS

The passage of the 1965 U.S. immigration reform, which eliminated the restrictive and discriminatory national-origins quota system, had an immediate effect on the number of immigrants admitted from Southeast Asian countries (Table 13.1). For the countries for which data are available, the sudden upsurge in the number of immigrants starting from the 1965–1969 period is clearly evident. In absolute terms, the Philippines stands out as the major source of immigrants from Southeast Asia: The flow from the country increased from just over 15,000 during the pre-amendment 1960–1964 period to more than 215,000 in the most recent 1980–1984 interval—an almost fifteenfold increase. The Thai immigrant stream is small compared with that of the Philippines, but the more than thirtyfold increase in its magnitude (from 703 in the 1960–1964 period to 25,306 in the 1980–1984 interval) is no less dramatic, a phenomenon that can be attributed, in part, to the political unrest in nearby Indochina (see Desbarats, 1979).

. For the purpose of this chapter, Southeast Asia is defined to exclude the countries in Indochina (Vietnam, Laos, and Kampuchea) that are discussed separately in Chapter 7 of this volume. The countries covered in the present chapter are the Philippines, Thailand, Burma, Malaysia, Indonesia, Singapore, and Brunei.

Table 13.1.   Southeast Asian Immigration to the United States, by
              Country of Birth: 1960–1984

Country of Birth	1960–1964	1965–1969	1970–1974	1975–1979	1980–1984
Philippines	15,753	57,563	152,706	196,397	215,683
Thailand	703	2,748	18,740	23,026	25,306
Burma	NA	NA	3,080[a]	5,558	4,559
Malaysia	NA	NA	1,307[a]	2,471	4,613
Indonesia	13,261	2,541	2,910[a]	3,426	5,261
Singapore	NA	NA	635[a]	1,459	1,866
Brunei	NA	NA	NA	84	80

Sources: 1960–1977: INS *Annual Reports;* 1978–1984: INS *Statistical Yearbook.*
[a]Data not available for 1970.

The responsiveness of the volume of immigration from the other
countries in the region is also evident, although much smaller in magnitude. During the intervals 1960–1964 and 1965–1969, immigration from
such countries as Burma, Malaysia, Singapore, and Brunei was apparently too negligible to warrant separate categories in the statistical
reports of the Immigration and Naturalization Service (INS). The numbers became significant in the 1975–1979 period, however, and have
generally increased through the 1980–1984 interval. The lone exception
to this trend is Burma, which experienced a decline from about 5,500
immigrants in the 1975–1979 interval to about 4,500 in the 1980–1984
period.

Beyond numerical increases, other studies have noted that the 1965
changes in immigration policy have also brought about changes in the
composition of the flows from Asia as a whole (see Keely, 1973; Boyd,
1971, 1974). Although data on the other Southeast Asian countries are
incomplete, the impact of the immigration reforms on the demographic
and occupational characteristics of the immigrant streams is evident in
the case of the Philippines. In particular, the changes in the law resulted in an increased proportion of males, especially those in prime
working ages, which may reflect the occupational preference provisions.
This shift has resulted in a more balanced sex composition of the flows,
as shown in an increase in the immigrant sex ratio (number of males
for every 100 females)—from 53 in the 1961–1964 period to 68 in the
1970–1974 interval, the latest five-year period for which complete age-
sex data are available. In absolute terms, however, immigrant females
far outnumber the males.

The proportion of immigrant professionals to total immigration from
the Philippines more than doubled in the years immediately following
the 1965 amendments—from about 12 percent between 1961 and 1965

to 28 percent in the 1966–1970 period. The absolute numbers are even more dramatic: The number of immigrant professionals from the Philippines grew from just over 1,900 in the pre-amendment 1961–1965 period to more than 17,000 in the 1965–1969 interval. Although no information on the pre-1965 period is available on the other countries in the region, the very high proportion of immigrants admitted on the basis of occupational skills (third preference) from these countries in the 1966–1970 period presumably reflects a sudden upsurge of professional migration (Table 13.2). The proportions of third-preference immigration have dropped considerably in recent years, however, apparently reflecting changes in the structure of the American economy, including increasing unemployment and, perhaps, as one study puts it, a certain amount of "racist hysteria" against immigrant workers (Surh et al., 1982). Increasing opportunities and rewards for professionals in Asian sending countries have also played a part.

The volume and trend of immigration from the countries in Southeast Asia have generally been responsive to the changes in U.S. immigration policy. It is also evident, however, that the effects of the immigration reforms have been uneven among the various countries in the region. The impact has clearly been most profound in the case of the Philippines. As will be seen in the sections that follow, other factors have apparently worked in combination with the policy changes to trigger the particularly large volume of immigration from the Philippines.

Ties between the Philippines and the United States

To understand why, among all countries in Southeast Asia, the Philippines is the largest contributor to U.S. immigration, it is important to take into account the country's long colonial experience with the United States. Although decolonization occurred several decades ago, the formal severing of political ties does not sunder overnight the social, cultural, and economic links that bind former colonies and mother countries and generate population movements between them. As observed in another study (U.S. Congress, 1974:34):

A fairly well demarcated pattern of immigration has taken place from former colonial areas to the imperial centers. By virtue of the former colonial–imperial link, the immigrant moves into what he believes to be familiar circles. The familiarity eases the burden of transition between the essentially different cultures. The imperial tradition may also engender the feeling that by migration to an imperial center, the former colonial is moving up into a superior and exciting culture.

For no two countries is this observation more true than for the United States and the Philippines. Indeed, the Americanization of Filipino cul-

Table 13.2. Southeast Asian Occupational-Preference Immigrants: 1966–1981

Region of Chargeability	Total Immigrants	Immigrants in Profession		Other Workers		Dependents		Total Occupational Preference	
		N	%	N	%	N	%	N	%
Philippines									
1966–1970	61,688	17,134	27.8	1,327	2.2	12,069	19.6	30,530	49.5
1971–1975	96,357	24,002	24.9	19	a	25,585	26.6	49,606	51.5
1976–1980	98,480	6,349	6.4	2,017	2.0	10,669	10.8	19,035	19.3
Thailand									
1966–1970	1,688	294	17.4	304	18.0	112	6.6	710	42.1
1971–1975	6,890	412	6.0	310	4.5	309	4.5	1,031	15.0
1976–1980	9,174	264	2.9	505	5.5	424	4.6	1,193	13.0
Burma									
1966–1970	1,580	249	15.8	89	5.6	352	22.3	69.0	43.7
1971–1975	3,697	130	3.5	58	1.6	209	5.7	897	10.7
1976–1980	5,530	89	1.6	43	0.8	244	4.4	376	6.8
Malaysia									
1966–1970[b]	819	22	2.7	33	4.0	32	3.9	87	10.6
1971–1975	1,202	52	4.3	91	7.6	89	7.4	232	19.3
1976–1980	2,000	155	7.8	100	5.0	185	9.3	440	22.0
Indonesia									
1966–1970	2,385	266	11.2	181	7.6	501	21.0	948	39.7
1971–1975	2,031	78	3.8	111	5.5	150	7.4	339	16.7
1976–1980	2,713	99	3.6	128	4.7	193	7.1	420	15.5

Sources: 1966–1977: INS Annual Reports (table 7A); 1978–1979: INS Statistical Yearbook (table 7A); 1980–1981: INS Statistical Yearbook (table 5).

Note: Data not available for Brunei.   aLess than 0.05 percent.   bData not available for 1966.

ture is pervasive and a major factor in the integration of Filipinos to the United States. One writer, in fact, observed that the recent graduate of a Philippine university "to a large extent patterns his expectations from life on his ideas of what his American counterpart receives" (Pirovano, 1977:74).

Beyond the Americanization of Filipino culture, there are other important features of the Philippine colonial experience that make the country particularly responsive to the changes in United States immigration policy. One such feature is that, prior to 1935, Filipinos were allowed to move to the United States freely as U.S. nationals. By 1930, the first year for which complete statistics were available, more than 100,000 Filipinos were in the United States, settled for the most part in California and the sugar plantations of Hawaii (Pirovano, 1977). Although small in number, these early streams of immigrants were significant in that they facilitated the entry of future immigrants through the family reunification provisions of the immigration law. As can be seen in Table 13.3, the proportion and numbers of Filipino immigrants who have entered the United States under the family preference system since passage of the 1965 immigration act have been much larger than for other countries in the region. The volume of family preference immigrants from the other countries has also grown in recent years, but the small numbers involved in earlier years has meant a slower pace of increase. The importance of chain migration has grown for all countries in the region, and the vast majority of Southeast Asian immigrants now enter the United States under the family preference categories.

The colonial status of the Philippines has also produced strong economic links with the United States. Many Philippine scholars regard this economic relationship as one of dependency, a legacy of colonialism that, in many ways, has grown even with decolonization. The economic presence of the United States in the Philippines is evident in the fact that more than 53 percent of total foreign investments in the country in 1983 can be attributed to the United States (CRC, 1985). The United States remains the Philippines' major trading partner and accounted for more than 28 percent of total Philippine trade in the same year (NEDA, 1984).

Although cause-and-effect relationships are difficult to establish, this strong economic tie has undoubtedly contributed to migration flows between the two countries by facilitating the movement of labor. Indeed, immigration to the United States has traditionally been tied to the demand for labor. As the American economy has expanded and shifted, the demand for labor has also changed. For the Philippines, the movement of labor to the United States started with the recruitment of agricultural workers in the early decades of the century, a period

Table 13.3. Southeast Asian Family-Preference Immigrants: 1966–1981

Region of Chargeability	Immigrants	1st Preference		2nd Preference		4th Preference		5th Preference		Total Family Preference	
		N	%	N	%	N	%	N	%	N	%
Philippines											
1966–1970	61,688	1,501	2.4	12,924	21.0	6,891	11.2	9,774	15.8	31,090	50.4
1971–1975	96,357	1,805	1.9	44,510	46.2	198	0.2	97	0.1	46,610	48.4
1976–1980	98,480	2,926	3.0	61,904	62.9	3,992	4.1	9,783	9.9	78,605	79.8
Thailand											
1966–1970	1,688	1	0.1	278	16.5	8	0.5	66	3.9	353	20.9
1971–1975	6,890	13	0.2	1,678	24.4	11	0.2	492	7.1	2,194	31.8
1976–1980	9,174	66	0.6	3,404	37.1	54	0.6	2,880	31.4	6,393	69.7
Burma											
1966–1970	1,580	2	0.1	165	10.4	26	1.6	259	16.4	452	28.6
1971–1975	3,697	2	0.1	992	26.8	29	0.8	587	15.9	1,610	43.5
1976–1980	5,530	15	0.3	1,238	22.4	87	1.6	3,426	62.0	4,766	86.2
Malaysia											
1966–1970[a]	819	1	0.2	85	10.4	29	3.5	205	25.0	320	39.1
1971–1975	1,202	2	0.2	206	17.1	23	1.9	272	22.6	503	41.8
1976–1980	2,000	4	0.2	383	19.2	73	3.7	911	45.6	1,371	68.6
Indonesia											
1966–1970	2,385	17	0.7	200	8.4	55	2.3	708	29.7	980	41.1
1971–1975	2,031	8	0.4	267	13.1	38	1.9	581	28.6	894	44.0
1976–1980	2,713	7	0.3	517	19.1	91	3.4	1,260	46.4	1,875	69.1

Sources: 1966–1977: INS *Annual Reports* (table 7A); 1978–1979: INS *Statistical Yearbook* (table 7A); 1980–1981: INS *Statistical Yearbook* (table 5).

Note: Data not available for Brunei.

[a]Data not available for 1966.

during which the United States was experiencing shortages of other Asian agricultural workers due to the effects of the country's Oriental exclusion policy.

The movement of agricultural labor has been supplanted in more recent years by the immigration of professionals, a pattern that seems to have been further facilitated by an educational system that "reflects American modes of learning, programs, and practices" (Abad and Eviota, 1984:6). By 1956, the Philippines had the second highest ratio of students to total population among all countries in the world (UNESCO, 1969). Given its underdeveloped economy, the country was producing college graduates much faster than its labor market could absorb them and with skills not entirely relevant to the needs of an agricultural economy (Pirovano, 1977; Tan, n.d.). In view of the similarity between the Philippine and American educational systems, it has not been difficult for the U.S. economy to absorb surplus professional labor from the Philippines (Pirovano, 1977). Indeed, the Philippines became the largest supplier of professional immigrants from the region soon after the U.S. immigration reform.

Related to professional immigration, student admissions from the Philippines have also contributed to the growth of immigrant flows to the United States. Many American schools are now vigorously recruiting foreign students to offset their declining enrollments. Because of its special ties with the United States, the Philippines has been a major source of these students. In 1981, an estimated 2,727 Filipino students were enrolled in American universities and colleges (UNESCO, 1983). As observed elsewhere (Fawcett et al., 1985), by recruiting foreign students, American schools are also unintentionally recruiting immigrants because many students eventually find a way to stay in the United States. During the period 1982–1984, some 690 Filipino students were adjusted to permanent resident status. The number is even bigger for Thailand: During the same period, 971 Thai students became permanent residents (INS, 1982–1984).

The American military presence in the Philippines is yet another legacy of the country's colonial experience. By agreement the United States continues to have legal jurisdiction over two major active military bases in the Philippines that contain the largest U.S. naval and air force fleet in the Asian–Pacific region (Wurfel, 1964). Although no direct evidence is available, this substantial military presence has apparently boosted U.S. immigration from the Philippines in at least two ways. First, U.S. forces in the Philippines have initiated kinship-based immigration through international marriages between American military personnel and Filipino women. Second, the U.S. military presence has facilitated the recruitment of Filipinos into the U.S. military. These recruits eventually qualify for American citizenship, a fact that must have an impact on the future immigration of Filipinos.

Internal Push Factors

Beyond international ties and changes in U.S. immigration policy, there are internal push factors that have reinforced the contemporary patterns of international migration from the Philippines. These factors include population growth trends, internal migration and urbanization, and, more recently, the worsening social and economic problems of the country.

The Philippines has about 51 million people living in an area of approximately 482,700 square kilometers. It has had one of the highest population growth rates in the world, reported to be about 3.5 percent in 1970 (Concepción, 1970). Despite a massive family planning outreach program launched in the mid-1970s, the country's population was still growing at a high 2.7 percent in 1980 (NEDA, 1984). The problem of rapid population increase becomes even more serious when viewed in the context of the country's economic problems. Already severe in the past two decades, these problems have taken on crisis proportions in recent years (see U.P. School of Economics, 1984), a trend that can only trigger further immigration in the future. The country's GNP growth has been declining in the past several years and was acknowledged to be a negative 5.5 percent in 1984 (Cariño, 1985).

The poor state of the economy is vividly illustrated by massive unemployment and layoffs. In 1984, some 86,000 workers were laid off by various corporations, and unemployment was officially (and conservatively) recorded at 6 percent. Along with unemployment are grave problems of poverty and inequality. In 1983, the reported threshold for a family of six was about P14,000 and 51 percent of families were at or below that threshold. The lowest quintile in 1983 was sharing 3.8 percent of total income, while the highest 20 percent were receiving as much as 57 percent (Cariño, 1985). The perceived instability of the political structure further exacerbates the country's economic problems and has been blamed for "capital flight" and "disinvestments."

In addition to the population's size and growth, its distribution is also a problem in the Philippines. Close to 15 percent of the population is concentrated in the Metro Manila area (NCSO, 1980). This uneven population distribution reflects the imbalance in welfare and development between Metro Manila and the rest of the country. In 1980, about 35 percent of the country's domestic output was contributed by Metro Manila (Cho and Bauer, 1985). Nevertheless, the country as a whole is urbanizing very quickly. It is projected that, by the year 2000, the Philippines will be about 50 percent urban, compared with only about 30 percent in 1960 (Cho and Bauer, 1985). For Metro Manila, a major component of the urban growth is rural-to-urban migration (Cariño, 1981).

The movement of people from rural areas to major urban centers, particularly Metro Manila, has contributed to a host of familiar urban growth problems: congestion and overcrowding, strained government services, unemployment and poverty, slums and squatters, and generally unsatisfactory environmental conditions. These problems have reached alarming proportions in Metro Manila, where urban growth has far outpaced the provision of basic government services.

In short, the Philippines is experiencing critical development problems: rapid population growth and increasing density; increasing scarcity of land; poor performance of the national economy; and problems related to urban growth. With worsening conditions in Metro Manila, the main destination of migrants within the country, many Filipinos have apparently headed for other countries. Given all these problems, the changes in U.S. immigration policy, and the special ties that exist between the Philippines and the United States, it is hardly surprising that Filipino immigration to the United States has grown dramatically in recent years.

The growth of contract-labor export from the Philippines has also been impressive. During the period 1975–1983, the number of overseas workers processed by the Ministry of Labor and Employment grew at an average of 37.2 percent per year (POEA, 1983a). In 1983, the Philippines Overseas Employment Administration (POEA) processed some 434,207 workers, a majority of whom were destined for the Middle East (POEA, 1983b).

CONSEQUENCES OF EMIGRATION

Emigration can have wide-ranging implications for the social and economic growth of the country of origin. These consequences are influenced by the volume and pace of emigration, the composition of the flows, and the extent of remittances and return migration. Focusing on the Philippines, the major source of U.S. immigrants from Southeast Asia, we shall now examine from a national perspective some of the principal impacts of emigration.

Demographic Selectivity

One major impact of emigration on the sending country is the age and sex selectivity that has characterized many emigrant flows, including those from the Philippines. On the Ilocos Coast, a major Philippine out-migration region, migrant flows have been uneven in sex composition. For example, in the period preceding World War II, out-migration from the Ilocos was heavily male-dominated—a trend that started with the recruitment of sugar planatation workers to Hawaii in the early decades of the century. In the postwar period, however, the trend has shifted to a female-dominant stream—a pattern that can also be observed in U.S. immigration streams from Thailand and Indonesia and one that apparently forms part of a widespread trend in more recent years (Eviota and Smith, 1983). In another major Philippine out-migration region, Bicol, migrants have tended to be young and single (Cariño, 1979).

The demographic consequences of this migrant selectivity process are easy to appreciate. On the Ilocos Coast, the male dominance of immigrant flows in earlier years resulted in highly imbalanced sex ratios in the region. As a consequence of their disproportionate contribution to out-migration, many of the lowland coastal towns had sex ratios of fewer than 850 males per 1,000 females during the period. These distortions in sex ratios, in turn, have been shown to be associated with delayed marriage and celibacy (Smith, 1981). In the Bicol region, one adverse consequence of out-migration of the young is the aging of the population—a process that, on the one hand, has depleted the region's labor resources and, on the other, has increased its dependency burden (Cariño, 1979).

Apart from their effects on marriage and fertility, evidence in the Philippines suggests that age–sex imbalances may also have important consequences for household structure. Data gathered by the Philippine Migration Study reveal that a much bigger proportion of migrant households (those with migrant members) have an extended structure when compared with stayer households (those without migrant members).[2] This pattern is consistent with the findings of an earlier study: Households of the extended type facilitate the departure of family members who have dependents because parents or older relatives in the area of origin can take over the guardianship function temporarily (Cariño and Cariño, 1976).

Emigration does not seem to have an adverse impact on household welfare in the Philippines, however. Results of the Philippine Migration Study show that migrant households have a higher socioeconomic status than stayer households—a phenomenon that can probably be

2. The Philippine Migration Study forms part of the migration research program of the East-West Population Institute and is being undertaken jointly with the Institute of Philippine Culture, Ateneo de Manila University. Investigators for the study are Ricardo G. Abad (Institute of Philippine Culture); Fred Arnold, James T. Fawcett, and Robert W. Gardner (East-West Population Institute); Benjamin V. Cariño (School of Urban and Regional Planning, University of the Philippines); and Gordon F. De Jong (Pennsylvania State University).

attributed to migrant remittances and to the fact that a certain amount of household wealth is required to enable a member to make a long-distance move.

The Brain Drain

One major consequence of the 1965 amendments to the U.S. immigration law is the so-called brain drain: the immigration of persons with professional and technical qualifications. The volume of the flow for this type of immigrant has been particularly large for the Philippines, the number of immigrant professional workers from the Philippines having grown from just over 1,900 in the period before the 1965 amendments (1960–1965) to more than 17,000 in the 1966–1970 period. For the other countries in Southeast Asia, immigrants in the professions have also increased, but the numbers involved are small when compared with the flow from the Philippines.

The extent of the brain drain from the Philippines is vividly illustrated by data on immigrant scientists, engineers, and physicians. Along with India (see Chapter 15), the Philippines has been a major supplier of these professionals to the United States (see also Chapter 17). The flow of immigrant professionals peaked in the years immediately following the 1965 amendments to the U.S. immigration law. Over the five-year period from 1966 to 1970, more than 4,300 Filipino engineers and scientists (including social scientists) and some 3,000 physicians and surgeons emigrated to the United States. During the pre-amendment period from 1962 to 1965, only 349 immigrant physicians and surgeons and 180 scientists and engineers had been admitted to United States. In a more recent three-year period, from 1976 to 1978, some 2,600 Filipino scientists and engineers emigrated to the United States (National Science Foundation, 1980; see also Pernia, 1976).

It is clear from these data that Philippine professionals responded vigorously to the changes in U.S. immigration law. Many argue that the departure of professionals constitutes a loss of valuable resources that, in the long run, will reduce the sending country's productive capacity. They point out that professional emigration represents lost educational investment in that the sending country bears the cost of educating this highly skilled labor but does not directly benefit from it.

These arguments are difficult to ignore. The departure of professionals does constitute a significant loss of expertise. As Pernia (1976) and Minocha (Chapter 15) have argued, however, the extent of the problem has to be qualified by taking into account the country's actual labor supply and the economy's capacity to absorb it. Using indicators of personnel/population ratios to reflect labor availability, and income per capita along with its rate of growth to mirror the economy's capacity to absorb additional supply, Pernia (1976:71) concludes there is *"prima facie* evidence that the Philippines' general 'brain-drain' problem stems from the basic inability of its economy to absorb the going supply of certain high-level skills." Conversely, the problem could be viewed as a case in which the supply of professionals—particularly engineers, scientists, physicians, and surgeons—has obviously outpaced the economy's absorptive capacity. The extent of the drain would therefore seem to be far less than the actual volume of immigrant professionals. More significantly, this view has an important policy implication: The remedy for the brain-drain problem seems to lie in a training and manpower policy that addresses itself to the sending country's actual development needs and objectives.

Remittances

Remittances have been viewed by many as a factor that may offset the harmful effects of the brain drain. The country of origin, it is argued, can benefit from the success of its immigrants abroad through repatriated earnings and other forms of support. Remittances to the Philippines have been reported to be substantial, especially when viewed in the context of the country's economy. A survey of Filipino immigrants in Honolulu in 1982 revealed that more than three-quarters of the households surveyed sent remittances to relatives in the Philippines. During the twelve-month period prior to the survey, the average remittance was $599 per sending household and $438 for all households in the sample. Over a one-year period, these remittances totaled more than $373,000 from 623 households (Caces, 1985:148).

For the Philippines, a substantial source of repatriated earnings is the social security payments to Filipino veterans and retired workers, a legacy of the country's long history of military and economic ties with the United States. In 1983, monthly U.S. social security payments to recipients in the Philippines amounted to almost $7 million, or about $84 million over a one-year period. Among all countries in the world, the Philippines ranks fourth (behind Mexico, Canada, and Italy) in total number of U.S. social security beneficiaries, including spouses and children (Social Security Administration, 1984).

It has been argued, that although remittances undoubtedly have had a favorable effect on household welfare in the Philippines, their benefit to the country's economy may be negligible in that only a small proportion of the funds are invested in productive enterprises. This is not to suggest that remittances have no beneficial effects at all beyond the household level. Griffiths (1979), for example, has observed that investments from remittances helped stimulate the growth of a local garlic industry in the Philippines. In general, however, remittances seem to be put mainly to nonproductive uses. In the survey of Filipino immigrants in Honolulu, two out of three of the sending households reported that their remittances were sent mainly for "daily needs," including food and clothing (Caces, 1985:150).

Repatriated earnings are also spent on housing and household appliances—often as a testimony to the immigrant's material success abroad. McArthur's (1979:93) description of how repatriated earnings are spent in Ilocos Norte may accurately portray the situation in other areas as well:

Nothing, for example, stands out more against the relative poverty of most Ilocos region towns and barrios than the brightly painted "luxury" houses of the *pensionados*. The appliances (stereo sets, electric refrigerators, televisions, fans, and gas stoves, etc.) which one commonly finds in these houses are prized more for the status that goes with their ownership than for their utility. The one "western" convenience which practically all of these houses share in common is a shower which invariably requires the construction of elevated tank to provide sufficient water pressure.

Another item for which remittances are spent in the Philippines is land. As noted by Griffiths (1979), the purchase of land in the Philippines is a reflection of a desire to gain security and social status; such purchases have little effect on production since no additional land is necessarily going into production. On the contrary, the increased demand for land in the face of its scarcity may result in severe local inflation of land prices, an effect that could work against the consolidation of holdings predicted by Griffiths.

Some have argued that the worth of remittances may lie not in their initial use but in the ultimate purpose to which they are put. Although a substantial proportion of remittances is destined to serve consumption needs, Arnold (1984) points out that the seller of consumption items may put the proceeds to productive investments. This argument could very well be valid, although there is apparently no evidence to substantiate it. Insofar as the initial use of funds is concerned, however, the evidence seems to suggest that, for the Philippines at least, remittances have negligible production effects.

Return Migration

Return migration can be an important source of change in the country of origin as migrants come home with new ideas and skills. Although some return migration to the Philippines is taking place, the evidence is rather fragmentary. A study by Jasso and Rosenzweig (1982) estimates that for immigrants who entered the United States in 1971, some 20 to 38 percent had returned to the Philippines as of January 1979. Kitano

(1981) reports that, in 1981, 39,000 of the approximately 113,000 Filipinos who emigrated to Hawaii returned to the Philippines while 18,000 moved on to the Pacific Coast states. Within a shorter four-year period—from July 1935 when the Philippine Repatriation Act was signed to December 1940 when the law expired—Arnold (1984) estimates that some 2,000 Filipinos were repatriated to the Philippines.

Proportionately, the magnitude of return migration to the Philippines in recent years appears to be smaller. On the basis of results from the Philippine Migration Study, Arnold (1984:9) reports that only 16 percent of the immigrant respondents in Honolulu expressed an intention to move again in the future. Among those who intended to move, however, the most popular choice was a return to their home region. It may be noted, in this connection, that return *visits* to the Philippines among the same informants are very common; a remarkable 61 percent have taken at least one trip since they first came to Hawaii (Caces, 1985:147). To some extent, the return migration and visits can be accounted for by such Philippine government programs as the *Balikbayan* (Return to Country), which is designed to encourage permanent emigrants to return with reduced fares, customs privileges, and tax exemptions, and the *Balikbahay* (Return Home) program for retirees, which grants returnees similar rights as citizens to purchase home lots (Marcelo, 1984).

Much less is known about the consequences of return migration. For instance, no information is available in the Philippines and in other parts of Southeast Asia on whether returnees are productive workers or dependents such as retirees and the elderly. Nor is there information on whether immigrant skills improve rather than deteriorate in the host society. Fragmentary evidence from other countries shows that, owing to limited opportunities abroad, few additional skills are acquired and those skills are often unsuitable to development conditions in the sending society. (See Swanson, 1979; Castles and Kosack, 1973.) Immigrant returnees may actually have an unfavorable influence on the sending society. They bring back materialistic values and often demand imported consumer goods, thereby shifting attention away from productive investments and possibly exerting inflationary pressure on the local economy (Abad and Eviota, 1984).

Political Activities

Filipinos in the United States have become more visible in recent years because of the political and lobbying activities of several Filipino American groups. Although the memberships of these groups are small relative to the size of the Filipino American population, their activities intensified with the 1983 assassination of opposition leader Benigno

Aquino and the subsequent revolution leading to the flight of former President Ferdinand Marcos into exile and the installation of Corazón Aquino as president. Belinda Aquino (1982), for instance, has described several underground movements that urged the withdrawal of American support from the Marcos regime and called attention to human rights violations in the country.

Many of these groups disseminated information aimed at increasing the Filipino peoples' awareness of the "abuses" of the previous Philippine regime and apprising them of the forms of opposition that existed. An article by a Filipino scholar in the United States, for instance, assessed the "state of the opposition" after several years of martial law in the Philippines and noted various forms of dissent (Muego, 1978). Several other lobby groups have reportedly exerted efforts to influence the nature of U.S. military and economic aid to the Philippines, while others have documented the extent to which the conduct of the economic and political affairs of the country is tied to pressures from international lending institutions such as USAID and the World Bank (Abad and Eviota, 1984).

The extent to which the governments of the Philippines and the United States react to these pressures is of great significance, of course, to the majority of Filipinos in the Philippines. For now, however, the impact of these political activities is difficult to measure because the 1986 revolution has led to drastic changes in domestic policy that will have far-reaching effects on the political and economic context.

SUMMARY AND CONCLUSION

In this chapter we have seen that among countries in Southeast Asia, the Philippines is the largest supplier of immigrants to the United States. Although the changes in U.S. immigration policy have apparently stimulated the phenomenal growth of Southeast Asian immigration, the policy changes alone do not fully explain the variations in size and composition of the immigrant streams from the countries in the region. In the case of the Philippines, its special economic, political, and military ties with the United States, along with its pressing internal development problems, have apparently interacted with the policy changes to produce the dramatic rise and shifting character of immigrant flows to the United States.

In turn, the massive immigration flows have important consequences for the sending society. The magnitude of these consequences, however, is difficult to determine because of the dearth of information on such aspects of the problem as remittances, return migration, the brain drain, and links between emigrants and their home country. To understand fully the impact of emigration on the sending country, we must have additional studies on these processes, as well as on the social and economic conditions in the countries of origin.

The need to undertake additional research is especially important for the Philippines in light of projections that Filipinos will soon edge out the Chinese as the largest Asian group in the United States. Currently just over 1 million in size, the Filipino population in the United States is projected to increase to more than 2 million by the year 2000 (EWPI and Operation Manong, 1985). Filipinos are also presently the largest Asian immigrant group to the United States, averaging about 40,000 admissions per year. The implications of these trends must be taken into account by the sending society, on the one hand, in formulating development and emigration-related policies, and by the host country, on the other, in considering future immigration reform and in dealing with the question of assimilation.

REFERENCES

Abad, R. G., and E. U. Eviota

    1984   "Reproducing Development Inequalities: Some Effects of Philippine Emigration to the United States." Paper prepared for the Conference on Asia–Pacific Immigration to the United States, East–West Center, Honolulu.

Aquino, B. A.

    1982   "Philippine Martial Law: Voices from the Underground." Special Paper No. 2. Washington, D.C.: Human Rights Internet.

Arnold, F.

    1984   "Birds of Passage No More: Migration Decision-Making and Filipinos in Hawaii." Paper presented at the Twelfth Annual Workshop on Psychosocial Factors in Population Research, Minneapolis.

    ————

    1985   "The Social Situation of Asian Migrant Workers and Their Families." Paper prepared for the Centre for Social Development and Humanitarian Affairs, Department of International Economic and Social Affairs, United Nations, Vienna.

Boyd, M.

    1971   "Oriental Immigration: The Experience of the Chinese, Japanese and Filipino Population in the U.S." *International Migration Review,* 5(1):48–60.

    ————

    1974   "The Changing Nature of Central and Southeast Asian Immigration to the United States, 1961-1972." *International Migration Review,* 8(4):507–519.

Caces, M. F. F.

    1985   "Personal Networks and the Material Adaptation of Recent Immigrants: A Study of Filipinos in Hawaii." Ph.D. dissertation, University of Hawaii.

Cariño, B. V.

    1979   "Migration and Development: The Bicol Region." In R. Pryor (ed.), *Migration and Development in Southeast Asia.* Kuala Lumpur: Oxford University Press.

    1981   "Socio-Economic Consequences of Migration in the Philippines." Paper prepared for the Conference on Migration and Adaptation for Environments Among Pacific Populations, East-West Center, Honolulu.

Cariño, B. V., and L. V. Cariño

    1976   "Rural Outmigration in the Philippines: An Analysis of Communities, Households, and Individuals." Research report prepared for the Population Center Foundation, Manila.

Cariño, L. V.

    1985   "Living in the Dark Times: How Ordinary Filipinos Cope with the Crises in the Philippines." Paper presented at the annual meeting of the Association of Asian Studies, Philadelphia, 22–24 March.

Castles, S., and G. Kosack

    1973   *Immigrant Workers and Class Structure in West Europe.* London: Oxford University Press.

Center for Research and Communication (CRC)

    1985   *CRC Executive Factbook 1985.* Manila: CRC Publications and Relations Office.

Cho, L. J., and J. G. Bauer

    1985   "Population Growth and Urbanization: What Does the Future Hold?" Paper prepared for the Conference on Population Growth, Urbanization, and Urban Policies in the Asia–Pacific Region, East-West Center, Honolulu.

Concepción, M.

    1970   *The Philippines: Country Profile.* New York: Population Council.

Desbarats, J.

    1979   "Thai Migration to Los Angeles." *Geographical Review,* 69:302–318.

East-West Population Institute (EWPI) and Operation Manong

    1985   *Filipino Immigrants in Hawaii: A Profile of Recent Arrivals.* Honolulu: East-West Population Institute, East-West Center, and Operation Manong, University of Hawaii.

Eviota, E., and P. C. Smith

1983   "The Migration of Women in the Philippines." In J. T. Fawcett et al.
(eds.), *Migration of Women in the Cities of Asia: Migration and Urban
Adaptation*. Boulder: Westview Press.

Fawcett, J. T., B. V. Cariño, and F. Arnold

1985   *Asia–Pacific Immigration to the United States: A Conference Report*.
Honolulu: East-West Population Institute, East-West Center.

Griffiths, S. L.

1979   "Emigration and Entrepreneurship in a Philippine Peasant Village."
Papers in Anthropology, 20(1):127–144.

Immigration and Naturalization Service (INS)

1982–   *Statistical Yearbook*. Washington, D.C.: Department of Justice.
1984

Jasso, G., and M. Rosenzweig

1982   "Estimating the Emigration Rates of Legal Immigrants Using Administrative and Survey Data: The 1971 Cohort of Immigrants to the U.S."
Demography, 19(3):279–290.

Kahin, G. M.

1964   *Governments and Politics of Southeast Asia*. Ithaca: Cornell University Press.

Keely, C. B.

1973   "Philippine Migration: Internal Movements and Emigration to the U.S."
International Migration Review, 7(2):177–187.

Kennedy, E. M.

1966   "The Immigration Act of 1965." *Annals of the American Academy of Political and Social Science,* 367:137–149.

Kitano, H. H. L.

1981   "Asian-Americans: The Chinese, Japanese, Koreans, Filipinos, and
Southeast Asians." *Annuals of the American Academy of Political and Social
Science,* 454:125–138.

Marcelo, T. I.

1984   "Emigration Policies and Domestic Development Goals of the Government of the Philippines Affecting Emigration to the United States." Paper
presented at the Conference on Asia–Pacific Immigration to the U.S.,
East-West Center, Honolulu.

McArthur, H. J., Jr.

1979   "The Effects of Overseas Work on Return Migrants and Their Home
Communities: A Philippine Case." *Papers in Anthropology,* 20(1):85–104.

Muego, B. N.

  1978   "The 'New Society' Five Years Later: The State of the Opposition." In
          Southeast Asian Affairs, 1978. Singapore: Institute of Southeast Asian
          Studies.

National Census and Statistics Office (NCSO)

  1980   *Census of the Population*. Manila: NCSO.

National Economic and Development Authority (NEDA)

  1984   *Philippine Statistical Yearbook, 1984*. Manila: NEDA.

National Science Foundation

  1980   *Scientists and Engineers from Abroad, 1976–78*. Surveys of Science and
          Resources Series. Washington, D.C.: National Science Foundation.

Pernia, E. M.

  1976   "The Question of the Brain Drain from the Philippines." *International
          Migration Review,* 10(1):63–72.

Philippine Overseas Employment Administration (POEA)

  1983a   *Annual Report for 1982*. Manila: Ministry of Labor and Employment.

  1983b   *Report of Operations in 1983*. Manila: Ministry of Labor and Employment.

Pirovano, E. V.

  1977   "Recent Arrivals from the Philippines in the United States." Ph.D. dis-
          sertation, University of Pennsylvania.

Smith, P. C.

  1981   *Population Pressure and Social Response on the Ilocos Coast in the Philip-
          pines*. Working Paper No. 2. Honolulu: East–West Population Insti-
          tute, East–West Center.

Social Security Administration

  1984   *Social Security Bulletin*. Washington, D.C.: Government Printing
          Office.

Surh, T., W. Chan, E. Yoshimura, A. Fernandez, J. Yoo, and W. Luk

  1982   "Asian Immigration." *Eastwind Journal,* 1(2):25–40. Fall/Winter.

Swanson, J. C.

  1979   "The Consequences of Emigration for Economic Development: A
          Review of the Literature." *Papers in Anthropology,* 20(1):57–74.

Tan, E. A.

  n.d.   "Philippine Market for Educated Labor." Report to the National
          Science Development Board. Manila: NSDB.

UNESCO

    1969   *UNESCO Statistical Yearbook 1968.* Paris: UNESCO.

    1985   *UNESCO Statistical Yearbook 1985.* Paris: UNESCO.

U.P. School of Economics

    1984   *The Philippine Economic Crisis.* Report prepared by faculty members of U.P. School of Economics. Diliman, Quezon City.

U.S. Congress, House Committee on Foreign Affairs

    1974   *The Brain Drain: A Study of the Persistent Issue of International Scientific Mobility.* Subcommittee on National Security and Scientific Development. Washington, D.C.: Government Printing Office.

Wurfel, D.

    1964   "The Philippines." In G. Kahin (ed.), *Governments and Politics of Southeast Asia.* Ithaca: Cornell University Press.

14

Korea and East Asia: Premigration Factors and U.S. Immigration Policy

Illsoo Kim

If U.S. immigration policy is designed to implement an egalitarian quota system of assigning an equal number of immigrants to each country, why have some nations sent larger numbers of immigrants to the United States than others? I contend that this differential pattern of immigration is due to the selective interplay between the premigration factors in home countries and U.S. immigration policy as stated in the Immigration Act of 1965 and its 1976 amendment. A structural analysis of how premigration factors in home countries—their degree of economic development and urbanization, their rapid population growth, their economic and political relations with the United States—would clarify the wide variation in the volume of immigrants from each country. It is my central thesis that premigration factors have interacted with specific aspects of U.S. immigration policy and thereby have contributed directly or indirectly to the formation of "emigration connections" that foster the establishment of entry mechanisms, legal or illegal, of emigrants into the United States. I shall advance my thesis by focusing on basic patterns of Korean emigration to the United States. To present basic similarities and dissimilarities of Asian immigration from a comparative perspective, I shall also show the prevailing trends of emigration from China (Mainland China, Taiwan, and Hong Kong) and Japan.

MULTIFACTOR APPROACH

Emphasis on the formation of emigration connections as a new dimension in contemporary immigration to the United States departs from general theories of international migration. The *equilibrium* theory of neoclassical economics views international migration as a natural and individual process of population movement, whereby sending and receiving regions achieve a balance in the supply and demand of labor, as well as in the incomes between the two regions. In this theory, predicated on the twin concepts of pull and push factors, the individual migrant is a free, utilitarian, rational, and well-informed agent trying to maximize differential income opportunities (Hawley, 1950:chap. 17; Lee, 1966). This theory does not address such macroscopic issues as immigration and emigration policy, class structure, or international political economy as institutional forces "pushing" and "pulling" people across national boundaries.

The *world-system* theory of international migration, like other variants of Marxist theory, treats international migration as a capitalistic organization of certain segments of labor across national boundaries. International migration is seen as the movement of labor from "peripheral" or "semiperipheral" to "core" nations driven by such capitalistic forces as "international division of labor," "peripheralization of underdeveloped economies," and creation of a "split" or "dual" labor market and an "industrial reserve army" in the receiving nation (Castles and Kosack, 1972; Bonacich, 1972; Piore, 1980; Petras, 1980, 1981; Sassen-Koob, 1980, 1981). Elizabeth M. Petras, for instance, notes (1980:439):

Within the framework of a modern world economy, bound together into one world capitalist system, the driving tendency towards capital accumulation is realized internationally as a single division of labor existing within a multiplicity of polities and cultures. Within a late stage of capitalist development, surplus or reserve labor is drawn across national barriers toward the most flourishing and healthy centers of accumulation. Cross-national labor flows are at times hindered and at times abetted by policies and economic cycles within the various nation states involved. The general pattern, however, is based on the attraction of free labor from those nations located in the peripheral and semiperipheral areas of production, to the core, or metropolitan centers.

Although this theoretical perspective has a vantage point of interpreting international migration in the context of international political economy, it is too abstract to be useful to the analysis of current immigration to the United States. (For specific limitations of the world-system theory, see Koo and Yu, 1981.) Migration theorists of Marxist orientation neglect noneconomic variables of international migration—

such as international marriage, kinship networks, international relations, foreign policy, and worldwide diffusion of postindustrial, bourgeois mass culture and consumption—as structural factors fostering emigration and immigration. (For a political dimension of contemporary international migration, see Zolberg, 1981, 1983). By attributing all aspects of migration to global capitalistic forces, they faithfully reify Marx's theory of economic determinism. In this chapter I prefer a multidimensional approach in order to explore the complex interplay of kinship, political, economic, and cultural factors as a basis for the formation of Asian, especially Korean, emigration connections to urban postindustrial America.

CHARACTERISTICS OF KOREAN IMMIGRANTS

The Volume of Korean Immigration

During the period 1962–1983, a total of 516,156 Koreans emigrated to foreign countries, of whom 416,679, or 81 percent, entered the United States as legal immigrants (Kim, 1984). Since the passage of the Immigration Act of 1965, South Korea has sent to the United States a larger number of immigrants than China and Japan, although its total population is much smaller than that of either of the two neighboring nations. From 1966 to 1981, South Korea sent to the United States 330,237 immigrants; China, 304,073; and Japan, 71,205 (U.S. Immigration and Naturalization Service, 1966–1977, 1977–1981). During the period 1979–1981, South Korea sent to the United States an annual average of 793 Koreans per million inhabitants of South Korea as of 1980. The South Korean emigration rate of 793 is high compared with 26 for China (excluding Hong Kong) and 34 for Japan (Winsberg, 1985:7). Differences in the formation and operation of premigration factors as they relate to U.S. immigration policy are a key to understanding the different rates of emigration from the three Asian nations to the United States.

Another group of Koreans entered the United States with nonmigrant statuses such as student, visitor, and businessman. Many of them wished to stay permanently. During the period 1960–1976, a total of 32,028 Koreans, who had previously entered with nonimmigrant status, managed to acquire permanent resident status (U.S. Immigration and Naturalization Service, 1960–1976). The influx of Korean students has been a major component of Korean immigration. According to the Korean Ministry of Education, from 1953 to 1980 a total of 15,147 Korean students left for the United States with student visas; fewer than 10 percent of them have returned to their home country. In 1985, some 13,000 were enrolled in American universities and colleges (*Dong-A Ilbo*, 17 May 1985). This pattern of student immigration is much more pronounced among Chinese than Koreans. During the period 1950–1983, some 70,000 Chinese students in Taiwan went to the United States, of whom 7,000, or 10 percent, returned to their homeland (Hwang, 1984:8). Moreover, a total of 33,649 students in Hong Kong came to the United States during the period 1963–1975 (U.S. Immigration and Naturalization Service, 1963–1975). Owing to this student immigration, China and Hong Kong have actually sent more immigrants to the United States than has South Korea. Most of these Asian students, especially those studying science and engineering, have acquired U.S. citizenship by virtue of their professional skills or by establishing an occupational connection with American industry and business.

Unbalanced Sex Ratio

Korean females outnumbered males by 2 to 1 during the period 1966–1975 (U.S. Immigration and Naturalization Service, 1966–1975). The sex imbalance has been narrowed since 1976, but in 1980 there were still 71 males per every 100 females (U.S. Bureau of the Census, 1983a). Both marriage connection and occupational connection have worked in favor of Korean females and mainly explain this imbalance. During 1950–1975, a total of 28,205 Korean women, most of whom had married American military personnel stationed in South Korea, came to the United States as wives of American citizens (Kim, 1977). Moreover, between 1966 and 1981 some 7,000 Korean nurses entered the United States by virtue of their nursing skills (Kim, 1981:148).

The sex imbalance due to women's marriage connection is quite striking among recent Japanese immigrants. During 1947–1976, some 58 percent of the 117,132 Japanese immigrants to the United States came as wives of American citizens, mostly American servicemen in Japan (Kim, 1977:99). Thus it is fair to say that the majority of post–World War II Japanese immigrants entered the United States via the marriage connection.

The sex imbalance is not so pronounced among Chinese immigrants, however. Females represented 52 percent of total Chinese immigrants during the period 1966–1975 (U.S. Immigration and Naturalization Service, 1966–1975). This lower proportion is due largely to the fact that Chinese females did not establish as many occupational and international marriage connections as Korean females.

Young Age Structure

Korean immigrants are mostly young and thus economically active. Some 87 percent of the Korean immigrants who entered the United States in 1977 were under age 40, compared with 64 percent for the U.S. population. In 1980, the median age for the Korean immigrants who had arrived in the United States between 1970 and 1980 was 27.3, compared with 36.1 for Chinese immigrants and 30 for the nation as a whole (U.S. Bureau of the Census, 1984). The young age structure of Korean immigrants is partly due to the adoption of Korean children by U.S. couples. Between 1962 and 1983, Americans adopted 45,142 Korean children (Kim, 1984:9). During the 1950s and 1960s, Americans adopted mainly the Amerasian children produced by the Korean War. Today they adopt mainly Korean children abandoned by urban poor parents, most of whom migrated to cities from rural areas.

Social Characteristics

A majority of Korean immigrants were drawn from the middle or upper middle classes in the South Korean primate cities of Seoul, Busan, and Taegu (Kim, 1981:38). Forty percent of the Koreans who came to the United States in 1974–1977 had previously held professional and technical occupations in their homeland (Yu, 1983:29). According to a sample survey on Koreans in the Los Angeles metropolitan area (Hurh and Kim, 1980:67), 65 percent of male and 53 percent of female respondents reported that they had finished college in their homeland. Korean immigration is also selective by religious affiliation. According to the same survey, about 50 percent of respondents were affiliated with Christian, particularly Protestant, churches in South Korea, although the Korean Christian population in South Korea represented only 24 percent of the total Korean population in 1984.

To sum up, Korean immigrants are selective and highly homogeneous in class, occupation, and religious affiliation. Chinese immigrants, by contrast, are heterogeneous in class and regional and linguistic background. Recent Chinese immigrants have been drawn from Taiwan, Hong Kong, Mainland China, Caribbean nations, and Vietnam, and their class and occupational status have varied widely (Sung, 1980).

U.S. IMMIGRATION POLICY AND OCCUPATIONAL CONNECTIONS

The Korean pattern of occupational and educational selectivity arose because the U.S. Immigration Act of 1965 gave the Department of Labor the authority to select immigrants with specific skills and thus initiated a definite institutional link between labor policy and immigration policy (Cassell, 1966:107). The linkage also opened the way for Chinese and Korean "nonimmigrant" students to acquire a green card because of their skills. As of 1984, the Korean Scientists and Engineers' Association in the United States listed some 3,500 Korean scientists and engineers, most of whom had earned doctoral degrees from American universities.

As we have seen, this student immigration is much more pronounced among Chinese than Koreans. In 1984, the Chinese students from China constituted the largest number of foreign-born engineering and science doctorates graduating from American universities (National Science Foundation, 1985). This pattern of immigration largely accounts for the bipolarity of occupational structure among Chinese immigrants. According to the 1980 U.S. census (U.S. Bureau of the Census, 1984), some 42 percent of 77,829 employed Chinese immigrants were engaged in managerial, technical, and administrative occupations and another 51 percent were found in menial, labor-intensive service occupations or in unskilled or semiskilled blue-collar jobs. This pattern of selective immigration among students and professionals cannot be found in the contemporary Japanese immigration to the United States. According to Shim (1978:164), "the basic reason was, of course, the growing labor shortage in Japan and the strong pressure exerted on the Japanese government by industry to reduce government support for emigration."

Given the linkage between labor policy and immigration policy, the influx of Korean medical professionals was conspicuous. Some 13,000 Korean doctors, nurses, and pharmacists entered the United States during the period 1966–1979 (Kim, 1981). In 1984 there were some 4,300 Korean immigrant doctors in the United States (*Dong-A Daily News*, 13 March 1984). Their influx has been reduced substantially since 1976, when the Health Professions Act provided for a phaseout of preferences to foreign doctors (Act of 12 October 1976, 90 Stat. 2243).

The international mobility of Korean medical professionals was a by-product of the expansion of the American medical economy (Kim, 1981:147–176). During the 1960s and the early 1970s the demand for medical personnel rose as a result of the emergence of a service-oriented economy, which has increasingly characterized contemporary American society. But the United States was not self-sufficient in the supply of medical workers—partly because the already large demand for them increased suddenly and partly because the American medical establishment had been unwilling or unable to produce enough medical workers to serve the growing number of Americans in need of treatment. This peculiar development in the American medical industry accidentally established an occupational connection with Korean emigrants and worked as the main factor drawing Korean medical professionals to the United States. Thus vast economic opportunities arose suddenly and serendipitously for South Koreans in this occupational category.

Facing such deep economic problems as the energy shortage, high unemployment, and inflation, the U.S. Congress in 1976 amended the Immigration Act of 1965 (Act of 20 October 1976, 90 Stat. 2703). One of the amendments downgraded professional immigrants (physicians, nurses, dentists) from the third preference to the sixth preference. This meant that the United States was virtually closing its door to skilled emigrants by almost abolishing the occupational preference. This shift in immigration policy has created a new pattern of Korean immigration. In 1972, some 45 percent of Korean immigrants had entered the United States under occupational and other nonfamily preferences; the percentage fell to 8 percent in 1977 and to 6 percent in 1983 (Kim, 1984). In 1983, some 94 percent of the Korean immigrants to the United States owed their entry to kinship preferences for reunion of immediate family members (57 percent), adoption of Korean children (19 percent), and international marriage (18 percent). Because of this new pattern of kinship-centered immigration, Korean immigrants of today are not so selective in terms of occupation, class, and educational background as their predecessors admitted prior to the 1976 amendment.

The dominant pattern of entry based upon kinship, however, reflects much of the old pattern of occupational and class selectivity, for the majority of new arrivals are close relatives of early comers who were professionals, students, businessmen, and government officials. The early immigrants laid the foundation for kinship-centered chain immigration. Since they were from the middle and upper classes of South Korean society, the families who followed them belonged to similar classes. Korean War brides and their families were an exception, however. Most of them came from the lower strata of South Korean society.

THE U.S. INVOLVEMENT WITH SOUTH KOREA

The four largest sending countries of immigrants to the United States—the Philippines, South Korea, China, and Vietnam—share a common premigration factor regarding the U.S. involvement with them. The historical, political, and military involvement of the United States with the Philippines, the two Koreas, the two Chinas, and the two Vietnams has fostered emigration from these nations to the United States. American intervention in these nations has unwittingly generated critical forces for their emigration to the United States: the creation of political refugees, international marriage, economic interdependence, and the diffusion of American mass culture. The operation of these factors differs from country to country, reflecting each country's unique relations with the United States. In the case of China, the U.S. political and military intervention contributed to the exodus of intellectuals, students, government officials, and businessmen from China, Taiwan, and Hong Kong for political reasons after the communists' overthrow of the Nationalist government in 1949. (For the effects of foreign policy on in-

ternational migration, see Hart, 1982; Teitelbaum, 1984.) Japanese immigration has also been greatly affected by the U.S. involvement with
Japan. The majority of Japanese immigrants, as I have indicated already,
achieved entry via marriage to U.S. servicemen stationed in Japan.

Korean immigration is a model case for these structural links between
U.S. foreign intervention and immigration. Since 1882, when Korea entered into a treaty with the United States, Korea (South Korea after
Korean independence from Japan in 1945) has been subject to American political, economic, and cultural influence. The political, economic,
and military involvement of the United States with South Korea since
the end of World War II has laid the foundation for the recent Korean
immigration to the United States. The effects of the U.S. involvement
on Korean immigration are interrelated and cumulative.

First, the U.S. forces in South Korea, which are maintained at an
authorized strength of 39,000, have greatly contributed to the kinship-
centered immigration as marriages have taken place between Korean
women and U.S. servicemen. In this context, it should be noted that
during the period 1962–1983 a total of 80,748 Koreans emigrated to the
United States through the entry mechanism of international marriage
(Kim, 1984). (The total figure includes the marriage between Koreans
and Korean American citizens.) The so-called Korean War brides are
one of the social groups who laid the foundation of the kinship-centered
immigration. Frauds have been frequently involved in the establishment
of this connection of international marriage. Many Korean women, who
wished to emigrate but could not gain access to a legal entry channel,
resorted to paying a fee to Korean emigration brokers in return for the
arrangement of a bogus marriage to an American citizen, usually a GI
in South Korea. (For a detailed description of this general pattern of
immigration to the United States, see Dec, 1981.) This illegal mechanism undoubtedly has facilitated the influx of Koreans into the United
States.

Second, the U.S. armed forces have transmitted American mass culture to South Korea. According to Lim (1982:30), "stationing of large-
scale American troops in Korea, especially during the Korean War,
provided another channel of Korean-American cultural contact. This
contact was significant in the sense that direct cultural contact was made
broadly between average citizens for the first time in the hundred years
of American-Korean relations." As a consequence, American goods,
movies, and popular songs have fascinated Korean urbanites. Learning English has become a major means by which businessmen, white-
collar workers, public officials, and military officers strive for upward
mobility. This cultural impact has been cumulative and has fostered
a desire for emigration to the United States. American military and

Table 14.1.   Demographic and Economic Indicators for Selected Asian
Nations

Nation	Average Annual Population Growth Rate, 1980–1985 (%)	Population Density (per Square Mile), 1984	Proportion of Population Urban (%)	Per Capita Income ($)
South Korea	1.5	1,061	63 (1983)	1,850 (1983)
Taiwan	1.8	1,348	71 (1980)	2,444 (1983)
Hong Kong	NA	13,188	86 (1981)	5,100 (1981)
China (Mainland)	1.4	291	28 (1985)	308 (1983)
Japan	0.6	823	76 (1980)	10,120 (1984)

Sources: Encyclopedia Britannica (1985); U.S. Bureau of the Census (1983b).

civilian personnel have played a key role in making a cultural connection with South Koreans by introducing to them an American consumption ideal.

Third, the continuous political and military involvement of the United States with South Korea—in particular the nuclear warheads deployed in South Korea by the United States against North Korea—has been a major source of tension between North and South Korea (Lee, 1983). In light of the fact that many middle-class and upper-middle-class Koreans have made a political exodus to the United States in fear of another Korean War, this is a push factor for emigration that the United States itself exported to South Korea.

So far I have considered the specific effects of U.S. political involvement on Korean emigration to the United States. This presentation, however, does not provide a complete picture of the premigration factors underlying Korean emigration to the United States. Since population and urban growth, internal migration, and economic development and international trade have increasingly shaped contemporary patterns of international migration, the impact of these macroscopic factors on the Korean movement to the United States deserves attention.

SOCIAL CHANGE AND EMIGRATION

As indicated in Table 14.1, South Korea, Taiwan, and Hong Kong share certain common demographic characteristics not shared with other developing nations. They have experienced moderate population growth rates but have high population densities. They are also much more urbanized than many other developing nations. In terms of per capita income they have become the "mid-advanced nations" as these nations, dubbed "little Japans," have undergone rapid but precarious economic growth. Their growth has been hampered by political uncertainty over the Taiwan issue, the Hong Kong issue, and the Korean problem. These political issues have caused an exodus of middle and upper classes from the countries to the United States (Kim, 1981; Kwong, 1984). South Korea, Taiwan, and Hong Kong also have the United States as a major trade partner—another premigration factor facilitating emigration to the United States.

Japan is significantly different from the "little Japans" only in the category of per capita income. Mainly because of the Japanese economic achievement, Japanese immigrants to the United States declined in number from 5,326 in 1971 to 3,896 in 1981. Like other Asian immigrants, however, Japanese immigrants consist largely of young, skilled, middle-class urbanites who "are seeking a challenge overseas that they cannot find in the comfortable confines of modern Japan" (*New York Times*, 7 November 1977). But Koreans are pushed to emigrate under different socioeconomic conditions.

The Population Explosion

The so-called population explosion has emerged as the most urgent domestic problem confronting South Korean society. Since 1962, the South Korean government has attempted to control population growth by relying upon family planning programs that encourage couples to use contraception. The Korean approach to family planning has been construed as a model for other developing nations (Keeny, 1967:4). Indeed, the annual rate of population increase was reduced from 2.9 percent in 1961 to 1.58 by 1980 (Republic of Korea Economic Planning Board, 1981). In absolute numbers, however, the population of South Korea grew from 25 million in 1960 to 38 million in 1980, increasing by 52 percent. South Korea's population density is the third highest in the world. As of 1984, more than 40 million people were competing with one another for the scarce resources of a country whose area is only slightly larger than the state of Maine.

To mitigate population pressure, the South Korean government in 1962 formulated an emigration policy designed to export its surplus population (Lee, 1976). The policy was an extension of the government's domestic population control policy. The South Korean emigration law, which was amended in 1962, stated: "This amendment, by encouraging people to emigrate to foreign countries, is designed to be geared to a population control policy and thus to contribute to the stability of the national economy" (*Yimin baeg-gwa*, 1964:361). And yet, in the face of its military confrontation with North Korea, the South Korean government imposed eligibility restrictions on emigration.

Seeing that Korean emigrants contributed to the South Korean economy by sending substantial remittances home—between 1970 and 1978, Korean immigrants in the United States remitted a total of $757 million (Koo and Yu, 1981:23)—as well as by facilitating trade between South Korea and their host country, the South Korean government has, since 1981, begun to liberalize emigration procedures. Emulating Japanese emigration policy, the South Korean government is permitting the establishment of a Korean base in receiving countries to facilitate trade and the acquisition of raw materials. South Korean emigration policy is also implicitly geared to South Korean foreign policy in the sense that the government wants to achieve its specific foreign policy objectives in receiving nations by relying upon Korean nationals. (For a discussion of the new direction of South Korean emigration policy, see *Dong-A Daily News,* 11 August 1984.)

Through the U.S. Immigration Act of 1965, South Korea, without exerting diplomatic pressure, was granted a substantial quota of emigrants to the United States. Koreans' entry to the United States was serendipitous. Although the South Korean government did not influence U.S. immigration policy, South Koreans have responded to the new immigration laws by taking individual initiatives to emigrate. Such initiatives include gathering information about residential and job opportunities in the new land, acquiring specific skills that can be sold in the American labor market, and amassing illegal dollars to be invested in business enterprises in the inner cities of America (Kim, 1981:chap. 2).

Urbanization and Economic Development

Population pressure is the primary premigration factor pushing South Koreans into the United States. However, it does not explain why a large number of South Koreans feel deprived and presume that their opportunities would be greater in the United States. Like other Asian emigrants from Hong Kong and Taiwan, most South Korean emigrants experienced in their own country a great deal of geographical and occupational mobility associated with rapid but hazardous economic growth and a corresponding process of urbanization. The Korean emigrants' sense of mobility was greatly intensified as a result of their experiences with a dramatic political change involving geographical and social dislocation. As Chinese immigrants from Hong Kong and Taiwan were drawn largely from among refugees (and their descendants) who fled Communist China, so a high proportion of Korean immigrants were North Korean refugees and their children, who took refuge in South Korea immediately before and during the Korean War. North Korean refugees were estimated to represent some 50 percent of those

Koreans who emigrated to foreign countries during the 1960s—mostly
to Latin American nations and the United States. (See Shrader, 1984;
for the marginal status of North Koreans in South Korea associated with
their emigration, see Kim, 1981.)

South Korea has been urbanizating at an unprecedented rate since
1960, and this transformation has produced vast social changes throughout the country. During 1960–1983, the proportion of the total population living in areas with populations of 50,000 or more increased from
28 percent to 70 percent owing largely to a massive influx of people
from rural areas (Lim, 1976:107–109; No, 1983:9). In 1983, some 23 percent of the nation's population was concentrated in Seoul, the capital
city, whose population had increased from 1.6 million to 9.2 million
since 1955. As of 1983, Seoul had, "on average, 36,000 people crammed
into every square mile, compared with 23,000 in New York City and
11,000 in London. At the present annual growth rate of 3 to 4 percent,
the population could reach 12 million in a decade and 15 million by
the year 2000" (*New York Times*, 13 June 1983). In short, South Korea
suffers from an overurbanization in which the rural-to-urban migration rate outstrips the expansion of urban economy, housing, and infrastructure, creating such typical urban problems as overcrowding, air
pollution, unemployment, and underemployment. According to a 1983
sample survey of Seoul citizens conducted jointly by Yonsei University
and the *Dong-A Daily News*, 61 percent of the respondents were unhappy with the quality of life in Seoul and wanted to leave; 42 percent
of them cited air pollution as the major reason for their desire to leave
Seoul. This sort of urban problem has certainly pushed unhappy Seoul
citizens to emigrate to the United States. Seoul has provided most of
the Korean immigrants to the United States.

The development of an export-oriented economy has largely effected
the massive rural-to-urban migration by creating economic opportunities in Korean urban centers. Since 1961, the entire South Korean economic structure has been reshuffled to encourage the development of
an export-oriented economy. According to the Republic of Korea Exchange Bank (1983:1), "real GNP has grown 8.3 percent per year on
average during the four five-year plans to 1981 and exports have risen
from just over US$50 million to more than US$21 billion." As a result,
South Korea is entirely dependent on the economic forces of a few advanced nations, especially the United States and Japan. Between 1975
and 1980, some 30 percent of all South Korean exports, or $20 billion
in goods, went to the United States while 21 percent, or $14.4 billion,
went to Japan. The two advanced nations have been the major suppliers of capital and technology to South Korean export industries (Saxonhouse, 1982). Economic aid from the United States, estimated at $5.9

billion from 1946 through 1979, has been invaluable to the Korean economy's development.

Nevertheless, South Korea has shown uneven rates of economic growth because the economy has been at the mercy of the vicissitudes of international trade, which is dominated by the United States and Japan. The sudden ups and downs of the South Korean economy during the past twenty years have influenced the migration flow of South Koreans to the United States. Between 1980 and 1983, for instance, the number of South Koreans applying to emigrate to the United States dropped from 33,638 to 24,015, owing partly to South Korea's impressive recovery from the economic recession of 1979–1980 (Kim, 1984; see also Shrader, 1984).

South Korean exports of labor-intensive consumer goods such as wigs, garments, shoes, and handbags to the United States have coincided with the entry of Korean immigrants to the United States. Korean immigrants have established economic entry points in American inner cities by importing such labor-intensive goods from South Korea (Kim, 1981:chap. 4). In facilitating South Korean exports to the United States, Korean immigrants have become both agents and beneficiaries of the trade between the two countries. In the Los Angeles metropolitan area, for instance, some 7,000 Korean business enterprises were identified in 1983, of which some 300 were trading companies dealing with South Korean products (*Dong-A Daily News,* 26 October 1983). The trading companies supply Korean goods to Korean retailers. (For a sample survey on this phenomenon in the Chicago area, see Kim and Hurh, 1984:36.)

The economic connection has facilitated the exodus of wealthy South Koreans to the United States. They have brought with them large sums of dollars. Many of them have entered the United States under a nonimmigrant status such as "businessman and investor" or "temporary visitor for pleasure" and have changed their status after entry to that of permanent resident. In acquiring permanent resident status, they have relied heavily on the technique of investing capital in business enterprises, a means by which both prospective immigrants and nonimmigrant aliens in the United States are entitled to become permanent residents.

CONCLUSION

The selective interactions of U.S. immigration policy with premigration factors of South Korea have determined the basic socioeconomic and demographic characteristics as well as the entry mechanisms of Korean immigrants to the United States. The political and economic dependence of South Korea on the United States since the end of World War II has generated specific "emigration connections" of South Koreans with the United States: marriage or kinship, occupational, and cultural connections. I have also considered other general premigration factors—the population explosion, overurbanization, development of an export economy, and international trade—and the extent to which they have contributed to Korean emigration to the United States.

Chinese immigration has shown quite similar premigration factors: the political issues surrounding Taiwan and Hong Kong, the urban population explosion, and rapid economic development. But the heavy influx of Chinese in the form of student immigration is a unique Chinese phenomenon. Some 90 percent of Chinese students became legal immigrants in the United States by establishing an occupational connection with certain segments of the American economy. Japan shares some basic premigration factors with South Korea: the U.S. military involvement, high population density, and an export-oriented economy. But Japan differs from South Korea in two premigration factors: political stability and awesome economic growth. Given this favorable domestic situation, Japanese immigration to the United States has been limited, and it declined during the 1970s—the decade of unprecedented Japanese economic expansion. Thus the primary candidates for Japanese emigration to the United States were predominantly Japanese brides of U.S. servicemen in Japan. The marriage connection was the principal entry mechanism for Japanese immigrants.

The patterns of Korean immigration to the United States are the unintended consequence of U.S. immigration policy. They are unexpected results because American policymakers did not anticipate the effects of the premigration factors on immigration. Furthermore, U.S. immigration laws are aimed at all nationalities, but the number of beneficiaries differs from country to country, depending upon the degree of its economic development and urbanization and the intensity of its economic, political, military, and cultural dependency on the United States. In this respect, the current national debate on a new U.S. immigration policy is myopic because it has focused on domestic issues without considering the interactions of a domestic immigration policy with the dramatic economic and social changes facing most Third World nations.

The patterns of Korean immigration to the United States cannot be explained by Marxist theories of international migration. The world-system theory and other variants of Marxist theory ignore the effects of U.S. foreign policy on the creation of premigration factors in Third World nations. This political dimension is relevant to almost all major sending countries of immigrants to the United States—Mexico, Cuba, the Dominican Republic, Jamaica, China, the Philippines, Vietnam, and South Korea. In the case of Asian immigration, the political involvement of the United States with the Philippines, the two Chinas, the two Koreas, and the two Vietnams has directly or indirectly contributed to the emigration of people from these nations to the United States. The involvement has created specific emigration connections within the framework of U.S. immigration laws.

REFERENCES

Abrams, E., and F. S. Abrams
   1975   "Immigration Policy—Who Gets In and Why?" *Public Interest*, 38:3–29.

Bonacich, E.
   1972   "A Theory of Ethnic Antagonism: The Split Labor Market." *American Sociological Review*, 37:547–559.

Cassell, F. H.
   1966   "Immigration and the Department of Labor." *Annals of the American Academy of Political and Social Science*, 367 (September):105–114.

Castles, S., and G. Kosack
   1972   "The Function of Labour Immigration in Western European Capitalism." *New Left Review*, 73 (May–June):3–21.

Chaney, E. M.
   1979   "The World Economy and Contemporary Migration." *International Migration Review*, 13:204–212.

Dec, D.
   1981   "Marriage Fraud." *INS Reporter* (Winter 1981–1982):8–9.

Encyclopedia Britannica
   1985   *1985 Britannica Book of the Year.* Chicago.

Fawcett, J. T., F. Arnold, and U. Minocha
   1984   "Asian Immigration to the United States: Flows and Processes." Paper presented at the Conference on Asia–Pacific Immigration to the United States, East-West Center, Honolulu.

Hart, G.
   1982   "Immigrants and the New Bill." *New York Times*, 24 August 1982.

Hawley, A. H.
   1950   *Human Ecology: A Theory of Community Structure.* New York: Ronald Press.

Hurh, W. M., and K. C. Kim
   1980   *Korean Immigrants in America: A Structural Analysis of Ethnic Confinement and Adhesive Adaptation.* Final report submitted to the National Institute of Mental Health, U.S. Department of Health and Human Services. Macomb, Ill.: Department of Sociology and Anthropology, Western Illinois University.

Hwang, C.-s.

  1984   "The Policy Meaning of Nonreturning U.S.-Educated Chinese Stu-
          dents and Scholars." Paper presented at the Conference on Asia–
          Pacific Immigration to the United States, East-West Center, Honolulu.

Keeny, S. M.

  1967   "Korea and Taiwan: The Score for 1966" *Studies in Family Planning,*
          5(19):4–15.

Kim, B.-L.

  1977   "Asian Wives of U.S. Servicemen: Women in Shadows." *Americas,*
          4(1):98–100.

Kim, I.

  1981   *New Urban Immigrants: The Korean Community in New York.* Prince-
          ton, N.J.: Princeton University Press.

Kim, J. K.

  1984   "The Trends and Policies of Korean Emigration." Paper presented at
          the Conference on Asia–Pacific Immigration to the United States,
          East-West Center, Honolulu.

Kim, K. C., and W. M. Hurh

  1984   *The Formation and Maintenance of Korean Small Business in the Chicago
          Minority Area.* Research Monograph. Macomb: Western Illinois
          University.

Koo, H., and E.-Y. Yu

  1981   *Korean Immigration to the United States: Its Demographic Pattern and So-
          cial Implications for Both Societies.* Papers of the East-West Population
          Institute, No. 74. Honolulu: East-West Center.

Kwong, P. C.-K.

  1984   "The 1997 Question and Emigration Problems in Hong Kong." Paper
          presented at the Conference on Asia–Pacific Immigration to the
          United States, East-West Center, Honolulu.

Lee, E.

  1966   "A Theory of Migration." *Demography,* 3:47–67.

Lee, G.-H.

  1976   "Ingu eogje wa imin jeongcheg" [Population control and emigration
          policy]. In S.-U. Kim (ed.), *Hangug eui ingu munje wa daechaeg* [Korean
          population problem and planning]. Seoul: Korea Development In-
          stitute.

Lee, M.

  1983   "How North Korea Sees Itself." In C.I.E. Kim and B.C. Koh (eds.),
          Journey to North Korea: Personal Perceptions. Berkeley: Institute of East
          Asian Studies, University of California.

Lim, H.

1982   "Acceptance of American Culture in Korea: Patterns of Cultural Contact and Koreans' Perception of American Culture." *Journal of Asiatic Studies,* 25(1):25–36.

Lim, H.-S.

1976   "Seoul si ingu jibjung e yeong yang eul michieun gujo yoin" [The psychological factor for the population concentration into Seoul]. Paper presented in a seminar report of the Korean Association of Population Studies, Seoul.

National Science Foundation

1985   *Participation of Foreign Citizens in U.S. Science and Engineering.* Washington, D.C.

No, J.-H.

1983   "Jongju dosi seoul seongjang e hangae" [The limit to the growth of primary city Seoul]. *Dong-Ilbo,* 6 (January).

Petras, E. M.

1980   "Toward a Theory of International Migration: The New Division of Labor." In R. S. Bryce-Laporte (ed.), *Sourcebook on the New Immigration.* New Brunswick, N.J.: Transaction Books.

———.

1981   "Modes of Structural Incorporation and Present Theories of Labor Immigration." In M. M. Kritz et al. (eds.), *Global Trends in Migration: Theory and Research on International Population Movements.* New York: Center for Migration Studies.

Piore, M. J.

1980   "The Economic Role of Migrants in the U.S. Labor Market." In R. S. Bryce-Laporte (ed.), *Sourcebook on the New Immigration.* New Brunswick, N.J.: Transaction Books.

Republic of Korea Economic Planning Board

1981   *Annual Report.*

Republic of Korea Exchange Bank

1983   *Monthly Review,* 16(4):1–10.

Sassen-Koob, S.

1980   "Immigrant and Minority Workers in the Organization of the Labor Process." *Journal of Ethnic Studies,* 8(1):1–33.

———.

1981   "Towards a Conceptualization of Migrant Labor." *Social Problems,* 29(1):65–85.

Saxonhouse, G. R.

1982   "Structural Changes and U.S.–Korean Economic Relations." *Journal of Asiatic Studies*, 25(1):16–31.

Shim, S.-J.

1978   "Japan and Latin America: A Changing Relationship." Ph.D. dissertation, Rutgers University.

Shrader, E.

1984   "Leaving the Homeland III." *Korea Herald*, 13 November 1984.

Sung, B. L.

1980   "Polarity in the Makeup of Chinese Immigrants." In R. S. Bryce-Laporte (ed.), *Sourcebook on the New Immigration*. New Brunswick, N.J.: Transaction Books.

Teitelbaum, M. S.

1984   "Asian Migrations and U.S.–Asia Relations." Paper presented at the Conference on Asia–Pacific Immigration to the United States, East–West Center, Honolulu.

U.S. Bureau of the Census

1983   *1980 Census of Population*. PC80-1-B1. Washington, D.C.: Government Printing Office.

————.

1983   *World Population 1983*. Washington, D.C.: Government Printing Office.

————.

1984   *1980 Census of Population*. PC80-1-d1-A. Washington, D.C.: Government Printing Office.

————.

1985   *Statistical Abstract of the U.S.* Washington, D.C.: Government Printing Office.

U.S. Immigration and Naturalization Service

1960–   *Annual Report: Immigration and Naturalization Service*. Washington,
1977   D.C.: Government Printing Office.

————.

1978–   *Statistical Yearbok of the Immigration and Naturalization Service*. Washing-
1981   ton, D.C.: Government Printing Office.

Wallerstein, I.

1974   *The Modern World-System, Capitalist Agriculture and the Origins of the European World-Economy in the Sixteenth Century*. New York: Academic Press.

Winsberg, M. D.

    1985   "1980 Rates of Emigration to the United States." *Population Today,* 13(2):6–7.

Yimin baeg gwa

    1964   *Yimin baeg gwa* [Emigration encyclopedia]. Seoul: Bak Moon Sa.

Yu, E.-Y.

    1983   "Korean Communities in America: Past, Present, and Future." *Amerasia Journal,* 10(2):23–51.

Zolberg, A. R.

    1981   "International Migrations in Political Perspective." In M. M. Kritz et al. (eds.), *Global Trends in Migration: Theory and Research on International Population Movements.* New York: Center for Migration Studies.

————— .

    1983   "The Formation of New States as a Refugee-Generating Process." *Annals of the American Academy and Political and Social Science,* 467:24–38.

15

South Asian Immigrants: Trends and Impacts on the Sending and Receiving Societies

Urmil Minocha

A new but seemingly permanent South Asian community is emerging in the United States. The South Asian region encompasses India, Pakistan, Bangladesh, Sri Lanka, Nepal, and Bhutan. According to the 1980 U.S. census, there were 387,223 Indians, 15,792 Pakistanis, 2,923 Sri Lankans, and 1,314 Bangladeshis living in the United States in 1980. However, this new and rapidly growing South Asian community has so far remained essentially uninvestigated. Drawing on the Immigration and Naturalization Service (INS) data on immigration and secondary data from the few existing surveys, this chapter traces the historical pattern of South Asian immigration to the United States and examines the demographic and economic profile of South Asian immigrants. It also considers some of the major factors bearing on the immigration of South Asians to the United States. Finally, it assesses the impact of the large-scale exodus of highly skilled South Asians on the socioeconomic structure of major sending countries.

HISTORICAL AND CURRENT TRENDS

A great majority of South Asian immigrants have come to the United States since the change in U.S. immigration laws in 1965. Fewer than one thousand South Asians entered the United States in 1965, whereas almost 32,000 entered in 1984 (Table 15.1). Despite these overall in-

Table 15.1. Historical Trend of South Asian Immigrants to the United States: 1946–1984

Year of Admission	Total Asia	Total South Asia	India	Pakistan	Bangla-desh	Sri Lanka	Nepal	Bhutan	Percentage South Asia of Total Asia	Percentage India of Total South Asia
1946–1964	238,750	7,629	6,319	1,310[a]					3.2	82.8
1965	17,080	769	582	187					4.5	75.7
1966	35,807	2,805	2,458	347					7.8	87.6
1967	53,403	5,288	4,642	646					9.9	87.8
1968	50,841	5,355	4,682	673					10.5	87.4
1969	65,111	6,814	5,963	851					10.5	87.5
1970	83,468	11,884	10,114	1,528		242			14.2	85.1
1971	92,165	16,667	14,317	2,125		180	40	5	18.1	85.9
1972	108,208	19,755	16,929	2,480		306	39	1	18.3	85.7
1973	111,927	16,309	13,128	2,525	154	455	46	1	14.6	80.5
1974	117,023	15,936	12,795	2,570	147	379	43	2	13.6	80.3
1975	118,952	19,297	15,785	2,620	404	432	56	—	16.2	81.8
1976	133,486	21,455	17,500	2,888	590	411	59	7	16.1	81.6
1977[b]	172,823	28,478	23,208	3,931	762	475	89	13	16.5	81.5
1978	232,141	25,811	20,772	3,876	716	375	68	4	11.1	80.5
1979	170,851	24,721	19,717	3,967	549	397	79	12	14.5	79.8
1980	217,353	27,912	22,607	4,265	532	397	98	13	12.8	81.0
1981	244,075	28,105	21,522	5,288	756	448	83	8	11.5	76.6
1982	293,872	27,529	21,738	4,536	639	505	97	14	9.4	79.0
1983	265,918	31,632	25,451	4,807	787	472	105	10	11.9	80.5
1984	239,722	31,925	24,964	5,509	823	554	75	—	13.3	78.2

Sources: INS (1955:table 13-A; 1959, 1969, 1970:table 14; 1980:table 13; 1984:table 1.3).

[a]Data for 1954–1964 only.

[b]Data for 1977 include the transition quarter (1 July 1976–30 September 1976) and therefore cover the fifteen months ending 30 September 1977.

creases, the South Asian share of the total Asian immigration has remained low. Since 1965, the proportion of South Asians in the annual flow of Asian immigrants has never exceeded 18 percent, and it was just over 13 percent in 1984.

Among South Asian sending countries, India ranks first and Pakistan a distant second. Since 1965, about 80 percent of South Asian immigrants have come from India and another 12 to 19 percent from Pakistan. Thus, between 1965 and 1984, Indians and Pakistanis composed over 90 percent of all South Asian immigrants.

The history of South Asian immigration to the United States can be delineated into three distinct phases. Indians were among the earliest South Asian immigrants to the United States. During the first few years of the twentieth century (roughly between 1900 and 1917) the number of Indian immigrants remained low. The first sizable influx of Indian immigrants occurred in 1907 when 1,072 entered; in 1908, an additional 1,710 Indians were admitted. These early immigrants came mostly from Punjab State and, to a lesser extent, from Bengal, Gujarat, and Uttar Pradesh. Most settled on the West Coast, primarily in California (Chandrasekhar, 1982). Contrary to their expectations, Indians encountered racial prejudice, discrimination, and extreme hostility from the host society (Chandrasekhar, 1982; Fisher, 1980; Hess, 1974). In late 1908, the U.S. immigration officials began to deny admission to Indians. With the exception of 1910, when some 1,782 Indians were admitted partly to meet the increased demand for construction workers on the Western Pacific Railroad, few Indians entered the United States between 1909 and 1916. Finally, the exclusion policy of the 1917 immigration law prohibited Indians from entering the country.

It was not until 1946, which marks the beginning of the second phase of South Asian immigration (1946–1964), that new amendments to the U.S. immigration law relaxed restrictions on the immigration of Asians in general and gave Indians, and subsequently Pakistanis, an annual quota of 100, thus ending almost thirty years of exclusion. This liberalization of the U.S. immigration policy facilitated an increase in the number of South Asian, primarily Indian, immigrants. Between 1946 and 1964, about 6,000 immigrants from India were admitted (Table 15.1). An additional 1,310 Pakistanis, including Bangladeshis, arrived in the country between 1954 and 1964. Throughout this period, the number of nonquota immigrants (spouses, children, and other dependents of American citizens) generally equaled or sometimes even exceeded the number admitted under the annual quota (Melendy, 1977; Hess, 1974).

The enactment of the 1965 immigration law marked the beginning of the third, and most important, phase of South Asian immigration to the United States. During this phase, the annual flow of new arrivals from India increased most dramatically. The number of Indian immigrants grew from 582 in 1965 to 24,964 in 1984, an increase of about 4,200 percent (Table 15.1). The increase in the annual flow was greatest during the first few years of this third phase. Since 1976, the annual number of Indians entering the country has leveled off at about 20,000 to 25,000. The growth in the annual flow of Pakistani immigrants during this period has been rather gradual, as the number of new arrivals from Pakistan increased from a low of 187 in 1965 to only 5,509 in 1984.

The annual flow of Pakistani immigrants, although numerically small, represents a somewhat higher proportion of Pakistan's total population than the annual flow of Indian immigrants. In 1981, for instance, 5,288 Pakistanis, or 0.006 percent of the total population of Pakistan for that year, immigrated to the United States, whereas 21,522 Indians who immigrated during the same year constituted an insignificant 0.003 percent of the total population of India. The immigration streams of the other South Asian countries have grown more slowly.

An overwhelming proportion of South Asian immigrants are admitted within the numerical limitation of 20,000 persons a year from any one country, though recently evidence has emerged of a modest increase in numbers admitted outside this limit (Table 15.2). All immigrants admitted within the numerical limitation are allocated to a seven-category preference system established in 1965. Table 15.3 illustrates the classification of South Asian immigrants by preference. The seventh preference, refugees, is not included in the table because the number of immigrants admitted under this category is negligible.

The preference classification of South Asian immigrants has changed substantially since 1970. At present a great majority of South Asians are admitted under the family (or relative) preferences—direct evidence of the emphasis placed on the reunification of families in the 1965 immigration law. In the early 1970s, nearly 25 percent of all immigrants came under occupational preferences and almost half came under the nonpreference category (a category to which any unused part of the total annual quota is assigned). Since 1980, virtually none have come under the nonpreference category and relatively few have entered under the occupational preferences, with the exception of immigrants from Sri Lanka and Nepal.

Within the family preferences, most South Asian immigrants are currently admitted under the fifth preference (brothers and sisters of U.S. citizens) and, to a lesser extent, the second preference (spouses and children of U.S. permanent resident aliens), though previously more South Asians entered under the second preference. It appears that, as soon as the new immigrants were settled in their new jobs and had accumulated resources, they first sent for their wives and children (sec-

Table 15.2. South Asian Immigrants Admitted, by Class: 1980–1984

Year of Admission	Total Immigrants	Immigrants Subject to Numerical Limitation	Immigrants Exempt from Numerical Limitation	Percentage of Immigrants Subject to Numerical Limitation
India				
1980	22,607	19,585	3,022	86.6
1981	21,522	18,203	3,319	84.6
1982	21,738	16,994	4,744	78.2
1983	25,451	19,348	6,103	76.0
1984	24,964	18,492	6,472	74.1
Pakistan				
1980	4,265	3,216	1,049	75.4
1981	5,288	4,264	1,024	80.6
1982	4,536	3,096	1,440	68.3
1983	4,807	3,133	1,674	65.2
1984	5,509	3,590	1,919	65.2
Bangladesh				
1980	532	410	122	77.1
1981	756	606	150	80.2
1982	639	436	203	68.2
1983	787	470	317	59.7
1984	823	478	345	58.1
Sri Lanka				
1980	397	303	94	76.3
1981	448	352	96	78.6
1982	505	360	145	71.3
1983	472	356	116	75.4
1984	554	359	195	64.8
Nepal				
1980	98	62	36	63.3
1981	83	63	20	75.9
1982	97	62	35	63.9
1983	105	67	38	63.8
1984	75	47	28	62.7
Bhutan				
1980	13	9	4	69.2
1981	8	6	2	75.0
1982	14	12	2	85.7
1983	10	4	6	40.0
1984	—	—	—	—

Sources: INS (1980, 1981:table 6; 1982–1984:table 2.2).

Table 15.3. South Asian Immigrants Admitted under the Numerical Limitation, by Preference Category: 1970-1984 (in Percentages)

Year of Admission	Total Immigrants	Family Preferences					Occupational Preferences					Non-preference Immigrants
		Total Family Preferences	1st Pref. Unmarried Sons and Daughters of U.S. Citizens[a]	2nd Pref. Spouses, Unmarried Sons and Daughters of Resident Aliens[a]	4th Pref. Married Sons and Daughters of U.S. Citizens[a]	5th Pref. Brothers and Sisters of U.S. Citizens[b]	Total Occupational Preferences	3rd Pref. Immigrants in Professions	3rd Pref. Dependents	6th Pref. Other Workers	6th Pref. Dependents	
India												
1970–1974	100.0	25.4	—	19.7	0.1	5.5	26.3	11.1	8.4	3.9	2.9	48.4
1975–1979	100.0	59.1	0.1	26.5	0.3	32.2	24.3	9.1	8.2	4.4	2.6	16.6
1980	100.0	83.2	0.1	19.7	0.6	62.9	16.7	7.7	7.2	1.1	0.7	—
1981	100.0	84.5	0.1	34.6	0.5	49.4	15.4	5.4	5.2	2.9	2.0	0.1
1982	100.0	76.5	0.1	30.8	0.9	44.6	23.5	11.8	9.5	1.2	1.1	—
1983	100.0	80.6	0.1	31.3	1.3	47.9	19.4	9.3	9.3	0.4	0.4	—
1984	100.0	84.1	0.2	28.5	1.7	53.7	15.9	5.2	6.3	2.1	2.2	—
Pakistan												
1970–1974	100.0	30.7	0.1	20.1	0.5	10.0	18.2	8.2	4.2	3.6	2.2	50.8
1975–1979	100.0	67.0	0.1	32.6	0.5	33.8	12.0	4.5	2.6	3.1	1.9	20.9
1980	100.0	81.8	0.1	20.7	1.3	59.7	17.9	5.8	3.7	4.4	4.1	0.2
1981	100.0	87.0	0.1	33.1	0.8	52.9	13.0	3.7	2.3	3.1	3.9	—
1982	100.0	81.5	0.2	38.8	1.9	40.6	18.5	6.8	4.6	3.6	3.6	—
1983	100.0	81.7	0.3	37.3	1.7	42.3	18.3	5.3	4.6	3.9	4.5	—
1984	100.0	83.0	0.3	33.6	1.8	47.2	17.0	4.4	3.6	3.3	5.7	—

Bangladesh												
1980	100.0	71.1	—	27.4	—	43.7	28.9	11.0	11.7	3.6	2.6	—
1981	100.0	80.4	0.8	32.0	1.0	46.5	19.6	8.6	5.8	2.8	2.5	—
1982	100.0	73.2	—	39.6	2.7	30.9	26.8	13.0	8.7	2.7	2.5	—
1983	100.0	68.8	0.2	32.8	2.6	33.2	31.3	16.2	8.4	4.3	2.4	—
1984	100.0	72.8	0.2	27.4	1.4	43.8	27.2	12.6	8.2	2.3	4.1	—
Sri Lanka												
1970–1974	100.0	31.3	0.2	17.8	0.3	13.1	29.8	7.1	6.9	7.1	8.6	38.1
1975–1979	100.0	58.6	0.1	26.2	0.8	31.5	25.1	5.0	4.8	8.7	6.6	15.4
1980	100.0	66.1	0.7	25.3	2.3	37.8	31.9	7.2	11.5	8.6	4.6	—
1981	100.0	80.4	—	31.3	0.9	48.3	19.6	6.5	6.0	4.8	2.3	—
1982	100.0	58.1	0.6	37.7	3.6	16.2	41.9	17.6	15.9	3.9	4.5	—
1983	100.0	53.1	0.5	31.2	0.5	20.9	46.9	13.3	10.6	11.9	11.1	—
1984	100.0	53.9	0.8	15.0	3.7	34.5	46.1	14.7	17.6	9.2	4.5	—
Nepal												
1980	100.0	73.3	—	33.3	—	40.0	26.7	6.7	4.4	11.1	4.4	—
1981	100.0	81.0	—	36.5	—	44.4	19.0	3.2	1.6	11.1	3.2	—
1982	100.0	70.0	—	39.2	2.0	29.4	29.4	11.8	13.7	3.9	—	—
1983	100.0	48.6	—	31.4	—	17.1	51.4	10.0	14.3	11.4	15.7	—
1984	100.0	68.8	—	18.8	—	50.0	31.2	6.2	14.6	8.3	2.1	—
Bhutan												
1980	100.0	75.0	—	41.7	8.3	25.0	25.0	—	25.0	—	—	—
1981	100.0	66.7	—	16.7	—	50.0	33.3	16.7	16.7	—	—	—
1982	100.0	75.0	—	50.0	25.0	—	—	—	25.0	—	—	—
1983	100.0	—	—	—	—	—	100.0	—	100.0	—	—	—
1984	100.0	—	—	—	—	—	100.0	100.0	—	—	—	—

Sources: INS (1980, 1981:table 5; 1982–1984:table 2.1).
[a]Includes children of this group.
[b]Includes spouses and children of this group.

ond preference) and in due course, as they became American citizens, began to sponsor their brothers and sisters (fifth preference).

MAIN CHARACTERISTICS OF IMMIGRATION FLOWS

Recent South Asian immigrants display a remarkable uniformity in their age–sex structure and occupational, educational, and income attainment status. They are predominantly young, highly educated, and well-trained professional or skilled male workers from urban areas. Thus they differ notably from their earlier counterparts, who were mainly middle-aged, illiterate, male farmers from rural areas (Hess, 1974; Patel, 1972). The demographic characteristics of South Asian immigrants admitted since 1965 are described in detail below using INS, census, and other secondary data from the few existing surveys.

Age and Sex Characteristics

Like most migrants, South Asian immigrants to the United States are young. As shown in Table 15.4, more than 60 percent of all recently admitted immigrants from each South Asian country, except Sri Lanka, were below age 30, and those between the ages of 20 and 39 composed over half of all immigrants. The predominance of young adults among South Asian immigrants is reflected in the age structure of this population in the United States. The 1980 U.S. census data reveal that most of the Indians were 25 to 44 years old, whereas only 13 percent were below age 15 and few were above age 65. Similarly, a survey of Pakistanis in the New York metropolitan area (Ghayur, 1984:18) found that 86.5 percent of the male respondents were in the 25 to 39 age group and few were 40 years old or over.

Although young adults have been predominant among South Asian immigrants, a trend toward the entry of increasing numbers of older persons has been developing. Almost 9 percent of all Indian immigrants in 1980 were age 50 and over, for instance, and in 1984 this proportion went up to 19 percent, of whom half were 60 and over.

The sex composition of South Asian immigrants, presented in Table 15.5, reveals a general preponderance of males. Among Indian immigrants, however, there is a growing trend toward convergence. Although males consistently outnumber females, the proportion of female Indian immigrants admitted since 1970 has been on the rise as well, thereby closing the gap between male and female entrants to the United States. From a low of 40 percent in 1970, the proportionate share of Indian female immigrants reached near parity in 1984. This was the consequence of ever greater numbers of dependents accounting for the substantial annual increase in the total number of immigrants from India.

Table 15.4. Age Distribution of South Asian Immigrants: 1980–1984 (in Percentages)

Country and Year of Admission	Total Immigrants	<20	20–29	30–39	40–49	50–59	60+
India							
1980	100.0	26.9	33.4	22.1	8.5	4.8	4.3
1981	100.0	25.0	36.3	19.7	7.8	5.5	5.7
1982	100.0	22.9	32.9	21.1	7.9	7.2	8.0
1983	100.0	23.4	30.8	19.1	8.7	9.1	8.9
1984	100.0	23.4	29.1	18.9	9.0	9.9	9.7
Pakistan							
1980	100.0	24.9	35.6	20.8	9.1	5.6	4.1
1981	100.0	28.7	36.2	18.2	7.9	5.3	3.8
1982	100.0	24.7	37.5	17.6	7.5	6.3	6.3
1983	100.0	23.9	37.6	17.4	7.4	6.7	7.1
1984	100.0	23.6	35.1	20.1	7.5	7.0	6.6
Bangladesh							
1980	100.0	24.8	40.8	23.3	5.8	3.6	1.7
1981	100.0	27.3	42.3	21.3	4.9	2.5	1.6
1982	100.0	28.2	40.5	18.2	6.6	2.8	3.8
1983	100.0	24.9	47.8	17.4	4.6	3.4	1.9
1984	100.0	17.4	47.0	22.7	5.0	3.9	4.0
Sri Lanka							
1980	100.0	21.6	29.7	25.4	13.1	4.3	5.8
1981	100.0	17.6	29.7	29.7	9.2	8.0	5.8
1982	100.0	17.4	29.1	30.7	10.1	5.7	6.9
1983	100.0	19.7	26.1	31.6	10.8	5.3	6.6
1984	100.0	21.1	22.9	30.5	13.9	5.2	6.4
Nepal							
1980	100.0	34.7	35.7	15.3	10.2	2.0	2.0
1981	100.0	28.9	33.7	25.3	3.6	4.8	3.6
1982	100.0	28.9	37.1	19.6	4.1	5.2	5.2
1983	100.0	27.6	39.0	23.8	3.8	4.8	1.0
1984	100.0	22.7	33.3	29.3	10.7	2.7	1.3
Bhutan							
1980	100.0	7.7	46.2	7.7	23.1	7.7	7.7
1981	100.0	12.5	25.0	25.0	12.5	12.5	12.5
1982	100.0	7.1	42.9	42.9	7.1	10.0	21.0
1983	100.0	10.0	60.0	—	—	10.0	20.0

Sources: INS (1980, 1981:table 15; 1982, 1983, 1984:table 4.3).

Table 15.5.   Sex Composition of South Asian Immigrants: 1970, 1979,
              1983, 1984

Country of Birth and Year of Admission	Total Immigrants	Males N	Males %	Females N	Females %	Unknown N	Unknown %
India							
1970	10,114	6,112	60.4	4,002	39.6	—	—
1979	19,708	9,986	50.7	9,722	49.3	—	—
1983	25,451	12,420	48.8	11,904	46.8	1,127	4.4
1984	24,964	12,655	50.7	12,309	49.3	—	—
Pakistan							
1970	1,528	1,029	67.3	499	32.7	—	—
1983	4,807	2,542	52.9	1,978	41.1	287	6.0
1984	5,509	3,214	58.3	2,295	41.7	—	—
Bangladesh							
1983	787	443	56.3	284	36.1	60	7.6
1984	823	554	67.3	269	32.7	—	—
Sri Lanka							
1983	472	237	50.2	211	44.7	24	5.1
1984	554	280	50.5	274	49.5	—	—
Nepal							
1983	105	56	53.3	44	41.9	5	4.8
1984	75	39	52.0	36	48.0	—	—
Bhutan							
1983	10	3	30.0	7	70.0	—	—

Sources: INS (1970, 1979:table 9; 1983, 1984:table 4.3).

Occupation and Education

The INS data do not provide information on the educational background of South Asian immigrants. Nevertheless, from the few existing studies and the 1980 census data on Asian Indians, it is apparent that most South Asian immigrants are highly educated. Leonhard-Spark and Saran (1980:151), for example, in a survey of 345 Indian households in the greater New York metropolitan area, reported that nearly 84 percent of all the respondents had college or postgraduate degrees. Another survey conducted by the National Science Foundation found that about two-thirds of the 1,074 Indian immigrant scientists and engineers included in this study had Ph.D. degrees (Datta, 1975:75). Consistent with the findings of these studies, the census data also reveal high education levels of Indian immigrants: 72 percent of the men and 52 percent of the women have a college degree. Similarly, Ghayur (1984:19), in

Table 15.6. Indian and Pakistani Immigrants, by Major Occupational
            Group: 1960–1984 (in Percentages)

Year of Admission	Immi- grants with Occupa- tion	Profes- sional, Technical, Kindred Workers	Mana- gers, Officials, Propri- etors	Clerical and Kindred Workers	Crafts- men, Foremen, Kindred Workers	Farm Laborers and Foremen
India						
1960–1964	100.0	67.3	4.0	12.0	2.3	2.6
1965–1969	100.0	85.8	2.4	3.8	1.9	0.5
1970–1974	100.0	86.1	3.3	3.9	2.0	0.4
1975–1979	100.0	66.9	10.1	7.3	3.7	3.1
1983–1984	100.0	45.3	16.4	7.7	5.6	8.9
Pakistan						
1965–1969	100.0	77.3	4.9	4.2	3.6	1.5
1970	100.0	78.6	5.5	5.3	3.0	0.4
1971	100.0	82.6	4.4	2.8	3.0	1.8
1983–1984	100.0	24.3	23.2	7.6	6.6	4.0

Sources: INS (1960–1977; 1978, 1979:table 8; 1983, 1984:table 6.1).

Note: Percentages do not sum to 100.0 because only selected occupational groups are included.

a survey of Pakistani immigrants in the New York metropolitan area,
reported that most of the male respondents had some university or
professional education and almost 39 percent had a master's, doctorate,
or professional degree.

These high educational attainment levels of South Asian immigrants
are reflected in the occupational profile of this community. Table 15.6
shows that an overwhelming majority of all Indian and Pakistani immigrants who reported having an occupation were professional, technical, and kindred workers. Even before 1965, professionals made up
a significant proportion of all immigrants from India.

Thus the pattern of immigration of highly qualified professionals
from India established in the second phase (1946–1964) continued during the third phase. In fact, visa priority given to professionals under
the new preference system immensely accelerated the flow of professionals from India, and from other South Asian countries as well. In
1971, professionals, technical, and kindred workers composed almost
91 percent of all Indians and about 83 percent of Pakistanis admitted
that year.

Two trends revealed by data on the occupational profile of Indian
immigrants (Table 15.6) are of great significance. First is the trend toward
a declining proportion of professionals among Indian immigrants. The

proportion of professional, technical, and kindred workers fell from 86 percent in 1970–1974 to about 45 percent in 1983–1984. Second is the long-term and recently accelerated trend toward a greater variety of skills possessed by Indians entering the United States. This trend is indicated by increasing numbers of Indian immigrants skilled in management and clerical occupations. The diversity in the occupational composition of Indian immigrants was evident in a study of South Asians in Southern California (Hossain, 1982), which found that, whereas 90 percent of Pakistanis and Bangladeshis in Southern California were professionals, the corresponding proportion for Indians was lower because of the diverse nature of this group.

Knowledge about the distribution of South Asian immigrants within the professional category is lacking. The U.S. census data on the occupational background of Asian Indians will remedy this gap in knowledge. Meanwhile the few existing studies indicate that engineers constitute the largest professional category, and the medical profession the next largest. A survey of Indians in the New York metropolitan area in 1978–1979, for example, showed that 22 percent were scientists and engineers, 16 percent doctors, and 13 percent managers and administrators (Leonhard-Spark and Saran, 1980:154). Similarly, Ghayur (1980:768) estimates that engineers and physicians comprise about 10 percent each of all Pakistani male immigrants in the United States, whereas most of the rest are scientists, academics, or businessmen.

As for the settlement patterns of South Asian immigrants, most of the immigrants tend to reside in urban areas of a few states, primarily in areas where there are large communities of other South Asians. New York and California are among the most popular states of destination for Indians and Pakistanis. According to Saran (1977:65), approximately 30,000 Indians are living in the tristate (New York, New Jersey, and Connecticut) area.

FACTORS INFLUENCING IMMIGRATION TRENDS

The immigration flows are influenced by several factors that either precede or follow the move itself. This section outlines some of these factors and explains their likely connection to immigration. The discussion encompasses development issues in South Asian countries, the political and economic ties between South Asia and the United States, relevant foreign policies and migration policies, and the economic and political activities of South Asian immigrants in the United States.

Development Issues in the Sending Countries

The wide range of problems in South Asia has led to an exodus of people from these countries. Centuries of British colonial rule left South

Asian countries in a state of utter poverty and underdevelopment. Immediately after independence, most South Asian countries, particularly India and Pakistan, launched plans to develop their economies, putting early emphasis on industrialization which required huge capital investments. Lacking domestic capital, these countries had to rely on foreign capital, primarily from the United States in direct investments or aid. The reliance on foreign capital has accentuated the problem of trade deficits and the need for foreign exchange to offset these deficits. Under these circumstances, South Asian countries have encouraged emigration, since remittances sent by overseas South Asians have become an increasingly important source of foreign exchange earnings. Moreover, the increased interdependency of nations has opened up new channels for the flow of information about opportunities in different locations.

Despite long-term efforts at development, the economies of most South Asian countries have remained stagnant and depressed, primarily because of extreme poverty and rapid population growth. In general, the lack of opportunities, discriminatory practices, inadequate facilities and amenities, and above all the economic and political uncertainty in these countries have pushed people to seek their fortunes elsewhere. Moreover, owing to the poor absorptive capacity of these stagnant economies, expansion of their educational systems has resulted in severe unemployment among the educated, leading to the exodus of many educated, skilled, and professionally trained people. An overwhelming majority of these South Asians have come to the United States, where their skills are in great demand.

In sum, then, the flow of South Asian immigrants to the United States is significantly related to the economic, political, and educational conditions in these countries. It also appears to be related to the level of development a country has achieved. The more developed South Asian countries, such as India and Pakistan, send relatively more immigrants to the United States—probably because of their ability to finance such moves but also because these countries have built closer political and economic relations with the United States.

Emigration Policies in the Sending Countries

There are no significant restrictions on the movement of South Asians in and out of their respective countries. Thus they have freedom to emigrate to any country of the world. According to Narayanaswami (1984:2): "The movement of professionals such as engineers, scientists, doctors, and other specialists, for the purpose of employment abroad, or of students possessing certain minimum qualifications intending to go abroad to pursue higher studies are not hindered, and their emigration from

India is unrestricted." The Indian Emigration Act of 1983, which was intended primarily to safeguard the unskilled and semiskilled workers taking temporary employment in the Middle East, made no provision for the emigrating professionals (Narayanaswami, 1984; Dasgupta, 1984). In fact, the Indian government has never seriously concerned itself with the emigration question. Two factors seem to account for this attitude of indifference. First, the Indian government has been unable to solve the problem of unemployment in general and that of its educated people in particular. Second, massive depletion in the foreign exchange reserves caused by foreign loans and the import of oil, heavy machinery, and technology has led to inflated significance of remittances sent by Indians abroad. I shall discuss both these matters in detail in the next section.

While pursuing a policy of freedom to emigrate, the Indian government did try to discourage the brain drain by taking certain actions in the early 1970s when professionals, especially physicians and engineers, began leaving the country in huge numbers. To halt the emigration of physicians, for instance, the Indian government, and subsequently the governments of other South Asian countries as well, banned the tests given by the Educational Council for Foreign Medical Graduates (ECFMG), which screened foreign medical graduates for work in U.S. hospitals. Moreover, the government required graduates from state medical colleges in India to serve the public health system for a specified period. Similar requirements were introduced in some vocational institutions, whereby graduates were required to take jobs in India for three to five years or pay a fee. None of these efforts proved effective in halting the exodus of professionals from India.

Relationships between Sending and Receiving Countries

Political and economic relations between South Asia and the United States have contributed to the immigration of South Asians to the United States, as these relationships enhanced mutual understanding between the sending and receiving countries. Prior to the 1950s, the United States was mainly concerned with East and Southeast Asia; South Asia was considered a low-priority area. With the ending of British colonial rule in South Asia in the late 1940s and new developments in Asia in the 1950s, however, this world region became increasingly important and the American involvement in the survival of these new democracies was enhanced. Accordingly, U.S. foreign policy toward South Asia was altered and the main emphasis was now placed on its economic development and the preservation of its noncommunist character. The strengthening of political ties involved an exchange of diplomats and other personnel that led to increased U.S. political visibility and interaction between Americans and South Asians. As a result, more South Asians became aware of the United States as an alternative destination for migrants.

The enhanced U.S. political influence in South Asia was accompanied by strengthening of economic relations between the United States and South Asian countries. In accordance with the basic objectives of American foreign policy—to assist South Asian countries in their efforts to develop economically and contain the expansion of communism in this region—the United States began in the early 1950s to provide extensive economic and technical assistance to these countries. That India and Pakistan, the two major South Asian sending countries, became the largest recipients of American assistance suggests a relationship between the magnitude of foreign assistance received by a country and the volume of emigration from that country.

The flow of South Asian immigrants, especially from India, accelerated immediately after U.S. assistance was received. When these countries began receiving American aid, a network was established through which information about opportunities in the United States became more widely diffused. In addition to the exchange of personnel to administer the economic aid, American technical assistance involved the need for specialists skilled in the new technology. Therefore a large number of South Asians had to be brought to the United States for either short-term training or degree study. The U.S. immigration policy was accordingly changed in the early 1950s partly to accommodate these moves.

Many of these South Asians, particularly Indians, who came to the United States in large numbers in the 1950s for training or degree study decided to stay on (Cummings, 1984). During the 1950s and the 1960s, more than half of all Indian immigrants who changed their status to resident aliens were students. The U.S. government programs provided the essential initiative, as increasing numbers of Indian and Pakistani students have continued to come to the United States, mostly at their own expense. And despite more restrictive U.S. immigration policies, a substantial number still manage to become permanent residents. This network of South Asian immigrants has facilitated further immigration to the United States by providing support (both financial and moral) and information to their kin and friends about career opportunities, research and study facilities, and other amenities that the United States offers to immigrants.

The U.S.–South Asian economic ties were further strengthened by increased trade and direct investment, especially between India, Pakistan, and the United States. With the increased volume of direct investments and exports to these countries, the United States, replacing the United Kingdom, began to exercise an overwhelming influence on the economies of these countries. The American dominance over the economies of South Asian countries, in particular the presence of American businesses and products, appears to have influenced the decision of many South Asians to immigrate to the United States.

Thus the flow of South Asian immigration to the United States has been reinforced by political, economic, and trade relations between these countries. Furthermore, the volume of immigration flow to the United States has steadily increased from the South Asian countries that have developed close political and economic relations with the United States.

Economic and Political Activities of Immigrants

The educational and occupational qualifications of South Asian immigrants appear to have greatly facilitated their rapid entry into the mainstream of the American economy. Studies on the economic achievements of South Asian immigrants consistently show that a vast majority of them are gainfully employed (Chandrasekhar, 1982; Fisher, 1980). Moreover, the labor force participation rate of this immigrant group is found to be very high—much higher, in fact, than the national average, primarily because of the age and educational composition of most South Asian immigrants but also because in most cases both spouses work.

These high labor force participation rates plus high employment levels of South Asian immigrants largely account for their high levels of income. Thottathil and Saran (1980:236), for instance, found that 68 percent of their 194 respondents had an annual income of more than $20,000; a sizable number of Indian immigrants were earning more than $30,000 and only 6 percent had incomes of less than $10,000. Equally high income levels of Indian immigrants were also observed in the NSF survey (Datta, 1975). The median family income of Indian immigrants ($25,644 in 1979), as revealed by the U.S. census, was higher than that of any other immigrant group or, indeed, the native U.S. population. Similarly, high income levels of Pakistani immigrants in the tristate New York, New Jersey, and Connecticut area have been reported by Ghayur (1984:21). In 1977–1978, about 63 percent earned between $10,000 and $24,999 a year, whereas 13 percent earned $25,000 to $29,999 and about 8 percent earned over $30,000 per year.

Though an overwhelmingly high proportion of South Asians are in professional occupations, a large number (especially, Punjabi and Gujarati Indians) have successfully entered the world of small business. Motels, Indian restaurants, South Asian grocery stores, and, more recently, car rentals and real estate are among the most popular small business enterprises ventured by South Asian immigrants. In fact, the economic success of South Asians in the United States becomes even more impressive when one considers that these people are young and have arrived in the country only recently. The economic success of South Asian immigrants has encouraged many potential immigrants to come to the United States and thus increased the flow of immigrants. Moreover, it has enabled South Asians in the United States to lend financial support to their friends and relatives who immigrate to the United States.

At first glance these high levels of income give the impression that South Asian immigrants have successfully achieved their economic goals and have been smoothly assimilated into the American economic structure. Yet the statistics conceal important information about the racial prejudice and job discrimination that many South Asians encounter in the United States. Chaddha (1978) and Elkhanialy and Nicholas (1977) have reported that an overwhelming majority of the Indians they studied believed that they were being discriminated against and that discrimination had hurt their careers. Similarly Hossain (1982), in a survey of South Asians in Southern California, observed that despite their high incomes most South Asian professionals believed that their prospects for further mobility in the professional hierarchy were meager.

Fisher (1980) and Leonhard-Spark and Saran (1980) found that large numbers of Indian immigrants, particularly scientists, managers, and administrators, were not employed in their occupational specialties. Although the Indian immigrants, with their high educational and skill levels, were able to find jobs and had good incomes, they were unable to obtain jobs commensurate with their qualifications. In other words, they were underemployed. Furthermore, even for those Indians (mostly physicians and engineers) who were able to retain their occupational positions, the transition often meant initial lowering of status, as their work entailed less responsibility and fewer rewards. These findings provide indirect evidence of job discrimination and indicate that economic adjustment for Indians, and other South Asians as well, has not been all that easy. No systematic attempt has yet been made to assess the extent of job discrimination among these immigrants, however, and its impact on career advancement and underemployment remains uninvestigated.

In their economic behavior, most Indian immigrants are exceptionally frugal. Thottathil and Saran (1980:236) observed that as many as half of the respondents they studied were saving up to 50 percent of their incomes, the average savings being 20 to 30 percent, which is quite high compared with the U.S. national average of 10 percent. Owing to this conservative economic behavior, the standard of living of most Indian immigrants is lower than that of their American counterparts.

In the political sphere, most South Asian immigrants have maintained a low profile by not participating actively in the political process of the host society (Fisher, 1980; Saran and Eames, 1980). Paradoxically, most South Asians living in the United States continue to take a keen interest in the politics of their homelands and many even participate actively. The Ghadar Movement, organized by Indian expatriates in the United States during the first few decades of the twentieth century to liberate India from British rule, and more recently, the strong support of greater political and religious autonomy for the state of Punjab shown by radical Sikhs in the United States are examples of such active participation.

The political apathy of South Asians toward their host country may be explained by the recency of their arrival in the United States and their preoccupation with settling into the new society. Moreover, their initial noncitizenship status has not afforded them a direct political experience either through aspiration to public office or participation in lobbying (Nimbark, 1980). In time, however, as they settle into their new environment and as more and more South Asians acquire citizenship, their participation is likely to increase and they will, no doubt, exert a greater influence in the political process of their newly adopted country.

COSTS AND BENEFITS TO THE SENDING COUNTRY

Brain Drain or Brain Overflow?

As pointed out earlier, immigration from South Asia—especially from India, the dominant sending country—has been primarily of highly qualified professional, technical, and kindred workers. This phenomenon, which began after World War II, gained momentum in the mid-1960s and experienced accelerated growth in the next few years. By the early 1970s, more than 50 percent of all Indian immigrants (and almost 86 percent of all those who indicated having an occupation) were classified as professional, technical, or kindred workers. During that period, immigrants from India (and the Philippines) constituted the leading external sources of professional, technical, and scientific workers in the United States.

In 1970, about 3,500 Indian scientists and engineers and 1,500 physicians, surgeons, and dentists immigrated to the United States (Datta, 1975:74). This massive exodus of highly qualified professionals continued during the next few years. In 1978, some 1,896 Indian scientists and engineers entered the United States; engineers represented about

68 percent, scientists (including social scientists) 26 percent, and mathematicians and computer specialists about 6 percent of this number (NSF, 1980:16). Physicians have also been predominant among professional immigrants from India. It is estimated that by 1978 some 26,000 Indian doctors were in the United States and India was still losing about one-fourth of its medical graduates to emigration (AID, 1979; Newland, 1979).

This heavy exodus, especially in the early 1970s, of highly qualified professionals from India and other developing Asian countries evoked grave concern from their governments and from academicians. In India, for example, many feared that this so-called brain drain was depriving the country of intellectual talent and skilled labor essential for its economic growth. Various studies provided estimates of the immense loss to India on account of the emigration of highly skilled labor. Amuzegar (1968:703) estimated that, on the basis of per capita average education cost of $20,000, India lost about $61 million through the emigration of 3,062 natural scientists, engineers, and physicians to the United States between 1962 and 1967. The findings of this study were further substantiated by the UNCTAD study (1974), which estimated that prior to 1967 India relinquished $1.7 million annually in the form of brain drain to the United States, Canada, and France, and in 1967 this annual loss rose to $5.5 million. Thus, on the basis of the average income forgone on account of the emigration of 5,439 engineers, physicians, and scientists, India lost about $188 million between 1958 and 1966 (Ghosh, 1979:283).

These studies on the brain drain highlighted the losses that India and other developing countries had suffered apparently in order to justify some kind of compensation from the receiving countries (Baghwati, 1976). Much of this early concern in India seems to have abated considerably—partly because of the declining numbers of professional, technical, and kindred workers among all Indian immigrants to the United States but mainly because of a more realistic approach to assessing the net effects of the outflow of highly qualified personnel from India. Most of the early studies on the brain drain focused exclusively on its cost—largely the money invested in the upbringing and education of the emigrating professionals or the average income they would have earned had they stayed in the home country. Few studies took into account the quality of people involved and the labor needs of the sending country.

More recent studies, however, indicate that India is not the victim of brain drain, since no evidence has yet been found that a shortage of highly skilled labor exists or that the country's development programs have been harmed by the exodus of professionals. In fact, India has a huge surplus of highly skilled labor that cannot be absorbed by its sluggish economy (Narayanaswami, 1984). In 1970, for instance, between 15,000 and 20,000 physicians in India were without jobs (Tinker, 1977) and the Institute of Applied Manpower Research of India estimated surplus engineers to number 100,000 in 1973–1974 (Ghosh, 1979:281).

The employment situation, especially that of educated and highly trained personnel, has even worsened in recent years. According to World Health Organization estimates, as many as 80,000 doctors in India were underemployed and 7.7 million educated job seekers were unemployed in 1980. These job seekers included, among others, 250,000 scientific and technical personnel, 190,000 graduates in engineering, 36,000 engineering diploma holders, and 3,500 graduates in medicine (Helweg, 1984:52). The major cause of this situation is the unplanned nature of the educational system in India, and in other developing countries as well, which is not oriented to the needs of the domestic economy. Moreover, the low cost of education in India makes it accessible to a large segment of the population. As a result, India produces more educated and highly skilled people than its stagnant economy can effectively use.

This dismal employment situation has led some researchers to question the appropriateness of viewing the emigration of professionals from India as a case of brain drain (Das, 1977; Ghosh, 1979). In the opinion of these researchers, the exodus of highly qualified individuals is more appropriately a case of "brain overflow" or "brain gain." Another point of controversy is the legitimacy of the term "brain drain" itself. Although the term refers to the loss of the most intelligent and talented individuals, doubts have been expressed over the intellectual qualifications of some emigrants. As Helweg (1984:51) has pointed out: "Emigration is a selective process where initially the most innovative and daring leave. Therefore, a receiving country gains capable, highly motivated individuals who may or may not have the formal qualifications of the 'brain drain.'" In the absence of hard evidence, it is not possible to draw any firm conclusions, but the issue warrants further investigation.

Effects on Resources, Employment, and Productivity

The emigration from India has influenced the Indian economy in several ways. Through increased flow of information and capital from abroad—the two by-products of the emigration process—it has provided India with better access to new technology, sophisticated machinery, and innovative ideas, the application of which has resulted in increased productivity and, in some cases, expanded employment opportunities, as in the establishment of new small-scale industries. In a study of the Punjabi village of Jandiali, Helweg (1983) found that remittances from abroad had led to increased productivity by enabling farmers to use more sophisticated and innovative techniques of cultivation; remittances also led to increased investments in small businesses and created new jobs. Moreover, Indian professional and technical workers living in the United States are a significant source of technological ideas for India. Many Indian professionals residing in the United States send the latest technological ideas to friends and colleagues in India and serve as consultants to the government of India and Indian universities. Finally, emigration has undoubtedly eased India's problem of unemployment, as the emigrating individuals no longer constitute a burden to the economy, though the extent to which emigration to the United States has solved India's unemployment problem remains to be assessed.

Effects of Remittances

The consequences of remittances from Indians in the United States have been pervasive and mostly positive. At the microlevel, remittances sent home have benefited the families and friends left behind, while at the macrolevel remittances from abroad have considerably lowered India's balance of payment deficits. Findings from various studies indicate that many Indian immigrants in the United States send money home to help families and friends. Glaser (1978:207) found that 84 percent of all the Indian immigrants he surveyed had sent money home; the average remittances amounted to $600 per year of work abroad. Similarly, another survey of Indian immigrants in the New York area revealed that close to 60 percent regularly sent money to families and friends in India; 30 percent sent up to $100 per month, whereas 26 percent sent more than $100 per month (Thottathil and Saran, 1980:241). By contrast, Ghayur (1984:25) found fewer Pakistani immigrants (49 percent) in the New York area who had ever sent money home.

With the rapid increase in the total number of Indians immigrating to the United States every year, especially in the early 1970s, there has been a concomitant growth in the proportion of total remittances to India coming from the United States. In the 1950s and 1960s, most of the overseas remittances came from the United Kingdom and Africa. According to a study by the Bombay Chamber of Commerce in 1978, some 21 percent of total overseas remittances for the state of Gujarat (which has sent the largest number of recent immigrants to the United States) came from the United States and Canada (Helweg, 1984:48). Moreover, substantially large amounts ($876,000 in 1983) are remitted annually in U.S. social security payments to beneficiaries residing in India.

The effects of these remittances are visible in rural areas as well as in large urban centers. For instance, capital from abroad has helped rural communities to build schools, roads, and other infrastructure and has provided resources for the purchase of sophisticated agricultural equipment. In other words, remittances from abroad have improved the quality of life and productivity in rural areas. In the urban areas, this capital from abroad has greatly facilitated the establishment of new industries and the creation of new jobs (Oberai and Singh, 1980; Trivedi and Dholka, 1981). Moreover, the state and local governments of Punjab and Gujarat (the two dominant sending states in India) are trying to industrialize by attracting direct investment from overseas Indians.

At the microlevel, however, the ramifications of remittances from the United States have been mixed. Although money sent home to families has enhanced socioeconomic status and the quality of life and has increased productivity, it has also produced exorbitant inflation and social tensions, particularly in areas with heavy emigration (Helweg, 1984; Mathew and Gopinathan, 1978).

Effects on Social Class Structures

Emigration to the United States has influenced South Asian societies and cultures in several other ways. It has led, for instance, to enhanced social status for the families of emigrating South Asians. Emigration to the United States has become not only a means of social enhancement but also a symbol of social enhancement in itself, as the prestige of a family in the social hierarchy is elevated just by having a member of the family in the United States (Ghayur, 1984; Helweg, 1984). Moreover, emigration to the United States widens the gap between the social classes, since most of the South Asian immigrants to the United States are urban elites whose prestige is enhanced by emigration.

The influx of Western goods—goods brought into India either by returning migrants or as gifts by visiting overseas Indians—has resulted in a strong preference for foreign, especially American, products (Helweg, 1984; Ishi, 1982). The idealization of American culture, moreover, has caused some Indians to deprecate their own culture.

Impact of Return Migration

The impact of return migration is difficult to assess primarily because of the lack of relevant information. The extent and character of return migration from the United States and the reassimilation of the returnees have received little attention from the Indian government and academicians. These returnees could make valuable contributions to India, for they have acquired new ideas abroad, yet also have a knowledge of Indian culture needed to successfully adapt the new ideas to the Indian situation.

The impact of return migration on the Indian educational system is quite apparent, however, as many of the top educational institutions have large cadres of scholars trained abroad. These returnees, who hold prestigious positions in the Indian institutions, have played a significant role in shaping India's educational system along the lines of the American model. Furthermore, the American influence on Indian educational and research institutions has led Indian students to seek higher education in the United States.

To sum up, then, the net impact of emigration from South Asia cannot be determined at this point owing to the lack of adequate knowledge about the costs and benefits of the process. From the existing literature, however, it appears that the positive effects of emigration somewhat outweigh the negative ones.

CONCLUSIONS AND POLICY IMPLICATIONS

Recent immigrants from South Asia are predominantly young, highly educated, and professionally well trained male urban elites who have come to the United States not to escape poverty or political turmoil in their homelands but mainly to seek educational and economic opportunities for themselves and their families. It appears that unless South Asians are offered equally good economic opportunities and other incentives in their homelands, thus rendering emigration less attractive, they will continue to immigrate to the United States. So far, there have been no signs of this happening and most South Asian countries are still faced with severe unemployment and underemployment. Given these circumstances, the immigration from South Asia is likely to continue. Although they are still a small fraction of the total U.S. population, South Asians have great potential to influence the economic, social, and political life of the United States because of their youth, education, skills, and motivation.

The process of U.S. immigration from South Asian countries has important implications for future policy since it affects the American economic and social situation. In particular, the immigration of South Asian professional and highly skilled workers has had a considerable impact on the American labor market. Although it may have deprived the home countries of intellectual talent, it has led to increased job competition between immigrants and the native U.S. population. The statistics already show that South Asian immigrants have lower unemployment rates and earn higher incomes, on average, than the native U.S. population. And as their numbers grow, job competition will become more intense. A major policy issue related to job scarcity in specific fields, therefore, is the protection of American workers against competition with immigrant workers for these scarce jobs. The provision of such protection would require a major overhauling of U.S. immigration policy that would restrict the entry of skilled immigrant workers to keep these jobs open for Americans. Such a policy would also keep foreign skilled workers at home and thus keep the brain drain in check.

REFERENCES

Agency for International Development (AID)

   1979   *Business Brief: Migrating to Work.* Washington, D.C.

Amuzegar, J.

   1968   "Brain Drain: The Irony of Foreign Aid Policy." *Economic Internationale,* Genoa.

Baghwati, J. N.

   1976   "The Brain Drain." Paper prepared for the ILO's Tripartite World Conference on Employment, Income Distribution, Social Progress, and the International Division of Labour, and presented at the International Institute for Labour Studies' World Symposium on the Social Implications of a New International Economic Order, 19–23 January, Geneva.

Chaddha, R. L.

   1978   "Problems and Perspectives of Career Advancement: A Cross-Section of Asian Indians." Paper presented at the Stanford Workshop, 20–25 August, Stanford University.

Chandrasekhar, S. (ed.)

   1982   *From India to America: A Brief History of Immigration; Problems of Discrimination; Admission and Assimilation.* La Jolla, California: Population Review Publications.

Cummings, W. K.

   1984   "Going Overseas for Higher Education: The Asian Experience." *Comparative Education Review,* 28(2):241–257.

Das, M. S.

   1977   "Brain Drain Controversy and Utilization of Returning Indian Scholars Trained Abroad." *Population Review,* 21(1 & 2):28–36.

Dasgupta, A. K.

   1984   "Review of Data Sources Concerning Emigration from India to the United States." Paper presented at the Conference on Asia–Pacific Immigration to the United States, East–West Center, Honolulu.

Datta, R. K.

1975   "Characteristics and Attitudes of Immigrant Indian Scientists and Engineers in the U.S.A." *Journal of Scientific and Industrial Research,* 34(2):74–79.

Elkhanialy, H., and R. W. Nicholas (eds.)

1977   *Racial and Ethnic Self-Identification and Desire for Legal Minority Status Among Indian Immigrants in the United States.* Chicago: University of Chicago Press.

Fisher, M. P.

1980   *The Indians of New York City.* New Delhi: Heritage Publishers.

Ghayur, M. A.

1980   "Pakistani Ethnic Group in the U.S." In S. Thernstrom (ed.), *Harvard Encyclopedia of American Ethnic Groups.* Cambridge, Mass.: Harvard University Press.

————.

1984   "Pakistani Immigrants in America: A Socio-Demographic Study." Department of Sociology, Sweet Briar College, Sweet Briar, Virginia. Mimeographed.

Ghosh, B. N.

1979   "Some Economic Aspects of India's Brain Drain into the U.S.A." *International Migration,* 17(3 & 4):280–289.

Glaser, W. A.

1978   *The Brain Drain: Emigration and Return.* New York: Pergamon Press.

Helweg, A. W.

1983   "Emigration from India: The Effects on a Village in Punjab." *New Community,* 10(3):435–443.

————.

1984   "Emigration and Return: Ramifications for India." *Population Review,* 28(1 & 2):45–57.

Hess, G. R.

1974   "The Forgotten Asian Americans: The East Indian Community in the United States." *Pacific Historical Review,* 43:577–596.

Hossain, M.

1982   "South Asians in Southern California: A Sociological Study of Immigrants from India, Pakistan, and Bangladesh." *South Asia Bulletin,* 2(1):74–83.

Immigration and Naturalization Service (INS)

1955–   *Annual Report: Immigration and Naturalization Service.* Annual.
1977   Washington, D.C.: Government Printing Office.

——————.

1978–   *Statistical Yearbook of the Immigration and Naturalization Service.* Annual.
1983   Washington, D.C.: Government Printing Office.

Ishi, T. K.

1982   "The Political Economy of International Migration: Indian Physicians
         to the United States." *South Asia Bulletin,* 2(1):39–57.

Leonhard-Spark, P. J., and P. Saran

1980   "The Indian Immigrant in America: A Demographic Profile." In P.
         Saran and E. Eames (eds.), *The New Ethnics: Asian Indians in the United
         States.* New York: Praeger.

Mathew, E. T., and P. R. Gopinathan

1978   "Emigrants and Emigrants' Household: A Case Study of Two Vil-
         lages in Kerala." *Economic and Political Weekly,* 13.

Melendy, B. H.

1977   *Asians in America.* Boston: Twayne Publishers.

Mookherjee, H. N.

1984   "Some Observations of the Assimilation of Asian Indians in the
         United States." *Population Review,* 28(1 & 2):58–79.

Narayanaswami, R.

1984   "Indian Immigration to the United States—Socio-Economic Conse-
         quences and Impact on India's Economic Development." Paper
         presented at the Conference on Asia–Pacific Immigration to the
         United States, East–West Center, Honolulu.

National Science Foundation (NSF)

1980   *Scientists and Engineers from Abroad, 1976–1978.* Surveys of Science
         Resources Series, NSF 80-324. Washington, D.C.: Government Print-
         ing Office.

Newland, K.

1979   *International Migration: The Search for Work.* Worldwatch Paper 33.
         Washington, D.C.: Worldwatch Institute.

Nimbark, A.

1980   "Some Observations on Asian Indians in an American Educational
         Setting." In P. Saran and E. Eames (eds.), *The New Ethnics: Asian In-
         dians in the United States.* New York: Praeger.

Oberai, A. S., and H. K. Manmohan Singh

1980   "Migration Remittance and Rural Development: Findings of a Case Study in the Indian Punjab." *International Labor Review,* 119(2). March/April.

Patel, N.

1972   "A Passage from India." *Society,* 9(6):25–29.

Saran, P.

1977   "Cosmopolitans from India." *Society,* 14(6):65–69.

Saran, P., and E. Eames (eds.)

1980   *The New Ethnics: Asian Indians in the United States.* New York: Praeger.

Thottathil, P. A., and P. Saran

1980   "An Economic Profile of Asian Indians." In P. Saran and E. Eames (eds.), *The New Ethnics: Asian Indians in the United States.* New York: Praeger.

Tinker, H.

1977   *The Banyan Tree: Overseas Emigrants from India, Pakistan, and Bangladesh.* London: Oxford University Press.

Trivedi, M. K., and R. V. Dholka

1981   "Impact of Foreign Remittances on the Economy of Baladia (District of Bhug-kutch): A Case Study." Unpublished report, Sheth Demodardas School of Commerce, Gujarat University, Ahmedabad.

United Nations Conference on Trade and Development (UNCTAD)

1974   *The Reverse Transfer of Technology: Economic Effects of the Outflow of Trained Personnel from Developing Countries (Brain Drain).* TD/B/AC. Geneva: Intergovernmental Group on Transfer of Technology, Trade and Development Board.

U.S. Bureau of the Census

1981   *Race of the Population by States: 1980.* 1980 Census of Population, Supplementary Reports (PC80-S1-3). Washington D.C.: Government Printing Office.

16

Paradise Left?
Pacific Island Voyagers
in the Modern World

John Connell

In little more than two decades there has been extensive migration from the small states of the South Pacific to the metropolitan countries that border the Pacific, resulting in absolute population decline in some states and new social and economic relationships between the peoples of the region. This chapter reviews the changing pattern of development in the region, the structure of international migration from the region, and the consequences of that migration for the migrants and the sending states. In short, it traces the rapid evolution of a new structure of international dependence.

In the remote microstates of the South Pacific, prospects for economic growth are unusually limited. Hence the now widely perceived disparities in economic welfare between the Pacific states, especially the smallest states of Polynesia and Micronesia, and the fringing metropolitan nations have contributed not only to substantial migration but also to increasing pressures for further migration. So extensive has this migration become that some of the greatest concentrations of Pacific Islanders are in cities such as Auckland, Honolulu, and Los Angeles rather than in the South Pacific. Some of the smallest states have more islanders overseas than at home, and currently populated small states and islands are likely to experience future depopulation. As emigration continues, small and vulnerable South Pacific states, in a region of unprecedented strategic significance, have become irrevocably a peripheral and dependent part of a wider world.

A conventional image of the South Pacific (especially Polynesia) is of island paradises where an idyllic existence in conditions of "subsistence affluence" (Fisk, 1966) is widespread. This perception of the region is certainly not the view from within the South Pacific, at least as reflected in the steady outflow of migrants from the region. In many areas "changes in natural trends due to declining mortality, the impact of the family planning program, and fertility decline from many causes are overlain completely by migration" (Brookfield, 1980:185). Small islands and small island-states are "beautiful but not places to live" (Bedford, 1980:57). Many aspects of social and economic life on the smaller islands of the South Pacific are affected and organized by migration; it is unlikely that this will change in the future. It might even be said that the Polynesian states are characterized by international emigration, the Melanesian states are characterized by internal migration (although across significant language and cultural boundaries), and the Micronesian states are experiencing both patterns of migration along with some immigration of migrant workers. These broad differences are elaborated elsewhere (Connell, 1985b, 1986).

THE SOUTH PACIFIC REGION

The South Pacific region, as defined here, includes some twenty-two states (Table 16.1 and Figure 16.1) and almost a thousand language groups; it is an area of exceptional geographical, cultural, and economic diversity. The region includes only 550,000 square kilometers of land amid 30 million square kilometers of ocean. It has three indigenous population groups—Melanesians, Polynesians, and Micronesians—and recent imigrants have included Europeans, Indians, and Chinese. The pattern of political organization in the region is also diverse. Many of the larger countries are independent, notably those of Melanesia; the exception is New Caledonia, which remains a territory of France but has a strong independence movement. In Micronesia only Kiribati and Nauru are independent; in Polynesia Western Samoa, Tonga, and Tuvalu are independent. Both American Samoa and Guam are territories of the United States. In Micronesia the Northern Marianas is a commonwealth of the United States, and the constituent states of the U.S.-administered Trust Territory of the Pacific Islands are in varying stages of negotiating self-government in "free association" with the United States. Both Wallis and Futuna and French Polynesia are overseas territories of France. Tokelau is administered by New Zealand, whereas the Cook Islands and Niue are self-governing in association with New Zealand. Pitcairn Island remains a British colony. The vari-

377

Table 16.1. Population, Land, and Urbanization: Pacific Islands, Recent Years

State	Estimated Population (Mid-1982)	Estimated Annual Growth Rate (%)	Land Area (km²)	Population Density (persons/km²)	Estimated Urban Population	Percentage Urban	Population in U.S.	Population in New Zealand	Population in Australia or Canada
American Samoa	33,900	1.9	197	172	11,399 (1980)	34	24,000	100	—
Cook Islands	16,900	-1.8	240	70	3,664 (1981)	22	250	25,000	1,200
Federated States of Micronesia	82,400	3.4	700	118	19,300 (1980)	23	2,000	—	—
Fiji	658,000	2.0	18,272	36	218,495 (1976)	38	7,000	4,000	29,000
French Polynesia	158,000	2.2	3,265	47	78,618 (1977)	51	1,200	220	120
Guam	108,400	2.0	540	200	108,400 (1982)	100	33,000	—	—
Kiribati	61,200	2.2	690	89	17,921 (1978)	29	150	50	80
Marshall Islands	32,800	3.2	180	182	15,296 (1980)	47	900	—	—
Nauru	8,400	2.8	21	400	8,400 (1982)	100	60	70	150
New Caledonia	145,000	1.3	19,103	8	76,205 (1979)	53	100	—	80
Niue	3,150	-3.5	259	12	—	0	60	8,250	120
Northern Marianas	18,400	4.4	470	39	14,585 (1980)	79	2,000	—	—
Palau	12,400	0.3	495	25	7,642 (1980)	62	1,200	—	—
Papua New Guinea	3,126,000	2.2	462,243	7	395,713 (1980)	13	100	120	1,650
Pitcairn Island	60	-5.0	5	12	—	0	—	140	—
Solomon Islands	243,000	3.4	28,530	9	18,314 (1976)	8	100	80	150
Tokelau	1,580	0.1	11	144	—	0	200	2,400	—

Table 16.1. (continued)

State	Estimated Population (Mid-1982)	Estimated Annual Growth Rate (%)	Land Area (km²)	Population Density (persons/ km²)	Estimated Urban Population	Percentage Urban	Popu- lation in U.S.	Popu- lation in New Zealand	Population in Australia or Canada
Tonga	98,000	0.2	700	140	25,589 (1976)	26	10,000	7,200	6,000
Tuvalu	7,700	2.0	26	296	2,191 (1979)	28	50	100	70
Vanuatu	125,600	3.7	11,800	11	15,102 (1979)	12	100	80	100
Wallis and Futuna	11,900	5.0	255	47	—	0	—	—	—
Western Samoa	157,000	0.7	2,935	53	32,099 (1976)	20	20,000	44,000	1,050
Total	5,106,190								

Source: Connell (1986).

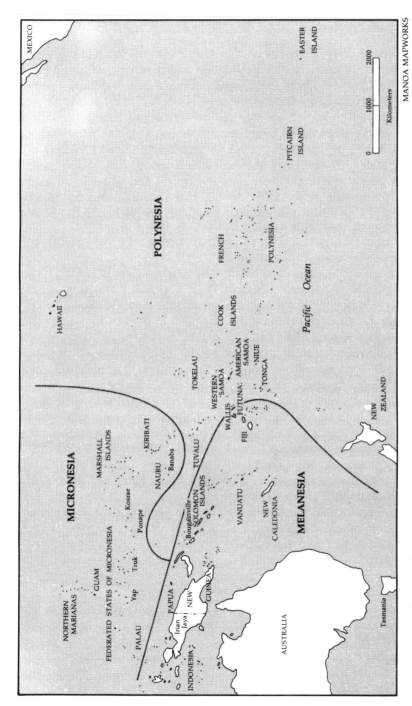

Figure 16.1. The Pacific Region

ety of political structures has major significance for international migration.

With the exception of Papua New Guinea, all the states in the region are extremely small, in both population and land area, although some countries have very large Exclusive Economic Zones. Economic and political jurisdiction over vast ocean areas has increased the economic and strategic significance of the region. Great distances separate countries and island groups within countries. Smallness, isolation, and fragmentation impose constraints on their development strategies. Even in the larger states the small size of the domestic market has hampered the development of import substitution industries, and only Fiji has a substantial industrial sector; consequently there is a high demand for imports and a consequent necessity to generate increased exports, but also considerable trade imbalances. In the case of the atoll states particularly, an extremely restricted physical environment severely limits the range of productive opportunities.

A negligible share in most commodity markets gives the island countries a weak negotiating position. Their economies are small, open, largely dependent on agricultural production and fisheries, and vulnerable to international economic changes. In the last few years, falling world prices for many basic commodities have seriously weakened the economic situation of most island-states. Some of the smallest states, especially the politically dependent territories, also depend on aid, principally from Australia, France, and the United States.

The significance of the agricultural and fisheries sector lies in its actual and potential contribution to employment, incomes, and welfare (specifically nutrition and health). Yet the fragmentary available figures suggest that the agricultural sector has performed poorly in recent years. Although most of the island-states' populations work in agriculture, usually combining subsistence and cash-cropping activities, some states have experienced an actual decline in food production per capita. Imports of foodstuffs, some of which can be produced locally, have increased in quantity and variety. Exploitation of the extensive fisheries resources of the region has been undertaken principally by distant fishing nations and has had limited benefit to the island-states. Yet fisheries have a greater unrealized economic potential for most countries in the region than any other sector of the economy.

Most nonagricultural employment in the region is in the services sector and especially with the government. Nowhere is this more apparent than in the constituent states of the Trust Territory of the Pacific Islands and some other dependent states, where productive employment constitutes a small proportion of total employment. Throughout the region there has been a shift in the labor force from the agricultural to the services sector. Economic recession at the start of the 1980s severely restricted the growth of new employment opportunities, and in many countries a growing problem has been urban and especially youth unemployment. Compared with other parts of the Third World, however, the region has high levels of income and welfare (health, education, social services, and nutrition). Although Western Samoa, Tuvalu, Kiribati, and Tonga are all included within the United Nations group of Least-Developed Countries, their development situations are no worse than those of other small Pacific states.

The larger independent Melanesian countries—Papua New Guinea and the Solomon Islands and, to a lesser extent, Vanuatu and Fiji—which have more diverse economies, are much less vulnerable to fluctuations in the external economy and hence have the best prospects for development. The dependent territories, especially the American territories, tend to have a narrow economic base, although they are supported by apparently long-term political agreements and hence external development assistance. The independent states of Kiribati and Tuvalu experience severe problems in maintaining basic subsistence levels for their dense populations; continued aid and emigration appear to be the only feasible solutions for them (Connell, 1985a).

Thus the region remains on the extreme periphery of the global economic system to the extent that:

The Pacific Island countries show all the signs of "underdevelopment" and "dependency": their economies are export orientated; there is little autonomous industrial development; political, public service, and private sector elites have a vested interest in the maintenance of present patterns of aid and development; foreign-owned companies have made handsome profits and still dominate some sectors of the economy; urbanization is running ahead of urban employment; most people are peasant producers with only a partial involvement in the cash economy (Macdonald, 1982a:57).

Despite these similarities, the countries of the region have had quite different economic and political pasts. Their population structures, migration experiences, and development plans reflect some of their differences.

The populations of most South Pacific states are now as large as they have ever been, and despite recent declines in fertility, the growth rates in most countries remain high. The current population growth rate for the South Pacific as a whole is around 2.5 percent a year, by world standards a high rate. For some observers it suggests the prospect of a Malthusian crisis as population outstrips resources. (See, for example, Fairbairn, 1982.) The postwar demographic pattern in most countries of the region has been one of continued high or only recently declining birthrates combined with substantially lower death rates; the on-set of the demographic transition has produced rapidly growing populations in many areas, especially in parts of Melanesia and Micronesia. In most parts of Polynesia, natural increase is very high, but population sizes are stable or declining as emigration siphons off the excess numbers. Higher life expectancy has resulted principally from a drop in infant mortality, and the decline in mortality has generally been accompanied by an epidemiological transition from infectious and parasitic diseases to chronic noncommunicable diseases.

·Several countries in the region have responded to high fertility levels with family planning policies and programs. In the 1970s, Fiji achieved such a substantial reduction in fertility levels that its program, with that of Singapore, was regarded as a model for the Third World. In recent years there have been indications not only of increasing fertility levels and declining contraceptive acceptance rates, but also of considerable national and individual resistance to family planning programs, especially in Melanesia. Thus a critical development issue for the region is that of maintaining, let alone improving, present standards of living in the face of rapid population increases.

CONTEMPORARY MIGRATION FROM THE SOUTH PACIFIC

International migration to the metropolitan nations on the fringes of the Pacific is primarily a Polynesian phenomenon. Many people from Niue, the Cook Islands, Tonga, Western Samoa, and American Samoa have moved either to New Zealand (whence some have gone on to Australia) or increasingly, as the New Zealand economy has stagnated and immigration restrictions have become tighter, to the United States. For the smallest states—Niue and the Cook Islands (and also American Samoa, Pitcairn Island, and Tokelau)—movement has been particularly dramatic since less than half the indigenous population remains. Only the Cook Islands, Niue, and Pitcairn are consistently losing population, however. In the largest countries of Melanesia emigration has nowhere reached such proportions. The larger countries are independent, rather than associated states; hence metropolitan immigration laws exert some control, and their economies are more viable. Two other significant migration streams to metropolitan nations are, first, that of Fiji Indians, who are moving primarily to Canada and, to a lesser extent, to the United States, and, second, that of Chamorros (from Guam and the Northern Marianas), who are moving to the United States. Political status affects migration in that the nationals of the Cook Islands, Niue, and Tokelau are New Zealand citizens and may move there freely. Similarly, American Samoans, Guamanians, and Northern Marianas islanders are free to enter the United States. The widespread migration from these states hints at the role of legal restrictions in constraining emigration from the South Pacific region.

Within the South Pacific, significant international migration movements also occur. Polynesians have moved from French Polynesia and Wallis and Futuna to New Caledonia, although in both cases this movement has been partially reversed since the end of the "nickel boom." A second important movement is that of i-Kiribati and Tuvaluans to Nauru (Figure 16.2). Although some regional population movements exist elsewhere, they are minor in number and significance. In every case the opportunities for international migration within the South Pacific are declining sharply, and migration movements are increasingly directed outward.

The scale of international migration currently appears to be more closely determined by the vicissitudes of the international economy (and specifically that in the United States and New Zealand), rather than the domestic island economies. It is also affected by the legal restrictions placed on international migration by the metropolitan nations, restrictions that are likely to be partly determined by the international economic situation. Thus the scale of future international migration is unpredictable. However, the signing of the Compact of Free Association between the former entities of the Trust Territory (Palau, the Marshall Islands, and the Federated States of Micronesia) allows free movement between those states and the United States. Although distance, language ability, and skills place Micronesians seeking American employment at a disadvantage, it is likely that out-migration will increase substantially within the next decade because local economies are particularly impoverished (Schwalbenberg, 1984). Beyond this, it is now unlikely that the Australian government will relax its restrictions on migration from the South Pacific. In every case the structure of migration will continue to be essentially determined by political and economic forces in the metropolitan nations.

The extent of migration from the South Pacific region is summarized in Table 16.1 and indicated graphically in Figure 16.2. This mid-1983 situation demonstrates the significance for the resident Polynesian population of the massive migration from all parts of Polynesia except French Polynesia; the total includes some immigrants. Except for Papua New Guinea, more than one-tenth of ethnic Pacific Islanders are residing in the metropolitan countries fringing the region; and except for French Polynesians, New Zealand Maoris, and Hawaiians, one-third of all Polynesians are overseas. Migration in the region has been characterized as circular mobility (Chapman and Prothero, 1985), but it is becoming increasingly permanent, both in the growing towns of the region and in the metropolitan cities on the fringe of the region. Only

384

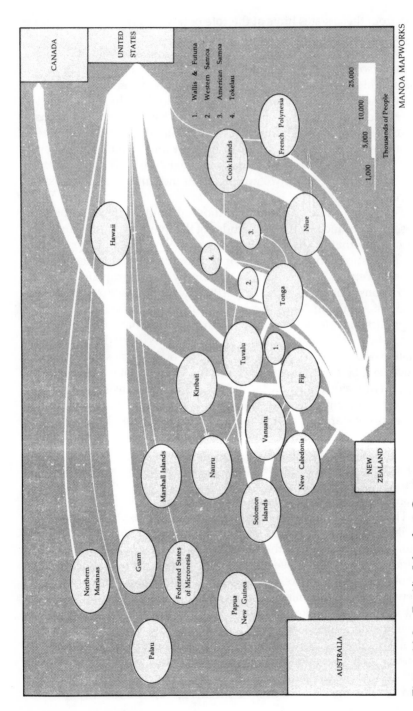

Figure 16.2.   Pacific Islanders Overseas

retrospectively can migration be considered permanent, however, and it is difficult to distinguish among contract workers, temporary migrants, and potentially permanent emigrants. Yet the impact of each migrant type on social and economic change is quite different. I shall not attempt to distinguish temporary from permanent migrants but argue that much international migration is effectively, if not intentionally, permanent and hence return migration is limited.

Since data on the flow of migrants from the region are inadequate, generalizations must be based on censuses taken in the metropolitan countries. In Australia the number of Pacific Islanders more than doubled between 1976 and 1981, although this rate of increase may have slowed in recent years with restrictions on migration from New Zealand. In New Zealand the number of Polynesians almost doubled between 1971 and 1981, although the growth rate slowed in the second half of the decade and may have remained lower in the present decade. In the United States the data are poor, but the number of Pacific Islanders at least doubled between 1970 and 1980, and this growth rate may have been maintained in the present decade. Overall, the rate of emigration remains at a high level, but the destination has tended to shift from New Zealand to North America.

The major influences on international migration are economic even when social forces are also significant. Migration is primarily a response to inequalities, both real and perceived, in socioeconomic opportunities that are themselves a result of dependent or uneven sectoral and regional development. Migration has been largely a function of the effective penetration of peripheral capitalism, the imposition of colonial administration, and perceptions of relative deprivation. But social influences on migration are also important, such as the desire for access to education and health services, and also as one element of the rite of transition to adulthood.

Family migration, often initiated by the male, now predominates, and sex ratios in most areas are balanced. As elsewhere, migration is generally characterized by the movement of young men and women, a situation that has contributed to transferred high fertility and dependency rates in some areas. Just as economic and social influences on migration cannot be easily distinguished, nor can the economic and social impacts of migration in the small states of the region.

Radical changes in expectations about what constitutes a satisfactory standard of living, a desirable occupation, and a suitable mix of accessible services and amenities have been a major cause of migration. Aspirations now almost always involve the availability of imported food and other goods and access to schools, hospitals, and even modern en-

tertainment—all of which demand cash income. In parallel with changing aspirations and the increased necessity to earn cash, agricultural
work throughout the Pacific has been losing prestige. Hence the limited participation of young men in the agricultural economy is declining further. Changes in values, following increased educational
opportunities and the expansion of bureaucratic (largely urban) employment within the region in the 1970s, have further oriented migration streams away from the region, as local employment opportunities
have not kept pace with population growth. These changes have also
contributed to the widening gap between expectations, which are themselves continually being revised upward, and the reality of limited
domestic employment and incomes.

In some countries, education is oriented to the needs of migrants
in their destinations rather than at home and hence proves a catalyst
to migration. In Kiribati, for example, attempts to introduce vocational
education in community high schools have been strongly opposed by
parents concerned that their children will be unable to obtain
bureaucratic employment. Moreover, many educational systems, notably those in U.S. territories, inevitably result in disdain for rural life
because "the exclusion of traditional skills and knowledge from western-
ized school curricula in many developing countries amounts to a constant tacit assumption that such things are not worth learning"
(Johannes, 1981:148). Tertiary education is usually undertaken outside
the home country, especially in the smaller states, a factor contributing to emigration. The title of this chapter is derived from a report on
Micronesian college education in America entitled "Island Voyagers in
New Quests" (Workman et al., 1981). A Tongan anthropologist, 'Epeli
Hau'ofa, has summarized the situation succinctly:

Once you are educated, once your mind is expanded, subsistence on a remote
little island is simply unacceptable. . . . Psychologically we are no longer islanders. Travel has changed our material values and expectations, drained us
of talent, changed outlooks within families and transformed eating habits.
. . . We have no future other than feeding ourselves, for nothing else is here
(cited by Dyson, 1982:120–121).

Consequently, "migrants seek in the West access to material goods, jobs
in the industrial sector, better education for their young, and social mobility in a society they have believed free of the traditional barriers of
rank and family status that made such mobility difficult at home"
(Shore, 1978:xiii). The experience of the wider world, its values, and
its material rewards further underlies the migratory experience.

THE IMPACT OF MIGRATION

Migration is both a catalyst and a consequence of social and economic change, and no society and few individuals in the South Pacific have been untouched by its influence. Few of its effects can be reviewed in any detail in this chapter, although migration has had a major influence in other spheres, such as politics, religion, nutrition (Connell, 1984a), health (Connell, 1987), and the lives of women (Connell, 1984b). The present focus on the relationship between migration and demographic and economic change emphasizes issues relevant to the future status and structure of international migration in the region.

Sex Selectivity

Sex selectivity in migration has implications for demographic change. There is much evidence that when men were the primary migrants, the birthrate was slowed; in some areas, such as Rotuma, migration was even regarded as one means of family planning (Howard, 1961). Recently, more balanced sex ratios in migration and the demise of long-term labor contracts have limited the impact of migration on fertility. Other trends in the region may have resulted in increases in fertility (and reductions in infant mortality) that counteract any population decline following migration (Connell, 1986). Indeed, in large parts of Polynesia natural increase is very high and international migration has proved to be a safety valve. The general argument that return migrants, through their contact with "modern" values favoring small families, induce lower fertility and thus reduce population growth in rural areas (see Standing, 1982:23; Simmons et al., 1977) is not validated in the South Pacific. The extent of emigration, the limited amount of return migration, and the strong influence of Christianity have all encouraged high fertility. The direct effect of migration on fertility levels in the region is now generally limited.

The major effect of migration on fertility in the region is through the transfer of fertility from one part of a country to another (usually from rural to urban areas) or outside the country. One result of this transfer is that migrants, and especially children born outside the home village or country, increasingly lose their native identity, experience problems of ethnicity, and, perhaps most important, find that they have only minimal residual claims to land and hence development opportunities in their home areas. This loss is exacerbated where marriages are increasingly across language boundaries and ethnic and cultural groups. Since alien birthplaces and loss of linguistic ability necessarily discourage return migration, transferred fertility is a major influence on the permanence of migration.

Education Selectivity

Throughout the South Pacific it is possible to demonstrate that it is the most educated who migrate first and, moreover, that many migrants have left rural areas to take advantage of superior urban and international educational facilities. These two factors of migration reinforce each other so that the bias is likely to be maintained (Connell, 1980:6). Invariably, migration results in the loss of the most energetic, skilled, and innovative individuals, and this loss is not compensated either by remittances or by any other trickle-down effect from urban and national development. In some small states the brain drain has been excessive; the Cook Islands, for example, lost more than half of its vocationally qualified population in the single decade of 1966–1976 (Cook Islands, 1984:23). The ubiquity of the education bias, despite the short history of formal education in parts of the Pacific, suggests that it is likely to continue (see Hezel, 1985). The combination of changing aspirations and the migration of the more educated young contributes to a brain or skill drain from national peripheries and from small states, perhaps ultimately worsening the welfare and bargaining position of those places.

Agricultural Change

There are complex and substantial variations in the impact of migration on the agricultural system. These differences derive principally from the extent to which the agricultural system depends on male or female labor, the length of absence of migrants, and the extent of compensatory remittances that may be used to hire labor or machinery (Connell, 1986). When migration takes place in a rural area characterized by low and perhaps diminishing returns due to population pressure on small landholdings, the reduction in population hypothetically can reduce any tendency toward diminishing returns and raise the productivity of rural labor. In the Pacific area, however, population pressure on resources is generally modest and the potential for mechanization is limited, so that rural land is subsequently worked by a smaller remaining population without an increase in productivity. Apart from the few states with declining populations, increased food production or purchases are required to support the growing population. Of seven larger Pacific countries (Fiji, French Polynesia, Papua New Guinea, Solomon Islands, Tonga, Vanuatu, Western Samoa), over the period 1965–1978 only Papua New Guinea actually increased its food production at a rate greater than that of population increase. The others suffered declines in their per capita food production, resulting in less food being available and greater compensatory imports (Yang, 1982), although such trends were only partly related to migration. During this transition, agricultural systems have gone from "subsistence affluence" to "subsistence malaise" (Grossman, 1981) and local economies from "village subsistence" to "monetary subservience" (Thomson, 1976:166) —and in much of Micronesia and also elsewhere, whole socioeconomies have gone from subsistence to subsidy. Again these trends have been strongly influenced by attitudinal changes, with discontent contributing to a downward spiral of the local economy.

A further result of the limited availability of labor and labor-saving technology has been a general decline in the use of marginal and distant land. In parts of Fiji, migration in the 1950s had already resulted in a declining area of cultivated land (Ward, 1961:270). Where a cash inflow from remittances or wages is considerable, some components of the agricultural system may simply be abandoned. Thus in the Cook Islands regular remittance payments appear to encourage many middle-aged and elderly people to abandon full-time agricultural activities and become dependent upon remittances (Curson, 1979:193–194); but only in exceptional circumstances, such as in parts of American Samoa, Micronesia, and Nauru, has subsistence agriculture effectively disappeared.

In some parts of the Pacific, especially in the smaller states, opportunities for productive investment in the agricultural economy range from severely restricted to virtually nonexistent. In these situations, typified in wholly atoll states like Kiribati, the Marshall Islands, and Tuvalu, conditions are such that "every migration creates greater consumer wants and diminishes the chance of satisfying them at home" (Wallman, 1977:111); lands are neglected and the idea of achieving self-sufficiency becomes more and more implausible. Even on larger islands, such as Western Samoa, it could be argued that migration is "a far more lucrative investment than anything available in the village" (Shankman, 1976:71) principally because of the lack of land, the unavailability of cash crops other than copra, and remoteness. In these conditions, income can be invested only in increased, if not necessarily improved, consumption. Moreover, if out-migration from small islands decreases, as is likely in the case of Tuvalu (because of declining employment opportunities in Nauru), cash incomes will fall; and although the subsistence sector should be able to support the increased population, cash crop production (of copra only) is likely to fall as coconuts are eaten rather than sold (Chambers, 1975:103), thus reducing the quality of life. Capital investment in agriculture is most appropriate to the larger islands; in the smaller atolls especially, the conservative use of income reflects the lack of productive investment opportunities.

The processes of agricultural decline that have gone on elsewhere, as in the smaller Caribbean islands (see Manners, 1965:186), are being replicated on the small islands of the Pacific and especially on those where international migration has been common. Niue is characterized by "dynamics of dependence": Many of the potential innovators in agriculture have migrated, and farmers have shortened their time horizons, believing that there is little point in planting coconut trees if they bear fruit when the owner has migrated or when he has a smaller family to support or inadequate labor to maintain the plantation (Pollard, 1978:82). Overall, then, migration and migrants' remittances have contributed to the disintensification of the traditional agricultural system (Brookfield, 1972, 1984) that has followed the expansion of cash cropping.

Although increased urban demand might have been expected to stimulate rural production, rapid urbanization is exacerbating these trends in the South Pacific. Earlier wants have become needs, and purchases must be partially financed by migration to wage employment. The shift away from production has been followed, more slowly and less obviously, by a decline in exchange and reciprocity. A parallel trend is the growing segregation of work from private life and the separation of public and private spheres of activity. The establishment of capitalism, and with it the emergence of cash cropping, wage labor, migration, and greater individualism within nuclear families, has tended to separate families from the community and women from men. Such trends are universal.

Remittances

The absence of migrants is usually balanced by some form of resource transfer from migrants to kin in the areas of origin. Such remittances, which maintain social ties and act as insurance premiums for migrants, are used principally to repay debts, finance migration moves for kin, and purchase consumer goods, including housing. Their use reinforces a traditional set of values. Thus migration, emerging out of inequality, may reinforce, rather than conflict with, the social hierarchy. Moreover, overseas migrants often have conservative attitudes toward development in their home areas; many Palauans in Hawaii have argued that it is important "to limit outside influences and hold onto traditional ways" (Vitarelli, 1981:22), and so remittances are aimed at conserving that tradition. The economic role of remittances has been discussed in detail elsewhere (Connell, 1980, 1986). In some of the poorer parts of the region, including Kiribati and Tuvalu, migrants are "sending home part of the means of subsistence. . . . This is quite a different pressure on urban incomes from one where gifts to people at home are luxuries and the timing of them [is] more or less immaterial to the recipients" (Morauta and Hasu, 1979:31).

The dependence on remittances is equally great, if not crucial to subsistence, in numerous parts of the South Pacific characterized by high levels of internal or international migration. Despite contributing to inflation, especially in the larger Polynesian countries, remittances have raised living standards and eased national balance-of-payment problems; they have also contributed to employment, especially in the construction and service sectors. In some small states, and on a number of islands, remittances constitute more than a quarter of the total income in normal circumstances (Connell, 1980, 1986) and in exceptional conditions (as in the aftermath of cyclones) and places (some outer islands of Kiribati and Tuvalu and many villages elsewhere) may constitute much more than double that proportion. The resultant dependence on remittances has reinforced the belief of individuals, households, and states in the necessity for continued migration. Indeed, increased demand for imported consumer goods can usually be met only by further migration where little of the remitted income is invested in economic growth.

Remittances and the elitist and consumer-oriented ideas of return migrants contribute to increased demands for high levels of consumption and welfare, although neither remittances nor return migrants may make significant contributions to increased production. Rising expectations in the wake of independence for many states in the 1970s and growing materialism have exacerbated the shift from production to consumption, the decline of exchange, and an increase in social tensions. The spreading taste for commodities has influenced work habits:

[The] allure of modernity is strongly linked to city life. . . . The mystique, however, tends to be stronger than the rational expectations. It survives the disappointment of the latter. Whatever its frustrations and degradations, the city continues to be the place where things are happening, where there is movement and a sense of future (Berger et al., 1974:128–129).

For many in the South Pacific, the largest cities and the metropolitan countries exercise the same allure, offer the same sense of future, and apparently validate migration.

Return Migration

Since migrants are generally younger, less traditional, and better educated than nonmigrants, they have a considerable potential for contributing to economic and social development in their villages and countries of origin. Elderly return migrants, however, are unlikely to be interested in development opportunities; in Wallis and Futuna, where by the 1970s the islands could be described as "holiday islands and havens for the retired" (Roux, 1980:174), return migrants have contributed little to development. Many of those who have returned have done so because of limited success abroad. This tendency is best documented in the case of American Samoa, where those who returned valued their family ties and the customary social organization of Samoa but also had been unsuccessful in some respect—usually in gaining long-term employment—in their adjustment to the U.S. economy and society (Lyons, 1980). Both nostalgia and reaction to discrimination also play a part. The available evidence suggests, however, that in comparison with situations elsewhere, return migration is limited and confined largely to "failures" or the retired. Moreover, the more successful return migrants tend to remain in the towns. Despite stated intentions, "it is probably unrealistic to expect more than a tiny fraction of those who have already escaped from the rural areas ever to go back. Many will want to go back but only provided that 'want' is never put to the task" (Crocombe, 1978:52).

All too often return migration is perceived as an admission of failure. Hence Shankman (1976:96) states bluntly that "Polynesian migrants do not return except for visitations, once they are overseas and have attained a degree of security." The limited extent of return migration is in part due to the great differences in income levels in Polynesia and in metropolitan nations and in part due to the difficulty of obtaining skilled jobs and the reluctance of return migrants to work in the agricultural sector. Consequently, widespread intentions to return may have more to do with nostalgia for the past than with a real plan for the future (Pitt and Macpherson, 1974:16). In general, despite occasional pressures on migrants overseas and occasional incentives from within the South Pacific, the volume of return migration is small.

Where rising expectations are combined with increased pressure on rural resources and static job opportunities in the formal sector, migration from rural areas is more likely to be permanent; this permanence may be in urban areas (and there are now third-generation urban residents in the South Pacific) or in metropolitan nations. In the United States, and certainly elsewhere, a signficant number of ethnic Pacific Islanders are unable to speak, or at least speak fluently, the language of their home country (Levin, 1985). This lack of facility is inevitably a deterrent to return migration, of either children or their parents, since all are embarrassed by the prospect of "young Samoans returning home and unable to speak their own language" (Emery, 1976:16). Such children are almost inevitably destined for an urban and international future.

The extent to which the impact of return migration is positive is doubtful. Although Pitt (1970) has argued that skills obtained from migration are valuable in the case of Western Samoa, considerable doubt exists about the transferability of skills obtained overseas to an economy like that of Western Samoa, where wages and salaries are much lower than in the metropolitan countries. It appears that those who have the skills most in demand in Western Samoa and the smaller states are least likely to return. A detailed analysis of attitudes toward return migration by Western Samoans concluded that there were four principal reasons for nonreturn. First, local businesses succeeded only rarely despite numerous attempts—partly because commerce was poorly understood and also because the social power of the 'aiga (extended family) ties eroded profitability. Second, wages and fringe benefits in Western Samoa were very low; third, New Zealand-born children had trouble adjusting to Western Samoa and hence parents were reluctant to return with them; and, fourth, the gerontocratic social organization limited individual aspirations (Macpherson, 1983). Moreover, in Western Samoa and other island states there is much evidence that actual return migrants are a "source of dissatisfaction with village life and the predominantly subsistence economy" despite, or more probably because of, the status they have gained from migration (Meleisea and Meleisea, 1980:37). They introduce new discontent, values, and aspirations, do not settle long themselves, and induce others to follow their lead.

Nevertheless, in recent decades return migrants to the countries of the South Pacific have included many of the principal political leaders in the region, including most of those who took a significant part in negotiating independence for their states. Thus return migrants to the Cook Islands include its three successive premiers (Albert Henry, Geoffrey Henry, and Tom Davis), and elsewhere in the region most political leaders have experienced education, training, and even employment abroad. For the molding of a political elite, the overseas experience has been vital. So too this return migration critically influences values; for many Cook Islands politicians, for example, "their life-style tends to be European in private and Maori in public" (Crocombe, 1979:54). These are the marginal men who were once the proponents of modernization and change. Those who might be future political leaders are now less likely to return, a situation that both emphasizes the conservative politics of the South Pacific and channels the frustrated away from inflexible systems of social and political stratification (as, particularly, in Tonga and Fiji).

Moreover, potential return migrants may face competition at home for the limited employment opportunities available and opposition from those who fear losing their jobs. For example: "Samoans who stayed at home will have taken over unused resources, especially in areas of rising population. Many rural Samoans feel that the migrants should not come back for long periods though they are welcome as visitors" (Pitt and Macpherson, 1974:15). The same attitudes are present in Niue and the Cook Islands. There are then few social, political, and economic incentives to return and, sometimes, not even the security of subsistence.

Many of the more positive comments on the impact of migration date from an earlier era when migration was less common, it was predominantly circular (thus producing a high level of remittances since return was almost certain), and there was no real demand for skilled labor in the region. Restless young men could earn money overseas, invest in the village, and return as responsible citizens. But the current context of migration is quite different. Whereas early migration was prestigious, it is now too common to be so. It has also produced a socioeconomy dependent upon migration. Expectations have risen and are increasingly difficult to meet within the confines of small national economies. Migration is thus viewed less as a means of diversifying economic risk within households than as a permanent transfer of human resources elsewhere. Migration is no longer so likely to be circular.

TOWARD A NEW DIASPORA

Undoubtedly, international migration has been of major benefit to destination countries, but for countries of origin the outcome is less clear. The prevalent use of remittances, the lack of economic growth, the failure to restructure economies, and the form of social change encouraged by emigration suggest minimal benefits at best. The impact of international migration on the migrants themselves, especially on their personal values and attitudes, is wide-ranging. On the positive side are the potential for gaining higher wages, education and other welfare benefits, experience, and new skills. Though there are social and psychological costs in the course of this acquisition, the conclusions suggest that many migrants benefit, although their children may be less fortunate. Because of limited return migration, the marginal value of many acquired skills in the sending countries, and the social conflicts between migrants and home societies, not all individual gains become gains for the sending countries.

At a national level, some evidence suggests that the source countries may suffer no net loss from high levels of emigration in the long run. Citing the case of a number of small countries, Blazic-Metzner and Hughes (1982:96) conclude that "the benefits nevertheless appear to exceed the costs for both individuals and countries." They note, however, that "the literature on this subject is large and emotive" (1982:101) and not wholly conclusive and that benefits will not occur if "the country concerned follows foolish policies" (1982:95). In the case of the small South Pacific states, few are large enough to have effective development policies. Consequently, international migration is often viewed as a significant source of income, as a safety valve that reduces pressure on national governments to provide employment opportunities and welfare services, and as a means of satisfying rising aspirations among political minorities and the poor and unemployed. Concern focuses on specific issues such as the brain or skill drain or, in the case of Niue, Pitcairn, and the Cook Islands, the overall population decline.

The safety-valve effect, limited economic growth, and arguments in favor of individual freedom of movement have created a steady migration from many countries. Constraints on international migration are posed by the destination countries rather than the source countries. International migration has thus become a substitute for development rather than a short-term support for increasing the effectiveness of national development efforts. Moreover, if migration were to become more restricted, and national socioeconomies were not restructured, the benefits would be even less apparent because of the inevitability of declining remittances in conditions of rapid population growth.

While international migration has had both positive and negative effects in the South Pacific region, the significance of the positive effects (notably increased standards of living) must be contrasted with the limited development potential of many countries in the region and their failure to achieve significant economic growth. The possibilities for agricultural and other forms of development vary substantially within the Pacific. A recent Asian Development Bank survey of choices and constraints in South Pacific agricultural development concluded:

The acceptance of a no-growth state of affairs may be the only realistic option for the small countries unless they are prepared to accept a state of permanent dependence on foreign aid. . . . No growth need not be synonymous with poverty if the possibility is established for people in stationary economies to migrate either temporarily or permanently to obtain access elsewhere to goods and services which cannot be made locally. . . . In the context of the limited physical resources of Polynesia this suggests a policy of unrestricted temporary or permanent migration of people from Polynesia, not only to New Zealand but also probably to Australia, the United States of America, and Canada where Polynesian communities are already established (Castle, 1980:136).

This is an extraordinary conclusion for a report on agricultural development, and as a policy recommendation it depends on decisions that Pacific countries can seek but cannot make. Moreover, the evidence presented here and elsewhere (Connell, 1986) suggests that migration is rarely beneficial to agricultural development.

Most countries in the South Pacific cannot guarantee perpetually unlimited migration and access to metropolitan countries; however, some, such as Kiribati and Tuvalu, now have effectively no outlets (other than Nauru in the short term) and, paradoxically, it is in those countries that a migration-based development strategy appears to be almost the only viable option. Even in the 1890s, labor migration was "the only alternative to starvation" (Macdonald, 1982b:53). In light of concern over the impending closure of the Nauru phosphate mines, a recent review of Australian aid gave particular emphasis to the special needs of the small states in the South Pacific. The executive summary attached sufficient importance to the problems of Kiribati and Tuvalu to give them a significance denied to all other states except Papua New Guinea:

Kiribati with a population of 60,000 and Tuvalu with a population of 8,000 have special problems. Their remote and minute land areas are heavily populated. They depend very much on remittances from their emigrants and on foreign aid. Their long-term development prospects are discouraging. In view of structural problems which are beyond their control and beyond the reach of aid, Australia should make available limited opportunities for immigration from Kiribati and Tuvalu (Australia, 1984:8; see also Blazic-Metzner and Hughes, 1982:94).

The review argued that Australia should "go beyond traditional ideas of aid" (1984:181) to provide a special immigration quota for two countries with which Australia has hitherto had few ties (Connell, 1985a). As in the case of the Asian Development Bank survey, external perceptions increasingly recognize the need for international migration from the South Pacific—a recognition that is likely to stimulate further pressures from other countries and reduce the dynamism of more self-reliant development initiatives.

In his introduction to an analysis of the impact of migration on Western Samoa, Shankman (1976:17) makes the sweeping statement that "there are no examples of countries that have developed through migration and remittances." The historical validity of this argument is highly doubtful, and in countries like Kiribati and Tuvalu, though migration may not have contributed greatly to development, it has certainly prevented nondevelopment. The principal advantages from international migration follow short-term or seasonal migration, but as migration becomes more pervasive and long-term these benefits may be reduced as dependence and uncertainty increases.

Concern over future metropolitan restrictions on immigration and issues of national pride and independence have produced a minority interest in the achievement of economic development in a more self-reliant context, possibly associated with a transition to low fertility. The economics of self-reliance have been considered elsewhere (Connell, 1986; Seers, 1983). In most states of the South Pacific, movement toward the self-sufficiency that reduction of migration and remittances implies would be difficult and painful. In many places aspirations are firmly directed toward the acquisition of modern goods. As has been argued for the small island of Rotuma, "with the prestige given to 'foreign' goods, it is doubtful, therefore, that Rotumans would *want* to be self-sufficient, even if it were a possibility" (Plant, 1977:174). In Tikopia, "from such a level of dependence on imported goods it becomes difficult to retreat without unease and a sense of deprivation" (Firth, 1971:69). In Ponape, too, villagers are not interested in adequate subsistence or even the "right to subsistence," but rather desire "continued and increased access to the goods and prestige provided by employment" (Petersen, 1979:37). These values from different parts of Polynesia and Micronesia are exceptionally widespread and attest to the serious local problems attached to even marginal movements toward greater self-reliance.

The limited prospects for economic development within the South Pacific are likely to be increasingly influenced by global economic cycles and the peripheral position of the region in that economy. Most economic forecasts for Third World countries in the next decade suggest a bleak future for the states of the South Pacific, although the states' isolation, their tenuous links with the international economy, and the strength of their subsistence sectors are likely to continue to dampen the regional impact of fluctuations in the world economy. Because of their growing dependence on depressed world markets, "the inherent vulnerability of Pacific island economies has become increasingly apparent" (Polson, 1983:21; see also Tisdell and Fairbairn, 1984). The traditional export crops of the region are less able to support Pacific Island populations and governments at their current expenditure levels, let alone support economic growth and the rising expectations of potentially growing populations. Even where there has been mining development, low market prices have prevented substantial gain. Owing to these economic trends, the South Pacific states have become increasingly dependent on the global economy for aid, trade, private investment, and, ultimately, migration. Their economic and cultural dependence will determine future trends in migration.

Virtually throughout the South Pacific, islanders have mobilized colonial ties to emigrate to the metropolitan countries; small states like American Samoa, the Cook Islands, Niue, and Tokelau have more islanders overseas than in their own countries. In larger Polynesian states the same trend exists, and the Micronesian states are likely to approach a point where Micronesian residents of the United States may outnumber the "folks back home" (Marshall, 1979:10-11). There has already been significant migration from Palau (and Guam and the Marianas) to the United States, and this movement is likely to be followed by more extensive migration from other parts of Micronesia (Connell, 1985b). The more often such choices are taken, the more difficult they will be to avoid for future generations of Pacific Islanders as the focus of life moves ever outward.

Individual aspirations in the South Pacific are as much focused on emigration now as they have ever been; there is no apparent reason why this focus should change. Despite the initial costs of migration, migrants usually reach the living standards of the host countries, or at least of the less affluent within those countries, within a generation or so. Long waiting lists for emigration and illegal migration demonstrate a large pent-up demand. Examination of development plans, policies, and practices in the "soft states" of the region further suggests that future economic development is unlikely to stimulate increased income and welfare levels in an equitable manner or to generate significant increases in wage employment. Moreover, not only is there no real opposition through policy to sustained emigration overseas but in many states policies actually favor labor migration and emigration.

Most migrants from the South Pacific, including some of those with skills, are in the secondary segment of the labor force of the metropolitan destination countries (mainly New Zealand and the United States), where social, institutional, and economic barriers prevent movement into the primary segment. Most Pacific Islanders remain in unskilled jobs with low wages (Levin, 1985), unstable tenure, poor working conditions, few benefits, high unemployment, and little unionization. Hence migrants from the region, whether temporary or effectively permanent, continue to function essentially as guest workers. As metropolitan economies are restructured and rationalized, the "secondary sector is most likely to experience a decline with a corresponding decline in the demand for labor" (Gibson, 1982); immigration policies of the metropolitan countries are therefore tending toward greater severity toward migrants and a skill bias. While global trends suggest increased national opposition to international immigration—as a political response to social and economic problems associated with high levels of unemployment—evidence from the principal destination countries for South Pacific migrants suggests that future policies are unlikely to discriminate further against the South Pacific states and that familial ties may enable Pacific Islanders to increase their immigration even if metropolitan immigration laws are strengthened.

As they have done for more than two decades, Polynesians especially, and many other Pacific Islanders, see emigration or overseas employment as a means of escaping limited domestic economic opportunities and maximizing their household development options. The voices of those who urge more self-reliant development strategies or those who contemplate with nostalgia enclosed village or island communities with their assumed immutable order are lonely voices in the wilderness; it is the new diaspora that extraordinarily rapidly has come to characterize the contemporary South Pacific. One of the last regions of the world to be settled has entered a period of potential population decline.

REFERENCES

Australia

   1984   *Report of the Committee to Review the Australian Overseas Aid Program.* Canberra: Australian Government Publishing Service.

Bedford, R. D.

   1980   "Demographic Processes in Small Islands: The Case of Internal Migration." In H. C. Brookfield (ed.), *Population–Environment Relations in Tropical Islands: The Case of Eastern Fiji.* Paris: UNESCO.

Berger, B., B. Berger, and H. Kellner

   1974   *The Homeless Mind: Modernization and Consciousness.* New York: Random House.

Blazic-Metzner, B., and H. Hughes

   1982   "Growth Experience of Small Economies." In B. Jalan (ed.), *Problems and Policies in Small Economies.* London: Croom Helm.

Brookfield, H. C.

   1972   "Intensification and Disintensification in Pacific Agriculture." *Pacific Viewpoint,* 13(1):30–48.

   1980   "The Fiji Study: Testing the MAB Approach." In H. C. Brookfield (ed.), *Population–Environment Relations in Tropical Islands: The Case of Eastern Fiji.* Paris: UNESCO.

   1984   "Intensification Revisited." *Pacific Viewpoint,* 25(1):15–44.

Castle, L. V.

   1980   "The Economic Context." In R. G. Ward and A. Proctor (eds.), *South Pacific Agriculture—Choices and Constraints.* Canberra and Manila: Australian National University Press and Asian Development Bank.

Chambers, A.

  1975   *Nanumea Report*. Wellington: Department of Geography, Victoria University of Wellington.

Chapman, M., and R. M. Prothero (eds.)

  1985   *Circulation in Population Movement: Substance and Concepts from the Melanesian Case*. London: Routledge & Kegan Paul.

Connell, J.

  1980   *Remittances and Rural Development: Migration, Dependency and Inequality in the South Pacific*. Occasional Paper No. 22. Canberra: Development Studies Centre, Australian National University.

————.

  1984a *Diets and Dependency: Food and Colonialism in the South Pacific*. 2nd ed. Occasional Paper No. 1. Sydney: Freedom from Hunger Ideas Centre.

————.

  1984b "Status or Subjugation? Women, Migration and Development in the South Pacific." *International Migration Review*, 18(4):965–983.

————.

  1985a "Islands on the Poverty Line." *Pacific Viewpoint*, 26(2):463–473.

————.

  1985b *Migration, Employment and Development*. Country Report No. 25. *North America*. Noumea: International Labour Organisation and South Pacific Commission.

————.

  1986   *Migration, Employment and Development in the South Pacific*. Noumea: International Labour Organisation and South Pacific Commission.

————.

  1987   "The Fatal Impact? Migration, Agriculture and Health in the South Pacific." In *The Effects of Urbanisation and Western Foods on the Health of Pacific Islands Populations*. Noumea: South Pacific Commission.

Cook Islands

  1984   *Cook Islands Development Plan, 1982–1985*. Rarotonga.

Crocombe, R.

  1978   "Rural Development." *Pacific Perspective*, 7(1–2):42–59.

————.

  1979   "Nepotism." In R. Crocombe (ed.), *Cook Island Politics: The Inside Story*. Auckland: South Pacific Social Science Association.

Curson, P.

1979 "Migration, Remittances and Social Networks Among Cook Islanders." *Pacific Viewpoint*, 20(2):185–198.

Dyson, J.

1982 *The South Seas Dream: An Adventure in Paradise.* London: Heinemann.

Emery, S.

1976 "The Samoans of Los Angeles: A Preliminary Study of Their Migration from Pago Pago to the South Bay." Los Angeles: University of Southern California. Mimeographed.

Fairbairn, I.

1982 "Second Thoughts on First Aid." *Islands Business*, 8(10):32–36.

Firth, R.

1971 "Economic Aspects of Modernization in Tikopia." In L. R. Hiatt and C. Jayawardena (eds.), *Anthropology in Oceania*. Sydney: Angus and Robertson.

Fisk, E. K.

1966 "The Economic Structure." In E. K. Fisk (ed.), *New Guinea on the Threshold*. Canberra: Australian National University Press.

Gibson, K.

1982 "Political Economy and International Labour Migration: The Case of Polynesians in New Zealand." *New Zealand Geographer*, 39(2):29–42.

Grossman, L.

1981 "The Cultural Ecology of Economic Development." *Annals of the Association of American Geographers*, 71(2):220–236.

Hezel, F. X.

1985 "In the Aftermath of the Education Explosion." Truk: Micronesian Seminar. Mimeographed.

Howard, A.

1961 "Rotuma as a Hinterland Community." *Journal of the Polynesian Society*, 70:272–299.

Johannes, R. E.

1981 *Words of the Lagoon: Fishing and Marine Lore in the Palau District of Micronesia.* Berkeley and Los Angeles: University of California Press.

Levin, M. J.

1985 "Pacific Islanders in the United States: A Demographic Profile Based on the 1980 Census." Paper presented at the Conference on Asian-Pacific Immigration to the United States, East-West Center, Honolulu.

Lyons, R.

  1980   "Emigration from American Samoa: A Study of Bicultural Assimi-
          lation and Migration." Ph.D. dissertation, University of Hawaii.

Macdonald, B.

  1982a   "Self-Determination and Self-Government." *Journal of Pacific History,*
          17(1):51–61.

  1982b   *Cinderellas of the Empire: Towards a History of Kiribati and Tuvalu.* Can-
          berra: Australian National Press.

Macpherson, C.

  1983   "The Skills Transfer Debate: Great Promise or Faint Hope for Western
          Samoa?" *New Zealand Population Review,* 9(2):47–76.

Manners, R. A.

  1965   "Remittances and the Unit of Analysis in Anthropological Research."
          Southwestern Journal of Anthropology, 21(3):179–195.

Marshall, M.

  1979   "Education and Depopulation on a Micronesian Atoll." *Micronesica,*
          15(1–2):1–11.

Meleisea, M., and P. Meleisea

  1980   "The Best Kept Secret: Tourism in Western Samoa." In F. Rajotte and
          R. Crocombe (eds.), *Pacific Tourism: As Islanders See It.* Suva: Insti-
          tute of Pacific Studies.

Morauta, L., and M. Hasu

  1979   "Rural–Urban Relationships in Papua New Guinea: Case Material
          from the Gulf Province on Net Flows." IASER Discussion Paper No.
          25. Port Moresby.

Morauta, L., and D. Ryan

  1982   "From Temporary to Permanent Townsmen: Migrants from the
          Malalaua District, Papua New Guinea." *Oceania,* 53(1):39–55.

Petersen, G.

  1979   "External Politics, Internal Economics and Ponapean Social Forma-
          tion." *American Ethnologist,* 6(1):25–40.

Pitt, D. C.

  1970   *Tradition and Economic Progress in Samoa.* Oxford: Oxford University
          Press.

Pitt, D. C., and C. Macpherson

  1974   *Emerging Pluralism: The Samoan Community in New Zealand.* Auckland:
          Longman Paul.

Plant, C.

1977 "The Development Dilemma." In C. Plant (ed.), *Rotuma: Split Island*. Suva: Institute of Pacific Studies.

Pollard, B.

1978 "The Problem of an Aid-Dependent Economy: The Case of Niue." In G. Woods (ed.), *South Pacific Dossier*. Canberra: Australian Council for Overseas Aid.

Polson, S.

1983 "Coconomics: Expert Agriculture Won't Pay the Bills." *Pacific Magazine*, 8(4):21–24.

Roux, J.-C.

1980 "Migration and Change in Wallisian Society." In R. T. Shand (ed.), *The Island States of the Pacific and Indian Oceans*. Canberra: Development Studies Centre, Australian National University.

Schwalbenberg, H.

1984 "Micronesians on the Move: Guam or Hawaii?" Compact of Free Association Memo No. 12. Truk: Micronesian Seminar.

Seers, D.

1983 *The Political Economy of Nationalism*. Oxford: Oxford University Press.

Shankman, P.

1976 *Migration and Underdevelopment: The Case of Western Samoa*. Boulder: Westview Press.

Shore, B.

1978 "Introduction." In C. Macpherson, B. Shore, and R. Franco (eds.), *New Neighbours . . . Islanders in Adaptation*. Santa Cruz: Center for South Pacific Studies.

Simmons, A., S. Diaz-Briquets, and A. R. Laquian

1977 *Social Change and Internal Migration*. Ottawa: International Development Research Centre.

Standing, G.

1982 *Circulation and Proletarianisation*. Working Paper No. 119. Geneva: International Labour Office and World Employment Programme.

Thomson, J. K.

1976 "Economic Development in the South Pacific: Some Problems and Prospects." In F. P. King (ed.), *Oceania and Beyond: Essays on the Pacific Since 1945*. Westport: Greenview Press.

Tisdell, G., and I. Fairbairn

1984 "Subsistence Economies and Unsustainable Development and Trade: Some Simple Theory." *Journal of Development Studies*, 20(2):227–241.

Vitarelli, M.

  1981   *A Pacific Island Migration Study: Palauans in Hawaii.* Honolulu: Pacific
          Islands Development Program, East–West Center.

Wallman, S.

  1977   "The Bind of Migration: Conditions of Non-Development in Lesotho."
          In S. Wallman (ed.), *Perceptions of Development.* Cambridge: Cambridge
          University Press.

Ward, R. G.

  1961   "Internal Migration in Fiji." *Journal of Polynesian Society,* 70(3):257–271.

Workman, R. L., C. O'Meara, J. Craig, J. Nagel, E. Robbins, and D. A. Ballendorf

  1981   *Island Voyagers in New Quests: An Assessment of Degree Completion
          Among Micronesian College Students.* Mangilao City: University of
          Guam, Micronesian Area Research Center.

Yang, Y. H.

  1982   "Agricultural Performance, Food Availability and Dietary Change in
          Asia and the Pacific." Paper submitted to Agri-Energy Roundtable,
          Maui.

PART V. RESEARCH ISSUES

17

Impacts of Emigration on Sending Countries

Benjamin V. Cariño

Emigration may either aid or hinder development in the sending society. Its impact involves a wide range of social, economic, demographic, and political phenomena. There may be short-term costs or benefits, or they may emerge over a longer period. Moreover, the effects of emigration can be measured at various levels: the individual, the household, the community, and the country as a whole. It is important to keep these various levels in mind, since the consequences of emigration may not be the same at all levels–that is, emigration may be beneficial for the individual and the household but less beneficial or even harmful for the community or the country at large. Remittances may, for instance, improve individual or household welfare but have negligible productivity effects at the national level if used mainly for consumption purposes. This chapter focuses primarily on the effects of emigration at the national level, although consequences at lower levels are also noted where appropriate.

The need to examine these consequences for Asian and Pacific countries is particularly important in light of the explosive growth of emigration from the region in recent years. Since the 1965 U.S. immigration reform, Asian immigration to the United States has dramatically risen from just over 17,000 in 1965 to an average of more than one-quarter of a million annually since 1981 (Chapter 6 in this volume). Similar trends in Asian immigration have been observed for Canada and Australia. With the easing of immigration restrictions, Asian immigrants in recent years have represented the largest proportion (more than 30 percent) of all immigrants to Canada (Chapter 10 in this volume). For Australia, the emphasis on family reunion, a nondiscriminatory immigration policy, and acceptance of responsibility for refugees have worked together to produce an increase in Asian and Pacific immigration of well over one-third of total immigrant movement to Australia in 1983–1984 (Chapter 8 in this volume). The effects of this emigration pattern on the sending countries may be dramatic and far-reaching.

As a proportion of the total population of the country of origin, the number of emigrants is small. For the Philippines and Korea, for instance (the two largest sources of Asian immigrants to the United States), the size of immigrant streams to the United States in 1984 represented only about 0.08 percent of their total populations. Regardless of its magnitude, however, emigration is likely to have some impact on the sending country. Emigration is generally tied to political and economic processes, and even though the initial magnitude may be small, emigration streams almost inevitably grow in time. Significant factors are the extent and nature of migrant selectivity, the amount of repatriated earnings and the manner in which they are used, the nature of the skills and ideas brought back by migrant returnees, and migrants' activities abroad and their linkages with the country of origin. The extent to which each of these factors is significant differs, of course, from country to country, accounting in part for the varying consequences of emigration for various sending nations.

Focusing upon Asian and Pacific countries, this chapter surveys the findings of the scattered literature on the consequences of emigration to the sending country. Attention is first given to labor force quality, economic productivity, foreign exchange earnings, and the like. Observations made in earlier chapters of the book are drawn upon, and other theoretical and empirical works that have examined the possible impacts of emigration for the sending country are examined. In the process, research gaps are identified and some suggestions are made about how such gaps can be at least partially narrowed.

It should be noted that this chapter is primarily concerned with emigration (which is more or less permanent) as distinguished from temporary labor migration.[1] Although some generalizations relating to

---

1. As part of its urbanization and migration research program, the East–West Population Institute is currently undertaking a research project on the labor market consequences of the flow of temporary contract workers from Asia. One result of this project is a recently completed book on Asian labor migration to the Middle East (Arnold and Shah, 1985).

both types of movement may be justified, by its very nature the effects of temporary labor migration on such matters as labor force quality, unemployment, and economic productivity are obviously different.

MIGRANT SELECTIVITY

Migrant selectivity is an important source of social change and often gives rise to certain development problems that are of great concern to social scientists and policymakers alike. These problems are shaped by the type of selectivity involved and its context. In this section, two major dimensions of migrant selectivity are examined: selectivity by age and sex, and selectivity in terms of educational and occupational skills, or manpower loss. As a salient feature of international migration, the latter has become known as the brain drain from the less developed to the more developed countries.

Age and Sex Selectivity

Selectivity by age and sex has been noted in some migration streams from Asia. A distinct characteristic of Korean immigrants to the United States after World War II, for instance, has been the predominance of women. For every 100 females, only 48 males were admitted to the United States in 1970, 63 males in 1973, and 64 males in 1977 (Koo and Yu, 1981:4). The imbalance in sex ratios was most pronounced in the 20–29 age group. The sex ratio was 23 in 1970, 32 during 1973, and 36 during 1977. This sex imbalance was attributed in earlier years to marriage of Korean women to American servicemen and, more recently, to the emigration of women married to Korean Americans.

The prewar out-migration experience of the Ilocos Coast region of the Philippines presents an interesting contrast. As noted in Chapter 13, out-migration from the region, especially the early migratory flows to Hawaii, was dominated by males (see also Smith, 1981). The trend has shifted to a female-dominant stream in the postwar period (Eviota and Smith, 1980), however, a pattern that is now similar to the emigration experience of Korea. This phenomenon also seems evident in emigrant flows from India, which similarly exhibited a predominantly male pattern in earlier years but have shifted to an almost even sex composition in recent times (Chapter 15 in this volume).

To the extent that they are permanent or long term, the demographic consequences of immigrant flows characterized by heavy imbalances in sex ratios are generally straightforward. First, these emigration patterns tend to disrupt the marriage process, as in the case of the Philippines (Chapter 13 in this volume). In turn, delayed marriage, lower nuptiality, and a high incidence of celibacy have almost mechanical consequences for total fertility rates and population growth. In several Pacific Island countries, there is much evidence that male-dominant emigration has slowed down the birthrate and, in some areas, emigration has been regarded as one means of family planning (Howard, 1961; also cited in Chapter 16 in this volume).

Not so straightforward, however, are the demographic consequences of single persons' temporary absences. These consequences may be much more complex and must be seen in the context of actual life processes in a given society. Data from some countries in Latin America indicate that the temporary labor migration of males is related, in many instances, to marriage plans, and the scarcity of resources available to young males may be the reason for marriage delays (Balan, 1983). The same pattern can be observed in rural areas in the Philippines and probably in other countries of Asia. To the extent that temporary absences due to wage employment increase the resources available to young males, they may reinforce a pattern of early household formation. As Balan (1983) suggests, marriage and childbearing may actually occur in anticipation of resources that can be realized from migration opportunities.

· Beyond demographic effects, age and sex imbalances in immigration and labor migration flows may also have important consequences for family relations. For example, they could alter household arrangements. Because of migration, the nuclear family is no longer as common a household pattern in many parts of the world; split and extended households are becoming increasingly common. Changes in the sex composition of households have also been observed. In turn, these changes may affect the division of labor within families. Research findings indicate that, at least among female workers, labor redundancy in rural areas is linked to the seasonal pattern of labor demand and to the absence of males during extended periods (Balan, 1983). In particular, the departure of males is one of the new pressures being exerted upon young women who are already in charge of various household activities. The result is a "double usage of time"—that is, young women engage in household and nonhousehold activities simultaneously, a phenomenon that should probably be reckoned with in efforts to improve the productivity of rural areas.

Evidence in the Philippines also shows that the departure of some household members has not had an adverse impact on household welfare. In fact, migrant households have higher socioeconomic status on the average than stayer households (Chapter 13 in this volume). For the Pacific Islands, however, the departure of some household members, especially the household head, appears to have serious implications for household welfare. A survey in Niue has found that villages with higher rates of out-migration also had the highest proportions of households with very low per capita incomes. Of these households, 65 percent seem to have been depleted and without sufficient support as a result of out-migration. Widows, widowers, and old people living with children constituted 40 percent of the households, and households lacking a father or other breadwinner comprised 25 percent (Walsh, 1981:8).

Emigration conceivably could affect other aspects of family life as well. The absence of a spouse could put strains on a marriage. For example, increasing evidence exists that male labor migration results in some stress on women who are left behind. Among spouses of contract laborers in the Middle East, emotional and psychosomatic problems are reported to be common in Pakistan and some areas in India (Arnold, 1984). Permanent immigration could put similar if not even more serious strains on a marriage. The findings of another study in West Sumatra show that the extended absences of migrant men may be responsible for the incidence of Oedipus complex among children and mental disorders among women (Naim, 1974:425).

Manpower Loss

Those concerned about the brain and skill drain argue that the departure of the economically active and productive segment of the population reduces a country's ability to produce and, hence, reduces income. Often this argument is made in the context of the "world system" theory which, as a derivative of Marxist theory, views international migration as a movement of labor from peripheral to core nations caused by the advanced capitalist economies' search for cheap labor and their desire to perpetuate economic and political dependency relationships (Portes, 1981; Petras, 1981). Related to this argument is the more pragmatic concern that the brain drain represents lost educational investment to sending countries. Lucas (1981:88) notes that these assertions of the negative effects of emigration are made entirely from a domestic perspective—that is, only from the perspective of those residing in the sending country. Emigration may have positive results for the migrants themselves and for the areas of destination.

Available data suggest that many countries in Asia are sending a considerable number of professional and highly qualified workers to the United States. Table 17.1 presents information on immigrant professional, technical, and kindred workers in the United States from major source countries in Asia during the 1960s and 1970s. The Philippines, India, and, to some extent, China and Korea stand out as the major suppliers of professional and technical workers during the period. During the intervals 1965–1969 and 1970–1974, the number of professional and technical immigrants from all Asian countries rose sharply. The

Table 17.1. Immigrant Professional, Technical, and Kindred Workers
            Entering the United States from Major Source Countries
            in Asia: Number and Ratio (per Thousand) to Total Im-
            migrants, 1960–1979

Origin	1960–1964	1965–1969	1970–1974	1975–1979
All Asia	12,381 (111)	53,078 (213)	131,872 (230)	117,853 (134)
China	2,457 (119)	10,571 (161)	17,095 (211)	14,083 (137)
Hong Kong	255 (82)	1,159 (61)	1,132 (55)	2,062 (81)
India	1,239 (392)	9,174 (501)	30,638 (456)	26,742 (290)
Iran	724 (245)	2,035 (343)	3,932 (305)	3,338 (141)
Japan	832 (39)	1,795 (99)	2,729 (114)	2,059 (99)
Korea	773 (81)	3,079 (167)	14,123 (151)	12,842 (86)
Philippines	1,916 (122)	16,773 (291)	42,634 (279)	32,088 (172)
Other Asia	4,185 (118)	8,492 (182)	19,589 (163)	24,639 (88)

Sources: INS Annual Reports (1960–1977); INS Statistical Yearbooks (1978–1979).

Note: Ratio figures (the number of professional, technical, and kindred workers for every 1,000 immigrants) are in parentheses.

rapid growth of immigrant professionals and technical workers is particularly prominent for India and the Philippines, which experienced more than a twentyfold increase over the fourteen-year period from 1960 to 1974. This turning point in international migration was ushered in by the 1965 U.S. immigration law reform, which favored professionals.

When compared with the total number of emigrants to the United States, the magnitude of emigrant professional and technical workers from these countries is not so staggering as when considered absolutely (Table 17.1). Nevertheless, the rates are still prominent for the major sending nations and particularly high for India, where professional and technical workers constituted more than half of the total immigrants in the 1965–1969 interval, the period in which revisions to the U.S. immigration law were introduced.

Data on immigrant scientists and engineers in recent years show essentially the same pattern, and India and the Philippines are again prominent as the major suppliers to the United States (Table 17.2). Together these two countries accounted for almost two-thirds of the total number of immigrant scientists and engineers from Asia during the 1976–1978 period. China and Korea also contributed a sizable number.

Several studies have likewise provided estimates of the immense loss to certain Asian countries caused by the emigration of highly qualified workers. In Korea, for instance, estimates in 1977 placed the country's loss at about 2.6 million years of schooling by virtue of emigration that

Table 17.2. Immigrant Scientists and Engineers in the United States from Selected Asian Countries: 1976–1978

Country	1976 N	1976 %	1977 N	1977 %	1978 N	1978 %	Total N	Total %
China	377	9.2	484	12.5	580	10.9	1,441	10.9
China (Taiwan)	217	5.4	49	1.3	327	6.2	593	4.5
Hong Kong	71	1.8	112	2.9	142	2.7	325	2.4
India	1,409	34.7	1,424	36.8	1,896	35.7	4,729	35.7
Japan	86	2.1	66	1.7	100	1.9	252	1.9
Korea	299	7.4	290	7.5	293	5.5	882	6.7
Pakistan	156	3.8	163	4.2	214	4.0	533	4.0
Philippines	1,201	29.6	778	20.1	682	12.9	2,661	20.1
Thailand	47	1.2	281	7.3	82	1.5	410	3.1
Other Asia	195	4.8	222	5.7	992	18.7	1,409	10.7
Total	4,058	100.0	3,869	100.0	5,308	100.0	13,235	100.0

Source: National Science Foundation (1980:tables 6–8).

Note: Scientists include social scientists and urban planners.

took place over a fifteen-year period (1962–1977), costing 220 billion won at its 1976 value ($458 million) in government expenditures (Koo and Yu, 1981:21–22). Similar estimates have been made for India. Until 1966, India gave up an estimated $1.7 million annually as a result of brain drain to the United States, Canada, and France, a figure that rose to $5.5 million in 1967 (Chapter 15 in this volume). Based on the median incomes of engineers, doctors, and scientists in India, it was calculated that the country lost about $188,419,000 through the emigration of some 5,439 of these workers between 1958 and 1966 (see Chapter 15).

The brain drain results partly from nonreturning Asian students in the United States. In 1984, American colleges and universities enrolled about 200,000 Asian students. It is estimated that about one-third of them will stay in the United States by marrying American citizens, obtaining immigrant visas based on skills or family relationships, or simply staying on illegally after the expiration of their student visas (Fawcett et al., 1985). This problem is particularly serious for Taiwan, where it is reported that only 13.2 percent of some 80,000 students who went to the United States from 1950 to 1983 have returned (Hwang, 1984).

That the departure of professionals and skilled laborers constitutes a loss for some countries in Asia is difficult to dismiss. As argued in earlier chapters, however, the extent of the problem has to be qualified (Chapters 13 and 15 in this volume). One must view the emigration of professionals in the context of the employment situation and economic circumstances of the country of origin. Some scholars have argued that only under certain conditions would emigration hamper the economic productivity of the sending country. Among those conditions are the employment status of the emigrants at the time of departure and the labor absorptive capacity of the sending country's economy (Lucas, 1981).

If one takes these factors into consideration, the brain drain may not be so harmful to the sending nations as the estimates of educational investments lost seem to suggest. Again the Philippines is an example of a country with a large stock of professionals and an economy that cannot fully absorb them because their skills apparently are not consistent with its development needs. Conditions in India are similar (Pernia, 1976; Chapters 13 and 15 in this volume). Emigration under these circumstances therefore may be viewed not as a brain drain but as a process that mitigates the problems of unemployment and underemployment so common among developing countries in Asia.

Related to the brain drain issue is the largescale departure of skilled agricultural labor and its impact on agricultural productivity, especially in rural countries of origin. Such an impact is influenced principally by the extent to which the agricultural system is dependent on male or female labor, the length of absence of the migrants, and the amount of compensatory remittances available to hire replacements for migrant laborers (Chapter 8 in this volume).

In some rural areas, the out-migration of agricultural labor may aid the sending country by easing the pressure on land and resources. Viewed in this light, emigration entails development in the passive sense—that is, the existing stock of resources will cover the remaining population more adequately (Bohning, 1983:40). Hugo (1985:18) reports that in Java the marginal productivity of agricultural labor is virtually zero and there has been little evidence until recently that rural out-migration produces labor shortages. Other scholars point out that, under these conditions, emigration reduces underemployment and induces rationalization of agriculture through the consolidation of landholdings, thus improving agricultural productivity (Kindleberger, 1967; Miracle and Berry, 1970; Friedlander, 1965).

Although emigration has enhanced agricultural productivity in some areas, in others it has led to the depopulation of villages. The experience of some Pacific Island countries is illustrative of this problem. Population pressure on resources in these countries has been observed to be low, and emigration has actually resulted in agricultural land being worked by a smaller remaining population. This situation, in turn, has given rise to less intensive use of land, declining agricultural productivity, and an increasing dependence on food imports from other countries (Chapter 16 in this volume). As Swanson (1979:47) notes, declining productivity may be attributed to factors that make it difficult to introduce mechanization—the inappropriateness of available machinery, for example, and land that can be farmed only by labor-intensive methods.

Clearly there is a need to establish the exact magnitude and nature of the brain drain and skill drain problem. The analysis presented here, however, suggests that the problem has to be assessed in the context of the social and economic framework of the sending nation. To the extent that the drain involves mainly labor in oversupply or not essential for important development needs, the problem is far less acute than the data imply. This view in no way suggests that the loss of skilled and highly qualified workers should be ignored, since the quality of the labor force will suffer. A common observation made about many Asian countries, however, may be usefully reiterated: Any remedy to the problem should focus attention on what seems to be its root cause— the lack of an effective training and manpower policy that is responsive not to external markets and demands but to the internal development needs of the sending nation. (See also Pernia, 1976.)

REPATRIATED EARNINGS

From the standpoint of the major sending countries in Asia and the Pacific, one beneficial effect of emigration may be the earnings repatriated by the emigrants to their home country. Repatriated earnings may take the form of remittances from emigrants while abroad, the savings brought back by returning migrants, or payments made to returnees (mostly social security benefits) by their employers abroad. For many countries in Asia, repatriated earnings have been reported to be considerable, especially when viewed in the context of the sending nations' economies.

Estimates of remittances from Koreans abroad totaled $1,124 million between 1970 and 1978, of which $757 million originated from the United States (Koo and Yu, 1981:23). Remittances from Asian Indian and Filipino immigrants also appear to be considerable. A survey of Indian immigrants in the United States reveals that an overwhelming majority of them had sent money home, with average remittances amounting to $600 a year (Glaser, 1978). As noted in Chapter 13, a similar survey of Filipino immigrants in Honolulu in 1982 shows that more than three-quarters of the households surveyed sent remittances to relatives in the Philippines and that the annual average remittance was $599 per sending household (see also Caces, 1985). These findings reveal that migrants earn far more abroad than they could in their home communities. Many of them are therefore able to save and return with relatively large sums of cash in addition to the remittances they send.

Repatriated earnings represent tangible gains to the households involved. The impact of these earnings beyond the household, however, depends on the manner in which they pass into the local economy. Research findings substantiate the claim made by many that earnings are primarily used for consumption and status mobility—much more than for productive capital investments (Swanson, 1979; Wiest, 1979). Studies in the Philippines show that expenditures out of remittances are devoted mainly to daily needs, housing and household appliances, and land (Caces, 1985; Chapter 13 in this volume).

Some researchers suggest that housing as a capital investment is beneficial because it generates local employment. Wiest (1979:172) points out, however, that additional employment created by housing expenditures usually depends upon the continuation of migratory wage labor and is often temporary and sporadic.

Wiest (1979) observes that the purchase of land may merely suggest that it is changing hands. Repatriated earnings, therefore, have only a *redistribution* effect in many cases, not a production effect. In the Pacific Islands, the impact of land purchases has in fact been more adverse: Regular remittance payments have encouraged middle-aged and elderly farmers to abandon their traditional agricultural activities and rely solely on remittances, with the result that the traditional agricultural system is weakened (Chapter 16 in this volume).

The foregoing discussion is in no way meant to suggest that repatriated earnings are never invested in productive enterprises. Moreover, a portion of remittances is invested in the education of the next generation, which can be viewed as an investment in the development of human capital (Caces, 1985). The failure, however, of many people with repatriated earnings to make productive investments has raised doubts about the economic value of migrant remittances (Watson, 1975; Paine, 1974). The dearth of viable investment opportunities in rural communities may partly account for this state of affairs. In the view of some scholars, the effects of these investments would probably be short-lived given the constraints faced by inexperienced producers in rural areas (Swanson, 1979; Wiest, 1979).

From a national standpoint, the experience of many Asian countries seems to suggest that repatriated earnings have only limited effects on production. However, other factors need to be taken into account in assessing the value of remittances beyond the household level. Certainly the ultimate purpose to which remittances are put should be examined (Arnold, 1984). Furthermore, as Stahl (1985) observes, although the marginal propensity to consume from remittances is high, funds left in demand deposits collectively may provide a good source of investable funds. In short, the development effects of repatriated earnings potentially could be maximized. Governments of sending nations should concentrate now on devising means (taxation, bonding schemes, and the like) to achieve this end.

SKILLS AND IDEAS BROUGHT BACK

Besides providing capital to underwrite productive investments, some scholars argue, the migrant can also bring changes by returning to his home village with new skills and ideas. Little is known about the exact number of migrants permanently returning to their home countries, although quite a few studies have been conducted on motivations for return. The return migrant has been characterized, for example, as one who sees the initial place of destination as a means rather than an end. Swanson (1979:39) claims that return migrants "may come to America in search of a better life, but a better life in their homeland, not in America." Other reasons for return migration have been cited, of course, including a peasant's attachment to land, failure in or expulsion from the host society, completion of the migrant's objectives, and even nostalgia (Rhoades, 1979; Bretell, 1979).

Fragmentary evidence is available on the extent of return migration in various countries in Asia and the Pacific. During the prewar period, for instance, the volume of return migration to the Philippines was fairly sizable (Chapter 13 in this volume). Some evidence of return migration among Indian professionals likewise exists. As part of its program to minimize the impact of professional emigration, the Indian government has encouraged Indian professionals abroad to register with the country's Council for Scientific and Industrial Research (CSIR) for possible job placement in India. Over the twenty-year period from 1960 to 1980, some 21,495 scientists, engineers, and doctors working abroad have registered with the CSIR. Of those registered, 11,276 were offered jobs; but only 7,300 accepted, of whom at least 227 went back abroad (Helweg, 1984:51).

Although little direct evidence is available, the volume of return migration to the Pacific Islands has been thought to be relatively small. In a study of Western Samoa, Shankman (1976:96) states categorically that "Polynesian migrants do not return." The wide differentials in wage and salary levels between the islands and places of destination and the difficulty of obtaining unskilled jobs outside the agricultural sector (to which the migrants are reluctant to return) help explain the limited flow of return migration to the Pacific Islands (Chapter 16 in this volume). These are mere assumptions, however, and in the absence of empirical data such assumptions are difficult to test. It seems, though, that at least some of those who return do remain in Western Samoa. Survey results in New Zealand show that migrants from Western Samoa intended to return home after their children were established there, although Connell (Chapter 16 in this volume, p. 392) points out that their intentions may be more a "nostalgia for the past than . . . a real plan for the future."

Information is likewise scanty on the acquisition of new skills among migrant returnees. The little evidence that exists indicates that negligible additional skills are acquired or at least few are applied. In his review of the literature, Swanson (1979:52) states that the unskilled generally remain unskilled. Castles and Kosack (1973:412) similarly take a pessimistic view of the effects of returnees' skills on the quality of the labor force. Not only are there limited opportunities to learn new skills abroad, but also returning workers often discover that the skills they have acquired are unsuitable to local needs. In other cases, returnees choose to relocate in rural settings where no market for their skills exists (Castles and Kosack, 1973:416).

Many writers argue that reintegration in the home country is particularly difficult among immigrants with essentially rural backgrounds who have moved to large industrial settings. Some have noted that many return migrants experience *backward* mobility, since a return to the area of origin often means a return to the occupation they formerly held. Reyneri and Mughini (1984) have observed that in Europe return migration often involves leaving the labor force—an observation that may apply equally to returnees in Asia and Pacific countries.

Emigrants who have acquired additional skills, moreover, may be the ones least likely to return. Two types of returnees are common: those who return because of failure and those who return for retirement. These returnees effectively transfer the dependency and employment burden back to the country of origin and subsequently compete with stayers for the limited resources available (see Kubat, 1984).

Besides using their skills, emigrants can effect change by returning to their home country with new ideas and attitudes. In North India, for instance, Patel (1972:28) found that returning migrants introduced certain variations (better light, ventilation, and bathroom facilities in their homes) that had been unknown to the village residents and apparently had a lasting influence on them. In Ilocos Norte, Philippines, McArthur (1979) found that the migrant returnees who had stayed longer in Hawaii were more likely than others to take risks in introducing new varieties of rice and fertilizer. But overall the evidence once again fails to indicate that return migration exerts a strong influence on places of origin.

In the view of some scholars, many of the innovations introduced by returnees reflect superficial consumerism rather than meaningful change (Watson, 1975; Philpott, 1973). To them, such innovations represent an attempt to recreate the life-style encountered abroad. Inasmuch as this consumerism is based mostly on imported goods, it contributes little to local economic development; it may even draw the home country deeper into a dependency relationship with the economically advanced countries.

IMMIGRANT ACTIVITIES ABROAD

Emigration could also have an impact on the sending nation through the economic and political activities of immigrant groups abroad. Asian American entrepreneurs have been reported to be forging trade links with their home countries through various enterprises and ownership of small businesses. This phenomenon seems to be particularly widespread among Koreans in the United States. A survey of Korean Americans in the Los Angeles area, for example, revealed that 40 percent of household heads and 34 percent of their spouses were proprietors (Yu, 1982:55). Most were engaged in trade and service enterprises (Bonacich and Jung, 1982). According to Koo and Yu (1981), Korean American businesses in the United States that merchandise such Korean-made products as wigs, clothes, and plastic items have benefited the Korean economy, and a close connection exists between manufacturing activities at home and the economic activities of immigrants in the United States. In general, the business activities of Korean Americans have assisted Korean immigrants' economic adaptation and benefited the home country in penetrating the American consumer market.

Other Asian American groups are forging trade links with their home countries as well. Although only informal evidence is available, it is reasonable to assume that the economic activities of Asian Americans have much to do with the rapid growth of Pacific Basin trade. There are, of course, other ways by which immigrant groups may induce demand for goods and services in the country of origin. As is common among Asians, immigrants may yearn for home-produced foodstuffs and other goods; or they may prefer to travel on a national carrier or with assistance from a national agency and, in the process, contribute to the country's export earnings. The Philippine government encourages travel on the country's flag carrier through the provision of a transportation discount package to returning immigrants (Chapter 13 in this volume; see also Marcelo, 1984).

The political activities of immigrant groups can have a decisive influence on policy. As observed in this volume, the political activities of Filipinos in the United States have intensified in recent years, although their impact on U.S. policy is difficult to measure (Chapter 13). In contrast, the Taiwanese lobby, which has drawn strength from Asian Americans, has had a clear impact on U.S. policy. It has influenced the American position concerning the status of Taiwan, prompting, for example, the U.S. Senate resolution stating that "Taiwan's future should be settled peacefully, free of coercion and in a manner acceptable to the people of Taiwan" (U.S. Senate Resolution No. 74). Through a lobbying group, Chinese Americans have been able to discuss with members of Congress such legislative concerns as the immigration issue. Their lobbying eventually resulted in the passage of legislation extending to Taiwan eligibility for its own quota of up to 20,000 U.S. immigrant visas per year.

CONCLUSION: RESEARCH IMPLICATIONS

As a proportion of the total population of the sending nation, the size of emigration streams is small. I have argued in the foregoing discussion, however, that emigration, regardless of its magnitude, is likely to have an impact on the social and economic development of the sending countries. It seems clear from this review of empirical and theoretical works that the nature of such an impact is still uncertain. The demographic, social, and economic effects of emigration are complex, and they can be both beneficial and detrimental to the sending nation. Different levels and types of emigration produce different consequences for countries with different sociocultural, economic, and political structures. For this reason, attempts at generalizing about the impact of emigration on sending countries have been, on the whole, futile. Hugo's (1985:65) observation concerning internal (rural–urban) migration applies to international movements as well: "What we should be doing is seeking to generalize not about particular impacts, but about impacts of particular types of movement in particular types of context."

The need to interpret these impacts in specific contexts has important implications for future research on the subject. Consistent with the "migration system" framework (see Chapter 19), this view implies, first of all, that data should be gathered not only on the circumstances of immigrants at the destination but also on conditions in the sending country—including information on what really happens to the stayers. Focus on sending-country conditions not only will be useful for assessing impacts but also will enhance our understanding of return migration, remittances, and immigrant expectations prior to departure.

To understand the changes that take place as a result of emigration, it is also important to introduce a time dimension into studies of its impact on the sending country. Most analyses of migration consequences have been based on one-shot surveys, and their implications for policy are often unclear. A longitudinal design would be more appropriate because it could take the analysis further to compare the "before" and "after" conditions in the country of origin. Moreover, a longitudinal approach would be useful in disentangling the complex interdependence between causes and consequences in the migratory process (Simmons et al., 1977:11). For instance, socioeconomic disparities between countries are often interpreted as causes of population movement, whereas they could be the *consequences* of emigration. A comparative design would enable researchers to assess the impact of emigration on countries of similar economic and sociocultural characteristics but different emigration experiences (and vice versa).

Moreover, there is a need to examine more closely the processes from which the consequences derive. Additional empirical studies should be undertaken on the key variables examined in this chapter: the brain and skill drain, remittances and other repatriated earnings, ideas and skills brought back by returning immigrants, and immigrant activities abroad. More information about these factors would help policymakers to devise ways of coping with the impacts of emigration.

Research on the brain drain should, first of all, be aimed at providing a more reliable measure of the true magnitude of the phenomenon. Previous studies have tended to assess the problem mainly in terms of educational investments lost and have paid little attention to the social and economic framework of the sending nation. Future research should try to assess the scale of the problem in relation to the actual supply of labor, as well as in relation to the sending nation's labor needs and labor absorptive capacity. Attention should also be focused on the appropriateness of training and educational curricula vis-a-vis the social and economic needs of the sending society. The aim should be to devise a manpower and training policy conducive to the development requirements of the country of origin rather than to external markets and demands. Thus the effectiveness of incentive and compensation schemes (taxation policies, bonding schemes, and the like) in reducing the loss of skilled labor should also be looked into.

Similar studies are needed on remittances and repatriated earnings. Stahl (1985) has observed that studies tend to focus on the initial use of these funds by household recipients. They reveal, in the process, that households have little propensity to invest the remittances productively and that these funds contribute little to development in the long run. What these studies ignore, however, is that investors may not necessarily be the same persons who initially receive the funds. If remittances are deposited in banks, for example, the banking sector may channel the funds to viable investment projects. As Arnold (1984) suggests, future studies must also look into the ultimate use of these funds. Likewise,.efforts must be made to determine the effectiveness of various schemes designed to divert repatriated earnings to more productive uses.

Information is critically lacking on the nature and impact of return migration. To study this phenomenon, macrolevel and microlevel data on both the destination and origin areas would again be useful. Information is needed on such matters as the timing and magnitude of return migration, the characteristics and motivations of the returning immigrants, the sectors of the economy into which migrants return, and their influence in changing the social and cultural attitudes of those who stay behind. Attention should also be given to return migration as an important element in the immigrants' decision-making process prior to departure and as an important factor affecting their behavior while abroad (Bretell, 1979:1).

Finally, more reliable evidence is needed on the economic and political activities of immigrants abroad as an important influence on the sending society. Much has been said about Asian American businesses and immigrant political lobbies in the United States, but there is only scattered evidence on these phenomena. Future studies on these topics should focus on the nature and scale of these activities, their influence on political and economic relations between the sending and receiving societies, the ways in which these linkages trigger further population movements, and the extent to which immigrant groups induce demand for goods and services in the country of origin.

Research in these substantive areas cannot, of course, proceed independently of efforts to understand the impact of policy on international migration and its consequences for the sending country. Policy alternatives include not only direct instruments such as emigration quotas and exit taxes but also programs aimed at improving conditions in the sending country (wages, employment, agricultural productivity, and so forth). These programs can also transform the composition and magnitude of flows and may be just as effective in changing the social desirability of emigration as policies directly aimed at either enhancing its benefits (diverting remittances to more productive uses, for example) or mitigating its costs (such as capital movement restrictions).

REFERENCES

Arnold, F.

    1984   "Birds of Passage No More: Migration Decision-Making and Filipinos in Hawaii." Paper presented at the Twelfth Annual Workshop on Psychosocial Factors in Population Research, Minneapolis. Available from the East–West Population Institute.

—————.

    1985   "The Social Situation of Asian Migrant Workers and Their Families." Paper prepared for the Centre for Social Development and Humanitarian Affairs, Department of International Economic and Social Affairs, United Nations, Vienna.

Arnold, F., and N. M. Shah

1985   *Asian Labor Migration: Pipeline to the Middle East.* Boulder: Westview Press.

Balan, J.

1983   "Selectivity of Migration in International and Internal Flows." Paper presented at the UNESCO Symposium on Issues and New Trends in Migration: Population Movements Within and Across Boundaries," Paris.

Bohning, W. R.

1983   "Elements of a Theory of International Economic Migration to Industrial Nation States." In M. M. Kritz et al. (eds.), *Global Trends in Migration: Theory and Research on International Population Movements.* New York: Center for Migration Studies.

Bonacich, E., and T. H. Jung

1982   "A Portrait of Korean Small Business in Los Angeles: 1977." In E.-Y. Yu et al. (eds.), *Koreans in Los Angeles: Prospects and Promises.* Los Angeles: Koryo Research Institute, California State University.

Bretell, C. B.

1979   "Emigrar Para Voltar: A Portuguese Ideology of Return Migration." *Papers in Anthropology,* 20(1):1-20.

Caces, M. F. F.

1985   "Personal Networks and the Material Adaptation of Recent Immigrants: A Study of Filipinos in Hawaii." Ph.D. dissertation, University of Hawaii.

Cariño, B. V.

1981   *Filipinos on Oahu, Hawaii.* Papers of the East-West Population Institute, No. 72. Honolulu: East-West Center.

Castles, S., and G. Kosack

1973   *Immigrant Workers and Class Structure in West Europe.* London: Oxford University Press.

Eviota, E., and P. C. Smith

1980   "The Migration of Women in the Philippines." In J. T. Fawcett et al. (eds.), *Women in the Cities of Asia: Migration and Urban Adaptation.* Boulder: Westview Press.

Fawcett, J. T., B. V. Cariño, and F. Arnold

1985   *Asia-Pacific Immigration to the United States: A Conference Report.* Honolulu: East-West Population Institute, East-West Center.

Friedlander, S.

1965   *Labor, Migration, and Economic Growth: A Case Study of Puerto Rico.* Cambridge, Mass.: M.I.T. Press.

Glaser, W.

    1978   *The Brain Drain: Emigration and Return.* Oxford and New York: Pergamon Press.

Helweg, A. W.

    1984   "Emigration and Return: Ramifications for India." *Population Review,* 28(1–2):45–57.

Howard, A.

    1961   "Rotuma as a Hinterland Community." *Journal of the Polynesian Society,* 70:272–299.

Hugo, G. J.

    1985   "Demographic and Welfare Implications of Urbanization: Direct and Indirect Effects on Sending and Receiving Areas." Paper prepared for the Conference on Population Growth, Urbanization, and Urban Policies in the Asia–Pacific Region, East–West Center, Honolulu.

Hume, I. M.

    1973   "Migrant Workers in Europe." *Finance and Development,* 10(1):2–6.

Hwang, C. S.

    1984   "The Policy Meaning of Non-Returning U.S.-Educated Chinese Students and Scholars." Paper presented at the Conference on Asia–Pacific Immigration to the United States, East–West Center, Honolulu.

Kindleberger, C. P.

    1967   *Europe's Postwar Growth—The Role of Labor Supply.* Cambridge, Mass.: Harvard University Press.

Koo, H., and E.-Y. Yu

    1981   *Korean Immigration to the United States.* Papers of the East–West Population Institute, No. 74. Honolulu: East–West Center.

Kubat, D. (ed.)

    1984   *The Politics of Return: International Return Migration in Europe.* New York: Center for Migration Studies.

Lucas, R. E. B.

    1981   "International Migration: Economic Causes, Consequences and Evaluation." In M. M. Kritz et al. (eds.), *Global Trends in Migration: Theory and Research on International Population Movements.* New York: Center for Migration Studies.

Marcelo, T.

    1984   "Emigration Policies and Domestic Development Goals of the Government of the Philippines Affecting Emigration to the United States." Paper presented at the Conference on Asia–Pacific Immigration to the United States, East–West Center, Honolulu.

McArthur, H. J.

   1979   "The Effects of Overseas Work on Return Migrants and Their Home
           Communities: A Philippine Case." *Papers in Anthropology*, 20(1):
           85–104.

Miracle, M. P., and S. S. Berry

   1970   "Migrant Labor and Economic Development." *Oxford Economic Papers*,
           22(1):86–108.

Naim, M.

   1974   "Merantau: Minangkabau Voluntary Migration." Ph.D. dissertation,
           University of Singapore.

National Science Foundation

   1980   *Scientists and Engineers from Abroad, 1976–78.* Surveys of Science and
           Resources Series. Washington, D.C.: National Science Foundation.

Paine, S.

   1974   *Exporting Workers: The Turkish Case.* London: Cambridge University
           Press.

Patel, N.

   1972   "A Passage from India." *Translation*, 9(6):25–29.

Pernia, E. M.

   1976   "The Question of the Brain Drain from the Philippines." *International
           Migration Review*, 10(1):63–72.

Petras, E. M.

   1981   "The Global Labor Market in the Modern World." In M. M. Kritz
           et al. (eds.), *Global Trends in Migration: Theory and Research on Inter-
           national Population Movements.* New York: Center for Migration
           Studies.

Philpott, S. B.

   1973   *West Indian Migration.* Monographs in Social Anthropology, No. 47.
           London: London School of Economics.

Portes, A.

   1981   "Modes of Structural Incorporation and Present Theories of Labor
           Immigration." In M. M. Kritz et al. (eds.), *Global Trends in Migration:
           Theory and Research on International Population Movements.* New York:
           Center for Migration Studies.

Reyneri, E., and C. Mughini

   1984   "Return Migration and Sending Areas: From the Myth of Develop-
           ment to the Reality of Stagnation." In D. Kubat (ed.), *The Politics of
           Return: International Return Migration in Europe.* New York: Center for
           Migration Studies.

Rhoades, R. E.

   1979   "From Caves to Main Street: Return Migration and the Transforma-
           tion of a Spanish Village." *Papers in Anthropology,* 20(1):40–57.

Shankman, P.

   1976   *Migration and Underdevelopment: The Case of Western Samoa.* Boulder:
           Westview Press.

Simmons, A., S. Diaz-Briquets, and A. A. Laquian

   1977   *Social Change and Internal Migration: A Review of Research Findings from
           Africa, Asia and Latin America.* Ottawa: International Development
           Research Centre.

Smith, P. C.

   1981   *Population Pressure and Social Response on the Ilocos Coast in the Philip-
           pines.* Working Paper No. 2. Honolulu: East–West Population Insti-
           tute, East–West Center.

Stahl, C. W.

   1985   "Southeast Asian Labor the Middle East." In F. Arnold and N. M.
           Shah (eds.), *Asian Labor Migration: Pipeline to the Middle East.* Boul-
           der: Westview Press.

Swanson, J. C.

   1979   "The Consequences of Emigration for Economic Development: A
           Review of the Literature." *Papers in Anthropology,* 20(1):39–56.

Walsh, A. C.

   1981   "Some Questions on the Effects of Migration in the Pacific Islands
           with Particular Reference to Source Areas." Paper presented at the
           Conference on the Consequences of Migration, East–West Center,
           Honolulu.

Watson, J. L.

   1975   *Emigration and the Chinese Lineage: The Maus in Hong Kong and Lon-
           don.* Berkeley: University of California Press.

Wiest, R.

   1979   "Anthropological Perspectives on Return Migration: A Critical Com-
           mentary." In R. E. Rhoades (ed.), *Papers in Anthropology,* 20(1):167–188.

Yu, E.-Y.

   1982   "Occupation and Work Patterns of Korean Immigrants." In E.-Y. Yu
           et al. (eds.), *Koreans in Los Angeles: Prospects and Promises.* Los An-
           geles: Koryo Research Institute, California State University.

18

Documenting Immigration: A Comparison of Research on Asian and Hispanic Immigrants

Teresa A. Sullivan

Immigration is a significant research issue to all receiving countries, but in the United States it has a special historical and contemporary significance. From the time of the first U.S. census in 1790 until the most recent 1980 census, all but a tiny fraction of the U.S. population have been immigrants or the descendants of immigrants. With the exception of the indigenous Native American (or American Indian) population, which represented only about 0.6 percent of the population in 1980, the history of the American people is a history of immigration, settlement, and assimilation. Probably the most important change in post–World War II immigration policy has been renewed access to immigration for Asians. Barred from immigrating by a series of laws that dated from the 1880s, Asians had been persistent victims of a discriminatory policy. Nearly twenty years later, we find that we know relatively little about the new Asian immigrants.

Many analysts would argue that we know relatively little about any contemporary immigrant group; from this perspective, studies of Asian immigrants are but an illustration of a more general neglect of the current processes of adaptation. The dominant research theme in American immigration studies has been adaptation, assimilation, and acculturation. Yet paradoxically—perhaps because immigration is so much a part of the texture of American life—specialized immigration statistics have rarely been available. The first objective of this chapter is to discuss how certain properties of the immigration statistics "system" make studies of immigrants, including Asian immigrants, difficult.

In addition, however, there are issues of particular salience to the study of Asian immigrants. Immigration studies could legitimately deal with *any* issue of human interest affecting immigrants or their children. The two largest groups of immigrants to the United States, the Asians and the Hispanics, are interesting to compare because of the differences in the emerging research traditions. An analysis of the recent research literature on Asian immigrants illustrates both how the research agenda differs from that on Hispanics and also how the extant data affect the continuities of the research. Compared with the Hispanic research agenda, research on Asian immigrants tends to emphasize issues that cannot always be addressed with existing data. The second objective of this chapter is to explore how the research tradition concerning Asian immigrants can be continued with existing data.

DATA PRODUCTION VERSUS DATA ANALYSIS

A system of statistics may be analyzed by separating data production from data analysis and official auspices from unofficial auspices (Figure 18.1). As applied to U.S. immigration statistics, Figure 18.1 illustrates the systematic, structural source of the data deficiencies. Later this analysis will be applied to research on Asian immigrants.

In the United States, most immigration data are collected under official auspices but analyzed under unofficial auspices (diagonal A–D). Thus from the beginning there is an important disjuncture between those who gather the information and those who later use it. For example, many of the extant immigration data are administrative by-products of routine paperwork produced by agents of the Immigration and Naturalization Service (INS). Some data are incidentally useful to analysts, but the data are collected principally for programmatic uses.

Cell *B* of Figure 18.1 is the analysis of data by official agencies. For the United States, at least, it is nearly an empty cell. Although an obscure provision of the present law calls for publication of many sorts of immigration data "with analytic comment thereon," in recent years there has been little analysis by permanent government agencies. Some ad hoc analysis has been undertaken by the various commissions and task forces charged with studying immigration policy—the Select Commission on Immigration and Refugee Policy, for example, and the Interagency Task Force on Immigration.

Cell *C* of Figure 18.1 also contains fewer types of data than cells *A* and *D* because the production of immigration data is so expensive that few unofficial organizations can manage more than very small samples.

	Data Production	Data Analysis
Official Auspices	*A*	*B*
Unofficial Auspices	*C*	*D*

Figure 18.1. Classification of Immigration Data

Indeed, two of the main types of data categorized in this cell are produced with official funds. The first case is that of government-financed but privately conducted national sample surveys, such as the General Social Survey, whose samples necessarily include a small number of the foreign-born and their descendants. The second case is data produced by other governments or by international agencies. These data, which are of course official within some contexts, are nevertheless "unofficial" in the United States. Cell C also contains many small studies with variables not covered in government data sources—data on religion, alcohol use, and so forth.

Cell *D* contains the analysis of data by unofficial analysts. This category includes both secondary analysis of official data (diagonal *A–D*) and primary or secondary analysis of unofficial data (row *C–D*). In the United States, the analysts consist predominantly of the academic community from several social science disciplines, although ethnic associations, church associations, and other not-for-profit firms also analyze immigration data. This research is guided by diverse research goals, and the result—as in any scholarly field—may be neither comprehensive nor satisfying.

This "system" of immigration statistics is further marked by a high degree of decentralization that is only implicit in Figure 18.1. For example, the production of official immigration data (cell *A*) is conducted by various agencies, often without consultation. Federal data are produced by the U.S. State Department, which issues the visas; by the Justice Department, of which the INS is a constituent agency; by the

Department of Health and Human Services, whose agencies assist refugees and screen all immigrants for health problems; by the Department of Transportation, which monitors tourists and international travel; and by the Treasury Department through its customs offices. The Labor Department certifies certain skilled immigrants. The Commerce Department, through its Bureau of the Census, estimates the volume of immigration and emigration. Moreover, the fifty states keep their own data on refugee use of public assistance, bilingual education needs, and other topics. The data are produced for different purposes, with quite different schedules and standards for quality, and in some cases even using different definitions of immigrant or refugee. Documentation, when it exists, varies in quality and extent.

Cell D is even more decentralized, with many scholars deciding, often on an ad hoc basis, to investigate certain questions about immigrants in general or about the immigrants from certain ethnic groups. If the data are unsatisfactory, as is often the case, the scholar may collect original data, thus augmenting what is available in cell C. It is almost certainly the case that the scholar's choice of research topics is affected by the data available in cells A and C. Current public policy debates, or the evaluation of recent policy changes, also motivate many studies.

Currently few formal links exist between the data analysts (cell D) and data producers (cell A and part of cell C). Thus the structure of the immigration data research system probably affects the extent to which the research agenda is completed and the data are satisfactory.

RACE AND NATIONALITY CODES:
A DATA PRODUCTION PROBLEM

Immigration analysts are perennially interested in comparing immigrant groups on a number of measures. Comparisons among Asian immigrant groups, however, are difficult because of the trade-off of sample size for substantive detail. Because the number of immigrants is relatively small, representative national surveys yield case bases too small for analysis. Unlike blacks and Hispanics, Asian Americans are rarely oversampled in such surveys. This is true regardless of whether the auspices are official or unofficial. For example, the General Social Surveys contain small numbers of English-speaking Asian immigrants. If aggregated over several years, the case base might be large enough to analyze but different entry cohorts will be grouped together. As a result, time-dependent phenomena, such as assimilation or refugee adaptation, cannot be studied. An example of an official survey that contains too few Asian Americans for analysis is the Survey of Income and Program Participation.

Even if the case base is sufficient in size, data codes may frustrate further analysis. In the officially produced Current Population Survey, for example, the "race" variable is coded as "white/black/other" although five types of Spanish origin can be identified. Unless a special question on ethnicity elicits specific Asian nationalities, therefore, the analyst will find Asian Americans grouped together with "other races": American Indians, Eskimos, and increasing numbers of Hispanics who identify their race as nonwhite.

Both the problem of size and the problem of identifying codes are solved by using the decennial census. The several public-use samples produced for each census may be aggregated to produce substantial case bases, and the "racial" identifier permits separate self-identification of Chinese, American Indians, Japanese, Koreans, Filipinos, Asian Indians, and Vietnamese. More detailed identifications are possible, depending upon the date of the census, including own birthplace, language other than English, self-identified ethnicity (in 1980), and parents' birthplace (except in 1980).

Even when codes are appropriate, however, other problems may occur. For example, the decennial census may be inappropriate to use late in the decade, especially if there have been major changes in immigration. Census questionnaires and codes change, complicating comparative studies. (See Chapter 12 in this volume for a detailed discussion.) Moreover, census questions do not cover many topics important to analysts. And studies of Asian immigrants in small geographic areas, such as counties, may again encounter the problem of small sample size. An example of a study for which the census was inappropriate was Loewen's (1971) study of Chinese grocers in Mississippi. This book, which made an important contribution to the understanding of Southern racial etiquette, required types of data and a case base that were not available from the census.

One conclusion to be drawn from this section is that generalizations about Asian immigrants can be made reliably for only a few topics. The cost of collecting primary data is too high, and the data available for secondary analysis are often inadequate. By contrast, data for specific Hispanic immigrant groups are easier to find. In Figure 18.1, cell A contains more data on Hispanics than on Asian Americans. The next three sections of this chapter investigate some reasons for this difference.

SETTING THE RESEARCH AGENDA: DIFFERENCES BETWEEN ASIANS AND HISPANICS

The 1965 amendments to the Immigration and Nationality Act were important both for Asian and for Hispanic immigrants. Asian immigrants

Table 18.1. Differences in Asian and Hispanic Immigration to the
United States

Differences	Asians	Hispanics
Cultural	Many languages; relatively quick adoption of English; religiously heterogeneous	One language; very high rates of language retention in second and third generations; mostly Catholic
Legislative	Historically restricted (until 1965 amendments)	Historically unrestricted (until 1965 amendments)
Perception of size	Size usually underestimated	Size often overestimated, perhaps through inclusion of Puerto Ricans and illegal entrants of Hispanic origin
Perception of permanence	Transoceanic immigration seen as more permanent, with greater commitment to U.S.	Immigration across adjacent land borders seen as circular or temporary, with less commitment to U.S.
Perception of assimilation	Called a "golden minority"; problems not emphasized	Perceived as a problem-ridden and disadvantaged minority

were allowed equal access; Hispanic immigrants, except for those from Spain, became subject for the first time to numerical restriction. (As Europeans, Spaniards had been numerically restricted for forty years.) Before the amendments, American immigration had remained predominantly European and Canadian. By 1979, however, Asians accounted for 41 percent of new immigrants and Latin American and Caribbean countries for only slightly less. (See Figure 6.4 in Chapter 6 in this volume.) Except for the Indochinese refugees, perhaps, public attention has tended to focus on the Hispanic immigrants and not on the Asians. Similarly, immigration studies have tended to emphasize Hispanics.

Table 18.1 suggests a number of reasons for the differential attention to Asians and Hispanics. The table is distilled from several years' close attention to the treatment of immigration in the mass media. The real and perceived differences between the two groups seem to be stronger than any of these real or perceived similarities:

- *Reason for immigrating:* Both groups are composed mostly of economic immigrants, but both groups contain refugees.

- *U.S. location:* Both groups have recently shown a preference for locating in large metropolitan areas; California is one destination the two groups share.

- *Legal status:* Both groups have used the family reunification provisions of current legislation; both groups contain at least some illegal entrants.

The first area of perceived difference (Table 18.1) is cultural homogeneity. There are certainly Americans who continue to claim that "all Asians look the same," and many Hispanic leaders draw attention to the differences among Puerto Ricans, Mexican Americans, and Cuban Americans. Nevertheless, there is a greater public recognition of differing national backgrounds among Asian Americans than among Hispanics. One reason for this awareness may be linguistic diversity; speakers of Chinese, Japanese, and Korean are not mutually comprehensible, whereas speakers with nationally or regionally accented Spanish are. A second example is religious diversity: Most Americans are aware of the variety of Asian religions as well as the Asian Christian communities. Most Americans are also aware that the vast majority of Hispanics (over 85 percent) are Roman Catholic by affiliation (Markides and Cole, 1984).

Within the research community, recognition of these differences may be translated into greater concern about appropriate heterogeneity in Asian samples. A sample of Cuban refugees probably would not require stratification by religion, for example, but a sample of Vietnamese refugees might. A questionnaire for Hispanic immigrants may need to be translated only into Spanish,[1] whereas a questionnaire for a large Asian sample might require translation into five or more languages. Thus the universe for each Asian study may be more restricted for reasons of cost and feasibility.

A second difference between Hispanic and Asian immigrants is the historical and legislative differences in their immigration. Asians were highly visible targets of bigotry in this country. Because Asian immigration was virtually eliminated for years, second- and third-generation Asian Americans were socialized in relative isolation from new immigrants. Mexicans, on the other hand, were the indigenous population when the Southwestern states became U.S. territories. Puerto Ricans are citizens and hence enjoy completely unrestricted migration. Restrictions on Latin American immigration are fairly recent and difficult to enforce. First-, second-, and third-generation Hispanics live together

---

1. Brazilians and Portuguese are not officially included in "Hispanic" data. Haitians, most of whom speak French, often are included.

in the same communities, and assimilation takes place in the context of continuing immigration. In future years, Asian American communities will also have many immigrants. In recent studies, however, researchers are still more likely to use generation as a control variable in studies of Asian Americans than they are in studies of Hispanics.

A third characteristic, size, is important in both absolute and relative terms. (See Lieberson, 1980, for a detailed exposition.) Although Asia is the largest single continent represented in current immigration, one rarely hears allegations of "growing hordes" of Asians, as one does with Hispanics. Perhaps this is due to recognition of the greater heterogeneity among Asian immigrants than among Hispanic immigrants. The presence of Puerto Ricans, concerns over illegal immigration, and perceptions of high Hispanic fertility may all lead to a greater concern about the size of the Hispanic population. One of the most common characterizations of Hispanics is that they are the "nation's fastest-growing minority." In the recent legislative debate over the proposed Simpson–Mazzoli immigration legislation, little was heard about the size of the Asian American population but much was heard about Mexico (Bean and Sullivan, 1985).

Related to the issue of size is proximity to the homeland. Correctly or incorrectly, immigration across a long, contiguous land border appears inherently more difficult to control than immigration across the Pacific Ocean. Furthermore, although air travel has made the comparison with the nineteenth-century Atlantic crossing obsolete, some Americans still associate transoceanic immigration with ambition, commitment, and perseverance. Immigration across the Mexican border or the Caribbean, on the other hand, allows for easy return migration. Some would argue that the easy return encourages ambivalence about the United States and discourages efforts to learn English and become assimilated. Thus immigration from Asia is perceived as a controllable process that brings ambitious immigrants for permanent residence. Immigration from Latin America is perceived as a volatile process with unpredictable results.

Size and proximity are both of concern because of the status that Asian Americans and Hispanics share as racial or ethnic minority groups. Asian Americans are often pictured as a "golden minority" who, if they have social problems, take care of their own. In previous years, to be sure, Asian American communities were characterized in unflattering terms about their cleanliness, density, crime rates, and clannishness. Today's fashion, at least for the present, is to portray Asian Americans as hard-working, family-oriented, intelligent, and successful.

Hispanics are more likely to be portrayed as a group with educational disadvantages and economic problems. There is at least some solid research evidence to support the contention that sons of Hispanic immigrants earn substantially less than the sons of other immigrants, including Asians, even after various controls have been applied. (For details see Chiswick, 1978; Featherman and Hauser, 1978; Martin and Poston, 1977.) Despite indications that the "golden minority" suffers economic disadvantages too (U.S. Civil Rights Commission, 1978, 1982), research on income and education has tended to focus on Hispanics.

The parallel between the problems of blacks and those of Hispanics has led to a variety of replications. (For some examples, contrast Poston and Alvirez, 1973, with Siegel, 1965; Borjas and Tienda, 1985, with Masters, 1975; see also Reimers 1983, 1984; Verdugo and Verdugo, 1984; Miller and Valdez, 1984.) And because the problems of disadvantaged minorities remain significant in the nation's research agenda, studies of Hispanic socioeconomic status have proliferated. Comparisons of blacks with Asian Americans are much more rare, although there are some exceptions (see Light, 1972). A more common theme in the literature considers Asian Americans as "brokers" or "middlemen," with the implication that the brokers are better off economically than the blacks or other groups who are their customers (Bonacich, 1973).

The geographic dispersion and concentration of new immigrants, both Asian and Hispanic, raises additional issues for the research agenda. Although only the federal government may admit immigrants and refugees to the United States, the individual states are expected to provide certain services to all residents, citizen or alien. With the growth and then curtailment of government services since 1965, much of the controversy about immigration has revolved about immigrants' use of government services. And because immigrants tend to migrate selectively to a few cities and states, disproportionate provision of goods and services by these localities has become a related issue (Cafferty et al., 1983).

Many of these services—bilingual education, public health services, and Medicaid—benefit both Asians and Hispanics. Moreover, policies such as affirmative action in employment may benefit both groups. Both groups also tend to reside in large cities in just a few states. On the other hand, the Hispanics, as a "disadvantaged" minority, are publicly identified as recipients. Among Asians, only the refugees are visible as recipients of federal funds. Thus the public at large may feel that the welfare "burden" of immigrants, especially the state and local "burden," is caused mostly by Hispanics. Even if this perception is wrong, it tends to steer the research agenda toward studies of Hispanics. (An exception is the research funded by the Office of Refugee Resettlement on the Asian refugees.)

RESEARCH ISSUES OF SALIENCE TO ASIAN IMMIGRANTS

So far I have tried to demonstrate why the data bases and research agendas have steered researchers toward Hispanics. With reference to Figure 18.1, the inadequacy of data in cells A and C and the development of the agenda in cell D have been the primary focuses.

Equally important, however, has been the emergence within the research community of a tradition of studying certain topics. To discover the topics especially germane to the study of Asian immigrants, I have analyzed a selection of the periodical literature appearing in the last fifteen years and the papers presented at the 1984 meetings of the American Sociological Association and the Society for the Study of Social Problems. Although this review is neither exhaustive nor detailed, it does reveal recurring themes.

The selection procedure identified forty-nine papers that dealt centrally with one or more Asian American groups.[2] Two of the papers were subsequently excluded because they dealt only with foreign-born students studying in the United States (Chang, 1973; Kang, 1972). Two more articles were excluded because they were reflections on earlier empirical work but did not report new data (Abbott and Abbott, 1968; Bonacich et al., 1977). Another two studies were excluded because the data were derived from case studies or participant observations, and thus the randomness or generalizability of the sample was not necessarily at issue (Gehrie, 1976; Kim and Hurh, 1980). Finally, two more studies were excluded because the size or nature of the data base was not entirely clear from the articles (Jung, 1976; Osako, 1976). The data sources and principal subjects of the remaining forty-one papers are reported in Tables 18.2 and 18.3.[3]

Table 18.2 lists studies with 1,000 or fewer Asian subjects. For the most part, these studies have been conducted within row C–D of Figure 18.1, for they involve the production and analysis of unofficial data. As their titles show, many of these articles could not be completed with official data sources because of the subjects studied. For example, the interaction patterns in Chinese clubs and the Chinese Americans' use

---

2. This procedure was by no means exhaustive. (Compare "A Selective Bibliography of Asian–Pacific Immigration to the United States," in Fawcett et al., 1985). It represents articles indexed in the *Social Science Index* and available in a large graduate school library collection. Researchers in specialized research centers would have access to more specialized journals, but this procedure is probably a fair representation of what is easily accessible to most social scientists in the United States.

3. Not included in either table are studies that comprehensively compare the experience of several ethnic or immigrant groups, including Asian American groups. For the most part, such studies use U.S. census or other official data. (For examples on several topics, see Bean and Marcum, 1978; Rindfuss and Sweet, 1977; Sullivan, 1978; U.S. Civil Rights Commission, 1978, 1982.)

Table 18.2. Small-Sample Research on Asian Immigrants

Author	General Topics	Asian Sample[a]
Beaudry (1971)	Chinese intermarriage	N = 100 in 70 households in upstate New York
Bourne (1975)	Acculturation and mental illness in Chinese students	N = 24 Chinese students seeking mental health counseling at a West Coast university
Chu (1972)	Drinking patterns of roominghouse Chinese	129 dwelling units in San Francisco
Connor (1974)	Value changes in three generations of Japanese	N = 83 Japanese immigrants N = 142 second generation N = 258 third generation
Connor (1975a)	Japanese student achievement	N = 130 third-generation Japanese students
Connor (1975b)	Japanese student values	N = 275 third-generation Japanese students
Connor (1976a)	Family bonds, maternal closeness, and suppressed sexuality	N = 359 and N = 514 Japanese American adults, three generations
Connor (1976b)	Achievement values of Japanese Americans	N = 234 Issei N = 241 Nisei N = 372 Sansei
Hayano (1981)	Japanese American views of Chinese Americans	N = 150 Japanese Americans in Los Angeles
Hessler et al. (1975)	Chinese American health care	N = 200 households in Boston's Chinatown
Homma-True (1976)	Chinese American attitudes toward mental health services	N = 100 in Oakland's Chinatown
Kim and Hurh (1984)	Role conflict in wives of Korean businessmen	N = 94 Korean immigrants running small businesses in Chicago
Kuo (1970)	Chinese social clubs	N = 50 Chinese (48 American-born) in Long Island, N.Y., belonging to at least two Chinese social clubs

Table 18.2. *(continued)*

Author	General Topics	Asian Sample[a]
Kuo (1976)	Migration and mental health	N = 170 Chinese Americans in D.C.
Kuo (1978)	Alienation among Chinese and Chinese Americans	N = 170 Chinese Americans in D.C.
Leonetti (1978)	Biocultural pattern of Japanese fertility	N = 94 second-generation Japanese American women in Seattle
Lincoln et al. (1978)	Cultural effects on organizational structure	N = 54 Japanese business organizations in Southern California
Mayovich (1972/1973)	Stereotypes and racial images	N = 100 Japanese adults, N = 100 Japanese students, N = 50 Japanese American students in an Asian study program
Min and Jaret (1984)	Cultural explanation for business success	N = 159 Korean immigrants running small businesses in Atlanta
Osako (1976)	Assimilation and intergenerational relations	N = 12 Issei and N = 46 Nisei from Chicago
Stella (1981)	Ethnic identity and friendship of Chinese Americans	N = 60 Chinese American students in New Brunswick, N.J.
Sue and Frank (1973)	Typology of psychological traits	N = 104 Chinese American male students, N = 50 Japanese American male students at University of California, Berkeley
Young (1972)	Independence training of sons	N = 52 Chinese mothers of sons aged 9–12 in Hawaii

[a]Some studies had additional samples of non-Asians.

of mental health services are topics that are inaccessible if the customary official data bases are used. Nevertheless, one disadvantage in generating unofficial data is apparent in the generalizability of the samples: Most were drawn from only one metropolitan area. It would be possible to make broader generalizations if the same study were repeated in many cities, but the constraints of time and energy, not to mention the patience of journal editors, usually discourage such replications.

Furthermore, any of these studies might properly be called studies in minority group sociology rather than studies of immigration per se. Except for those that explicitly include several generations, conclusions about assimilation and acculturation are not the principal focus.

Table 18.3 presents a similar summary of large-scale studies. These studies are more likely to follow the *A–D* diagonal of Figure 18.1. Although some use unofficial data, many involve secondary analysis of U.S. census data or other official data sets. A few studies combine small numbers of interviews with official sources of data. These studies tend to examine more objective dependent variables such as exogamy, earnings, and occupational status. Included in this set of papers are several that deal specifically with issues of assimilation, acculturation, and acceptance into American society.

Several themes found in the small studies are elaborated in the large ones. For example, Berk and Hirata (1973) elaborate on the theme of mental health among the Chinese that was later addressed with smaller data bases by Bourne (1975) and Homma-True (1976) and Kuo (1976, 1978). Intermarriage is studied with both small data sets (Beaudry, 1971) and large ones (Kikumura and Kitano, 1973; Leonetti and Newell-Morris, 1982; Yuan, 1980). Fertility patterns can be investigated by means of large data bases to establish trends and differentials (Johnson and Nishida, 1980; Rhodes and Woodrum, 1980) or with attitudinal data from small samples (Leonetti, 1978).

One advantage of comparing the two types of data bases is that they can provide checks and cross-validation. For example, Boyd's (1971) study of socioeconomic status among Chinese Americans showed that Chinese males in Hawaii have higher educational attainment and higher proportions of workers in the professions than do Chinese males in New York. This is an important observation in light of the many studies made with location-specific small samples (see Kuo 1976, 1978); it also provides a context for interpreting nationwide trends (Wong, 1982).

SOME ISSUES FOR THE FUTURE

All the issues considered so far have implications for future studies of Asian immigration. One of the first issues likely to have serious ramifications is the relative isolation of data producers from data analysts. Without more systematic ways to inform the data production procedures, analysts will find themselves with unsatisfactory official data. Two examples will demonstrate how this may happen. First, needed data may be discontinued—either because a specific datum is no longer collected or because an entire data series is terminated. The recent federal budget cuts to several statistical agencies have raised fears that immigration statistics, already inadequate, may be further curtailed. An

Table 18.3. Large-Sample Research on Asian Immigrants

Author	General Topics	Data Source
Berk and Hirata (1973)	Mental illness among the Chinese	California State Department of Mental Hygiene official hospital records; U.S. census
Boyd (1971)	Chinese socioeconomic status in three locales	1960 U.S. census; INS data
Johnson and Nishida (1980)	Minority group status and fertility of Chinese and Japanese	1970 U.S. census
Kikumura and Kitano (1973)	Japanese American patterns of interracial marriage	1924–1972 marriage license data for Los Angeles County
Kim (1974)	Social demography of Korean Americans	1970 U.S. census
Kuroda, et al. (1978)	Japanese character	1971 list of registered voters in Hawaii
Leonetti and Newell-Morris (1982)	Japanese intermarriage	2,769 marriage license applications of Japanese Americans (1930–1975)
Levine and Montero (1973)	Socioeconomic mobility of Japanese Americans	Three-generational survey of Japanese Americans (see Montero and Tsukashima, 1977; Montero, 1980, 1981)
Li (1977)	Kinship among Chinese immigrants	U.S. congressional records and interviews ($N = 180$)
Light and Wong (1975)	Tourist industry in Chinatown	1965–1972 INS data; U.S. census
Montero (1980)	Elderly Japanese Americans	$N = 1,002$ first-generation Japanese Americans
Montero (1981)	Changing patterns of assimilation in three generations of Japanese Americans	$N = 4,012$ Japanese Americans (three generations)
Montero and Tsukashima (1977)	Educational achievement among second-generation Japanese Americans	$N = 2,304$ second-generation Japanese Americans
Rhodes and Woodrum (1980)	Minority fertility	$N = 4,153$ Japanese Americans (three generations)

Table 18.3.   (*continued*)

Author	General Topics	Data Source
Taylor and Kim (1980)	Federal employment of Asian Americans	1% sample of U.S. Civil Service records
Wong (1982)	Earnings of Chinese, Japanese, and Filipinos	1960, 1970 U.S. census data; 1976 SIE
Woodrum et al. (1980)	Economic behavior of Japanese Americans	$N = 1,047$ first-generation Japanese Americans
Yuan (1980)	Chinese exogamy	1970 U.S. census

example of a datum that is no longer collected is parents' birthplace, discontinued from the 1980 census after several decades' use. Although the question was replaced with an ancestry question, the specific issue of generational assimilation—an important topic heretofore in Asian immigration studies—cannot be easily studied among the new immigrants.

A second problem is that a needed datum may not be available. One example of such information is identification of the legal justification under which the immigrant was admitted. For many reasons, analysts would like to compare the experience of Asians admitted as skilled workers with those admitted under family reunification policies. Further, it would be most useful to be able to compare, let us say, Vietnamese admitted as refugees with those admitted under some other justification. Additional data that would be useful are indicators of the determinants of migration, including more detailed information on the place of origin, education and work experience in the home country, and any "transitional experiences"— for example, in a country of first asylum. No single official data set now contains these data, and the merging of data sets—which in theory could produce such a data base— is apparently unlikely given current privacy statutes and the limited time and resources available to the federal agencies.

As these two examples suggest, the scarcity of official data (cell *A* of Figure 18.1) may continue to force analysts of Asian immigration to collect their own data (cell *C*), with the resulting small sample sizes and limited geographic scope. So long as researchers must worry about having even minimally adequate data available, additional issues that should be on the research agenda will be ignored. Such basic concepts as adaptation or adjustment remain inadequately developed and difficult to measure.

The greater heterogeneity among the new immigrants in their nationality and culture will be another major issue for research. A recent

study has shown important differences among four Indochinese refugee groups: the Hmong, the Khmer, the Vietnamese Chinese, and the
Vietnamese (Rumbaut, 1984; Blumberg and Rumbaut, 1984). Such work
almost surely will command continued attention, if only because the
parallel work among Hispanics has shown substantial differences between Cuban refugees and the economic immigrants from Mexico
(Portes and Bach, 1980, 1985; Sullivan and Pedraza-Bailey, 1979). Because much of the Indochinese settlement has been quite recent, and
because some of the groups have been quite mobile geographically (especially, perhaps, the Hmong), 1980 census data may be inadequate
for continuing the analysis. Other data bases, such as those of the Office
of Refugee Resettlement, look more promising.

The issues of changing immigrant composition implicit in this discussion also suggest that it may be time to shift from repeated cross-
sectional studies of immigration to true panel or longitudinal designs.
(A major study of this type for several Hispanic groups is being conducted by Alejandro Portes and his colleagues; see Portes and Bach,
1985.) Longitudinal studies may be particularly needed for the new
Asian immigrants because their experience is likely to be quite different from that of the earlier immigrant cohorts. Cynics might argue that
if the immigration experience is so affected by secular events, then even
a longitudinal study would have little generalizability for future cohorts.
This resort to empirical agnosticism, however, seems to leave us with
little information for evaluating and planning U.S. immigration policy
for the remainder of the century.

While a longitudinal design might be the most important design in-
novation, other new approaches to research design need to be considered. The issue of cyclical or return immigration—important for studying
Hispanics and possibly also important for the study of Asians—has been
virtually impossible to address with official data bases and too expensive to address with unofficial data. The difficulty currently encountered in estimating "stocks" versus "flows" of immigrants is one aspect
of the more general difficulty in tracking emigration of either the native-
born or the foreign-born.

Researchers need to consider further the appropriate unit of analysis in studying immigration. Partly because of our individualist ideology, partly because of the availability of microdata, we have tended to
emphasize the individual while ignoring the significance of the household and the community. To be sure, some recent research on Hispanics has tried to overcome this bias (see, for example, Portes and Bach,
1985) and there has been some effort to analyze spatial distribution and
its relationship to community among some Asian groups (see Young,
1983).

Most of these research issues cannot be addressed in isolation by either the official producers of data or by the research community. The recently released report of the Panel on Immigration Statistics of the National Research Council recognized the need for greater communication among the producers of data and between producers and consumers of data (Levine et al., 1985). Many of its recommendations, if adopted, would go far toward improving the current research on immigration in the United States. Among its suggestions for improving communication among data producers, the panel recommended:

- That Congress and the attorney general strongly affirm the significance of reliable, accurate, and timely immigration information.

- That the Office of Management and Budget exercise its responsibilities to monitor and review statistical activities and budgets concerning immigration and emigration statistics and establish an interagency review group to examine consistency and comparability in concepts and definitions and introduce standard approaches.

- That the INS commissioner establish a Division of Immigration Statistics with a full complement of trained professionals and formal liaison with other federal and state agencies that collect data on immigrants.

- That the commissioner for refugee affairs establish an interagency task force for all federal offices concerned with refugee issues. This task force would standardize the currently collected data, eliminate duplication, and recommend priorities for new data to be collected.

To improve communication among users and producers of data, the panel recommended:

- Establishment of an INS advisory committee to advise the proposed Division of Immigration Statistics on needs for new or different types of data, to assess existing data and data collection methods, and to provide independent evaluation of statistical products, plans, and performance

- Development of an INS fellows program to bring outstanding researchers into the agency for one or two years to conduct original research on published or unpublished immigration data

- Initiation of a program of contract research that emphasizes the evaluation of data production and data quality

- Encouragement to government funding agencies to pay particular attention to the need for well-done studies of immigration

The panel also recommended that certain types of data be made available. It urged the Census Bureau to reinstate the question on parents' birthplace in the 1990 census, for example, and it urged the Labor Department to publish summary information on employers who petition the admission of foreign workers. Specific suggestions for improved data were directed to the U.S. Travel and Tourism Administration (for information on tourists), to the Social Security Administration (to include country of birth and to make some of its data available to outside researchers), and to the National Center for Health Statistics (to initiate coding of country of birth for vital events).

The panel also recommended, in particular, the development of a five-year longitudinal study of aliens. Data would be collected from a sample of persons legally admitted under regular immigrant preferences, persons granted entry visas as nonimmigrants, and aliens given legal status under any amnesty programs. The data base wou' concentrate on the geographic dispersion and subsequent migration of the sample, the sample's income and labor market experience, and the sample's program participation and service use. If even a small number of the panel's recommendations are followed, the quality and quantity of data available for immigration research will be substantially increased—principally by improving the data contained in cell A of Figure 18.1 and by facilitating the interchange with private researchers along the A–D diagonal.

CONCLUSION

Many key questions concerning the new Asian immigrants and the effects of readmitting Asians to the United States remain unanswered. Some of the blame may lie with the academic community, where the formation of a research agenda tends to be a decentralized process subject to idiosyncrasy. Probably of greater importance, however, are the unsuitability of available data and the unavailability of suitable data. The current statistical system, in which data production and data analysis are often separated, remains a structural obstacle to improving study designs.

REFERENCES

Abbott, K. A., and E. L. Abbott

1968   "Juvenile Delinquency in San Francisco's Chinese–American Community: 1961–1966." *National Taiwan University Journal of Sociology*, 4:45–56. April.

Bean, F. D., and J. P. Marcum

1978 "Differential Fertility and the Minority Group Status Hypothesis: An Assessment and Review." In F. D. Bean and W. Parker Frisbie (eds.), *The Demography of Racial and Ethnic Groups.* New York: Academic Press.

Bean, F. D., and T. A. Sullivan

1985 "Immigration Policy and Its Consequences: Confronting the Problem." *Society,* 22(4):67–73.

Beaudry, J. A.

1971 "Some Observations on Chinese Intermarriage in the United States." *International Journal of Sociology of the Family,* Special Issue (May):59–68.

Berk, B. B., and L. C. Hirata

1973 "Mental Illness Among the Chinese: Myth or Reality?" *Journal of Social Issues,* 29(2):149–166.

Blumberg, R. L., and R. Rumbaut

1984 "Manchild Versus Womanchild in the Promised Land: Sex Differences in Household Variables Among Four Indochinese Refugee Groups." Paper presented at the annual meeting of the American Sociological Association, San Antonio, 27–31 August.

Bonacich, E.

1973 "A Theory of Middleman Minorities." *American Sociological Review,* 38(5):583–594.

Bonacich, E., I. H. Light, and C. C. Wong

1977 "Koreans in Business." *Society,* 14(6):54–59.

Borjas, G., and M. Tienda (eds.)

1985 *Hispanics in the U.S. Economy.* New York: Academic Press.

Bourne, P. G.

1975 "The Chinese Student—Acculturation and Mental Illness." *Psychiatry,* 38(3):269–277.

Boyd, M.

1971 "The Chinese in New York, California, and Hawaii: A Study of Socioeconomic Differentials." *Phylon,* 32(2):198–206.

Cafferty, P. S. J., B. Chiswick, A. M. Greeley, and T. A. Sullivan

1983 *The Dilemma of American Immigration: Beyond the Golden Door.* New Brunswick, N.J.: Transaction Books.

Chang, H. B.

1973 "A Study of Attitudes of Chinese Students in the United States." *Sociology and Social Research,* 58(1):66–77.

Chiswick, B.

1978   "The Effect of Americanization on the Earnings of Foreign-Born Men."
        Journal of Political Economy, 86:897–921. October.

Chu, G.

1972   "Drinking Patterns and Attitudes of Rooming-House Chinese in San
        Francisco." *Quarterly Journal of Studies on Alcohol,* 6:58–68. May.

Connor, J. W.

1974   "Value Continuities and Change in Three Generations of Japanese
        Americans." *Ethos,* 2(3):232–264.

———— .

1975a   "Changing Trends in Japanese American Academic Achievement."
        Journal of Ethnic Attitudes, 2(4):95–98.

———— .

1975b   "Value Changes in Third-Generation Japanese Americans." *Journal
        of Personality Assessment,* 39(6):597–600.

———— .

1976a   "Family Bonds, Maternal Closeness, and the Suppression of Sexu-
        ality in Three Generations of Japanese Americans." *Ethos,*
        4(2):189–221.

———— .

1976b   "Joge Kankei: A Key Concept for an Understanding of Japanese-
        American Achievement." *Psychiatry,* 39(3):266–279.

Fawcett, J. T., B. V. Cariño, and F. Arnold

1985   *Asia–Pacific Immigration to the United States: A Conference Report.*
        Honolulu: East–West Population Instiute, East–West Center.

Featherman, D. L., and R. B. Hauser

1978   *Opportunity and Change.* New York: Academic Press.

Gehrie, M. J.

1976   "Childhood and Community: On the Experience of Young Japanese
        Americans in Chicago." *Ethos,* 4(3):353–383.

Hayano, D. D.

1981   "Ethnic Identification and Disidentification: Japanese-American Views
        of Chinese-Americans." *Ethnic Groups,* 3(2):157–171.

Hessler, R. M., M. F. Nolan, B. Ogbru, and P. K. M. New

1975   "Intraethnic Diversity: Health Care of the Chinese-Americans." *Hu-
        man Organization,* 24(3):253–262.

Homma-True, R.

1976 "Characteristics of Contrasting Chinatowns, Part 2: Oakland, California." *Social Casework*, 57(3):155–159.

Johnson, N. E., and R. Nishida

1980 "Minority-Group Status and Fertility: A Study of Japanese and Chinese in Hawaii and California." *American Journal of Socioloqy*, 86(3):496–511.

Jung, M.

1976 "Characteristics of Contrasting Chinatowns, Part 1: Philadelphia, Pennsylvania." *Social Casework*, 57(3):149–154.

Kang, T. S.

1972 "A Foreign Student Group as an Ethnic Community." *International Review of Modern Sociology*, 2(1):72–82.

Kikumura, A., and H. H. L. Kitano

1973 "Interracial Marriage: A Picture of the Japanese Americans." *Journal of Social Issues*, 29(2):67–81.

Kim, H. C.

1974 "Some Aspects of Social Demography of Korean Americans." *International Migration Review*, 8(1):23–42.

Kim, K. C., and W. M. Hurh

1980 "Social and Occupational Assimilation of Korean Immigrant Workers in the United States." *California Sociologist*, 3(2):125–142.

————.

1984 "The Wives of Korean Small Businessmen in the U.S.: Business Involvement and Family Roles." Paper presented at the annual meeting of the American Sociological Association, San Antonio, 27–31 August.

Kuo, C. L.

1970 "The Chinese on Long Island—A Pilot Study. *Phylon*, 31(3):280–289.

Kuo, W.

1976 "Theories of Migration and Mental Health: An Empirical Testing on Chinese-Americans." *Social Science and Medicine*, 10(6):297–306.

————.

1978 "Immigrant/Minority Status and Alienation." *Sociological Focus*, 11(4):271–289.

Kuroda, Y., T. Suzuki, and C. Hayashi

1978 "A Cross-National Analysis of the Japanese Character Among Japanese-Americans in Honolulu." *Ethnicity*, 5(1):42–59.

Leonetti, D. L.

1978   "The Biocultural Pattern of Japanese-American Fertility. *Social Biology,* 25(1):38–51.

Leonetti, D. L., and L. Newell-Morris

1982   "Exogamy and Change in the Biosocial Structure of a Modern Urban Population." *American Anthropologist,* 84(1):19–31.

Levine, D. B., K. Hill, and R. Warren (eds.)

1985   *Immigration Statistics: A Story of Neglect.* Washington, D.C.: National Academy Press.

Levine, G. N., and D. M. Montero

1973   "Socioeconomic Mobility Among Three Generations of Japanese Americans." *Journal of Social Issues,* 29(2):33–48.

Li, P. S.

1977   "Fictive Kinship, Conjugal Tie and Kinship Chain Among Chinese Immigrants in the United States." *Journal of Comparative Family Studies,* 8(1):47–63.

Lieberson, S.

1980   *A Piece of the Pie: Black and White Immigrants Since 1880.* Berkeley: University of California Press.

Light, I. H.

1972   *Ethnic Enterprise in America.* Berkeley: University of California Press.

Light, I. H., and C. C. Wong

1975   "Protest or Work: Dilemmas of the Tourist Industry in American Chinatowns." *American Journal of Sociology,* 80(6):1342–1368.

Lincoln, J. R., J. Olson, and M. Hanada

1978   "Cultural Effects on Organizational Structure: The Case of Japanese Firms in the United States." *American Sociological Review,* 43(6):829–847.

Loewen, J. H.

1971   *The Mississippi Chinese: Between Black and White.* Cambridge, Mass.: Harvard University Press.

Markides, K. S., and T. Cole

1984   "Change and Continuity in Mexican American Religious Behavior: A Three Generation Study. *Social Science Quarterly,* 65(2):618–625.

Martin, W. T., and D. L. Poston, Jr.

1977   "Differentials in the Ability to Convert Education into Income: The Case of the European Ethnics." *International Migration Review,* 2(2):215–231.

Masters, S.

1975   *Black-White Income Differentials: Empirical Studies and Policy Implications.*
        New York: Academic Press.

Mayovich, M. K.

1972/   "Stereotypes and Racial Images—White, Black and Yellow." *Interna-*
1973   *tional Journal of Social Psychiatry,* 18(4):239–253.

Miller, M. V., and A. Valdez

1984   "Immigration and Perceptions of Economic Deprivation Among
        Working-Class Mexican American Men." *Social Science Quarterly,*
        65(2):455–464.

Min, P. G., and C. Jaret

1984   "Korean Immigrants' Success in Small Business: Some Cultural Ex-
        planations." Paper presented at the annual meeting of the Ameri-
        can Sociological Association, San Antonio, 27–31 August.

Montero, D.

1980   "The Elderly Japanese American: Aging Among the First Genera-
        tion Immigrants." *Genetic Psychology Monographs,* 101(1):99–118.

————— .

1981   "The Japanese Americans: Changing Patterns of Assimilation Over
        Three Generations." *American Sociological Review,* 46(6):829–839.

Montero, D., and R. Tsukashima

1977   "Assimilation and Educational Achievement: The Case of the Second
        Generation Japanese-American." *Sociological Quarterly,* 18(4):490–503.

Osako, M. M.

1976   "Intergenerational Relations as an Aspect Case of Assimilation: The
        Case of Japanese-Americans." *Sociological Inquiry,* 46(1):67–72.

Portes, A., and R. L. Bach

1980   "Immigrant Earnings: Cuban and Mexican Immigrants in the U.S."
        International Migration Review, 14(3):315–337.

————— .

1985   *Latin Journey: Cuban and Mexican Immigrants in the United States.* Berke-
        ley: University of California Press.

Poston, D. L., and D. Alvirez

1973   "On the Cost of Being a Mexican-American Worker. *Social Science
        Quarterly,* 65(1):697–709.

Reimers, C.

1983   "Labor Market Discrimination Against Hispanic and Black Men."
        Review of Economics and Statistics, 65:580–579. November.

─────── .

1984   "The Wage Structure of Hispanic Men: Implications for Policy." *Social Science Quarterly*, 65(2):401–416.

Rhodes, C., and E. Woodrum

1980   "Contending Hypotheses of Minority Fertility: Three Generations of Japanese Americans." *California Sociologist*, 3(2):166–183.

Rindfuss, R. R., and J. A. Sweet

1977   *Postwar Fertility Trends and Differentials in the United States.* New York: Academic Press.

Rumbaut, R. G.

1984   "Migration, Adaptation, and Age: A Comparative Study of Hmong, Khmer, Chinese-Vietnamese, and Vietnamese Refugee Families." Paper presented at the annual meeting of the Society for the Study of Social Problems, San Antonio, 25 August.

Siegel, P. M.

1965   "On the Cost of Being a Negro." *Sociological Inquiry*, 35:41–57.

Stella, T.-T.

1981   "Ethnic Identity and Close Friendship in Chinese-American College Students." *International Journal of Intercultural Relations*, 5(4):383–406.

Sue, D. W., and A. C. Frank

1973   "A Typological Approach to the Psychological Study of Chinese and Japanese American College Males." *Journal of Social Issues*, 29(2): 129–148.

Sullivan, T. A.

1978   "Racial-Ethnic Differences in Labor Force Participation: An Ethnic Stratification Perspective." In F. D. Bean and W. P. Frisbie (eds.), *The Demography of Racial and Ethnic Groups.* New York: Academic Press.

Sullivan, T. A., and S. Pedraza-Bailey

1979   *Differential Success Among Cuban-American and Mexican-American Immigrants: The Role of Policy and Community.* Washington, D.C.: National Technical Information Service.

Taylor, P. A., and S. S. Kim

1980   "Asian-Americans in the Federal Civil Service." *California Sociologist*, 3(1):1–16.

U.S. Civil Rights Commision

1978   *Social Indicators of Equality for Minorities and Women.* Washington, D.C.: U.S. Civil Rights Commission.

———— .

1982   *Indicators of Unemployment and Underemployment for Minorities and Women*. Washington, D.C.: U.S. Civil Rights Commission.

Verdugo, N. T., and R. R. Verdugo

1984   "Earnings Differentials Between Mexican American, Black and White Male Workers." *Social Science Quarterly,* 65(2):417–425.

Wong, M. G.

1982   "The Cost of Being Chinese, Japanese, and Filipino in the United States: 1960, 1970, 1976." *Pacific Sociological Review,* 25(1):59–78.

Woodrum, E., C. Rhodes, and J. R. Feagin

1980   "Japanese American Economic Behavior: Its Types, Determinants, and Consequences. *Social Forces,* 58(4):1235–1254.

Young, N. F.

1972   "Independence Training from a Cross-Cultural Perspective." *American Anthropologist,* 74(3):629–638.

Young, P. K. Y.

1983   "Family Labor, Sacrifice, and Competition: Korean Greengrocers in New York City." *Amerasia,* 10(2):53–71.

Yuan, D. Y.

1980   "Significant Demographic Characteristics of Chinese Who Intermarry in the United States." *California Sociologist,* 3(2):184–196.

19

Explaining Diversity: Asian and Pacific Immigration Systems

James T. Fawcett
and Fred Arnold

The most evident fact about Asian and Pacific immigration is its diversity. Whether one looks at the political and economic status of the countries of origin, the characteristics of the immigrants themselves, or their modes of adaptation in the host society, differences are more striking than similarities. Sending countries include socialist Vietnam, capitalist South Korea, and colonial American Samoa—each having quite different economic resources and strategies for development. Significant groups of immigrants include Hmong hill farmers, Indian scientists and engineers, Chinese businessmen, and Filipino service workers—as well as Thai, Filipino, and Korean women immigrating as marriage partners. After these various immigrant groups have arrived at their main destinations—the United States, Canada, Australia, or New Zealand— they find economic and social niches almost as diverse as their origins.

From the perspective of social science, the differences among immigration flows discussed in this book offer a challenge to theorists who seek general models to explain the causes and consequences of international migration. Although immigration laws obviously regulate the gross volume of flows and labor market conditions can explain some differentials within flows, "Currently, there is no general theory that would explain diverse movements, let alone historical immigration trends. . . . most theoretical work on international migration is devoid of its applicabilty to differing types of flows" (Kritz, 1985:23).

Chapter 3 by Portes categorizes analytically a large number of theoretical or quasi-theoretical ideas that have appeared in the literature on international migration, as a step toward theoretical integration. Each approach is incorporated under one of four rubrics, according to what it mainly seeks to explain: the origins of migration flows, the causes of the stability of flows, the uses of immigrant labor, and the adaptation of immigrants to the host society. This review alerts us to a problem, namely, that proponents of theories that are conceptually limited have a tendency to generalize their conclusions beyond appropriate boundaries. For example, a conclusion derived from the application of a labor market theory to a set of data on immigrant service-sector workers may be formulated as a general proposition pertaining to all immigration. Such an inference is clearly not justified, and the comprehensive model into which such partial findings should fit continues to elude us. As noted by Portes (p. 66),

What the sum total of research findings indicates is, above all, the wide diversity of immigration histories and experiences, a fact that precludes blanket generalizations and compels us to draw on different theoretical traditions for their understanding.

The absence of a comprehensive explanatory framework is also attributable to the paucity of empirical data that would correspond to such an approach. It is fairly obvious, for example, that an adequate explanation for an immigration flow must take into account conditions in the areas of both origin and destination. Yet, immigration studies seldom give equal attention to the relevant factors at both ends of the stream. Or, if attention is given to the place of origin as well as the destination, the data typically are quite limited in scope and pertain only to an aggregate level of analysis. These limitations of empirical studies are dictated to a large extent by the constraints of readily available data, coupled with the logistic and financial barriers to collection of new data on an international scale. They also reflect the prevailing interests of researchers and policymakers in one location or the other.

With respect to areas of origin, for example, Cariño points out in Chapter 17 that practically all the research on emigration has been conducted from the perspective of loss of human resources, especially resources representing high levels of educational investment. Because of this preoccupation, little attention has been given until recently to the next logical question: What are the connections between emigrants and the home country after their departure? When this topic is examined, a rather different picture emerges. The remittances from emigrants are often found to be substantial, and sometimes remittances are used to support the education of relatives at home, where they partially offset the human resource loss. Moreover, emigrants frequently establish business linkages that support economic development at home, they sometimes return and engage in direct investment in their native country, and their presence abroad may serve the national interest in the sphere of international relations.

The limitations of empirical studies in destination areas are discussed by Sullivan in Chapter 18, with particular reference to research on Asian and Hispanic immigrants in the United States. Because of its historic openness to immigrants, the United States has a long tradition of public policy debate about the costs and benefits of immigration. Given this highly visible concern, it is both ironic and remarkable that the knowledge base about immigration to the United States continues to be so weak. As Sullivan points out, this lack of knowledge can be attributed to structural deficiencies in both data collection and data analysis, some of which are now being remedied. It remains starkly apparent, however, that immigration is much lower on the nation's research agenda than it is on the nation's policy agenda, an anomaly that defies easy explanation. The result is a fragmented data base unconducive to the kind of integrated theoretical development that is needed. The information that is available, moreover, pertains almost exclusively to the postarrival characteristics of the immigrant population. The few studies that combine comprehensive predeparture and postarrival data serve only to highlight the enormous gaps in knowledge about the U.S. immigrant population as a whole. (See also the discussion in Chapter 14 by Kim.) Similar assessments could be made regarding the state of knowledge about immigration in other receiving countries, although some—notably Australia—have given greater official recognition to the role of research on this topic.

A reciprocal relationship obviously exists between theory and research, with advances in one stimulating advances in the other. If our theories of immigration were more comprehensive, we would be more ambitious about collecting data to test those theories. If we had data available on immigration that were wider in scope and more varied in scale, we would undoubtedly be prompted to devise more encompassing theoretical perspectives. Our purpose in the remainder of this chapter is to discuss some of the building blocks that we see as essential to the development of a comprehensive theory.

A MIGRATION SYSTEMS PARADIGM

The most fundamental criticism of immigration studies (as well as immigration theories) is their fragmentary nature. Many studies deal with a small and unrepresentative group of immigrants, and no real effort is made to relate their situation to the immigrant population from which they are drawn. Where a whole immigration stream is studied, the data typically are limited to a few demographic variables. Moreover, it is rare for an immigration study to look at changes over time in *both* the immigration flow and the factors identified as causes or consequences of the flow at the origin and at the destination. As discussed earlier, these shortcomings are partly attributable to inadequacies of existing data. In addition, however, we believe that fragmentary studies persist in part because of a lack of conceptual frameworks that provide a comprehensive view of the immigration process.

We propose such a conceptual framework in this chapter. It is not a theory, because we make no effort to specify functional relationships or propose hyphotheses. Rather, it is a heuristic device, a loosely structured set of concepts that we hope will provide some stimulation and guidance for future research efforts. We refer to this framework as a migration systems paradigm.

A migration system is a set of places linked by flows and counterflows of people. The advantages of a migration systems approach are several. First, it forces attention to both ends of a migration flow, with a corresponding necessity to explain stability and mobility in each location. Second, it examines one flow in the context of other flows, or one destination as part of a set of alternative destinations. Third, a migration systems perspective inevitably highlights the diverse linkages between places—not only flows and counterflows of people, but also transactions involving information, goods, services, and ideas. Looking at two (or more) places and their linkages also implies comparisons, and it is comparisons—or, more accurately, disparities—between places that seem to provide the energy underlying migration flows. Further, the migration systems paradigm, in which one part is sensitive to changes elsewhere, serves as a reminder that immigration is an intrinsically dynamic process. An understanding of historical conditions is important, and since the conditions we study today are transient, we must seek explanations based on general principles, not specific events.

Goldscheider (1971:57–58) has made a similar argument:

. . . at a minimum, it is important to know exactly where limited research foci fit into a broader, comprehensive portrait of the migration process. Without a perspective on migration that includes stability as well as mobility and that fits specific migratory streams into a systems approach, we are not able to see how migration is interrelated with more generalized social processes, nor are we able to interpret adequately the determinants and consequences of mobility. Most important, migration research will not be cumulative.

The "generalized social processes" cited by Goldscheider are similar to the contextual factors discussed by Fawcett and Cariño in Chapter 1, where recent trends in the Pacific Basin are highlighted. In the present chapter, we approach these contextual factors more systematically, organizing them under three conceptual categories:

• state-to-state relations and comparisons
• mass culture connections
• family and social networks

After discussing this essentially structural framework, we present a social–psychological paradigm for a migration systems approach. The central element here is a sequential model of the individual immigration process, involving three stages: decision, transition, and adaptation. This model, in which individual processes are conditioned by relevant contextual factors at each stage, is offered as one means to encourage more comprehensive studies of immigration systems. Along similar lines, Papademetriou (1984:414) has urged that those studying international migration should be:

. . . constantly aware of the interdependence between the international politico-economic system and migration and of the economic and socio-political implications of such interdependence; at the same time, focusing on the manner in which such actions impact upon the position of individuals (migrants and non-migrants) both within the household and [within] the social structure of the community of origin.

STRUCTURAL AND CONTEXTUAL FACTORS

In this section we discuss mainly the linkages between places that reflect levels of aggregation "above" the individual: the family, the culture, the polity, the economy, and so on. These linkages, in our paradigm, are conditions that influence individual immigration decisions. Other scholars would prefer to focus on the macroprocesses themselves, ignoring the actions of individuals. Either approach is legitimate, of course, and in principle it should be possible to shift from one level of aggregation to another in explaining the same social phenomenon—an immigration flow. In practice, however, the gap looms large between those who explain immigration through a combination of historical and structural analyses and those who focus more on contemporary conditions and the available "hard" data that can be used for quantitative evaluations of causes and consequences.

A practical use of the broad migration systems paradigm discussed here is as a "scanning device," to serve as a reminder of factors that ought to be considered in studying any migration flow, regardless of   .

the researcher's theoretical or empirical orientation. We have attempted to identify in fairly concise terms the major categories of factors that influence international migration flows. Here we discuss each of these categories illustratively, drawing mainly on material presented in this book. To help focus the discussion, illustrations are drawn particularly from Korea and the Philippines, which are currently the top source countries for Asian immigration to the United States. However, other immigration flows are cited selectively in connection with particular points.

State-to-State Relations and Comparisons

The relationships between nations included under this category are mainly economic and political. Considerable theoretical attention has been devoted to international economic relationships as a factor in immigration theory, most recently as an offshoot of world systems theory or dependency theory. These approaches have a political dimension too, usually ascribing dominance (or exploitation) to capitalist societies. But there are many other dimensions of economic and political relations, including legal agreements, alliances, and the levels of development that are important in equilibrium theories of migration. Subcategories of state-to-state relations and comparisons might include:

- differences between internal political systems
- mutual political recognition
- political dependency or dominance and military alliances
- economic dependency or dominance and trade agreements
- emigration and immigration policies
- economic and technical assistance programs
- disparities in level of economic development

Because international migration by definition involves a border crossing, there is a transition from one political system to another. Whether this is an important aspect of immigration depends on the extent and nature of the differences between two political regimes. Microstudies tell us, for example, that some Korean emigrants are motivated by the political repression at home and the promise of greater freedom of political expression elsewhere. Refugees come immediately to mind when political regimes are cited as a factor in international migration, although it is sometimes difficult in practice to distinguish between a regime's political orientation and its economic policies as providing impetus to refugee flows. Nonetheless, it is undeniable that people do "vote with their feet" as immigrants and refugees. The major Pacific Basin receiving countries—the United States, Canada, Australia, and New Zealand—are all stable democratic states with strong guarantees of individual rights, and these political conditions are an important factor in international migration in the region.

Border crossings call for documentation and bureaucratic permissions to leave or to enter, unless the migration is clandestine. The factor of mutual political recognition between countries comes to the fore here. In the absence of state-to-state political relationships, legal immigration may be precluded. This political reality is dramatically illustrated in the Asian case by the United States' nonrecognition for many years of the People's Republic of China, which entailed among other things the absence of consular facilities needed to enable easy legal movement between the two countries. Beyond this basic legal and logistical requirement, immigration flows naturally tend to be more vigorous between countries with close political and economic ties.

For Asia-to-U.S. immigration, for example, rapid growth in recent years has been observed for the Philippines, a former U.S. dependency. Notably fast growth has also occurred in immigration from Vietnam and South Korea, countries in which American troops have been directly engaged in military operations. Political affinity is evident in patterns of immigration to Canada, Australia, and New Zealand, where linkages with British Commonwealth sending countries are important. India is among the top-ranked sources of Asian immigrants for all three receiving countries; Malaysia is another important source for Australia and New Zealand, and Hong Kong is important for Canada. In the Pacific, free movement occurs between certain island-states and New Zealand, the United States, and Australia, owing to the islands' former or current status as political dependencies.

Political and military dependency is perhaps most clearly a factor in Korea-to-U.S. immigration. The presence of American troops in South Korea—about 40,000 currently—has been an important element in bolstering the strength of regimes in power there, while serving as a microlevel connection that has fostered emigration through the marriage of large numbers of Korean women to American G.I.'s and the adoption by U.S. residents of thousands of Korean (or Korean American) children. The military connection has also served as a bridgehead for the diffusion of American culture to South Korea, the effects of which will be discussed later.

Economic dependency is apparent in the case of the Philippines, owing to its previous status as a colony of the United States. Many Philippine businesses and natural resources are owned by Americans. In a recent year, 53 percent of foreign investment in the Philippines was from the United States. In addition, the United States is the Philippines' major trading partner, accounting for 28 percent of all foreign trade. The Filipino elite have also invested heavily in the United States, as revealed through the tracing of assets belonging to former Philippine president Ferdinand Marcos and his cronies when they fled into exile in 1986. Both economic dependency and political affinity are factors in the flows and counterflows of people between the Philippines and the United States.

Trade patterns in the region are of growing importance for temporary migration and, to a lesser extent, for immigration. Japan, a nation dependent on international trade, provides a striking example. According to government statistics, the number of Japanese working overseas for Japanese companies grew from about 10,000 in 1960 to more than 110,000 in 1980. It is noteworthy that this trend is partly attributable to the movement of Japanese factories overseas, which in turn was made necessary by Japan's reluctance to admit foreign workers into its homogeneous society. The trend is evident in admission statistics in countries that are Japan's major trading partners. In the United States, the number of Japanese entering annually on temporary business visas grew from 61,000 to 193,000 during a recent twelve-year period. Other evidence on the importance of international trade can be found in the business activities of immigrants. More than five thousand Korean-owned businesses are found in the Los Angeles area alone, for example, and a substantial number of them specialize in the import of Korean-made goods.

Weiner (1985:441) has pointed out the neglect of political dimensions in relation to population movements:

Theories of international migration pay remarkably little attention to state interventions, while the literature on international relations says relatively little about population movements, except insofar as the refugee phenomenon is described as an outcome of conflicts. How do state actions shape population movements, when do such actions lead to conflicts and when to cooperation, and what do governments do in their domestic policies to adjust to or influence population flows are questions that have received far too little attention.

The state actions that most directly influence international migration are, of course, policies on immigration, emigration, and temporary migration for business, pleasure, or employment. From a political perspective, it is surprising that such policies are usually enacted unilaterally, rather than through consultations between sending and receiving countries. Perhaps there is a need for an international tribunal that could facilitate such consultations, with the goal of enhancing both international understanding of policy goals and the effectiveness of specific policy measures. The existing hodgepodge of written and unwritten policies and complicated administrative procedures at both origins and destinations does not serve the best interest of any party.

Among the other state actions that deserve study are foreign aid programs. Although hard to quantify, the immigration-facilitating effects of bilateral economic and technical assistance programs must be substantial. Many such programs include provisions for student scholarships in the donor country. The governments of Australia, New Zealand, Canada, and the United States all provide substantial scholarship support to Third World students. Such programs normally include provisions requiring the scholars to return to their home countries, but these requirements are not fully effective. The government of Taiwan estimates, on the basis of past experience, that only one out of ten of its overseas students will return. India is another Asian country that has experienced a significant outflow of foreign-trained scholars, as has the Philippines. With over 200,000 Asian students enrolled in the United States, Canada, Australia, and New Zealand, international education must be recognized as a potentially important influence on Asian immigration. Scholarship-supported education is a major factor in outmigration from the Pacific Islands, too.

A traditional structural view of international migration would highlight disparities in economic development or societal modernization as the key factors in Asian immigration in the Pacific Basin. All four of the major receiving countries have highly developed capitalist economies, with rewards for entrepreneurship as well as diversified labor markets and substantial opportunities for job mobility. Although some scholars would question the extent to which this characterization holds for immigrant labor, the point here is that the *image* of an open economic system induces immigration from Asia, especially when it is buttressed by widely-publicized success stories of Asians in the receiving countries. The open economic structure and modern amenities of receiving countries are also important for many immigrants with professional and technical qualifications, such as those from India and the Philippines. For immigrants and refugees with rural backgrounds and low education, however, whose aspirations may not extend beyond a secure job in the service sector, the difference in levels of economic development between origin and destination may be more pertinent than the structure of the economic system.

The role of economic disparities is particularly interesting in the case of Japan, because Japanese immigration to the United States has remained essentially stable at a low level over the past thirty years, while immigration from virtually every other Asian country has increased. During this period Japan has joined the ranks of the major industrialized nations, with a per capita GNP equal to that of the United Kingdom and just below that of Canada. It seems that in the absence of an economic inducement, emigration has not been an attractive option for the Japanese.

The factors discussed illustratively above typify the problems inherent in studying systematically the influence of state-to-state relations and comparisons on immigration flows. Although it is often possible to cite a particular case to make a point, the body of data does not exist that would allow careful testing of a hypothesis about the importance of one factor vis-à-vis other factors. Some kinds of economic data seem solid—trade balances, for example—but other important facts are missing, such as the extent to which immigrant populations are engaged in businesses involving international trade. Further, relevant data are available on some important topics but have not been pulled together in this context. Examples are the scholarship components of international assistance programs, the flows of military personnel, and the flows of capital and people through various locations within transnational corporations. A complete matrix of state-to-state relations and comparisons is neither necessary nor feasible, but an effort to look at these dimensions more comprehensively should add substantially to our understanding of immigration flows in a migration systems context.

Mass Culture Connections

The economic and political linkages just discussed clearly provide much of the driving force behind immigration, given the great disparities in wealth and individual liberties that exist in today's world. But other forces are at work too, involving linkages in the cultural and social spheres. One way to appreciate these forces is to recognize that cultural and linguistic differences once served as formidable barriers to immigration. These barriers have greatly diminished in the modern era, owing to such factors as the internationalization of the mass media, the accessibility of international travel to large numbers of people, and the rapid spread of English as the major international language. One effect of these changes has been to increase awareness of economic and political differences. At the same time, however, different customs and lifestyles have become less "foreign." In general, the cultural distance between places is diminishing, as indicated through analysis of the following factors:

- cultural similarity or dissimilarity, value systems
- cultural dependency or dominance, "Westernization"
- media diffusion—television, radio, film, music, print media
- use of a common language

- common religion or compatible religious beliefs
- similarity of educational systems
- face-to-face contacts through international travel

Korea provides a dramatic example of decreasing cultural distances. Once known as the "hermit kingdom" because of its isolation, Korea had limited international connections until the 1950s (apart from its contacts with Japan and China). The breakthrough for Korea came as a result of the Korean war, with its heavy influx of foreign troops—mainly American—under the United Nations flag. Thirty years later, South Korea has a substantial American military presence, English-language television and radio stations and newspapers, a constant inflow of foreign business people engaged in international trade, and a growing tourist industry that is gearing up to handle the 1988 Olympics. There can be little doubt that Koreans exposed to these immense changes over the past thirty years have a greater propensity to immigrate than previous generations, owing in part to a more sophisticated world view and the concomitant reduction of cultural barriers. The number of Koreans applying to their government for permission to emigrate grew from fewer than 3,000 in 1963 to more than 30,000 in 1983, despite the expanding economic opportunities within South Korea. (An easing of government restrictions on emigration also occurred during that period.) Overseas Korean communities are now prominent in several Latin American countries, as well as in Australia, Canada, and the United States. With respect to similarity of value systems, it is relevant that Korean immigrants to the United States are disproportionately Christian, as compared with the population of Korea.

Cultural dependency is exemplified by the relationship between the Philippines and the United States, its former colonial ruler. "Americanization" is both a widely recognized phenomenon and a hotly debated topic in the Philippines, with polar positions taken by those who work toward a resurgence of traditional culture and those who seek admission of the Philippines as the fifty-first American state. The influence of American mass culture in the Philippines is evident in television programming, popular music, dress styles, and other mass phenomena. The educational system is modeled after that of the United States, English is the medium of instruction, most of the population is Christian (mainly Catholic), the political system and constitution at the time of independence were similar to those of the United States, and a strong circular flow of people, including students, tourists, business people, and workers, links the two countries. The Philippines is the fourth-ranked recipient among foreign countries to which U.S. social security payments are sent (after Italy, Mexico, and Canada), receiving $84 million paid annually to eligible retirees in the Philippines. These mass culture connections are, we believe, critical to an understanding of why Filipinos represent the second-largest flow of U.S. immigrants world-wide (after Mexicans) and why Filipinos are on the verge of becoming the largest Asian group in the United States.

The spread of a "global culture" through mass media is bound to have a continuing impact on *potential* immigration, in the sense that ever-growing numbers of people are exposed vividly to other lifestyles and more comfortable economic and political circumstances. As noted by Richmond (1984:525–526):

Most contemporary forms of recreation, sport, entertainment, and popular culture are independent of language, nationality or cultural boundaries. Modern mass communications have enabled millions of people throughout the world to enjoy leisure-time activities that have universal appeal.

Images are not necessarily role models, however, and a place perception does not translate directly into a motivation to migrate. For the vast majority of people in Asia, such images of distant places and leisure-time activities will have no effect on their future mobility, owing to their deep and abiding ties to their homelands and native cultures, which provide an essential sense of security. For a selective minority, however, media images and other cultural connections serve as a bridge in the migration system, easing the way for international moves that may have underlying economic or political motives but are likely to be triggered by family connections.

Family and Social Networks

Under today's immigration laws, the main mode of entry is through specific family reunification provisions. Moreover, a significant proportion of admissions on other grounds, such as "needed skills," are attributable to arrangements made by relatives or friends at the destination. Recent statistics demonstrate the point. In the United States, 92 percent of Asian admissions in 1980–1984 were due to family reunification, compared with 60 percent in 1970–1974. Similar increases in family-based admissions have occurred in Australia. As detailed in earlier chapters, this shift toward family connections as a basis for entry is a result of similar provisions in immigration law that have been enacted in the two countries since 1965.

Connections with friends and former community members in destination countries are also potent elements in prompting a move and facilitating settlement by providing help with jobs and housing. Further, these factors may sustain an immigration flow after the initial impetus from economic or political disparities has declined. A migration system, once started, has considerable momentum. Any comprehensive theoretical perspective should take into account the following aspects of family and social networks related to immigration:

- geographic dispersion of relatives and friends
- geographic dispersion of members of home country or community
- historical depth of family and community migration
- visiting and communication pattern of absent family and friends
- occupational niches of earlier waves of migrants
- social and economic status of previous migrants
- frequency and amount of remittances
- normative household and family structure
- normative family obligations and commitments

The familiar phenomenon of chain migration is of course a function of the geographic dispersion of relatives, friends, and compatriots. Once the pioneering wave of immigrants has settled, linkages are established that motivate and facilitate further migration. Often immigrants develop complex family strategies to maximize the opportunities available under prevailing immigration laws. In the United States, for example, current provisions give higher priority to reunification of parents and children than to reunification of siblings. Thus, if an immigrant wants to bring in his siblings, a common strategy is first to petition the parents, who will be admitted quickly and who can subsequently bring in the rest of their children under high priority status. The parents then may return to the home country to live, having used a chain migration strategy to settle their children in a country of greater opportunity.

These processes also promote geographic clustering in the country of destination. Many immigrants who enter the United States under family reunification provisions do not have a prearranged job. Rather, they tend to rely on their relatives for arranging initial employment, as well as for providing housing and other assistance. Their destination is therefore the community where their relatives live, which is often an enclave of their fellow countrymen as well.

The longer the migration stream has been established, the stronger will be the effects of these family and social networks. One reason for this is the cumulative impact of visiting and communication patterns between the area of origin and the destination, which increase information and reduce uncertainty among potential new migrants. A study of post-1965 Filipino immigrants in Hawaii showed, for example, that seven out of ten had returned to their home community in the Philippines for at least one visit, and many had returned several times (Caces

et al., 1985). With modern air transportation and the emergence of relatively low fares for transpacific travel, the contemporary Asian or Pacific Island international migrant often circulates freely between old and
new homes, quite unlike immigrants in earlier times.

One result of this circulation is the transmission of knowledge about
labor markets and specific job opportunities in destination areas. Just
as Mexican villagers are aware of jobs and wage rates in specific U.S.
communities, so Filipinos in some rural provinces are quite well informed about the duties and pay scales for maids in Hawaii's hotels
and Koreans know about the investment needed for a small business
or a franchise in Los Angeles. Effective formal channels do not exist
for such information; it is nearly all transmitted by family and social
networks.

Besides person-to-person communication and correspondence, important messages are sent implicitly through remittance channels. The
very fact that immigrants can send money home says something about
comparative opportunities and standards of living. When the amounts
are relatively large, the motivational impacts are correspondingly substantial. Looking again at the Philippines as an example, we found that
households in the province of Ilocos Norte that benefit from remittances
from the United States receive about $250 per year, whereas the an-
nual average household income in that part of the Philippines is only
$367. A study at the other end of this migration system showed that
three-fourths of Ilokano immigrant households in Hawaii sent remittances home, the average amount being $600 per year. Clearly, such
remittance flows contribute substantially to the information context in
which immigration decisions are made.

The strength and extensiveness of family obligations, which differ
considerably among Asian and Pacific countries, are also important in
understanding the immigration effects of family networks. Some cultures place greater emphasis on the welfare of members of the immediate family, such as parents, spouses, and children, whereas other
cultures stress obligations to virtually all relatives, even those somewhat distant in lineage. Such cultural differences could· have important implications for immigration patterns if, for example, Korean
immigrants tended to accumulate resources to finance the education
of their children, whereas Filipino immigrants tended to use their
resources to expand the inflow of eligible family members. We have
previously introduced the term *shadow households* in connection with
Filipino immigration (Caces et al., 1985), to highlight the importance
of continuing obligations and commitments between an immigrant and
his or her former household of residence. Cultural influences have a
role in economic migration too, with many immigrants admitted to work

in family-owned enterprises. The Asian propensity for family-held businesses, together with the trend toward multinational expansion of such enterprises, also has an effect on immigration through special preferences for investors. Further, the relatively high economic status of Asian immigrant families is attributable to the close family ties that keep the family together as an economic unit, thus producing an above-average number of income earners per household. The Asian family ethic thus reverberates in many ways throughout the immigration system.

Relevant data on family and social networks are not generally available from official data sources, such as immigration statistics or the census. At best, these sources may identify accompanying family members, members of the same household, and the family member who petitioned or sponsored an immigrant. Such data leave unanswered vital questions about the overall geographic dispersion of family and community members, the queuing sequence for immigration, the pattern of visiting, communications, and remittances between households at the origin and at the destination, the dynamics of providing auspices for housing and jobs, and so on. For these phenomena it is necessary to conduct special microlevel research, usually based on sample surveys or community studies that involve a combination of direct questioning and observation. Because of the financial and time costs of such studies, they are rare and usually quite limited in scope. As a result, the family and social network—arguably the most critical element in contemporary immigration systems—is inadequately documented.

A SOCIAL–PSYCHOLOGICAL PERSPECTIVE

The social–psychological perspective follows naturally from a discussion of the family context, since the family usually plays a key role in decisions about immigration. Figure 19.1 provides a schematic view of the social–psychological processes within an immigration system, beginning with the decision stage and proceeding through the transition and adaptation stages. We briefly discuss the scheme as a whole and then each stage.

An advantage of this microlevel view is its dynamic emphasis; it highlights the *process* of immigration. The process appears most clearly in the boxes running horizontally across the center of Figure 19.1, showing activities or events occurring over time that are instrumentally related to the goal of moving or are an intrinsic aspect of the actual movement. These activities and events are directly linked to proximate barriers and facilitators, as shown by the boxes above and below the central line, and are connected more distantly to structural factors at origin and destination and intercountry linkages. The process depicted in Figure 19.1

468

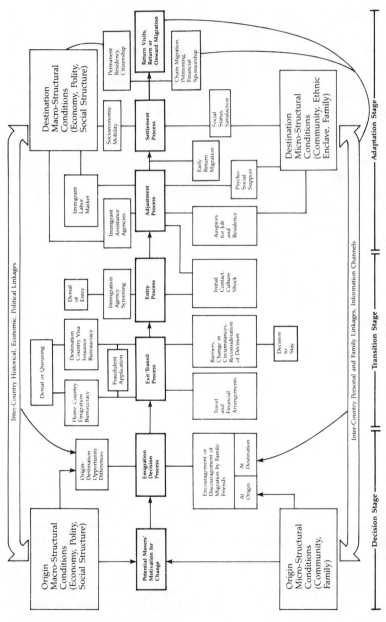

Figure 19.1. Processes in an Immigration System

is thus complementary to the structural perspective described in the preceding section.

The *decision stage* (as marked off at the bottom of the diagram) contains two main components: the potential mover's motivation for change, and the emigration decision process. As in most migration models, we see motivation for change (or dissatisfaction) arising from the relative position of the individual or family in the socioeconomic structure of the area of origin. The decision process, however, is triggered only in the presence of two other powerful factors: the differences in opportunity (real or perceived) between the area of origin and potential destinations, and the family and friend influences that provide crucial incentives or disincentives for moving. It is thus the interaction of three factors—motivation, opportunity for improvement, and family incentive—that determines progress through the decision stage of the migration system.

Although decision making is usually regarded as an individual action, migration decisions may be better conceptualized as family phenomena. The family may move as a unit, or the initial decision may involve a chain migration strategy involving a sequence of moves. The decision-making process may entail extensive discussions and consultations among family members, including those not involved in the move. And, most important, the utility expected as a result of the move may be a joint utility; that is, the decision may be made for the purpose of family rather than individual gains. Empirical applications of the social–psychological framework discussed here should make allowance for both individual and family decisions.

The decision stage always entails a choice about whether to move or to stay and sometimes involves a choice among alternative destinations. In the case of immigration, it should not be assumed that these are independent decisions. When a relative petitions for a teenager's admission to the United States, for example, the teenager may have a choice between going to the place where the relative lives or not going at all. Nonetheless, in modeling the decision process, one can treat the decision to move and the choice of destination as analytically distinct events.

The period between the initial decision (formation of an intention to move) and the actual move is of great practical importance, yet it has been little studied (Fawcett, 1985–1986). This *transition stage* entails a variety of explorations, encounters, and adjustments that can determine whether a move really occurs, the final choice of destination, the timing of the move, and the nature of the adjustment process after the move. The events that occur in the transition stage constitute the essential inner workings of an immigration system, although they are less visible than what occurs at the endpoints.

Notable features of the transition stage involve encounters with bureaucracies and individual bureaucrats, for both emigration and immigration. The official gatekeepers can affect the process decisively, allowing some family members to go but not others, putting the applicant at the end of a long queue, or denying exit or entry altogether. It is the power of the gatekeepers that provides an important impetus for fraud at the transition stage of an immigration system. Other kinds of barriers besides legal ones may stop the process at the transition stage, including costs of travel, recognition of the psychic costs of separation, and culture shock at entry. Recent studies have shown striking discrepancies between the number of people intending to emigrate and those who have actually moved after a given period, pointing to the need for greater understanding of events occurring in the transition stage.

In the field of immigrant studies, more attention has been given to the *adaptation stage* (adjustment, assimilation, acculturation) than to any other aspect of the immigration system. Recent work has focused on the role of the immigrant labor market in imposing constraints on the selection of jobs and on the prospects for upward mobility. In our scheme, the labor market and institutional factors are important, but no less so than the psychosocial support and other assistance provided by family and friends at the destination. These auspices too can have negative consequences, often channeling new immigrants into the same limited-opportunity niches filled by earlier immigrant cohorts. Although return migration may result from a failure of adjustment, it is also recognized that immigrants can return after a successful move (for example, returning at retirement). Once the immigrant is settled, new dynamics are fed back into the process through remittances, visits to the home country, and encouragement of others to immigrate, including formal immigration petitioning and financial sponsorship.

As shown in Figure 19.1, these social–psychological events take place within a framework that includes intercountry historical, economic, and political linkages at the macrolevel and intercountry personal and family linkages and information channels at the microlevel. (These linkages are represented by the wide arrows and large boxes across the top and bottom of Figure 19.1.) By analyzing these macrolinkages, as discussed earlier, and combining that information with individual-level data on the processes just described, we believe that researchers can produce the comprehensive picture that is required to understand the dynamics of an immigration system.

There is growing recognition of the need to assess premigration factors to achieve analytic insights into the roles and achievements of immigrants in the host society. Portes and Bach (1985:48), for example, have called attention to the class composition of early U.S. immigrant flows as the critical factor that "played a decisive role in determining their modes of incorporation and subsequent economic destiny in the United States."

A similar argument is made by Nee and Wong (1985), who make use of an analogy from economics, referring to the need to examine in historical perspective both the supply side and the demand side of immigration streams. The supply side incorporates various premigration characteristics of the group, notably cultural factors (such as the neo-Confucian ethic) and socioeconomic background factors, including educational attainment. The demand side includes structural aspects of the host society, particularly the labor market. According to Nee and Wong, immigration trends and adaptation patterns can be understood only by examining historical interactions of demand and supply factors, both of which are changing over time.

The basic concepts of a migration system approach have also recently been cited by Richmond (1984:520) as necessary ingredients in achieving an adequate understanding of adaptation:

The immigrant adaptation process is influenced by pre-migration conditions, the transitional experience in moving from one country to another, the characteristics of the migrants themselves and conditions in the receiving country, including government policies and economic factors. . . . The process of adaptation is a multidimensional one in which acculturation interacts with economic adaptation, social integration, satisfaction and degree of identification with the new country.

CONCLUSIONS

We started this chapter by noting the diversity in Asian and Pacific immigration and observing that the widely differing circumstances in which it occurs provide a challenge to the immigration theorist. As a step toward theoretical development, we have argued for the application of a broad migration systems paradigm within which diverse bits of knowledge can be integrated and compared. This paradigm requires the use of macro- and microdata, it presupposes a knowledge of history as well as of contemporary conditions at the origin and at alternative destinations, it seeks to explain both stability and different forms of mobility, it pays particular attention to the linkages between places, and it recognizes that the parts of a migration system are dynamically interconnected.

These are not novel ideas. Indeed, the best work on immigration—from the classic study of the Polish peasant class (Thomas and Znaniecki, 1927) to the recent work on Cubans and Mexicans in the United States (Portes and Bach, 1985)—has reflected a migration systems approach, along the lines discussed above. We are not calling for anything new so much as we are urging greater ambition in migration theories and research, with the goal of creating a body of knowledge whose worth matches the importance of the topic it seeks to address.

REFERENCES

Allen, R., and H. R. Hiller

1985 "The Social Organization of Migration: An Analysis of the Uprooting and Flight of Vietnamese Refugees." *International Migration*, 23(4):439–451.

Arnold, F., and N. M. Shah

1986 *Asian Labor Migration: Pipeline to the Middle East.* Boulder: Westview Press.

Caces, F., F. Arnold, J. T. Fawcett, and R. W. Gardner

1985 "Shadow Households and Competing Auspices: Migration Behavior in the Philippines." *Journal of Development Economics*, 17(1):5–25.

Fawcett, J. T. (ed.)

1985– *Migration Intentions and Behavior: Third World Perspectives.* Special is-
1986 sue of *Population and Environment*, 8(1 and 2).

Goldscheider, C.

1971 *Population, Modernization, and Social Structure.* Boston: Little, Brown and Co.

Kritz, M. M.

1985 "International Migration Theories: Conceptual and Definitional Issues." Paper presented at the IUSSP Seminar on Emerging Issues in International Migration, Bellagio, Italy, April 22–26.

Nee, V., and H. Y. Wong

1985 "Asian American Socioeconomic Achievement: The Strength of the Family Bond." *Sociological Perspectives*, 28(3):281–306.

Papademetriou, D. G.

1984 "International Migration in a Changing World." *International Social Science Journal*, 36(3):409–423.

Portes, A., and R. L. Bach

1985 *Latin Journey: Cuban and Mexican Immigrants in the United States.* Berkeley: University of California Press.

Richmond, A. H.

    1984   "Socio-cultural Adaptation and Conflict in Immigrant-Receiving Countries." *International Social Science Journal*, 36(3):519–536.

Thomas, W. I., and F. Znaniecki

    1927   *The Polish Peasant in Europe and America*. New York: Knopf.

Weiner, M.

    1985   "On International Migration and International Relations." *Population and Development Review*, 11(3):441–455.

Contributors

Anthony J. Agresta
Demographer
CACI, Inc.
Fairfax, Virginia

Fred Arnold
Research Associate
East–West Population Institute
East–West Center
Honolulu

Herbert R. Barringer
Professor
Department of Sociology
University of Hawaii
Honolulu

Leon F. Bouvier
Vice President (retired)
Population Reference Bureau
Washington, D.C.

Benjamin V. Carino
Professor
School of Urban and Regional
    Planning
University of the Philippines

John Connell
Senior Lecturer
Department of Geography
Institute Building
University of Sydney
Australia

James T. Fawcett
Research Associate
East–West Population Institute
East–West Center
Honolulu

Robert W. Gardner
Research Associate
East–West Population Institute
East–West Center
Honolulu

Linda W. Gordon
Chief Statistician
Office of Refugee Resettlement
U.S. Department of Health and
    Human Services
Washington, D.C.

Illsoo Kim
Assistant Professor
Department of Sociology
Drew University
Madison, New Jersey

Frank Klink
Doctoral candidate
School of International Service
American University
Washington, D.C.

Mary M. Kritz
Associate Director
Population Sciences
Rockefeller Foundation
New York City

Daniel Kubat
Professor and Chair
Department of Sociology
University of Waterloo
Canada

Michael J. Levin
Population Division
U.S. Bureau of the Census
Washington, D.C.

Urmil Minocha
Former Fellow
East-West Population Institute
East-West Center
Honolulu

Alejandro Portes
Professor
Department of Sociology
Johns Hopkins University
Baltimore

Charles A. Price
Professorial Fellow (retired)
Department of Demography
Australian National University
Canberra

Astri Suhrke
Professor of International
    Relations
American University
Washington, D.C.
and Visiting Fellow
School of International Studies
Jawaharlal Nehru University
New Delhi

Teresa A. Sullivan
Associate Professor of Sociology
    and Training Director
Population Research Center
University of Texas at Austin

Michael S. Teitelbaum
Program Officer
Alfred P. Sloan Foundation
New York City

Andrew D. Trlin
Reader in Sociology
Department of Sociology
Massey University
Palmerston North, New Zealand

Peter S. Xenos
Research Associate
East-West Population Institute
East-West Center
Honolulu

Author Index

477

Subject Index